CHOSEN TALES

CHOSEN TALES

Stories Told by Jewish Storytellers

edited by
Peninnah Schram

JASON ARONSON INC.
Northvale, New Jersey
London

For credits, see page 435.

This book was set in 11 pt. Bookman by Alpha Graphics in Pittsfield, New Hampshire, and printed by Haddon Craftsmen in Scranton, Pennsylvania.

Library of Congress Cataloging-in-Publication Data

Chosen tales : stories told by Jewish storytellers / edited by
    Peninnah Schram.
        p. cm.
    Includes bibliographical references.
    ISBN 1-56821-352-2
    1. Short stories, Jewish.   2. Short stories, American—Jewish
authors.   3. Legends, Jewish.   4. Jews—Anecdotes.   5. Jews—
Fiction.   6. Judaism—Fiction.   I. Schram, Peninnah.
PN6120.95.J6C48   1995
813'.01088924—dc20   94-43612

Manufactured in the United States of America. Jason Aronson Inc. offers books and cassettes. For information and catalog write to Jason Aronson Inc., 230 Livingston Street, Northvale, New Jersey 07647.

To all the storytellers everywhere—
and to all who are inspired to read and retell our stories!

The voice is the heart's pen and the mind's messenger.
—Bahya ibn Pakuda, *Duties of the Heart*

CONTENTS

FOREWORD
  Black Fire on White Fire: The Power of Story   xv
    Rabbi Avraham Weiss

PREFACE   xxxv
  Peninnah Schram

ACKNOWLEDGMENTS   xli
  Peninnah Schram

PROLOGUE: THE APPLE TREE'S DISCOVERY   1
  Peninnah Schram and Rachayl Eckstein Davis

EVERY NAME HAS A STORY   5
  Penina V. Adelman

THE CAR THAT RAN FROM MITZVAHS   11
  Hanna Bandes

A STORY FROM THE JEWISH CEMETERY IN JAPAN   20
  Joel ben Izzy

REMEMBERING RACHEL   26
  Suzanne Benton

FABLES OF THE MISNAGDIM   31
  The Eagles   32
  Ephram the Elephant   34
  Shep the Sheep   36
  Faige the Fawn   39
    Saul J. Berman

NOAH'S WIFE   41
  Judith Black

THE STORY OF BRYAN   47
    Tsvi Blanchard

THE LIGHT IN THE WALL   50
    Renée Brachfeld

GO FISHING   54
    Jay Brand

RIDING WITH THE MOON   58
    Roslyn Bresnick-Perry

TELLING JOKES FOR THE SAKE OF GOD   66
    Yitzhak Buxbaum

THE GHETTO REBBE AND
HIS "KINGDOM OF CHILDREN"   70
    Shlomo Carlebach

THE SHEPHERD'S PRAYER   76
    Susan Danoff

REST AREA   81
    Yitzchak Etshalom

NETTIE BLUMENTHAL   89
    Gerald Fierst

FEATHERS   93
    Heather Forest

REVIVAL OF THE DEAD   97
    Ellen Frankel

THE PATH   104
    Nancy R. Ginsberg

THE STORYTELLER 107
   Two Stories from Reuven Gold 109
    In Memory of Reuven Gold

THE BURNING PIANO 112
   Karen Golden

LEON'S PLAN FOR PEACE 120
   James Stone Goodman

THE JOURNEY OF THE LOST PRINCESS 126
   Debra Gordon-Zaslow

MARIA RAEL: A JEWISH STORY FROM NEW MEXICO 132
   Lynn Gottlieb

THE CHICKEN'S TALE 138
   Daniel T. Grossman

"HABERES BUENOS" 142
   Naftali Haleva

PENNIES FROM HEAVEN 145
   Annette Harrison

A TASTE OF HONEY, A TASTE FOR LOVE 150
   Lynn Hazan

THE WISDOM OF SOLOMON 155
   Merna Ann Hecht

THE MOUNTAIN AND THE CLIFF 161
   David Holtz

A TALE OF REB NAHUM CHERNOBLER
—AND A *TIKKUN* 166
   Eve Penner Ilsen

THE NEVER-ENDING SONG   173
  Nina Jaffe

RASPBERRIES FOR SIMA   179
  Betty Lehrman

RAPS   187
  Walk Like an Israelite: A Passover Adaptation   189
  Shavuot Rap   191
  Chanukah Rap   195
  Suri Levow-Krieger and Eva Grayzel

THE OLD MAN   198
  Syd Lieberman

A NEW YORKER'S GUIDE TO EDEN   202
  Lisa Lipkin

HOW I LEARNED TO STUDY TORAH   205
  Doug Lipman

THE BOOKSELLER FROM GEHENNA   210
  Lennie Major

THE FOURTH CANDLE   217
  Mara

THE PEKL STORY   222
  Helen Mintz

GRANDMA'S CHALLAH   226
  Marilyn Price

HOW I LOST MY DIAMOND RING   231
  Leslie Robbins

IF YOU THINK YOU ARE A CHICKEN   237
  Steven M. Rosman

AYNENI YODAYA   241
   Donald B. Rossoff

I ALREADY HAVE WHAT I WANT AND NEED   245
   Charles Roth

THE DAY THE RABBI STOPPED THE SUN   250
   Robert E. Rubinstein

THE MIDWIFE'S REWARD   256
   Barbara Rush

COULD THIS BE PARADISE?   261
   Steve Sanfield

WINEDROPS ON THE EYELASHES   265
   Zalman M. Schachter-Shalomi

GOING ALONG WITH JOHA: A MEDLEY OF MIRTH   279
   Peninnah Schram

THE MIRACLE OF THE BLACK PEPPER   286
   Rebecca Schram-Zafrany

THREE STORIES FROM THE HEAVENS   291
   Turning: A Midrash of the Sun and Moon   293
   The Sign: A Midrash of the Rainbow   295
   Midrash of Mayim: A Water Story   297
   Cherie Karo Schwartz

THE COTTAGE OF CANDLES   301
   Howard Schwartz

Y. L. PERETZ IN THE ISRAELI ARMY   305
   Shai Schwartz

MESSIAH MAN   313
   Rami M. Shapiro

THE UNTOUCHED OIL   336
  Eliezer Shore

A TALE OF DIAMOND LISTENING   344
  Laura Simms

THE CANDLE MAKER OF LIGHT   349
  Devorah Spilman

SHOSA LAYA, THE WISE   356
  Susan Stone

A LAMED VAVNIK   363
  Arthur Strimling

THE MOST PRECIOUS THING IN THE WORLD   371
  Joan Sutton

MY GRANDPARENTS   376
  Sarika's Story   377
  Charoset   381
  Susan Talve

LOOK NOT UPON THE FLASK   384
  Hanoch Teller

"EXCUSE ME, I HEVE AN APPOINTMENT
WITH THE PRIME MINISTER"   391
  Dvorah Menashe Telushkin

THE REST OF CREATION   396
  Arthur Waskow

BARKING DOGS   400
  Peretz Wolf-Prusan

THE SEER OF LUBLIN'S SHIRT   402
  Diane Wolkstein

APPENDIX 1: Other Works by the Contributors 408

APPENDIX 2: Storytelling Organizations 420

APPENDIX 3: Contributors' Addresses 421

GLOSSARY 425

CREDITS 435

FOREWORD

Black Fire on White Fire: The Power of Story
Rabbi Avraham Weiss

This foreword is dedicated to the sweet singer and story-teller Rav Shlomo Carlebach, of blessed memory.

Avraham (Avi) Weiss *is senior rabbi of the Hebrew Institute of Riverdale, national president of the Coalition for Jewish Concerns (AMCHA), and assistant professor of Judaic Studies at Stern College of Yeshiva University. His essays and articles have appeared in national publica-tions. He is the author of* Women at Prayer: A Halakhic Analysis of Women's Prayer Groups. *Avi and his wife, Toby, have a family that includes Dena and Mark and their child Ariella, Elana and Michael and their children Gilad and Eitan, and Dov.*

 ish Da'at, the fiery law, is one of the more esoteric phrases describing the Torah. Says the Midrash: "*Eish shahor al gabei eish lavan*—black fire on white fire."[1] On the simplest level, black fire is the letters of Torah, white fire the spaces between the letters. On another level, the black represents what is clearly written in the Torah, the *peshat*, while the white represents what we bring into the text when we interact with it—interpretations, ap-plications, and expansions of the text. This is the *d'rash*, the messages we read in between the lines.

And on yet another level, the black letters represent the cog-nitive message, while the white spaces represent that which goes beyond the world of the intellect. The black letters are limited, limiting, and fixed. The white spaces, on the other hand, catapult us into the realm of the limitless and the ever-changing, ever-growing. They are the silence, the song, the story.

A precious chain of words and voices links the stories we were told to the stories that we tell. That chain, that tradition, or *masoret*, is mutable yet unbreakable. It is mutable because, unlike the holy words of God received at Mount Sinai, the language used for storytelling is personal, inflected, and contextual. When we hear a story that captivates or compels, we take ownership of it, molding it with nuances and importance from our individual hearts, souls, and memories.

How, then, can the *masoret* be unbreakable as well? It would seem that if we don't retell a tale in the way it was originally told, then the chain is broken. And, even more, it would seem that if the story is never retold at all, in any form, the chain is certainly broken. Yet this is not so, for a story heard or read is still internalized. Even if we don't pass it on with intent, we often communicate its meaning or message through an action or through our own stories. And that is what stories and storytelling are about: fanning the white fire to its limits.

Just what do these stories—whether personal or retold—do for us, for our children? Above all, they enrich and enhance. They enrich and enhance so well because stories, in a universal sense, can arouse powerful feelings; they can make bitter pills palatable; they can teach softly and sensitively. In a particularly Jewish framework, stories can help us grow in Torah; they can even show us the way to redemption.

WHY STORYTELLING?[2]

Feeling the Experience

One can receive a message on an intellectual level, just as one can receive a message on an experiential level. A well-told story is a bridge between the two; it is an attempt to give people a sense of the experience.

If one were teaching *mussar*, an ethical lesson, on the intellectual level, he or she would share the principle that is operative. For example, if one were teaching about the law of not engaging in insult, he or she might *teach* texts that explain the details of the law and the reasons behind it. On the experiential level, on the other hand, one might ask the listener to *experience* the pain of an offended person.

A story, however, can bridge these two approaches. Even if it is impossible to subject the listener to the actual experience, to the real pain of the insult, the listener can, through the story, *feel the experience*.

For example, the Torah states: "*Lo tov heyot ha-Adam le-vado*; it is not good that the human being is alone" (Genesis 2:18). "Aloneness" is not "loneliness," notes the late Rav Yosef Dov ha-Levi Soloveitchik (the Rav) of blessed memory.[3] Aloneness is a physical condition—literally, being without company. Loneliness is a metaphysical state. One can share a home, a room, a bed, with someone, and still be lonely. The antidote to loneliness, says the Torah, is "*Ve-davak be-ishto*, to cleave to his wife" (Genesis 2:24), or to her husband, as the case may be. Even as we maintain our individual uniqueness, couples are encouraged to share each others' beings, destinies, and dreams.

Cognitively, one can teach the idea of love. But to actually help the listener who has never in his or her life experienced love, come close to understanding the concept of love on a deeper level, and even perhaps identify with the experience, a story is required:

> After the death of Tonya Soloveitchik, her husband, Rav Yosef Dov ha-Levi Soloveitchik, spoke of the prophet Jeremiah, who prophesied the destruction of the First Temple. God commands Jeremiah to leave Jerusalem and travel to Anatot to buy a field from his cousin Chanamel (Jeremiah 32). Jeremiah obeys God's word. By the time he returns, Jerusalem was destroyed.[4]
>
> It can be suggested that when God told Jeremiah the Temple was doomed, Jeremiah knew the word of God was true. But his love for the Temple was so great that he felt that by remaining nearby, he would be able to infuse his very life, his very spirit, his very breath, into the Temple.
>
> Then, as an act of faith, Jeremiah left to buy a field—a statement that even in the midst of doom, one must always believe that the Jewish people will prevail. While well intentioned,

Jeremiah, by leaving Jerusalem, broke the umbilical cord between himself and the Temple, and the Temple was destroyed.[5]

The Rav often spoke of his wife in the most romantic terms. She was his *bayit*, his home, his Temple. And when the doctors told the Rav that Tonya was terminally ill, he knew the prognosis was bleak. But like Jeremiah, he felt he would always remain near and infuse part of his being into her.

And so it was. For months, the Rav remained at his wife's side. He prayed, studied, and conducted his business there, until one day when Tonya urged him to travel to New York to finalize a contribution made by a generous philanthropist to increase the salaries of the rabbis teaching at Yeshiva University, Rav Soloveitchik's yeshiva. The Rav hesitated, but in the end, the doctors assured him that Tonya was not in danger that day. He flew to New York and was successful in securing the gift. But as he stepped from the plane in Boston, he was notified that Tonya had lapsed into a coma. Entering his wife's hospital room, the Rav found her unconscious. A short time later, Tonya Soloveitchik died.[6]

Here is a story of love, of "*ve-davak be-ishto*."

Saying Radical Things

A story is also a means to communicate radical messages without saying them in explicit words. This allows for selective hearing. Thus, people who are open to the story's message will hear it, and those who are not will not. While in the above approach, the story is a means of more effective communication, in this approach, the story is really a way of clouding communication. As the saying goes, "*Hameivin yavin*; the one who understands will understand."

For example, many of Rav Nachman's tales contain an extraordinary amount of hidden radical thinking. But not every listener will understand his stories on that level. To the less-attuned ear, the story will sound like no more than a moral tale, while the more astute listener will catch the theological radicalism in the story's message. The following midrash is a wonderful illustration of this point:

When God denied Moses entry into Israel, God told Moses: "You can see the land from the mountain, but here you will die."

But Moses begged God to permit him to live forever. "Everyone must die," was God's response.

"I'm better than everyone!" Moses argued.

"Are you better than Adam, whom I created?" God asked.

"Yes," responded Moses. "Adam disobeyed you. He ate from the tree. I never disobeyed Your word."

God then asked: "Are you better than Noah? He obeyed My command and built the ark. Even he died."

"Yes," answered Moses. "When told the world would be destroyed, Noah did not intercede to save humankind. I, however, challenged Your decree to destroy the Jewish people after they built the golden calf."

"What about Abraham?" God continued. "He argued for Sodom after hearing it would be razed. Still, he died."

Moses argued: "Abraham had a wicked child, Ishmael. My children, while not great, are not evil."

"But you killed the Egyptian who was smiting the Jew," God retorted. "You overreacted and therefore must die."

Moses snapped back: "Look how many Egyptians You killed. I killed only one. Why should I be punished?"

Exasperated, God declared, "You, Moses, are not God. You do not give life and therefore cannot take life. I give life, and therefore I can take life."[7]

On the surface, this is a feisty story that ends with an explanation for Moses' seemingly unjust death before entering the Land of Israel. God gave Moses life and only God can be the judge of when it is time for Moses' life to end. On another level, this lesson can be applied to all people and all deaths that seem untimely. But there is yet another level on which one can understand this story.

Unlike leaders of other faith communities, Jewish leaders are not subdeities. But were the Jews in the desert confusing Moses with God? Was it necessary for Moses to die dramatically for the people—and even Moses—to realize that he too was mortal, that he was not God? Was it not necessary for Moses to die, right then, at such an ironic time, so that it would be understood by all those present and all those in generations to come that even the great Moses, the Moses who was in many ways the most righteous, committed, and selfless leader of the Jewish people, could not live forever?

Stories as a Nonthreatening Way to Teach

Storytelling can also be a nonthreatening way to say something that people need to hear, particularly when teaching *midot*, positive traits. If you communicate the message directly and straightforwardly, people will often hear it as a critique and, therefore, as an attack. A story enables the same message to come through in a way that does not talk *at* people but rather, enables them to appreciate or share in the goodness of a particular path. In this way, it can have a far greater impact on people's values and behavior. We are all more willing to look at ourselves critically if we feel the impetus is imposed not from the outside but from ourselves. Because stories require a certain amount of active interpretation on the part of the listener, they have a magical way of helping the listener come to a realization on his or her own.

Rav Yisrael Salanter told this story:

> On Friday night, the custom is to cover the loaves of *challah* when reciting the *kiddush* blessing over the wine. Some suggest we do this so the *challah*, which is normally the most important food of the meal, will not be "embarrassed" as we place emphasis on the *kiddush* wine.
>
> It happened once that Rav Salanter was a Sabbath guest at the home of a rich couple. As Rav Salanter's host was about ready to recite the *kiddush*, he scolded his wife for not having covered the *challah*. Rav Salanter couldn't contain himself. Calling the man aside, he said: "Listen well. The purpose of covering the *challah* is not to embarrass it. If in the process of not embarrassing the *challah* you shame your wife, you're better off not covering the *challah* at all."

What a masterful and nonthreatening way of communicating to the listener the *midah* of not shaming another in public!

Yet another story:

> The editor of a weekly journal came with a photographer to in-
> terview Reb Aryeh Levin, the "Tzadik of Yerushalayim, the righ-
> teous man of Jerusalem." As the interview progressed, the pho-
> tographer attempted to take a picture of the rabbi. Motivated by
> his innate modesty and religious objection to being photographed,
> Reb Aryeh used his hands to hide his face from the camera.
> Finally, the photographer became exasperated.
> "Rabbi," the editor explained, "by your actions, you are depriv-
> ing this man of his livelihood."
> Asked Reb Aryeh: "You make your living from taking pictures?"
> "Yes," answered the photographer.
> "In that case, take as many pictures as you like."
> And the rabbi posed for the photographer, suppressing his own
> extra strict religious scruples so as not to cause another Jew even
> the slightest loss of earnings.[8]

And what is the important lesson of this story? Sometimes it
is more righteous to put aside the strictures we impose upon
ourselves—especially when those strictures may in a certain circumstance fly in the face of other, more basic, Torah principles
of *ben adam l'haveiroh*, between a person and his or her friend.

STORIES AND TEACHING TORAH

Stories Simplify

Stories can clarify complicated Torah ideas and help us discover their meaning for our every day lives. In *Lonely Man of
Faith*, Rav Yosef Dov Soloveitchik gives a profound explanation
for why there are two stories of the creation of Adam in Genesis. Calling them Adam I and Adam II, he contrasts two contra-
dictory elements of human nature. Adam I, he writes, is driven
by God's mandate to humankind to "fill the earth and subdue it"
(Genesis 1:28). Adam I's goal is to master the universe. Adam I is
provoked by the cosmos to quest for power and control, thus
asking the functional "How?" question, while Adam II is provoked
by that same cosmos to ask the metaphysical questions of "Why?,"

"Who?," and "What?" Adam II is interested in the deeper reason of humankind's existence; Adam II's quest is to attempt to discover the meaning of it all; Adam II yearns to fulfill God's command "to serve and guard the earth" (Genesis 2:15).[9]

But what does this all mean? As the Gemarah often asks: "*Mai nafkah minah*? What is the practical application of this principle?" A story can help illustrate:

> There once was a king who told one of his subjects: "I love you and wish to give you a part of my kingdom. Tomorrow at sunrise you will set forth from the palace. Wherever you walk, the land is yours. There is one condition, however: You must return by sunset."
>
> Starting precisely on time, the man began walking. Then, wanting more and more, he began to jog and then run. As he moved along, his child called out for some help in doing his schoolwork; his wife pleaded for some time to share a thought; his rabbi implored him to be the tenth man at a synagogue service; the heavens, the trees, the lakes beckoned him to notice them. But for all this, he had no time.
>
> The sun began to fade, and the man, remembering that he had to be back by sunset, dashed toward the palace. He reached the threshold precisely as the sun dipped over the horizon. But just at that moment, he collapsed in exhaustion and gasped his last breath.
>
> The next day at the man's funeral, the king granted his wife a modest home. After all, that's all one really needs anyway.[10]

While this man was so busy being Adam I, he missed out on the opportunity to also be Adam II. While he strived to acquire more possessions, he neglected his own need to step back and examine the meaning of his existence. He died without an appreciation for the really good things in life. He died without understanding that physical comforts, power, and control are only a means to an end, not an end in themselves.

The Elliptical Biblical Phrase

Biblical texts often contain elliptical passages, lacking what we think of as "connecting thoughts." The story, in this case a

Midrashic tale, fills in the empty spaces. For example, in the story of Cain and Abel, the Bible says: "And Cain said to his brother Abel, and it was when they were in the field that Cain rose up against Abel his brother and killed him" (Genesis 4:8). The obvious question is, what did Cain say to Abel? A Midrashic tale provides some possibilities:

> Cain and Abel felt the world was too small for both of them. Imagine, with only them and Adam and Eve alive, there wasn't enough room. The missing text, says the Midrash, alludes to how they bargained to split the world.
> Says one rabbi: "Cain said he'd take the movable property; Abel agreed to take all the immovable objects. Days later, Cain said to Abel: 'Take off your clothes; they're movable, and therefore, they're mine.' Abel responded: 'Then fly. The land you're standing on is mine.'"
> A second rabbi says: "It didn't happen that way. What they were really arguing about was where the Temple should be built."
> A third rabbi adds: "You're both incorrect. With few women in the world, perhaps only Eve, they argued about Eve."[11]

My teacher in Bible, Nehama Leibowitz, suggests this interpretation: The story of Cain and Abel is not only the story of Cain and Abel. It is, rather, the story of the nature of violence. The first rabbi argues that the root cause of bloodshed is economic. The second rabbi maintains that confrontation is promoted by ideological disputes. The third rabbi says that violence is caused by passion.[12]

The text purposely lacks words. Had the precise argument been presented, it would have limited the text's application. The empty spaces in the Bible allow for a more universal message, one not bound by time or space.

The Contrary Message

Stories, especially Midrashic ones, often teach ideas that run contrary to the literal meaning, the *peshat*, of the biblical text. Consider the well-known narrative of the binding of Isaac (Genesis 22).

God commands Abraham to sacrifice his son. Abraham doesn't hesitate. He takes Isaac to Mt. Moriah, binds him, and lifts his knife to kill him. At the last moment, an angel calls out to Abraham: "Stop!" Abraham has passed the test; he is truly a servant of God.

Noting the virtual silence of Abraham and Isaac in the narrative, the Midrash tells this story:

> An old man appeared to Abraham on his way to Moriah. "Where are you going?" he asked.
>
> "To pray," answered Abraham.
>
> "If so," the old man asked, "why are you carrying a knife, fire, and wood?"
>
> "In case we are delayed and need to prepare food."
>
> "But," the old man persisted, "wasn't I there when God told you to sacrifice your son? At the age of 137, are you prepared to do so?"
>
> "Even so," Abraham sighed, "I will follow God's wishes, whatever they are."
>
> "But tomorrow, after you've sacrificed Isaac, God will say you are guilty of murder."
>
> "Even so," concluded Abraham, "I will follow God's wishes."[13]

In the surface narrative, Abraham seems without question ready to sacrifice his son. In the Midrash, however, it happens differently. God tells Abraham to dedicate Isaac to God. Abraham assumes that dedication means dying for God. He treks to Moriah, but his conscience (represented by the old man)[14] begins to bother him. He wonders: "Is this what God wants? As the child's father, is this something I can do? And, from a moral perspective, isn't child sacrifice wrong?"[15]

Rather than walk to Moriah without hesitation, the Midrash tells us, Abraham is torn and uncertain. He doubts, and doubting has its merits. If you doubt, you ask difficult questions and grow and come to know more.[16]

As Abraham painfully binds Isaac and lifts the knife, an angel —an inner voice—calls out: "Abraham, you've misunderstood. When God told you to dedicate Isaac, God did not mean through death, but through life!"[17] The Midrash turns the *peshat* of the narrative on its heel. The message of the binding of Isaac is that the ultimate sanctification of God comes through living every day for God, not dying for God.[18]

Trigger Tales

Stories can trigger novel ideas in the listener. The following tale, a kind of modern Midrash, is told by Rabbi Moshe Sokolow. "Listen" to the story. Can you identify the character being described?

> A young Jewish man was taken from Israel by force and grew up in a foreign country. In spite of difficulties, he persevered and succeeded, but not without bringing about a noticeable measure of jealousy and hostility. Eventually, he used his abilities to provide the King with some lifesaving advice and was rewarded by being appointed Viceroy, second to the King. The King gave him a royal ring, symbolizing his high office, and, dressed in royal garments, he was driven around in a royal chariot while a page went before him, announcing his promotion. The young man did not let all of this go to his head. He remained a loyal Jew, faithful to his God, and he used his position and influence for the benefit of the Jewish people.[19]

This story echoes the key events in the lives of Joseph, the favored son of Jacob, and of Mordechai, the uncle of Esther in the events that led to Purim. It plants the seed in the listener's head that these two stories are similar and serves as a catalyst to further comparison and study.[20]

ILLUMINATING THE PATH TO REDEMPTION

Stories can help us understand the ultimate goal of Judaism—to create a faith community that "perfects the world under the reign of the Almighty," as we say three times each day in the Aleinu prayer.[21] This will be the Messianic era, when humankind will be at peace—redeemed.

In Jewish philosophy, there are two approaches to understanding the era of redemption. One approach suggests that redemption will come when God is ready. Human beings play no role in the process; it's all in God's hands.[22]

The other approach insists that redemption involves a partnership between God and people.[23] Thus, the last word of the creation story is *"la'asot*, to do" (Genesis 2:3). God, in effect, tells us, "I've created the world incompletely, imperfectly, and leave it to you to finish that which I have started. In partnership we will redeem the world." As much as we yearn for redemption, this theory says, redemption yearns for us. As much as we await the Messiah, the Messiah awaits us. As much as we search for God, God, says Rabbi Abraham Joshua Heschel, searches for us.

God Alone Redeems

A tale about a Hasidic rebbe helps amplify the former approach:

> The Klausenberger Rebbe lost his entire family, his wife and eleven children, during the Holocaust. After the war, he emigrated to America. Once, on a Sabbath morning, when the portion of the *tokhaha* (curse) was being read, the Torah reader read at a fast pace and in a low voice, as is the custom. Suddenly, the Rebbe began to scream: "*Hecher*! Louder!" His disciples were stunned. The *tokhaha* was always read quickly and in a hushed tone as a way of declaring that we want no part of the curse. In fact, even a reader's mistake is never corrected. Who would want to hear the curse twice? But the Rebbe insisted, and so it was—the *tokhaha* was read aloud.
>
> After the Sabbath, the students sought an explanation from the Rebbe, who answered: "I lost my entire family in Europe. I know this curse well—not only as prediction, but also as that which has already happened. I, therefore, insist that it be read aloud as my way of telling God: 'Listen closely, Almighty God, the curse has already come true. Now it is time for all of us to experience your blessing of redemption!'"[24]

The Klausenberger Rebbe understood that only God brings redemption. He, a survivor of the Holocaust, understood that human beings are often at the mercy of history and God's greater plan. Yet the Rebbe insisted that we have the right, and even the obligation, to demand that God, who alone brings redemption, bring it now.

Human Beings as Partners in the Redemption Process

Yet there are also stories that tell of the human role in the redemption process. For instance, this Hasidic tale told by Rav Shlomo Carlebach, of blessed memory, demands that we do our share in bringing redemption. (I retain many of Rav Shlomo's inflections and words to preserve his unique manner of story telling.)

When the *heilege* (holy) Reb Moshe Leib Sassov died, it was decided to send him to heaven. But everybody knows that on the way to heaven, you have to go through hell and the way you do it is the following: The angels walk you through hell, quickly. You go through and all at once you're on your way to heaven.

As the *heilege* Reb Moshe Leib was being walked through hell, he saw the pain, the brokenness of all the *neshamos* (souls) in hell. He stopped. The heavenly policeman, the tourist guide, so to speak, who was walking him through, said: "Reb Moshe Leib, let's go, let's hurry, we have to go to heaven!" Reb Moshe Leib responded: "I'm not leaving hell unless I can take all the souls who are here with me."

You can imagine the commotion. "Look," the guide said. "It's tough enough to run hell. Think about the complaints, all the yelling here. We have enough trouble without your demands. Please, Reb Moshe Leib, this is not your place. Your place is in heaven. Just go through."

Reb Moshe Leib answered: "I'm not leaving until all the souls come with me."

The heavenly tribunal had no choice but to convene to hear Reb Moshe Leib's argument. And this is what he claimed: "If it's true, if God really wants me to live in heaven, what kind of heaven can I have if these poor souls remain in pain in hell? How can I live in bliss when I know there is suffering? So, if you want me in heaven, the only way I will go is if I can take all the souls with me."

There are two versions to the end of this story. In the first, the holy court decides that if Reb Moshe Leib never ever in his life missed an opportunity to do someone else a favor, he merits bringing all the souls from hell with him. The record is checked, and sure enough, Reb Moshe Leib never missed a chance to help someone in need. Rabbi Moshe Leib takes all the souls with him out of hell. However, Rav Shlomo notes, it doesn't take long for hell to be filled again.

In the second version, the heavenly court decides that Reb Moshe Leib can take with him to heaven as many souls as righteous deeds he performed for others in his life. The holy court counts his deeds, and sure enough, there are exactly the same number of deeds as souls in hell.

"Awesome, amazing!" concludes Rav Shlomo Carlebach. "This means each time you do an act of kindness, you may be getting somebody out of hell."

Believing Redemption Will Come

Regardless of the challenges we face, Jews have always lived with an abiding belief that redemption will come. A personal story illustrates this point:

In November of 1985, I travelled to Geneva together with Yosef Mendelevich—who spent eleven years in a Soviet prison—to demonstrate for Soviet Jewry at the first Reagan-Gorbachev summit. We entered the Soviet Aereflot office, demanding a ticket to Israel for Natan Sharansky, from the Chistopol prison where he was being held.

We insisted we would not leave until our request for Sharansky's ticket was met. Within minutes, the office was ringed with KGB agents. Just moments before we were arrested, Mendelevich took a picture of Roald Zelichonok, one of the Soviet Jewish Prisoners of Zion, and placed it over a portrait of Lenin, which adorned the Aereflot office wall. Turning around to face us. Yosef lifted his hands like a fighter who had just won the heavyweight championship. For me, this was a most extraordinary moment. It was Yosef's way of saying, "In the end, we will prevail. Even Lenin will be overcome. Soviet Jews will be free."

Upon my return to New York, I shared this experience with

family and friends at our Sabbath table. Sitting at my side, our youngest child, Dov, not yet bar-mitzvah, looked puzzled. Turning to me, he said, "*Abba*, what does Yosef Mendelevich want with John Lennon?"

Lenin thought he would control the world, especially the minds of the young; but in Dov's mind, the only Lenin he knew was the Beatle John Lennon.

And who would have imagined that just a few years later, Lenin statues would be disposed of, communism would be dead, the iron wall would be shattered, and hundreds of thousands of Soviet Jews would emigrate—they would taste from the sweet cup of redemption. In the words of a Hasidic master: "A little bit of light has the power to remove all the darkness in the world."

Everyone Can Make the Difference

Redemption seems overwhelming, beyond the grasp of any individual. What can a simple human being do to help usher in the Messiah? Everything, insists Maimonides. Every person can make the difference. One should see the world as an evenly balanced scale. A single action by any one of us can tip the scale.[25] A favorite story of mine speaks best on this topic:

> Once there was a travelling rabbi who had the ability to answer every question. Never once was he wrong. Then, one day, he came to a town where thousands came to hear him. One little girl raised her hand. "I have the question you can't answer," she said. "I have in my hand a bird. Tell me, is this bird alive or dead?"
>
> She thought, if he says it's alive, I'll close my hand and kill the bird. If he says it's dead, I'll open my hand and let the bird live.
>
> The rabbi, aware of the trick behind this question, was stumped. Here was the question he couldn't answer. But then, all at once, the answer hit him. Tears came streaming down his cheeks, even as his face broke into a cherubic smile, much like rain falling in the midday sun. Here, he knew, was the secret of Jewish destiny.
>
> Looking at the girl in the midst of the huge crowd, he said: "My

precious, precious child. You hold in your hand a bird. You ask
if it's alive or dead. I can only tell you one thing: The fate of this
bird lies in your hands. You can let it live, or you can let it die."

The bird is the metaphor for the Jewish people, for all humankind. It's in our hands, yours and mine, and everyone, with the
help of God, can make the difference.

* * *

And so, we have passed through an experience together,
woven together stories and secrets of white fire. Sometimes I
wonder which speaks more powerfully, the black, rationalistic
letters or the white, mystical spaces between them.

The rabbis say that in Divine poetry the black letters rest on
the frame of the white empty spaces. "Half bricks on whole
bricks," the Talmud notes.[26] It's the white fire that gives the black
fire its foundation.

In the end, fire differs from water. Water flows toward the
lowest level, while fire seeks a higher plateau. It reaches high,
higher, and higher still, burning past our eyes and ears into our
hearts and souls and memories.

Especially the white fire. It soars heavenward, linking the finite
human being with the infinite God.

Such is the power of stories.

Notes

1. See Rashi, Deuteronomy 33:2, s.v. *eish da'at*, quoting *Midrash
Tanhuma*, Genesis 1.
2. Many thanks to my dear friend Rabbi Saul Berman, who shared
with me insights contained in this section regarding the underlying
power of stories as an educational medium.
3. Rav Joseph B. Soloveitchik in *The Lonely Man of Faith* (New York:
Doubleday, 1992), pp. 28–33.
4. See *Pesikta Rabbati*, ed. Meir Ish Shalom (Tel Aviv, 1963), 131b.
It states that when returning from Anatot, Jeremiah did not see the
smoke rising from the Temple. See Ethics 5:5.
5. Some rabbis maintain that Jerusalem could never have been
destroyed had Jeremiah and other righteous people remained in the
city. See Louis Ginzberg, *The Legends of the Jews* (Philadelphia: Jewish Publication Society, 1936), iv, 303, 322.

6. I heard this story from various individuals. See Rabbi Jacob J. Schacter, "Rabbi Joseph B. Soloveitchik *z'l* on the *Tisha B'Av Kinos*," *Jewish Action* 54:4 (Summer 1994):10, whose footnotes directed me to the sources quoted in notes 4 and 5.

7. See Nehama Leibowitz in *Studies in Shemot* (Jerusalem: World Zionist Organization Department for Torah Education and Culture in the Diaspora, 1976), pp. 44–46, quoting *Midrash Petirat Moshe—the Midrash of the Passing of Moses*. The Midrash is found in *Ozar ha-Midrashim* (New York: Eisenstein, 1915), part 2, p. 363. I've paraphrased the Midrash using my own words.

8. Simcha Raz, *A Tzaddik in Our Time—The Life of Rabbi Aryeh Levin* (New York: Feldheim, 1976), p. 8. The story as told here includes some direct quotes from *A Tzaddik in Our Time*.

9. Rav Joseph B. Soloveitchik in *The Lonely Man of Faith* (New York: Doubleday, 1992), pp. 19–22.

10. I first heard this story at Torah Leadership Seminar, a program of outreach sponsored by Yeshiva University for Jewish teenagers. Some people have told me that a version of this story has been attributed to Tolstoy. See also Rabbi Joseph Lookstein, *Faith and Destiny of Man* (New York: Bloch, 1967), pp. 54–62.

11. *Midrash Genesis Rabbah*, 22:7. Here, too, I've paraphrased the Midrash.

12. See Nehama Lebowitz, *Studies in Genesis* (Jerusalem: The World Zionist Organization Department for Torah Education and Culture in the Diaspora, 1976), p. 39.

13. *Midrash Tanhuma*, Genesis 22. Once again, I've paraphrased.

14. See Nehama Lebowitz, *Studies in Genesis* (Jerusalem: The World Zionist Organization Department for Torah Education and Culture in the Diaspora, 1976), p. 198.

15. Note the sentences: "And Isaac spoke to Abraham his father, and said: 'My father.' And he said: 'Here am I, my son.' And he said: 'Behold the fire and the wood; but where is the lamb for a burnt-offering?' And Abraham said: 'God will provide Himself the lamb for a burnt-offering, my son'" (Genesis 22:7–8).

Could the first exchange of "'My father.' And he said: 'Here am I, my son,'" relate to Abraham's doubts as a father? And could the second exchange, where Isaac asked: "Behold the fire and the wood; but where is the lamb for a burnt-offering?" and Abraham answers: "God will provide Himself the lamb for a burnt-offering," relate to Abraham's moral dilemma?

16. See Rabbi Norman Lamm in *Faith and Doubt* (New York: Ktav, 1986), pp. 1–40.

Rabbi Emanuel Rackman writes in *The Condition of Jewish Belief* (Milton Himmelfarb, ed. [New York: Macmillan, 1966]): "God may have His own reasons for denying us certainty with regard to His existence and nature. One reason apparent to us is that man's certainty with regard to anything is poison to his soul. Who knows this better than moderns who have had to cope with dogmatic Fascists, Communists, and even scientists?"

See also Dennis Prager and Joseph Telushkin in *Eight Questions People Ask About Judaism* (New York: Tze Ulmad Press, 1975), pp. 1–22.

17. Rashi, Genesis 22:12, s.v. *ki atah yadati* quoting *Midrash Genesis Rabbah* 56:8.

18. See Rambam, *Code*, Laws of Fundamentals of Torah 5:1–2. Rav Aharon Soloveichik argues that the order of presentation of these laws indicates that for Maimonides the highest sanctification of God is to live for God. See Rabbi Avraham Weiss, *Women at Prayer* (New York: Ktav, 1990), p. 52.

19. See Rabbi Moshe Sokolow, *Text and Topics in the Teaching of Limudei Kodesh* (Torah Education Network), Purim, p. 1.

20. Note the thematic parallels. In both stories, a key event is forgotten for a time: Joseph's interpretation of the baker's and butler's dream; Mordechai's saving of King Achashveirosh from the plot to kill him.

In both, there are hangings: the baker in the Joseph story; Haman and his sons in the Purim story.

In both, sleep, or the inability to sleep, plays a key role: Joseph's interpretation of Pharaoh's dreams catapult him to leadership; Mordechai is paraded through the streets by Haman himself after King Achashveirosh—unable to sleep—has his Book of Chronicles read aloud, reminding him that Mordechai had saved the King's life.

In both, the crescendo is reached after a party: Joseph reveals himself after sharing a meal with his brothers; King Achashveirosh decides to hang Haman after Esther makes her plea to save the Jewish people at the King's lavish party.

The listener may also begin to detect a parallel message in the stories. In both narratives, a Jew, living in the exile (Joseph in Egypt, Mordechai in Shushan), courageously defends his people without fear.

And more—God's name does not appear in the *Megillah* story, and aside from Joseph's mentioning that God is the source for interpreting dreams (Genesis 39:9, 40:8, 41:16), God's name is not mentioned in the Joseph story. Both episodes appear to be a series of coincidences.

First the Purim story: Vashti *just happens* to be removed; Esther *just happens* to replace her; Mordechai *just happens* to overhear the plot against the King; Haman *just happens* to enter the palace after the King has read of how Mordechai rescued him.

So, too, the Joseph story: Joseph *just happens* to meet a stranger who directs him to his brothers; Joseph *just happens* to be sold to the chief executioner in Egypt; Joseph *just happens* to be placed in prison, where he interprets the dreams of the butler and baker; this *just happens* to lead to his being brought before Pharaoh, interpreting Pharaoh's dream, and becoming second to the King.

God's name is missing in both stories, but He is present everywhere, weaving the tapestry of redemption itself.

Note also the textual parallels between the stories:

Genesis 41:34 and *Megillat Esther* 2:3;

Genesis 39:10 and *Megillat Esther* 3:4;

Genesis 43:14 and *Megillat Esther* 4:16.

21. See the second paragraph of the *Aleinu* prayer recited at the conclusion of the morning, afternoon, and evening services.

22. See Rabbi Isaac de Leon in his *Megillat Esther* commentary to Maimonides *Book of Commandments*, affirmative commandment 4.

23. See *Sanhedrin* 98a.

24. I first read this story in notes taken on a lecture given by Rabbi Shlomo Riskin at the Lincoln Square Synagogue in New York City.

25. See Rambam, *Code*, Laws of Repentance 3:4.

26. *Megillah* 16b and Rashi's commentary s.v. *leveinah*.

PREFACE

It is always a great pleasure to participate in a storytelling festival or conference with other storytellers! At these events, we all get to share stories, hear each other's stories, and get to know each other better through the stories we choose to tell for the occasion. In a way, this book presents a Jewish Storytelling Festival in print, beginning with a foreword by Rabbi Avraham Weiss that sets the tone as it places stories as "apples of gold in a frame of silver." By the time you finish reading all the introductions to the stories and the stories themselves, you will feel a special friendship with these storytellers.

How did such a collection of tellers and tales come about? There is a story to tell. A number of years ago, Seymour Rossel suggested the idea of bringing out a book that would be a collection of stories by Jewish storytellers. Coincidentally, it was at about the same time that I became the founding director of The Jewish Storytelling Center in New York City, an outgrowth of the first Jewish Storytelling Festival in May 1984. Soon after, I also became the first coordinator of the Jewish Storytelling Network of the Coalition for the Advancement of Jewish Education (CAJE). However, for several reasons, that wonderful book idea just sat on the proverbial shelf for many years.

More recently, Arthur Kurzweil, vice-president of Jason Aronson Inc., approached me, independently, with a similar idea, and I thought that this was the absolutely right time to do it. By now, the number of Jewish storytellers had grown, thanks to a great extent to the CAJE Network, which allowed us the opportunity to bring storytellers together each summer at the annual national conference. As you can see from this volume, there are now many professional storytellers, educator-storytellers, author-storytellers, and rabbi/cantor-storytellers. Yes, it was a good time to have such a collection of stories! I set only a few criteria for the storytellers. I asked that the storytellers themselves choose stories with Jewish themes that are important to them. I also requested that the stories be written in an oral style so that others could tell or read them aloud. That's what storytelling is all about, the sharing of stories so that stories can continue to be told.

In March 1992, at the second Jewish Storytelling Celebration, "Continuing the Teaching Tradition," which was held once again at Yeshiva University's Stern College, Rabbi Weiss was the keynote speaker and his topic was the power of Jewish story. His talk, "Black Fire on White Fire: The Power of Story," set the tone masterfully. As we in the audience were listening and understanding the stories on one level, we were also experiencing their impact on other levels. What better way to begin this book than through the inspired voice of this wise storyteller! We not only have a series of stories that teach us, he also uses the stories to illuminate his points. After reading his foreword, you will feel as though you have been on a journey, with Avi Weiss as your guide, to discover for yourselves through story what is truly the enlightening dynamism imbedded therein. That is also what storytelling is all about, the hearing and experiencing of the stories—as well as the words about stories—in our heads, in our mouths, and in our hearts.

In this book, you will find a variety of stories, as well as a broad spectrum of storytellers who were invited to submit stories. While the storytellers represented here are among the most active tellers in the Jewish world, and highly accomplished and talented in the oral art of storytelling, there are certainly many others in your communities who are as accomplished and experienced. In my travels and at storytelling festivals, I meet new as well as experienced Jewish storytellers about whom I had not known before. Wherever I travel, I meet teachers and librarians who integrate stories into their sessions. I know that there are numerous storytelling rabbis and cantors who continually interweave *midrashim* and parables into their sermons and talks. And there are certainly many more people, and youngsters, too, who are bursting to tell stories but may need more encouragement or who have not yet discovered this very Jewish tradition.

Therefore, I hope this book will accomplish several things: acquaint you with the great variety of stories found in our Jewish oral tradition (in the past and in contemporary life); introduce you to some of the Jewish storytellers and their individual and collective voices; inspire you to retell or read aloud these stories to yourselves and to others; retrieve your own important stories that you need to remember; and bring more story-telling into our Jewish world, in the home, in the classroom, and in the synagogue—and anywhere you walk.

In this collection you will find a rich variety of stories chosen by the contributors. Some are personal or family stories; others are folktales. Some are based on remembered events, and some on biblical or talmudic accounts. Some focus on an individual true-life character, and some on a biblical or folktale hero. Some are told in contemporary times, some in historic times, and some in "Once upon a time." Most are serious in tone, but several are humorous. Some are mystical, others are magical, and still others reality-based and earth-bound. All of the stories mean something to the teller, and each one has expressed those thoughts and connections in the introduction that precedes each story. These introductory comments put each story into a context for the reader or listener. However, several contributors preferred to add an afterword to their stories instead of, or in addition to, the introductions.

While about fifteen of these stories have been recorded elsewhere, in print or on cassette, the rest have not. Most of the stories are written in prose, but four are in verse form (Suzanne Benton, Lynn Gottlieb, Heather Forest, Suri Levow-Krieger/Eva Grayzel) and two incorporate music (Jay Brand, Heather Forest). The length of each story varies from less than one page to many. Most are single stories, but a few are a string of stories tied together by the same character (Rami M. Shapiro, Peninnah Schram), by their similar images or holidays (Renée Brachfeld, Cherie Karo Schwartz, Suri Levow-Krieger/Eva Grayzel), or by the same genre of parable (Saul J. Berman). All the stories in the book have been arranged in alphabetical order of the story-teller's name, except for the prologue story. Although "The Storyteller—In Memory of Reuven Gold" is not authored by Reuven, it is about him, so we kept it as "his" story.

What is most interesting is that while there is a most extraordinary variety, there are no duplications of stories. Again, there is one exception, but even here, while the kernel of the story is the same, the styles, the approaches, and also the endings are marvelously different (Saul J. Berman, Steven M. Rosman). The themes of the stories offer a literal smorgasbord. What are some of the themes found in this collection? Here are only a sampling: we can learn from everything (Hanna Bandes, Rami M. Shapiro, Susan Stone); remembering (Eliezer Shore, Yitzchak Etshalom); justice (Howard Schwartz); the power of dreams (Roslyn Bresnick-Perry, James Stone Goodman, Steven M. Rosman, Laura Simms); names (Penina V. Adelman, Judith Black, Lynn Hazan); water/tears (Cherie Karo Schwartz, Joan Sutton); holidays (Renée Brachfeld, Nina Jaffe, Suri Levow-Krieger/Eva Grayzel, Debra Gordon-Zaslow, Mara, Joan Sutton, Marilyn Price, Devorah Spilman); and so on. There are portraits of various people in the storytellers' lives: grandparents (Annette Harrison, Betty Lehrman, Syd Lieberman, Laura Simms, Susan Talve), a cousin (Roslyn Bresnick-Perry), a father-in-law (Tsvi Blanchard). All the characters come alive with vibrancy and heart in these stories.

What emerges in all the stories is that the storytellers are teachers. And what more beautiful way of teaching exists to celebrate life and Judaism than through stories! As important as the teller of the story is the one who listens. We need to become listeners to our own stories, as well as to those of others. How do we do this? I would like to suggest that we dialogue with the story! Stories, no matter whether humorous or serious, pose important life questions and, in turn, answer those questions. It is here that we can connect the questions and responses to our own lives. Wrestle with the story and its theme; with the characters and their actions; create a *tikkun* ("repair"), a different ending that can work (as in the stories by Eve Penner Ilsen and Charles Roth), or else create a different story. This is part of the fluid nature of folklore and the oral tradition.

Sources have been cited in the introductions to the stories, which can be traced, if not to their original sources, then to other variants of the story. Our tradition says that when all the sources will be cited, then Moshiach/Messiah will come. We storytellers are trying to do our part. But this raises some questions: Can every story be traced to its origins? What is a "truly original" story?

It is difficult to be certain of the first version for every tale. Wherever Jews have lived, stories have been borrowed, adapted, transformed, shared, and exchanged, Thus, there are many Jewish variants of stories classified in the Israel Folktale Archives, in addition to all of the variants in world folktales. Surely, some of these stories will remind you of similar tales, perhaps ones that you had forgotten for years. Others will bring to your attention the fact that, as humans, we all tell similar kinds of stories. Thus, there are only a few "original" plots embroidered with variations.

Even when events actually happen in real life, these occurrences are often interpreted by drawing on the folk tradition. Therefore, similar stories have been told throughout the ages, although sometimes with different main acting characters or protagonists. An example of this phenomenon appears as the kernel of the story "Look Not upon the Flask." Here, Hanoch Teller identifies the bridegroom who exchanges his beauty for the physical deformity of his future bride, which is part of a bargain made in heaven before his birth, as the Sanzer Rav (d. 1876). In fact, this story is often attributed to the Sanzer Rav. But this story type also appears in *Me'otzranu Hayashan* (Hebrew), edited by B. Yushzon (Sifriyat Maariv, 1976). Here, this supposedly true historical tale is told of Moses Mendelssohn (1729–1786). Mendelssohn, a man with physical deformities, was hired by a wealthy Berliner named Guggenheim to tutor his daughter. Guggenheim felt that Mendelssohn would pose no threat to the affections of his daughter. However, one day, as they were studying Rachel and Leah, Mendelssohn, who loved her but was afraid she would reject his proposal, asked her if she believed that matches were made in heaven. Then he told her the story. At the end, the beautiful student agreed to marry him.

Many years ago, I heard Elie Wiesel tell a version of this story, also with the unattractive Moses Mendelssohn as the protagonist but with him meeting his beautiful bride for the first time at their arranged wedding. When the bride sees how ugly her bridegroom is, she refuses to enter into the marriage. And, as with the other variants, it is only when he tells her the story that she consents, happily, to the marriage. Apparently, this story has been told in Eastern Europe for many generations.

Recently, a version of the Mendelssohn story was transformed into an illustrated Japanese fairy tale. And so it goes: a good story always triggers another version.

There have been reports that this story has helped bring couples to the wedding canopy. Cherie Karo Schwartz was leading a story swap at a conference once, and an old woman told her: "I was very beautiful, and a suitor was very homely, so I wanted nothing to do with him. But then, one day, as we walked in the garden, he said, 'Let me tell you a story,' and he told me the story of Moses Mendelssohn. And we've been happily married for over forty years now." I, too, have heard that this story, in some version, has indeed brought couples to the marriage canopy, just as Hanoch Teller writes in his introduction. That is the power of a beautiful story!

Like the shepherd who offers his own kind of prayer rather than the traditional ones (as in Susan Danoff's story), so, too, we must write or recite the story in our own way. It is a folk way; it is a Jewish way. As Walter Benjamin wrote in his essay "The Storyteller," "Counsel woven into the fabric of real life is wisdom." (Walter Benjamin and Hannah Arendt, *Illuminations*, tr. H. Zorn [New York: Harcourt, Brace, 1968].) By delving into stories—personal, family, folk, and traditional—we retrieve so much good counsel provided we listen and tell and remember. Talking is remembering. It is then up to us to weave that good counsel into our lives.

All the storytellers in the book feel strongly that you, the readers, should retell or read aloud our stories. However, the introductions as well as the stories are copyrighted by each of the authors. Therefore, they can be reprinted or recorded only with the written permission of the specific author.

I believe the storytellers have chosen their stories wisely. May we continue the telling!

Peninnah Schram

ACKNOWLEDGMENTS

A book is never a solo adventure. Therefore, there are many people who encouraged me and helped to make this book possible. First of all, my heartfelt thanks and gratitude go to my dear friend Arthur Kurzweil. It is his love of story that has spurred so many of us to collect and write our stories for publication by Jason Aronson Inc. He has achieved the distinction of publishing more Jewish collections of stories than any other publisher. My profound gratitude goes to the sixty-eight contributors whose stories make up this book. Every one of them contributed worthwhile and inspiring stories with open hearts! This is indeed an international group which includes five storytellers who live in Israel, one from Turkey, and two from Canada. I want to also express my *nakhat* (Jewish pride) that several students from my various workshops and Yeshiva University storytelling courses who have continued telling stories are also part of this collection: Rachayl Eckstein Davis, Cantor Nancy R. Ginsberg, Naftali Haleva, Rabbi David Holtz, Nina Jaffe, Eliezer Shore, and also my daughter Rebecca Schram-Zafrany. It is from my students, and from all of the storytellers, that I continue to learn. I am delighted that the talented artist Lisa Rauchwerger has given permission to include her wondrous "apple tree in 4 seasons" illustration. I am very fortunate to know all the people who have contributed to this book.

There are two friends I wish to thank for the time they took to brainstorm ideas with me and to offer their good suggestions (which I always respect) in regard to this book: Howard Schwartz and Cherie Karo Schwartz. I feel especially grateful that Rabbi Avi Weiss said yes when I asked him to adapt his keynote address as the foreword to this book. He has continually inspired me personally with his manner, his voice, his listening, his learning, and his stories. They are all part of his *neshamah*, which reaches out to teach in a most beautiful way—and I listen and learn.

I want to express my appreciation to Gioia Timpanelli for her idea to include a story in memory of Reuven Gold, a storyteller whose voice is still heard through his remembered stories by many. In her introduction and in Howard Schwartz's story, "The Storyteller" (listed alphabetically under "Gold"), they capture the essence of Reuven and his spiritual storytelling legacy.

While this book was being edited, we heard the news of the death of the rebbe of rebbes of storytelling and singing, Reb Shlomo Carlebach, on October 20, 1994. His voice remains in our memories and in our hearts as the master teller of tales and sweet singer of Israel. I feel fortunate that he had contributed one of his special stories to this collection.

Since a book is a cooperative effort, there are many talented and skilled people who helped to produce this book, including the production editor, Janet Warner, the copy editor, Nicole Balant, and the director of editorial production, Muriel Jorgensen.

I continue to be appreciative of my husband, Jerry Thaler, who is always there with insights and encouragement for me to continue with all of my storytelling ventures. I respect his wisdom and perspective. On a personal note, I am also *qvelling* that my son, Michael Schram, has now discovered the excitement of telling stories he has listened to all his life. This has given me added impetus to gather more stories from storytellers everywhere so that we can continue, with strength, to transmit our wonderful Jewish legacy.

PROLOGUE: THE APPLE TREE'S DISCOVERY

Peninnah Schram and
Rachayl Eckstein Davis

Rachayl Eckstein Davis *received her formal introduction to storytelling in a storytelling course at Stern College coordinated with a program, "Kernels of a Pomegranate," at the 92nd Street Y, both of which were organized and taught by Peninnah Schram. After completing her B.A. in education, she received an M.A. in educational theater from New York University. Currently she teaches high school drama and leads creative dramatics and storytelling programs in day schools and summer camps. Rachayl lives in Oceanside, New York, with her husband, Hillel, and their four children, Nahva, Ariel, Leora, and Avital.*

See page 279 for bio and photo of Peninnah Schram.

We first heard Rabbi Avi Weiss tell "the apple story" during his workshop on Midrash at the first Jewish Storytelling Festival, which was held at Stern College in 1984. When we asked him what was the source of this "midrash," as he referred to it, he told us that he had heard it at a Marriage Encounter, and said that the story probably originated as a Chinese parable.

Yet, "the apple story" speaks in a particularly Jewish voice, for it describes the inner beauty, the *tselem Elokim*, that God has planted in each of us and the challenge we have in discovering that goodness, that *kedusha*.

In addition, even though we think of the six-pointed star, the star of David, as Jewish, it is rather the five-pointed star in the apple that could be compared to the Seal of Solomon, which has been documented as having actually existed.

1

"The apple story"—as a wonderful story should—appeals to a broad range of audiences. It has been told and retold in preschools and at high schools, from rabbis' pulpits and at holiday tables, on university campuses and at senior residences. Two years ago it was published by the Coalition for Advancement in Jewish Education (CAJE) as a Rosh Hashanah card. The artwork for the card, created by Lisa Rauchwerger, was also commissioned by CAJE.[1] This story conveys a message that every audience can appreciate and, in turn, wishes to share with others.

Stories speak to the very soul of the person. They appeal to the heart and to the head. They open a door to that inner core we each possess. They are told and retold—passed from parent to child, friend to friend, teacher to student—because they help us discover the beauty in others and in ourselves.

Stories are in each of us; they are our treasure!

May we continue to share our stories so that the spark that ignites the star inside of each of us can grow brighter and create stronger bonds between us all.

Note

1. Lisa Rauchwerger, illustrator and graphic designer, specializes in Jewish papercuts, paper sculpture, and calligraphy. Originally from California, she now lives and works in New York.

Illustration by Lisa Rauchwerger

n a great oak forest where the trees grew tall and majestic, there was a little apple tree. It was the only apple tree in that forest and so it stood alone.

Winter came. As the snow fell to the forest floor, it covered the branches of the little apple tree. The forest was quiet and peaceful.

One night the little apple tree looked up at the sky and saw a wonderful sight. Between the branches of all the trees, the little apple tree saw the stars in the sky, which appeared to be hanging on the branches of the oak trees.

"Oh God, Oh God," whispered the little apple tree, "how lucky those oak trees are to have such beautiful stars hanging on their branches. I want more than anything in the world to have stars on my branches, just like the oak trees have! Then I would feel truly special."

God looked down at the little apple tree and said gently, "Have patience! Have patience, little apple tree!"

Time passed. The snows melted and spring came to the land. Tiny white and pink apple blossoms appeared on the branches of the little apple tree. Birds came to rest on its branches. People walked by the little apple tree and admired its beautiful blossoms.

All summer long, the apple tree continued to grow. The branches of the tree formed a canopy overhead as they filled with leaves and blossoms.

But night after night, the little apple tree looked up at the sky with the millions, and millions, and millions—and millions of stars and cried out, "Oh God, I want more than *anything* in the world to have stars in my tree and on my branches and in my leaves—just like those oak trees."

And God looked down at the little apple tree and said, "You already have gifts. Isn't it enough to have shade to offer people, and fragrant blossoms, and branches for birds to nest on so they can sing you their song?"

The apple tree sighed and answered simply, "Dear God, I don't mean to sound ungrateful, but that is not special enough! I do appreciate how much pleasure I give to others, but what I really want more than anything in the world is to have *stars*, not blossoms, on my branches. Then I would feel truly special!"

God smiled and answered, "Be patient, little apple tree."

The seasons changed again. Soon the apple tree was filled with many beautiful apples. People walked in the forest. Whoever saw the apple tree would reach up to pick an apple and eat it.

And still, when night came to the forest, the apple tree looked at the stars in the oak trees and called out, "Oh God, I want more than *anything* in the world to have stars on my branches! Then I would feel truly special."

And God asked, "But apple tree, isn't it enough that you now have such wonderful apples to offer people? Doesn't that satisfy you? Doesn't that give you enough pleasure and make you feel special?"

Without saying a word, the apple tree answered by shaking its branches from side to side.

At that moment, God caused a wind to blow. The great oak trees began to sway and the apple tree began to shake. From the top of the apple tree an apple fell. When it hit the ground, it split open.

"Look," commanded God, "look inside yourself. What do you see?"

The little apple tree looked down and saw that right in the middle of the apple—was a star. And the apple tree answered, "A star! I have a star!"

And God laughed a gentle laugh and added, "So you do have stars on your branches. They've been there all along, you just didn't know it."

EPILOGUE

Usually, when we want to cut an apple, we cut it by holding the apple with its stem up. But in order to find its star, we must turn it on its side. If we change our direction a little bit, we too can find the spark that ignites the star inside each of us. The stars are right there within each one of us. Look carefully, look closely, and you'll find that beautiful star.

EVERY NAME
HAS A STORY

Penina V. Adelman

Penina V. Adelman *is a social worker and folklorist and the author of* Miriam's Well: Rituals for Jewish Women Around the Year. *She has collected stories from elderly Jews, Ethiopian immigrants in Israel, and women who are spiritual seekers. Her most recent work is a Bible for very young children. Penina lives in Newton, Massachusetts, with her husband and two children.*

In the fall of 1981, I met Eli Levine, the source of this story. He was a student of mine in a class on Jewish folklore that I was teaching at Hebrew College in Brookline, Massachusetts. But he was a student in name only. An elderly gentleman whose whole being came to life as soon as he started speaking, Eli was an expert on Jewish folklore. He had lived it, breathed it, and passed it on, both in *di alter haim* (the Old Country) in Volkovisk, Poland, and here in *di goldene medine* (the United States).

I know I learned more from Eli than he learned from me. As the class progressed, he remembered more and more anecdotes, stories, sayings, jokes, and customs. It was as if he needed the class only as a memory jog. Once, we were discussing the expressiveness of hasidic *nigunum* (melodies without words), how a *nign* was so versatile that it could convey whatever the mood and intention of the singer happened to be at the time.

Eli spoke up: "It's the same with the word 'Oy.' It can mean, 'Oy, I'm worried about my son—I haven't heard from him in weeks,' or 'Oy, imagine how it must be to lose a child while you're still alive,' or 'Oy, isn't this the most beautiful *simcha* (joyous occasion)?' All this in one such tiny word. The entire history of the Jewish People could be summed up with 'Oy.'"

When the semester ended, Eli confided to me that he was writing a book about his life and could use some help. "It's for my children and my grandchildren, so they should know how I grew up. So they should understand what it means to be a Jew." He was concerned that his grandchildren would not receive an adequate Jewish education and felt it was his duty to remedy that. I was to learn months later that he was suffering from cancer and didn't have very long to live. Hence, the urgency in his request for help in putting together the story of his life.

He showed me the manuscript. I could see in the written account that he was bursting with stories but that his writing just did not convey the vitality of his oral tellings. Eli needed a listener in order to tell his story properly. I suggested that we meet together weekly. I would ask him questions and tape his answers. Then, I explained, he would have a richer manuscript, with the stories told in his inimitable style. He agreed.

I had been waiting for this opportunity for many years. When my own grandparents were alive, I had been too young and timid to ask certain questions about their earlier lives. Eli was the storytelling grandfather of my adulthood. Ironically, I felt closer than ever to my grandparents while listening to his accounts of life in Poland as a young boy, and then in Boston as an immigrant in his twenties.

As for Eli, I think he was able to die with greater ease knowing that his stories would live on, even though he never did get his manuscript published. I promised him that I would tell his stories as often as I could and, indeed, I am still telling Eli's stories to children and adults in schools and synagogues, and to my own children as well.

"Every Name Has a Story" is my favorite story of Eli's to tell. Everyone has a name with some kind of a story behind it. The universal quality of a name story makes it easy for people in the audience to respond to such a story by telling one of their own. Isn't this one of the greatest gifts stories have to offer—to make story-listeners into storytellers?

I have added some explanatory material to Eli's original version in order to make it easier to understand and more accessible to Jews who are not over sixty, were not born in Eastern Europe, do not understand Yiddish, and did not migrate to the United States two generations ago.

Every time you tell a story of a person who has died, you are keeping alive the memory of their name. You are honoring that person, just as Eli's father was honoring the name of the grandfather whose name Eli received. Please remember this when you read or tell this story.

any years ago, in a faraway village named Volkovisk, in a faraway country named Poland, there lived a little boy named Eli.

Eli and his mother and his father lived together in a little house on the edge of town. It was a pretty little house, with wildflowers in many colors growing all around in spring and summer. Two tall pine trees guarded it carefully all year. Sometimes, on the coldest days, the goat and chickens would come and stay inside to keep warm by the stove. Eli's family didn't have much, but there was enough to eat and a roof over their heads at night.

Eli and his mother and his father did not speak English the way you do. They spoke Yiddish. When Eli wanted his mother, he would say, "Mameh," and when he wanted his father, he would say, "Tateh."

Every morning, for as far back as Eli could remember, as soon as breakfast was over, Tateh would take him on his knee and teach him the alphabet, the *aleph-beis* as it was called in Yiddish. Tateh and Eli sat at the table, while Mameh kneaded bread dough or peeled potatoes and onions to put into the big soup pot on the stove. Especially on Friday morning, just before the Sabbath or a big holiday, there was nothing Eli liked better than to sing the alphabet with Tateh while Mameh made delicious smells come from the stove.

First, Tateh would sing in his big, low voice, "A-LEPH, A-LEPH," the first letter of the alphabet, and then Eli would answer in his little, high voice "a-leph, a-leph." Then, Tateh would sing, "BEIS, BEIS," and Eli would answer, "beis, beis." Then, "GI-MEL, GI-MEL," and "gi-mel, gi-mel." And they would keep singing in this way until they reached the last letter of the alphabet. Later, Tateh wrote the letters down for Eli so that he could see what they looked like as he sang them.

Every single day Tateh sang the alphabet with Eli, until he knew it by heart. Then, on Sukkoth, the holiday when we eat and sleep in a little hut all decorated with apples and pears and squash and gourds from the fall harvest, Tateh and Mameh did something very special with Eli.

They all sat down together at the table, where a book lay open to the first page. It was the Torah, the story of the Jewish People, the family tree of our ancestors, Adam and Eve, Abraham and Sarah, Isaac and Rebecca, Jacob, Rachel, and Leah. Next to the book was a little bowl of sweet honey that Mameh had bought to make honey cake for the New Year. Mameh took a spoon and dripped a few drops of the sweet honey onto the letters of the first word of the Torah.

"Now, Eli, let's sing those letters that Mameh has covered with honey," said Tateh.

"But, Tateh, I can't see them!" complained Eli.

"Well, I guess you'll just have to lick off the honey, then," laughed Tateh.

Eli stretched his head over the book, stuck out his tongue as far as he could reach and, before you could say "*a-leph-beis*," the honey was gone.

"And now what do the letters say?" asked Tateh again.

Eli sang, "*Beis, Resh, A-leph, Shin, Yud, Tav. . . .*"

"That's right!" beamed Tateh.

"My smart little boy!" exclaimed Mameh as she gave Eli a big kiss.

"Now, what do those letters mean?" Tateh wanted to know.

"I don't know, Tateh."

"They spell the word, *Be-rei-shis*, and that means, 'In the Beginning. . . .' *Be-rei-shis* is the first word of the story of How the World Began in the Torah," explained Tateh.

"It's like the, 'Once upon a time . . .' of the stories I tell you at night before you go to sleep," explained Mameh.

"Oh," said Eli, and he licked his lips once more as he thought about how good that *Be-rei-shis* tasted on his tongue.

"Tomorrow will be a 'Beginning' for you, Eli. Tomorrow is the day you will start school and learn to read the Torah on your own," said Tateh, and he put his arm around Eli, who suddenly looked sad.

"But, no, Tateh, I don't want to go to school. I want to stay right here with you and Mameh."

"You are a big boy now, Eli," Tateh explained. "I've taught you all I can. It's time for you to go and learn with the other boys your age and to have your own teacher. Just the way I did when I was a little boy."

"And the way my father did when *he* was a little boy," echoed Mameh.

But Eli was still not convinced it would be such a good thing to go to school.

"How do I know I'll like it?" he asked.

Then Tateh knew that Eli needed to hear a special story, one that would help him feel good about going to school.

"Eli, when you go to school tomorrow, I'll tell you the story of how you got your name," promised Tateh.

"Tell me now, Tateh! Tell me now!" Eli begged. He loved to hear stories.

"Tateh will tell you on the way to school tomorrow," Mameh said in a firm voice. "You'll be walking down the road together and he'll tell you all about your name." And Eli had to be content with this.

That night, he dreamt that all the letters of the alphabet had faces and arms and legs. They walked to school with him because they were his friends. That made him feel not so lonely after all. But when he woke up the next morning and remembered that this was the day he was going to school, he became worried again.

"Are you all dressed and ready to go, Eli?" Tateh wanted to know.

"Oh, do I have to go, Tateh?"

"Yes," said Tateh, "I'm walking to school with you right now."

So Eli took Tateh's hand, and in the other hand Mameh stuffed some cookies she had baked in the shapes of the letters. As father and son walked to town, Eli munched on the sweet honey and raisin cookies. When he had finished the last crumb, he started thinking again about school. Then he remembered Tateh's promise.

"Tateh, I want you to tell me the story of my name."

"Certainly, Eli, I'll tell it to you. Remember, a story is like a cookie. Only you chew it with your ears," explained Tateh.

"Chew it with my ears?" wondered Eli. "How can I do that? My ears don't even have teeth."

"I don't mean you really chew on it with your ears," said Tateh. "I mean you listen very, very hard. You let the story come way inside you and feed you with sweetness the way a cookie does. So . . . here is the story of your name."

And as Tateh told the story, Eli stopped thinking about where they were walking or how soon they would get there. All his thoughts were on the words coming from Tateh's mouth.

TATEH'S STORY

A long, long time ago, before you were born, there lived a very good and wise man. People came from all over to talk to this man and ask him questions. And he had an answer for everyone. You see, he knew all the stories in the Torah by heart. And in these stories were all the answers to all the questions in the world.

So . . . as it happened, this wise man was your great-grandfather. My grandfather. And his name was Eli too. He was named for Elijah the prophet, who wanders all over the world, helping people; Elijah whose cup we drink from at the Passover *seder* because he stands for hope, for the time when the world will be at peace.

Mameh and I named you after your great-grandfather because he was a great scholar. He studied so that he could help people understand the ways of this world and the ways of the Creator. Today you are starting school, and you carry your great grandfather's name with you. That means you must make yourself *worthy* of his name. If you can learn to love study, then you will be a great scholar, too. Now, there's your school, just ahead of us.

Sure enough, there it was, a small wooden building not much bigger than their home. Eli stared and stared at it. But he wasn't worried anymore. He had chewed on Tateh's story the way he chewed on one of Mameh's delicious honey and raisin cookies. Now he felt proud to be taking his name to school with him.

THE CAR THAT RAN FROM MITZVAHS

Hanna Bandes

Hanna Bandes, *a profes-sional storyteller since 1987, has ignited sparks of Jewish-ness in audiences from Maine to Alaska. The found-ing editor and publisher of* Neshama *and a columnist for* K'fari, *she also offers work-shops on Jewish women's spirituality, storytelling, and writing for children. Her two published children's books are* Sleepy River *and* Reb Aharon's Treasure, *winner of the 1991 Sydney Taylor Manuscript Prize.*

The Car that Ran from Mitzvahs" is based on a true story, slightly dramatized to make a more tellable tale. The details have been changed to protect the anonymity of the characters, but the under-lying story truly happened and truly made a dramatic difference in the protagonist's life.

As a religious person, I like the story because it demonstrates *hashgacha pratit,* God's guiding hand, and shows spiritual struggle and growth. The world shown in this story is unfamiliar to many people, particularly the discipline of Shabbat and *shiva* (mourn-ing), which are governed by laws that are sometimes uncomfort-able for the people who follow them. Also, many people think that the Orthodox Jews have intense, yet stable, spiritual lives; this story provides a glimpse into the way in which deeply religious people sometimes wrestle with their spiritual development, and even with their basic faith.

Yet while giving a glimpse of the Orthodox world, the story is universal. Everyone can relate to the importance of doing *hesed,* deeds of loving-kindness, although sometimes they relate with surprise. I've had listeners tell me they hadn't realized how self-ishly they've lived their lives! Most city folks appreciate what this story says about community, a concept that is too often neglected in our fast-paced modern world. Finally, Jews and non-Jews re-late to the story because they can identify with Chaya's struggles and how it takes her so long to realize what's really happening in her life. I've had people come up to me after a performance and say, "You know, I think I've been too much like Chaya, too inde-pendent. You've given me a lot to think about."

The woman to whom this happened loves the idea that lots of people will hear, and perhaps tell, her story. She says, "People can be lectured at forever without it touching them, but when they hear the same lesson in a story, sometimes it can change their life. The events in this story changed my life. If they can change anyone else's, or start anyone thinking in ways that even-tually precipitate positive change, then my difficult years will not have been wasted."

---

he other day I ran into someone I hadn't seen in a long time. I knew her as a closed, bitter woman, but that day she radiated peaceful joy. I said, "Chaya, you look great! What's up?"

She smiled and said, "If you'd asked me six months ago what would improve my life, I would probably have said, 'Winning the lottery.' I'd never have said, 'Car trouble.' But that's the truth: car trouble turned my life around." And she told me this story.

I've had a lot of trouble in the last few years. My boyfriend was killed in an auto accident, everything I owned was destroyed in a fire, I was laid off—more than enough trouble for a lifetime, much less a couple of years. I stopped calling friends and hardly went out any more. My life was work-worry-sleep, work-worry-sleep. I barely had energy for what I *had* to do; everything else went out the window.

About that time, my car started to give me trouble. Sporadic trouble. At first it was a dead battery, a broken fan belt, the windshield wiper motor. Little things, easily diagnosed, easily fixed. Then, with no pattern I could see, the car started to stall. It felt like when I was a kid, learning to drive a standard and forgetting to downshift. So I kept saying, "Transmission," but the mechanics kept saying,"Engine." Within four months I'd shelled out over four hundred dollars and still couldn't trust the car. By now, this had become something other than simple car trouble. It seemed to be a metaphor for the way bad things kept happening to me.

Well, one day I had to make a shiva call, to comfort a mourner. I hated making shiva calls. Just a few days before my boyfriend, Arnie, was killed, we'd decided to get married. We hadn't told anyone. Like a couple of foolish teenagers, we were waiting until my ring was ready. Then the accident. His family whisked him away for burial in their city, at a private ceremony. They made it clear that I wasn't welcome. And since there wasn't anything formal between us, I couldn't sit shiva. I was so hurt and angry that I shut my door and didn't come out for almost two weeks. I'd suffered with my grief all alone, so visiting other mourners brought up a lot of pain. But Tamar was a good friend, and her mother had been sick for a long time. I had to go, even though I didn't want to and even though she was sitting shiva at her sister's home, about ten miles away.

The day I was going, someone called me to ask, "If you visit Tamar today, could you take Evelyn?"

Evelyn is one of those very sweet, good people with whom I have nothing in common. But you can't say no to requests like this. "I'll call her," I said, hoping I sounded happy to have the chance to give her a ride, the opportunity to do a mitzvah.

Evelyn bent her busy schedule to fit mine, and we started off. But about three miles before we got to the house of mourning, the car stalled. When I finally got it started, I pulled into a gas station and called Triple A.

Evelyn and I sat in that car for an hour while we waited for the tow. I felt guilty that I'd made her change her schedule to fit mine, especially since we weren't even going to make it to the house of mourning! But when I apologized, she said, "We don't know why this happened, but clearly it's God's will." There wasn't the slightest irritation in her voice, and gradually, my frustration eased and I felt some of her calmness creeping in.

The dealer kept my car for two days before he called. "We can't find anything wrong with your car, lady," he told me. Lady? The language I wanted to use was anything but ladylike. Then I thought of Evelyn. Was this all God's will? I took a deep breath. At least, this time they didn't charge me.

The next day, like a bolt of lightening, I thought, "It feels like the transmission; I should call a transmission shop." The transmission specialist said my description was very clear, and he explained what the problem was and how much the repair would cost. He could see the car in two weeks.

I called the dealer back and spoke to the service manager. He begged me to give his shop another chance, and when he offered to loan me a car, I agreed. I dropped my car off Thursday morning and drove off in the loaner.

Friday at 3:00 P.M. just as I was about to leave work to get home before Shabbat, the service manager called. His diagnosis and price matched those the transmission man had given me; the car would be ready Tuesday. I was about to hang up when he added, "Oh, and we need the loaner back tonight, or we have to charge you thirty dollars per night or ninety dollars for the weekend."

Return the car? I barely had time to get home and prepare for Shabbat! How could I get to the dealer and then home before Shabbat came? As a Sabbath observer, I couldn't drive, ride in a bus, or even carry my handbag after Shabbat started. I ran out of the office, zoomed to the dealer, and dropped off the loaner. That left me about twenty-five minutes to get home. I called a cab but was told that, due to rush hour and the rain, I'd have a half-hour wait. Thank God, the bus came along. I ran all the way home from the bus stop, bursting through the door a minute before Shabbat. No time to heat my dinner or even put up hot water for tea. It was more than I could bear. I thought of Arnie and wished I'd been with him in the car when that truck jumped the median.

I lit my Sabbath candles, sat down, and cried like a baby.

Tuesday after work I took the bus—three buses, actually—to the shop, paid the five hundred dollars, and drove off. As I started home I thought, "The car sounds great!" But as I got closer to home, I thought, "Maybe it doesn't sound so good." And as I pulled up in front of my building, I thought, "I'd better call them in the morning."

Even so, fool that I was, after dinner I drove to my exercise class. The car sounded awful, and after class, when I tried to start it, it would not go into any gear.

I locked the car and walked the mile home. I was seething, and I thought that the walk through the chilly drizzle would calm me down. But as I walked, I thought of Evelyn's words. I felt like screaming, "God, if this is Your will, why? Why do You keep hurting me? Haven't You done enough?"

By the time I reached my street, I was really ripping. I wanted answers, and I wanted them now. So instead of going home, I went to the rabbi's house. He was out, so I told the rebbetzin the whole story. "Why do these things happen to me?" I cried. "I have so much trouble. Why?"

"Why didn't you call me? I'd have picked you up at your class," she said.

"This isn't about me asking for a ride, it's about the bad things that happen to me."

"You should have called," she repeated. "If you didn't want to call *me*, you could have called half a dozen other people."

"I didn't want to bother anyone. That's not the . . ."

She interrupted: "It's not a bother. That's what we're here for. We're here to help each other. That's what community is all about."

"But I don't like to be beholden, and I don't like to have others owe me anything," I said. "I know it's a mitzvah to help others, and I try, but I barely have energy for myself, let alone everyone else. I'm *tired*. Anyway, that's not the issue. I want to know why . . ."

She interrupted again: "Ask for help, Chaya. That's all I can say."

I went home even madder, furious that I hadn't been able to make her understand. I had had it—with the car, with religion, with God, with everyone and everything.

For the next two days I held myself together by focusing on the car. The dealer had towed it to the shop Wednesday morning, but by 5:00 P.M. Thursday he still hadn't told me what was wrong. In fact, every time I called, I was disconnected! I was sure they'd screwed up the five hundred dollar job, ruined the whole transmission, and were planning to stick me with the bill for a total rebuild. It would be just my luck!

I needed advice, so I called Bruce Williams on talk radio and told him my story. He said, "You're right, they may try to rip you off. I hate to sound sexist, but you need a man to call for you. Got a husband?"

"No."

"Got a boyfriend?"

"No."

"You must have a male friend."

"Well . . ."

"Look lady, if you don't have any friends, there isn't much I can do." And he hung up on me.

I stared at the phone. His words reverberated with the rebbetzin's: theme and variations. "Have a friend, be a friend. Ask for help. Helping others—that's why we're here." And as a quiet counterpoint, I heard Evelyn: "It's God's will, God's will."

For the first time I really *thought* about all those times the car had failed. Dead battery—when I was on my way to work at the synagogue rummage sale. Broken fan belt—when I was bringing a meal to a new mother. Windshield wiper motor—when I was picking up my neighbor's husband at the trolley during the early hours of a hurricane. Stalling while driving folks to an engagement party; my unexpected passengers had meant I couldn't stop at the mall en route. Stalling on my way to visit my housebound Great-Aunt Tilly; I'd turned around because I was afraid of getting stuck in her small town. Stalling three times on my way to my cousin's wedding, which made me so late I missed the *chuppa*—the wedding ceremony—an event that had promised to be bittersweet, since it would be my first wedding since Arnie's death. Each and every time the car had stalled, I'd been doing a mitzvah reluctantly, with resentment. I'd been giving because I felt I should, but I'd felt I had nothing left to give. I was giving while my heart screamed, "Stop!"

Was it surprising that my car kept quitting? It had been acting out my inner thoughts!

But—I slowly admitted to myself—part of the equation was missing. I was being a friend by helping, by doing mitzvahs. But when had I let anyone help me?

Had the rebbetzin misunderstood me? Or had she focused right in on the problem? Could my "I'll take care of myself" attitude be preventing the universe from fulfilling *my* needs?

I made myself a cup of tea, then sat staring at the cup until it got cold.

After a while I pulled myself together and made a fresh cup of tea. Then I started telephoning. I didn't even know which friend, or friend's husband, might know something about cars! On the second call I struck gold, someone who discussed the angles of the situation with me for half an hour. When I hung up, with the name and number of a reliable transmission man in hand, I felt supported and hopeful for the first time in years.

In the morning, I called the transmission man and told him the story. "Sounds like the dealer screwed up," he said. "Let me call him for you."

Half an hour later, the dealer called. "Lady, your transmission died—no relation to the problem we fixed earlier this week—and we've worked out a deal with the manufacturer. As a good will gesture, we'll rebuild your transmission, a one thousand dollar job, and all you have to pay is one hundred dollars. We'll have the car done by next Wednesday."

A nine hundred dollar goodwill gesture? Right. But I pretended to believe him and accepted the offer. And I arranged for the rebbetzin to pick me up at work on Wednesday and drive me to the shop.

The car wasn't ready Wednesday, so I canceled my ride. The rebbetzin wasn't available Thursday, so I called someone else. This woman said, "I'm so glad you called! I'd never have landed my new job if you hadn't helped me rewrite my resume last summer, but I couldn't think of a way to say thank you."

But the car wasn't ready Thursday either.

Friday was the first Friday after daylight saving ended, the first short Friday and a day of crisis for all Sabbath observers, who suddenly have an hour less to get everything done. My hand reached for the phone half a dozen times, then pulled back: if I asked for help today, would I make people angry? But finally I dialed the rebbetzin's number—not to ask for a ride, but to ask what to do. Her son, home for the weekend, answered the phone. She wasn't available, so I spilled my story to him. And he said, "I'm not busy and my mother's not using the car. Where should I pick you up?"

We picked up the car, and it's run just fine ever since. It sounds great and drives well. I think its troubles are over.

I think mine are over, too. I've been asking people for help and making myself available to help them. The phone's been ringing—people asking for help, people offering to do things for me, and people just calling to say hello. And somehow, everything else has been going better, too. I even got a note from Arnie's mother. She'd been going through his papers and had come to understand how important we'd been to each other. She even apologized for keeping me from his funeral!

Chaya smiled, a calm, almost beatific smile. She was silent for a moment, then said, "Do you know the story of the Persian who bought an ox from a Jew? The ox worked well for a couple of days. But one day, the ox wouldn't even stand up. The Persian screamed at it and finally hit it; still, it just lay in its stall and chewed its cud. The Persian stormed off to the Jew's house and demanded a refund. The Jew said, 'I think I know what the problem is,' and went with the Persian to the barn. He bent over the ox and whispered in its ear. The ox then lumbered to its feet and let the Persian yoke it.

"All day it worked hard, and all day the Persian wondered. That night, he returned to the home of the Jew. 'What did you say to the ox?' he demanded.

"'I told him that when he belonged to me, he rested on the Sabbath because I rest on the Sabbath. Now, I told him, he belongs to you, and since Persians don't have a Sabbath, he has to work whenever you do. You won't have any more trouble from him.'

"The Persian went home and thought about this. The next night, he came back to the Jew and asked about the Sabbath.

Soon he was studying with the Jew, and shortly, he became Jewish. At his conversion he took the name 'ben Torta,' 'son of an ox,' because he said the ox had been his greatest spiritual teacher."

There was a long pause as Chaya stared into the distance. "I think," she said slowly, "I should take the name 'bat Auto,' 'daughter of a car,' because the car has been my great spiritual teacher. It taught me the importance of running to do mitzvahs— and of letting others run to do mitzvahs for me."

A STORY FROM THE JEWISH CEMETERY IN JAPAN

Joel ben Izzy

Joel ben Izzy *travels the world, gathering and telling stories. Recent performances have taken him to Paris, Rome, Athens, Madrid, Zurich, Tel Aviv, Haifa, Jerusalem, Hong Kong, Tokyo, and throughout the United States. He has pro-duced two tapes,* Stories from Far Away *and* The Beggar King and Other Tales from Around the World, *both of which have received Parents' Choice Gold Awards. Joel is a native Californian and attended Stanford University. He now lives in Berkeley, California, with his wife, Taly, and their son, Elijah.*

I first became interested in Jewish stories when my second-grade Sunday school teacher, Mrs. Malatsky, assigned me to read *Zlateh the Goat* by Isaac Bashevis Singer. I have been searching for more stories ever since.

Looking for stories is a tricky thing. There are some stories that I find, and others that find me. Still others lie buried, waiting to be found and passed on. What follows includes one story of each type.

20

ome years ago, I was invited to tell stories at the Tokyo Jewish Community Center. It's an odd place, as you might imagine. When people think of Tokyo, they don't generally think of Jews. Yet there are Jews in Tokyo, as there are in any country in the world, and a handful of them showed up on a Saturday night in November to hear stories.

Afterward, the Rabbi came up to me and told me how much he had enjoyed the stories. He asked what I planned to do the next day.

I explained that I had a flight to Hong Kong in the evening and I thought that until then, I might catch some of Tokyo's most famous sights—the Meijii shrine, the department stores in the Ginza, and the Emperor's palace.

"You could do that," he said, nodding politely. "Sure you could." Something in his voice told me he wasn't recommending it.

"But wouldn't you rather come with us tomorrow? We're going to go clean out the Jewish graveyard in Yokohama."

I had to admit that the thought had not occurred to me. He saw my hesitation and added, "It's a big mitzvah, you know, honoring the dead. And the Jewish graveyard is the only dirty place in all of Japan."

I did know that it was a big mitzvah. I thought about how many times I had told groups of Jewish students about the mitzvah of cleaning up a graveyard and realized that I myself had never done it.

Then, the Rabbi added, "Besides which, you could meet Mr. Shimkin."

"Oh!" I said, with no idea who he was talking about. "*The* Mr. Shimkin?"

"Look," he said. "You're a storyteller. Maybe you'll get a story out of this. Besides, the Meijii shrine will be here the next time you come to Tokyo, but Mr. Shimkin may not be."

The next morning found a motley group of about fifteen of us equipped with sponges, mops, brooms, and buckets. There were a few college students, some businesspeople, a couple of wandering Jews, and one frail, elderly man who looked a little like Isaac Bashevis Singer and walked with a cane.

The Rabbi pointed and whispered, "That's him. Joseph Shimkin. Go talk to him."

As we descended into the subway, I struck up a conversation with the old man. He spoke English with a Yiddish accent so thick that I could even hear it when he added phrases in Japanese.

He looked me up and down. "You're a storyteller? Very nice. What are you doing in Japan?"

I told him that I was looking for stories and asked him if he knew any.

He thought a while, cocked his head, and then asked, "Have you ever heard of Senpo Sugihara?"

I shook my head.

"You should have. Everyone should have. The man was a hero. He saved my life."

When he saw he had my interest, Mr. Shimkin continued.

"I am not from around here," he said. I had gathered as much. "I was born in Poland. When the war came and we realized what was happening to Jews, I went from embassy to embassy, looking for a visa, any visa. As happened to so many Jews, door after door slammed in my face. Ambassadors laughed at me. England, America, they all said the same thing. 'Jews?' they asked. 'We have plenty of Jews.' Finally, with no place else to go, I came to the door of the Japanese consul to Lithuania in Kaunas.

"He listened politely to my story and told me that it was very unlikely that his country would issue me a visa because, after all, it was about to become allied with the Nazis. But he said he would wire and ask. Three times he wired, and three times the Japanese government said no. He said he was very sorry. Then he asked what would happen to me if I stayed.

"I told him I would be killed.

"'And are there many in your position?'

"'Thousands,' I told him.

"He looked at a large box in his office and told me to return the next day. When I did, I found him at his desk, with stacks and stacks of signed, stamped visas and his pen in hand, signing more. Japanese visas then had to be written by hand. Over the next twenty days, he wrote sixteen hundred transit visas to Japan, and as the Japanese government demanded that he leave his post he wrote more, as many as he could. His arm shook with exhaustion. They carried him to the train. I remember his face as he left. He was still writing visas and passing them out the window as the train left the station.

"Those were transit visas, and we used them to escape to Japan. Some we were able to duplicate to save more Jews. Six thousand in all. And of all those Jews that came to Japan fifty years ago, some went on to Australia and some to the United States, some to Israel and some to England. But I am the last one left in Tokyo that Senpo Sugihara brought in. I like it here."

He handed me his card. It read, "Joshim Trading Company." At the top it said, "Exports: electronics, general merchandise, cultured pearls." Below that, it read, "Imports—Joseph Shimkin, President."

"And that ambassador, Senpo Sugihara, was punished in this country for his actions. He died a shamed man—*hi-ji sarashi*—and his family was dishonored. Senpo Sugihara—you should tell his story."

I was so involved in the story that I had not noticed that we had arrived in the graveyard in Yokohama. The Jewish section was small and overgrown with plants; the gravestones were covered with mud and moss.

As we scoured out the names and dates with toothbrushes and soapy water, Mr. Shimkin began to tell me about the people who lay buried there. "Every Jew who comes to Japan has a story," he said. "Look here, at this one."

He pointed to a gravestone, the cleanest in the yard. "This man showed up at the Jewish Community Center at High Holiday services. There are only two thousand Jews in all of Tokyo and we all know each other, but no one knew him. We asked who he was and where he was from.

"He said his name was Avram, and never mind where he was from—it was far away.

"He spoke good English and we asked him if maybe he was from England. 'No.' The United States? 'Feh,' he said. He refused to talk about it.

"He was an odd sort, an older man, and a spark of life in our congregation. After services he would start to sing old Yiddish songs and tell stories and jokes, but he refused to say anything about who he was and where he was from. His favorite subject was Esperanto, and he would go on and on about how if only the world would all learn to speak the same language we could live in peace. He offered Esperanto classes at the JCC, and people actually came and studied. Can you imagine? Esperanto in Japan?

"The years went on and he became sick. Now the questions of where he was from and who his family was became more important. He refused to talk about the past, only discussing the future. He spoke only of his dreams. He said, 'Someday there will be peace in the world, and we will fight no more! Someday we will all speak the same language—Esperanto!' Finally, he died. A mystery to us.

"There is no Jewish undertaker in Japan. He would do no business—there are so few Jews, and you could never make a living waiting for us to die. You'd die first. So when one of us dies, we gather a Chevrah Kaddisha and wash the body ourselves, in that little hut over there." He pointed to a tiny shack, small even by Japanese standards, with a window looking out into the graveyard. "And so we laid him to rest, right here."

"Three days later, we received a phone call from two women in New York. They were his sisters, they said, and they wanted to thank us for giving their brother a Jewish life and a Jewish burial.

"'Such an end to such a life,' they said. 'And such a brilliant scientist.'

"We asked what they meant. They said that he had been a physicist at the University of California at Los Angeles in the 1940s. He worked on the atomic bomb. When the bombs fell on Hiroshima and Nagasaki, he felt he could never go on living in the United States. He became miserably depressed and said that the only way he could live with himself was to go and make peace in Japan. He became a teacher of Esperanto. . . .

"So you see, every grave has a story, because every Jew has a story."

He was quiet for a moment. Then he pointed to the next space over. "You see this one here?"

I did not see anything. I looked at him and wondered how good his eyes were. I looked again, and there was nothing.

"Look, right here. Do you see?"

It was a judgment call. I did not want to embarrass him, saying there was nothing there. But after some thought, I told him that I saw nothing.

"No," he said. "Of course you don't. That one's mine. That's where they'll bury me. And maybe someday, Mr. Storyteller, you'll tell my story."

This past year I returned to Tokyo, to tell stories again at the Tokyo Jewish Community Center. I asked about Joseph Shimkin.

The Rabbi smiled and shook his head. "It's funny you ask about him. We buried him just last week. The last time I saw him alive was just before that, at a ceremony honoring Senpo Sugihara. The Japanese government revised its position on Sugihara. Did you know they've made him a hero?"

REMEMBERING RACHEL

Suzanne Benton

Suzanne Benton, *sculptor, mask performer, and print-maker, has worked through-out the world for twenty-two years, absorbing and retell-ing the myths and legends of diverse cultures. Her deeply philosophical work urges us to consider the contemporary meanings of sacred texts and ancient stories. Her honors include numerous artist-in-residencies and grants worldwide: a recent Fulbright Lecturer to India; Thanks be to Grandmother Winifred Grantee, East Africa; and exhibitor, "Mythic Works," National Museum of Ameri-can Jewish History, Phila-*

delphia. She has produced a cassette, Myths, Masks, Legends and Lifestory. *Suzanne resides in Ridgefield, Connecticut.*

I believe in the power of the artist as culture maker. Throughout the years, I have chosen to develop my work as a bridge between cultures, and to absorb the myths and the mask forms of East-ern and Western worlds.

As a Jew, I've had to reclaim and retell the myths and life sto-ries of Judaism to be comfortable with my own culture. In order to honor my Jewish identity as a woman and as a feminist, I've had to transform the stories.

I create metal masks and usc them in portraying the powerful stories of the women of the Bible. Although these women were limited by the social constructs of their time, they nevertheless have an enduring role in the course of Jewish history. I began with the story of Sarah and Hagar, performing it as a mask tale at Lincoln Center in 1969.

My metal masks are works of art in themselves, and they also come alive in performance. Masks possess a visceral symbolism, which adds dimension and power to the stories that I cull and reshape in the process of creating Midrash.

I continue the midrashic tradition in my work with other cul-tures by reinterpreting their mythic, religious, literary, and folk-loric texts according to the issues of our time. When I tell the tragic tales, I am not creating a model for repetition, but exposing the universality of oppressive patterns so that we may change them.

From 1983 to 1985, I created twenty-five masks and tales on the theme of the Holocaust in order to personally come to terms with this profound crisis for Jews and modern society. I established a studio in Koln (then in West Germany) and welded archetypal masks of victim, perpetrator, innocence, witness, and so on. I use these masks to perform the "Tales of Tragedy."

"Remembering Rachel" is one of my thirteen mask tales of women of the Bible. I developed this story for a 1989 performance at the Women in Spirituality conference at Mercy College in Detroit. My biblical feminist retellings begin with the study of biblical text and Midrash. Then, I create the welded mask. The mask is used in movement and with voice improvisation as the next step in unlocking the tale. Scenes from the story are played out until the mask tale is cohesively developed. Eileen Jones, a specialist in Laban movement, worked with me in the initial stages of developing the Rachel tale. I also conducted workshops in improvisational mask storytelling as part of the process of this work.

As the story takes form, stylized movements are choreographed and the script takes form in free verse. The work remains in process, with further refinements growing out of repeated performance.

I feel that what I am doing is really Midrash. We need to share the texts of our culture again and again. It is the present-time transformations of our cultural heritage that keep our spirit alive and invigorated.

The story of Rachel can be found in Genesis 29–33 of the Bible. I also referred to Louis Ginsberg's book, *Legends of the Bible*, published by the Jewish Publication Society of America (Philadelphia, 1968).

Proud woman,
Beloved woman
Rode a camel,
And Jacob worked fourteen years
To have her as his bride.

I'm Rachel
Fair of form and face, they say.
They look at me; they touch me.
Jacob kissed me hot, wet
When he met me.
I ran home to tell.

He could have me, my father said,
He could have me.
Seven years labor,
My price.

Who wanted him
Staring, touching, pulling.
Because I'm beautiful
They think I want them near me.

My mother died when I was young.
Leah could help me.
Leah wanted him.
Her tender eyes
Longing to be mother of nations.

Our father gave her to Jacob.
After seven years
He sent Leah into the bridal tent.
In the morning
Jacob saw that he was cheated.

Laban, the Syrian, our father said,
"Fulfill Leah for a week,
And you can have Rachel.
Promise me another seven years."

Leah was fulfilled.
Then, he took me.
I said no, I'm tired, I have cramps,
I've put henna in my hair
You must wait three hours.

Leah has made babies for six years,
Six sets of twins.
We number the boys.
She named them.
She named their future.

Reuben, the first, came seven months
After the night of the tent.
Normal she called him.
She liked it.
The sailors by the sea,

The travelers on the road,
The women by the looms spoke about it.

I saw her pain, her tiredness.
Jacob didn't want me to have children.
His couch is in my tent.
It is convenient.
He does the talking,
Fourteen years of labor for me
And six more for the cattle.

I live with the oracular voices.
The teraphin I stole from my father,
After the twenty years labor,
When we fled to Jacob's mother, Rebeccah.

My mother is dead
Leah hates me.
I am childless.
Bilhah is my bondsmaid,
As old as Leah.
I say to Jacob,
"Go in unto Bilhah, my sister,
So that I may have a child through her."
And Jacob harkened to that.

Young Zilpah is Leah's bondsmaid.
Her father is our father.
Leah gives her to Jacob
Between us we will make twelve tribes.

I am barren.
I live with the teraphin,
Heads, of firstborn slain,
Salted, oiled, copper and gold tablets
Under their tongues.
They speak on all matters asked.
I am to have children, two.

Jacob will not help me.
He says it is God's doing.
His God reprimands him.
Still, I am cursed.

The mandrake root
Looks like a man,
Can kill or make wonders.
I buy it from Leah,
Wizard with the herbs.

"Give it to me," I say.
"Why?" she asks, (what would you kill?).
"You can have Jacob for the night."
He is mine to give.

When he comes from the field, Leah says,
"I have bought you for a mandrake root."
Jacob says yes to Leah.

She thinks I am the beloved.
He gazes at me.
He dreams of me when he is with her.
What does he dream with me?

I have no life.
I have the mandrake root.
It will make me laugh.
It will make me loose.
It will make me like Leah.

Leah prays for me.
I bear my son, Joseph.
He is a dreamer, like me.
Jacob loves him.

In twelve years
I will have another son.
I will fast twelve days.
I shall die
Bearing my second son,
Benjamin, the peace maker.

I am Rachel, beloved,
Remember me.
I have given you
The dreamer,
Given you, the Peacemaker.
Remember me.

FABLES OF THE MISNAGDIM

The Eagles

Ephram the Elephant

Shep the Sheep

Faige the Fawn

Saul J. Berman

Saul J. Berman *is an associate professor of Jewish Studies at Stern College of Yeshiva University and an adjunct professor at Columbia University School of Law, where he teaches a seminar in Jewish law. He served as rabbi of the Orthodox Congregation in Berkeley, California, after his completion of ordination at Yeshiva University and receipt of a J.D. from New York University School of Law. From 1984 until 1990, he was the senior rabbi at Lincoln Square Synagogue in New York City. He has since returned to full-time teaching, learning, writing, and parenting. He and his wife, Shellee, have four children—Shama, Efrath, Akiva, and Esther Golda.*

It was almost ten years ago that I began serving as Rabbi of Camp Morasha. I was intimidated only by the prospect of delivering a *derash* every Shabbat morning to some seven hundred campers and staff members, the majority of whom were between the ages of ten and fifteen. With the knowledge that my predecessor had somehow done it, I entered upon my responsibility with a mixture of confidence and trepidation.

My initial *derash* was a disaster. It was probably interesting for the adults present, but its only merit for the children was its brevity. I simply didn't connect with any level of their conscious-

31

ness. Distressed, I thought carefully about what I should do on the following Shabbat. However, another unsatisfactory connection with the kids led me to radically reconsider what I might do.

On my third Shabbat, with some degree of desperation, I decided that I would try telling a story. Many stories came to mind, since I had in childhood voraciously read entire collections of fairy tales, fables, and other assorted collections of stories. I finally decided that I would try a fable that I had heard my father tell in a *derash* that he delivered in his Synagogue when I was yet a child. It was the only fable I ever heard him tell of which I never read any echo, and I assume that he made it up.

My father's fable, "The Eagles," which I retell in these pages, lent itself to a particular connection to the weekly Torah reading, providing in its moral an answer to a question that I posed at the outset of my talk. It went gangbusters. The adults as well as the kids were fully engaged with the tale during my telling of it. Moreover, for the rest of Shabbat and for days afterward, children would stop me to discuss exactly what I had meant by various subtle elements of the story.

For the following Shabbat, I defined a problem in the Parasha and began to create a fable in which the answer to the moral dilemma would be embedded. The excitement, for me and for the campers, was wondrous, and a standard form was born. For these past many years, I have been composing a new fable for almost every Shabbat of the summer. For the first few years I did not even take notes on my fables, and every now and then I meet a former camper who reminds me of a story I had completely forgotten. More recently, I have been recording the fables after Shabbat. The following are four samples of my fables.

The Eagles

 flock of eagles was flying high over the land. In their view, they were able to see the dense forests and the villages, the rivers and the lakes; all of the beauties of the world lay beneath them. As they were flying gently, one of the eagles suddenly felt a sharp pull in his wing as if something had snapped. And so he began to fly downward toward the earth so that he could examine himself and discover what had happened. When he landed, he found himself in the middle of a chicken coop. He wasn't distressed because he knew that he simply had to examine himself to find

out what was wrong and then fly on. But as he examined himself, he realized that his wing had snapped and that it would
take time to recuperate and to heal. The eagle, therefore, began
to look around himself, and the more he saw, the more he disliked the place where he found himself.

"Why, these chickens," he said to himself, "just look at what
disgusting birds they are. They call themselves birds and yet
they don't even fly. They just flap their wings and hop up and
down. And when they need food they actually peck in the ground,
digging their food out of the dirt. And they cackle at one another in those unpleasant sounds." And so the eagle isolated
himself off in a corner of the chicken coop, knowing that his
recuperation period would be short and that eventually, he
would rejoin his proud fellow eagles.

But time passed and the eagle became lonely, and so gradually, over the course of time, he ventured out of his corner and
began to communicate with the chickens in the coop. And slowly
but surely, he began to imitate their ways.

The year passed, and the original flock of eagles was again
flying over that same area of the land, looking down again at
the beautiful mountains and the villages, the rivers and the
streams and the lakes. And suddenly, one of the eagles in the
flock noticed, down below, one of his fellow eagles. And so he
quickly descended, circled the area, ascertained that it was in
fact a fellow eagle, and flew down and landed next to the first
eagle. And the first eagle didn't even respond. Indeed, the first
eagle was flapping his wings, jumping up and down, hopping,
and pecking in the ground for his food.

And the second eagle said to the first eagle, "Come, you don't
belong here. You're an eagle, not a chicken. You don't belong
here in the midst of all of these strange birds. Come fly away
with me."

And the first eagle said, "No, don't be silly. This is my place.
This is where I belong."

And the second eagle said, "No, this is not where you belong.
Don't you understand? You're not a chicken—you're an eagle.
You don't have to just flap your wings and hop. You can fly and
soar to the highest places. You don't have to peck the ground

and the dirt for your food. You can take your food wherever it's to be found. Don't you understand?" said the second eagle to the first. "You're an eagle. You can soar to the highest places." And gently and slowly the second eagle began to persuade the first eagle that, in fact, the habits that he had taken on himself over the intervening year were not of his nature and that he was, indeed, an eagle who could soar and achieve great heights, until eventually, the two eagles soared off together high up into the sky, where they could see the land, the dense forests, the lakes and the rivers—all that God had created.

The eagle had resumed his destiny.

Ephram the Elephant

Deep in the forest there lived a wonderful beast named Ephram— Ephram the elephant. Ephram the elephant loved all of the other animals of the forest and, since he was big and strong, always wanted to do things to help others. And he did. One time, Ephram the elephant was walking in the forest. He saw a whole family of monkeys chattering, excited and upset, in a tree. Ephram walked over to them and asked, "Is there a problem?"

They said, "Yes, there is a very serious problem. The tree in which we usually reside—we can't stay there anymore because a nest of vipers has settled right near the tree. That has driven us away."

"Well," Ephram said, "don't worry. I'll go there and I'll take care of it because, after all, I have very thick skin and I'm not afraid of the vipers. I'll drive them away so that you'll be able to go live in your tree again."

The monkeys were very relieved, and they began chattering happily amongst themselves as Ephram walked away to take care of the problem. As Ephram was leaving, he noticed a group of young monkeys playing baseball with some coconuts. Ephram thought that was very funny and decided that he would watch, just for a few minutes. After all, he knew that he had a responsibility to take care of and he would do it—but just a little bit later. So Ephram sat down, thinking that he would watch just one inning. But it was really exciting and fun to watch. He watched the second inning, and the third, and pretty soon Ephram found himself staying to watch the entire game. Indeed, by the time the game was over, Ephram had completely forgotten that he was supposed to take care of a problem.

The next morning, as Ephram was walking through the forest, he came upon a lioness living in a cave. Ephram began talking to the lioness, and the lioness said that she really had a serious problem. One of her lion cubs was ill and she had to stay nearby to take care of him. But that meant that she was not able to go out and hunt to provide food for her cubs. "Well," Ephram said, "that's no problem. I'll take care of that for you. I'll go out and hunt for you, and I'll come back and I'll provide you the food for your family." The lioness was very relieved and she turned and went back into her cave to take care of her sick cub, knowing that food would soon arrive.

Ephram, meanwhile, girded himself to get ready to hunt so that he would be able to bring food back for the lioness and her cubs. As Ephram completed all of his preparations to go out and hunt, he suddenly realized that he was very tired. If he was going to go out to hunt he needed to be refreshed, and now was the time to take a nap. Of course, Ephram knew that he would have to wake up soon in order to go hunting, and he really meant to do what he had said he would do—but he would do it a little bit later.

So Ephram lay down to take a short nap. But lo and behold, Ephram's short nap lasted all through the night. The next morning, when Ephram awoke, he awoke to the sounds of the forest—alive with the chattering of all different kinds of animals. He realized that all of the animals of the forest were gathering, excited and upset. Ephram marched over and asked, "What's the problem?" The animals said that news had just arrived that hunters were on their way to that segment of the forest, and all of the animals were afraid that the hunters would come in and kill them all. Ephram thought for a moment, and then he said: "Don't worry. I'll take care of the problem. Why, I'll go out to the beginning of the path that leads into our section of the forest, and there I will uproot some trees with my trunk. I'll lay them across the path so that the hunters will not be able to get by. In that way, I will protect the forest."

Everyone was very excited about Ephram's plan. They thought it was a marvelous idea and, relieved that they would now be protected, they went on their way. Ephram started going toward the head of the path that led into the forest. Just before he got there, Ephram noticed that there was a beautiful stream—one he had never seen before. Oh, how beautiful it was. The water was so clear, and the flowers growing on the banks were so beautiful. Ephram, as he stood there, realized that he ought to stop and praise Hashem for having created such beautiful flowers and such a beautiful stream. So Ephram walked closer and sat down at the side of the stream to offer praise and thanks to Hashem for the beautiful world he had created. Ephram became so engrossed in his appreciation of the beauty of the place, and so engrossed in his praise of Hashem for having created such beauty, that he didn't realize the hunters had already come up the path. Lo and behold, the hunters saw Ephram the elephant, and this was exactly what they were hunting for. And so they shot and killed Ephram the elephant. When Ephram fell, he fell right on the spot where the nest of vipers was located. Sure enough, Ephram had destroyed the nest of vipers and the monkeys would now be able to come back to their original home in the tree that they loved. And indeed, the place where Ephram fell was very close to the cave where the lioness lived. The lioness was able to come out of her cave and tear pieces of flesh out of the body of Ephram the elephant to feed her cubs. Since the hunters had taken his tusks, which were what they had come for, Ephram had really protected all the animals of the forest.

Indeed, everything that Ephram had said he was going to do but put off for later was eventually done. But how sad that it had to happen through Ephram's death.

Shep the Sheep

Once upon a time, there was a sheep named Shep. Shep was a very simple sheep who pranced through the grass, eating and living a very simple life. One day, Shep was down near the pond. He happened to see a beautiful peacock, which had a magnificent tail filled with all the colors of the rainbow. Shep looked at the tail of the peacock, and he said to himself: "I want that. How marvelous it would be if I had a tail like a peacock instead of the simple grey tail that hangs at my back."

Shep began to pine for the tail of a peacock. He kept telling all of his friends how much he would love to have the tail of a peacock. They laughed at him. But then, eventually, one of his friends said to him, "Well, don't you know that there is an old, wise, and magical owl deep in the forest who is able to grant all wishes?"

Enthusiastically, Shep the sheep began to search for the owl and, indeed, he eventually found him. He said to the owl, "Oh, Mr. Owl, won't you grant my wish and give me the tail of a peacock?" The owl raised one eyelid and said to Shep the sheep: "Shep, do you really need that tail? Or, do you simply want to have it because the peacock has it?" Well, Shep was furious, and he stamped his back feet, and he stamped his front feet, and he said, "Mr. Owl, don't ask me silly questions like that. I just want the tail of a peacock. Please give me the tail of a peacock." The owl said, "If that's what you want." He snapped the feathers of one of his wings and, lo and behold, attached to the back of Shep the sheep was a magnificent, beautiful rainbow-colored tail.

With that new tail, Shep returned to his pasture. His friends looked at him as if he were a little bit odd but, on the other hand, they praised him for the beauty of his new tail.

Some time passed, and one day, Shep the sheep was walking in the pasture when he noticed a snake and saw a fly flying over the head of the snake. Suddenly the snake's tongue snapped out of his mouth, grabbed the fly, and swallowed it. Shep watched, amazed. He saw another fly come by, buzz over the head of the snake and, again, the snake's tongue came flashing out, grabbed the fly, and swallowed it. Said Shep to himself: "Wouldn't it be wonderful if I had a tongue like a snake? Why, then all of the flies that now buzz around my head, and around my back, and around my underside—I could get rid of them in no time at all. I know what I'll do. I'll go again to visit the wise and magical owl who lives deep in the forest."

So, Shep the sheep went again to the owl and told the owl

that this time, he would like to have the tongue of a snake. The owl raised one heavy eyelid, looked at Shep, and asked: "Shep, do you really need that tongue? Or do you simply want it because someone else has it?" Well, Shep was infuriated. He stamped his rear legs, and stamped his front legs, and he yelled out at the owl: "Don't ask me silly questions like that. Just give me what I want." So the owl snapped the feathers of his wing and, lo and behold, Shep the sheep had not only the tail of a peacock but also the tongue of a snake.

So Shep returned proudly to his pasture once again. This time, the other sheep looked at him as if he were quite strange—with the tail of a peacock and the tongue of a snake. More time passed and, one day, when Shep was again down near the pond, he saw a large turtle. As Shep approached the turtle, the turtle pulled his legs and his head into the shell so that he was completely covered and completely protected. Shep said to himself: "My goodness! Would it not be wonderful if I had a shell like that? Then, whenever it rained I would be protected, and whenever I wanted to rest and be safe, I could simply pull my legs and my head into my shell, and I could rest peacefully and calmly. I know what I'll do: I'll go again to the wise and magical owl who lives deep in the forest."

So, once again, Shep made the trek to visit the wise and magical owl. He came before him and he said, "Mr. Owl, I would like to have the shell of a turtle." The owl raised one very heavy eyelid and looked wonderingly at Shep the sheep standing before him, already with the tail of a peacock and the tongue of a snake. The owl said to Shep, "Shep, do you really need that shell, or do you simply want it because someone else has it?" Well, Shep was very angry, and he stomped his rear legs, and he stomped his front legs. He called out to the owl: "Mr. Owl, don't ask me silly questions like that. Just give me what I want." And so, ever compliant, the owl snapped the feathers of his wing and, lo and behold, Shep the sheep now had a shell covering him, bottom and top.

Shep then returned to the pasture. This time, when he returned to the pasture with the tail of a peacock and the tongue of a snake and the shell of a turtle, the other sheep didn't even know who Shep was. Saddest of all, Shep himself didn't know who he was, either.

Faige the Fawn

Deep in the forest, there was a family of deer. They were a wonderful, joyous family. Boruch, the buck, and Dassie, the doe, were the parents of many children, many little deer. They took their responsibilities as parents very seriously. They knew that the most important thing that they could convey to their children was the skill of survival, and that while the deer wasn't very strong and couldn't fight off larger animals like the lion, they could be very swift and outrun the lion. Therefore, from the time when their children were very young, they tried to teach them to run fast. They made up games that involved running and did all sorts of activities to make sure their children, without feeling overburdened, would learn how to run fast. Indeed, all of their children did learn how to run fast except for Faige the fawn. Faige, you see, felt put upon by this whole business of having to learn how to run fast. Faige said to herself: "It's not fair; it's just not fair that I should have to learn how to run fast. There must be better ways to escape the lion." And so, Faige, instead of participating in all of the other activities to learn how to run fast, would go off on her own, seeking out different ways to escape. Indeed, one day, Faige saw a snake being chased by a mongoose. She saw the snake slither quickly into the underbrush and escape. Faige said to herself, "Why, that is a wonderful way to escape." So Faige the fawn decided that she, too, was going to learn how to slither. She got down on her stomach, and she began to practice. Day after day, and week after week, Faige the fawn would be down on the ground, practicing slithering into the underbrush.

Time passed and one day Faige saw a kangaroo. She saw a wolf chasing the kangaroo and the kangaroo getting back on its rear legs and leaping long distances to escape. Faige the fawn said to herself: "My goodness, that is a wonderful way to escape. I can do that also." So Faige the fawn began to practice leaping. Well, it was very clumsy for Faige the fawn to do. But nevertheless, she worked hard at it. She had worked hard to learn how to slither—yet she wouldn't learn how to run. Now she worked hard at learning how to leap great distances—but she wouldn't learn how to run.

After a while, Faige the fawn saw a monkey being chased by a tiger. The monkey ran directly over to a tree, and grabbed it with all four legs, climbed rapidly right up into the top branches of the tree, and escaped. Faige the fawn said to herself: "My goodness, that is the most wonderful way to escape. I can do that, too." So Faige the fawn began to practice climbing trees. It was very cumbersome for Faige to get up and even get all four legs around the tree, but she was insistent and she was determined. Faige the fawn practiced climbing. She wouldn't learn how to run fast, but she practiced climbing trees.

Time passed, and then one day in the forest, a rumor spread. Someone said, "The lion is coming." Suddenly, all of the deer began to run to escape from the lion. Faige got down on her belly and began to slither into the underbrush, and from behind her she heard persistent voices calling, "The lion is coming." Off in the distance, she could already see her family members, who had run very far away. So Faige began to leap as well as she could. The sound of the lion got closer, and her family appeared smaller and smaller in the distance. Finally, Faige realized that she wasn't getting very far at all and that the lion was catching up with her. So she quickly rushed over to the nearest tree, wrapped all four of her legs around it, and began to try climbing it. As she began climbing up the tree, she turned back and she saw the lion almost upon her, while off in the distance, her family had escaped by running. Faige the fawn said to herself: "If only I had perfected the gift that God gave to me instead of attempting to imitate everyone else around me. If only I had." This was the last thought of Faige the fawn as the lion sank his claws into her back.

NOAH'S WIFE
Judith Black

Judith Black is a storyteller,
writer, teacher, and parent
based in Marblehead, Massachusetts. She has performed
in venues ranging from the
Montreal Comedy Festival to
the National Storytelling
Festival in Jonesborough,
Tennessee, and is a long-
time adjunct faculty member
of Leslie College's Arts
Institute. She has recorded
several tapes, including
Waiting for Elijah and Glad
to Be Who I Am, which won
the Parents' Choice Gold
Award. Judith is one of the
founding board members of
the Three Apples Storytelling
Festival in the Boston area.

The Bible reminds us again and again of lineage. Abraham begot
Jacob, and Jacob begot Joseph, and Joseph begot. . . . It is truly
important to know from whence you came. How can you map out
a future without a past? When the matriarchs take their place,
in prayer, study, and memory, alongside the patriarchs, then we
will have a balanced past from which to grow our future.

My first job out of college was teaching arts and crafts at Ohabai
Shalom, a large synagogue on Beacon Street in Brookline, Massachusetts. Like many of us, I was very busy being a socialist, feminist, and intellectual during the collegiate years and had a lot of
catching up to do on Judaism. When a third-grade teacher said
her students would be studying Abraham and could I please come
up with a project that integrated themes from his life, I did what
any good socialist, feminist, and intellectual does: I went back to
the source and read the Bible. No sooner was this done than I
found myself knocking angrily on the rabbi's study door.

"Exactly, what am I supposed to teach third-graders about our
father Abraham?" I demanded angrily. "This man gave his wife
away, not once, not twice, but three times to other men, claim-
ing she was his sister!" The rabbi—as they all do—took a deep
breath and said patiently: "This is a book of stories, human experiences. Our job is not to copy their lives, but to learn from
them." And so it has been ever since.

The story of Noah is a universal story. Every major culture has a tale reflecting a conflict between a creator and the creations. Ours needs to present the balance that history and theology should represent. Thus, I offer you Mrs. Noah and the hidden knowledge that God likes organic farmers!

And Adam begat a son in his own likeness and called his name Seth. . . . And Seth begat Enosh. . . . And Enosh begat Kenan. . . . And Kenan begat Mahalalel. . . . And Mahalalel begat Jared . . . and Jared begat Enoch . . . and Enoch begat Methuselah . . . and Methuselah begat Lamach . . . and Lamach begat Noah. . . .

he Lord looked down from the heavens and said: "Oooowee, have I got a mess down here! Lying, cheating, slaving, wasting . . . I blew it—gotta get the understudy and get rid of this model. But wait, what's this?"

And Noah found grace in the eyes of the Lord.

Noah, friends, was an organic farmer, and on this day he happened to be hoeing around the carrots and singing, "Inch by inch, row by row, gonna make . . ." when the "big" voice interrupted: "Noah!"

Noah, like most of us, had a hard time identifying the voice of the Lord.

"Must be indigestion . . ." and he went on singing: "gonna make this garden grow. All it takes is a rake and a . . ."

"Noah! . . . I am talking to you!"

"Definitely the leek and eggplant stew I had for lunch, more kickback than I thought . . . piece of fertile ground! . . ."

The Lord is occasionally willing to adapt so that people can hear, and so He sang, "Inch by inch, row by row, the Lord will bless the seeds you sow. . . ."

"Nice harmony," commented Noah, just a split second before realizing its origins. "Oh my God!"

"Exactly, Noah. Noah—it wasn't the eggplant talking to you. Actually, the stew smelled pretty good. It makes me think that

I should have been more appreciative of Cain. Vegetables and grains are actually a better use of the land than grazing cattle, a lot more protein per acre, but never mind, I was a young God then. I'll make it up to him with this. I love your eggplants, and we are going to keep your boat from leaking." Noah couldn't keep up with the Almighty's sense of biblical irony.

"Lord, dear Lord, slow down. What are you talking about?"

"Noah, the world's full of lying, cheating wasters and no-goodniks, but you have found grace in my eyes."

"Thank you, Lord."

"So, Noah, I want you to build an ark."

"I'm a farmer, Lord."

"I want it should be three hundred cubits long, fifty cubits wide, and thirty cubits high, with a little lookout hut on the top."

"I'm a farmer, Lord."

"Put it up with gopher wood and tar the outside."

"I'm a farmer, Lord."

"Take seven pairs of clean animals and seven pairs of unclean animals."

"I'm not a zoologist, Lord."

"Do all this in seven days . . . when I will bring a rain that will destroy the earth and all that's on the land."

"I'm a carpenter, zoologist, a fast learner, whatever you say, Lord. . . ."

"Noah, man, knew I could rely on you."

And the countenance of the Lord left.
Thus did Noah, according to all that God commanded him, so did he.

"Wife, Wife, Mrs. Noah!" Now, do you know why they called her that? Because she didn't have a name. "Wife, wife—ach, you are here! Did you hear what the Lord asked? This is impossible. In one week, he wants it. Can you believe?"

Mrs. Noah (we'll call her that because she didn't have a name) knew this man well.

"Now Noah, breathe in deeply through the nose. That's good, dear." You see, she understood immediately. Noah could do one thing at a time, but to organize for a planetwide flood it would take a woman, a good woman. And so, she set out to divvy up the work among her sons, daughters-in-law, herself, and Noah, whom she set to designing the ark.

"Wife!" (He called her that because she didn't have a name.) "I have the plans here. Look!"

She nodded her head back and forth slowly. "Three floors! That's it? Husband, where have you been? You can't have the mouse stay with the snake or the fawn with the mountain lion. We need a seating arrangement." And Mrs. Noah (you know why they called her that—because she didn't have a name) did it all, even putting two little bins in each space, filled with corn husks. Once you have raised children you know how to prepare for all possibilities.

"Now, wife" (you know why they called her that—because she didn't have a name), "this is terribly fancy and, I think, unnecessary. Wife, why the little bins?"

"Noah, why do you think the Lord chose an organic farmer? Now, go get the animals." And he did.

The fountains of the great deep burst forth and the windows of heaven were opened.

Now, much is known about the preparations for the flood, but who was there to report on the 40 days and 40 nights of rain and the subsequent 190 days aboard the ark? Not Noah, that's for sure. After only three days of storm: "Wife, wife (you know why they called her that . . .) I'm . . . sick . . . I need to . . ."

"Please, lean over the second bin of corn husks, dear." Ham, Shem, and Japheth, the couple's three sons, were not in any better shape. Meanwhile, Mrs. Noah (you know why they called her that . . .) got to the task of making the ark work. "Mammal aerobics at sunup, reptile stretches at noon . . . tonight will be our first ark dance." Noah built the structure, but Mrs. Noah refined the infrastructure. It was in the social hall at night that Mrs. Noah taught all the creatures how to do-si-do, bow to their partner, and honor their corners. Another night featured line dances where snakes and serpents allowed their heads and tails to be held by the hooves, wings, and claws of other creatures, thus connecting them. Yet another night was given to moving to the pulsating rhythms created by the monkeys and apes beating the ark's sides to the tempos of the water's currents that carried it. It was at these dances that the creatures learned to respect and appreciate their world and one another. Indeed, to this day, animals do not kill or injure one another for sport or pride. And Mrs. Noah and her daughters-in-law (you know why they called them that—because they didn't have names) maintained a compost pile that would have been the envy of any organic farmer.

When the rains finally subsided, Noah's wife said: "Noah dear, it's calm now. You can take to measuring the water levels. And as soon as it is possible to lay anchor, so to speak . . . the snake needs more stretching; the panther, more running; and the giraffe, just more space."

Finally, one day, the dove returned with an olive branch in its beak. Soon after, when released again from the ark's top, it did not return at all. Noah and his wife opened the ark door, and all were joyous.

And God spoke unto Noah, saying "Go forth of the ark, thou, and thy wife, and . . ."

"Wife, Wife . . . Wife!"

"Noah!" His wife spoke in a voice almost as loud as the Lord's. "I've had it. I want a name."

"Wife, please, not now. This is a historic moment."

"It will wait, Noah." A silence fell around them. Noah did not understand.

"You want what?"

"A name. When our story is recorded for all to learn from, I want people to know who I am. They will know that the Lord spoke to you, and you built the ark, and you sent out the raven and then the doves, and you brought us safely back. But will they know what the daughters of men have done?"

Noah felt a little hurt. "You are my wife. Isn't that enough?"

"No, Noah, I am also myself." And the voice of this woman, as would many others, touched the Lord, and God spoke: "You are without fault. Choose a name and you will be known by it, but know that the book is already inscribed. Your name will be known for its essence rather than its fact."

"I can live with that," said the woman who'd been known as Mrs. Noah. "Call me Flo."

"Flo!" Noah was surprised.

"Yes," she said, smiling. "I kept the 'flow' of things going." Now you won't find it in the book, but Flo it was, because she enabled life to "Flo" so smoothly. Noah waited a few seconds, and it was then that a bow appeared in the sky, with many colors drawn from one side of the earth to the other. Noah and Flo, and their sons and daughters-in-law, and all the animals stood, just looking.

> I will remember my covenant, and the waters shall no more become a flood to destroy all flesh.

"Excuse me, Lord." Flo was on a first-name basis now. "How about fire? Would you also promise never to take us by fire?"

And Noah added, "And pestilence and famine. . . . We organic farmers are always worried about that."

"And Lord, who knows what might happen? Would you promise to not take us because of war, pollution, hunger . . ."

"Flo, Flo, slow down. Listen, you two, the rainbow is my promise to never destroy by water. Flo, you did a great job there with the animals; they will only kill out of hunger, they will never waste, and they will use my earth sparsely—but people are another story."

"But Lord," Flo was headed toward a legal definition of the Lord's promise, "you promised to not destroy flesh again."

"Flo, I promised to not destroy flesh by flood. What you do to each other, I can't control. It's up to you . . . but good luck. If you need me, I'll always be here." And so it was that from that day on, wives had their own names and humans were left, for better or worse, in charge of their own affairs.

THE STORY OF BRYAN

Tsvi Blanchard

Tsvi Blanchard *is a Senior Teaching Fellow at the National Jewish Center for Learning and Leadership (CLAL). He holds Ph.D.s in psychology and philosophy and received his rabbinic ordination from St. Louis Rabbinical College. Currently he is a practicing psychologist. He lectures and teaches extensively and has also appeared on many television programs, including the "Oprah Winfrey Show," where his expertise as an ethicist was central to a panel discussion of moral dilemmas. His own stories and parables have been widely anthologized. Tsvi lives in New York City with his family.*

I like telling the following story about my father-in-law because, as all good stories should, it works on many levels. To begin with, it is an inspiring story about an especially sensitive, loving healer whose professional life was dedicated to the relief of pain and suffering.[1] It also reminds us that sometimes, the best we can do for another human being is "just being there." In this sense, it is a teaching story that belongs equally to everyone.

But the story also works within our family in special ways. Telling it responds to the deepest, perhaps even unasked, question of any physician's children (especially a doctor as devoted to his patients as my father-in-law): where are you when we need you? First, the story reminds them that their father was doing something important and valuable. He wasn't just out having a good time, unconcerned about them. Second, it suggests to them that although there were many nights when their father could not be at home to care for them, he nonetheless loved them very much, just as he loved the little boy in the story.

And, paradoxically, the story also covertly expresses the idea that their father was really "there for them," as he was for that boy, despite the fact that he couldn't always take away their pain at his absence. Perhaps this is why the story created a "ritual object." The pencil in the breakfront came to symbolize, and hence, make present to all, the special, caring father whose necessary absences were so hard for the children to fully understand. The best family stories create these kinds of rituals and ritual objects, just as the telling of the stories themselves becomes a sacred family ritual.

This last paradoxical "message" allows the story to work for us all on a level more profound than the story's more obviously inspiring surface meaning. It speaks to our painful sense of forsakenness in a world that cannot meet all our needs for security and protection. Telling this story can, if we allow it, evoke our deepest sense that, despite everything, "we are all in this together." In this sense, telling this story reminds us that mutual caring and support—that simply holding each other tightly—can be intensely healing.

Note

1. Dr. Mortimer Mark, of whom this story is told, passed away on May 26, 1994. As the story shows, he was a remarkable human being.

---

 y father-in-law was a pediatrician who also specialized in pediatric anesthesiology. One of his patients, a young boy named Bryan, was fighting a running battle against cancer. Although the treatments my father-in-law gave him were quite painful, especially as he actually injected the medicine, he was able to relieve Bryan's agony with anesthesia.

Once, however, when Bryan was due for a treatment, he developed a bad cold. This infection made giving him an anesthetic too risky. My father-in-law sat down with him and explained: "Bryan, I have to give you this treatment. There is no way to put it off. Because you have a cold, I can't take away your pain by giving you the anesthetic. But whenever I have to put in the medicine, I am going to hold you very very tightly in my arms. I love you very much and I will hold you close whenever the pain comes."

And so it was. My father-in-law watched the monitor carefully. Whenever the moments of greatest pain would come, he would hold Bryan tightly. Somehow, they both got through it.

After the treatment, Bryan insisted on giving my father-in-law a present to express his love and gratitude. He gave him an oversized pencil. It was his favorite. My father-in-law didn't really need the pencil, but to make Bryan happy, he took it.

When he got home, he shared the story of Bryan's treatment with the family and showed them the pencil. The oldest child took the pencil, went to the family breakfront, and said, "Take out all this glass and silver and put Bryan's pencil in their place. This is what we have to show everybody." And then he put Bryan's gift in the breakfront. The family felt that this was just the right thing to do. And that pencil has remained right where it was put, right next to the kiddush cups and other holy objects.

THE LIGHT IN THE WALL
Renée Brachfeld

Renée Brachfeld *began performing as a juggler in 1985. She began interspersing stories as a way to fill the time, and then found herself and her audiences captivated by the power of the tales. Gradually, she told stories more and juggled less. She now earns her living as a professional storyteller. She performs solo at schools, synagogues, community events, and weddings, telling folktales from around the world as well as contemporary and original stories. Together with her husband, cantor and musician Mark Novak, she also performs "Stories and Songs from the Jewish Tradition." Renée resides in Washington, D.C., with her husband and her cat, Benjamin. She still juggles a little bit, too.*

This is, as far as I know, an original story. It was suggested to me by a question. A number of years ago I was preparing stories for a holiday concert in Atlanta and mentioned to a friend that I was seeking a short, Chanukah-related story for a concert aimed at adults. "Did you ever hear the story about someone who tried to light Chanukah candles in the concentration camp?" she asked. I hadn't, and I asked her to tell it to me. She said that she could neither remember the story nor recall where she had heard or read it, but that it had something to do with the guards not being able to extinguish the flame.

I liked the idea of that story and checked the various sources where I thought such a story might be found, but without success. Usually, I tell traditional tales or stories written by others. Most of my original tales are personal or family stories, so it did not immediately occur to me to write this story. Then, one day, this story simply . . . appeared. I woke up with it complete, and in essentially its present form. It is as though I received the story as a gift.

I told this story at that December concert, and the woman who had first mentioned the story came to talk to me after the performance. "That was a great story," she told me. I told her it was based on the story she had herself suggested to me. "I don't know what you're talking about," she insisted. "I've never heard of a story like that before in my life."

---

t was wintertime in the concentration camp, the dark, dreary, bone-chilling cold of December. Even in the camp, though it seemed impossible, Chanukah was approaching. It seemed impossible that Chanukah could exist in such a place. Some inmates rarely thought about it; some did not believe a holiday of light could find its way inside such a place. Others consciously acknowledged it but despaired. How were they to observe the holiday in any meaningful way? They had no candles, and the prayers and songs of celebration were forbidden to them.

One young man, however, thought a great deal about the holiday. He yearned for those lights and remembered the warmth and comfort and strength he had felt in looking at the candlelit menorah during his childhood. He longed to light the candles, to say the blessings, to celebrate again the triumphs of the Jews. But there were no triumphs there in the camp—no warmth, no lights. Just hard work, endless cold, and the constant torment from the prison guards.

Still, the young man made up his mind that he would observe the holiday. In the weeks preceding Chanukah he kept a constant watch, and he was at last able to obtain a candle. He slipped the tiny piece of candle into the folds of his clothes. He knew that he could lose his life if he was discovered with this contraband, but his desire to observe the holiday was strong. For several more days, he awaited the opportunity to obtain a match. Finally, he found one. This, too, he kept hidden in his clothes. He carried the match and candle with him everywhere, despite the great peril of this act of daring.

Finally, the holiday arrived. The young man knew that it was the first night of Chanukah. All day he waited anxiously for evening to come. He was nervous about openly defying the rules but felt compelled by his desire to continue the tradition of lighting the Chanukah candles.

As darkness fell, word spread through the barracks that the young man intended to kindle a light in honor of the holiday. With that knowledge, fear spread through the barracks, but pride and the spirit of defiance spread, too. The young man looked around, searching for a suitable chanukiah, a place to light his candle. Finally, he found it, a crack in the wall that formed a small niche or crevice—the perfect spot to hold the candle.

The young man pulled the candle from its hiding place. He placed the precious candle in the crevice in the wall and fished the match from the folds of his clothes. He stood alone by the barrack wall, engrossed in his own actions and not asking anyone to join him. The others watched and then, slowly, cautiously, came forward—first one and then another and another, until all the men had left their bunks and stood gathered around the young man.

The young man lit the match, cupping the flame gently in his hand. It cast the only light in the dark room. Slowly, lovingly, he lit the candle. The flame sprang to life, filling the small crevice in which the candle sat with a light that danced over the walls and over the gaunt faces of the assembled men. The yellow flame lit those tired, cold faces and shone in each pair of eyes.

Quietly, the men began the blessing over the Chanukah candles. With their voices joined together, they began: "Baruch Atah Adonai Eloheinu. . . ." They blessed God, who commanded the kindling of the Chanukah lights. Then, continuing together, they began the second prayer, praying to God, "who did miracles for our ancestors in days of old, and in our day," when the barrack door slammed open, and a guard stomped in.

The singing ceased instantly as the men stood for one frozen moment in the candlelight and then fled silently to their separate bunks. Only the young man remained standing, quiet and still, beside his burning candle. Slowly, the guard approached him.

Large and menacing, the guard towered over the slight young man, who stood regarding him calmly. The guard glared at the candle and then motioned toward the young man: "Put it out!"

The young man shook his head slightly and replied very quietly, "No."

The guard quivered with rage at having his command ignored and ordered harshly, "I said put it out!"

Once again, the young man looked at the candle, shook his head, and responded with a quiet, "No."

Outraged at being disobeyed, the guard removed his pistol from its holster, raised it, and shot the young man in the head. The young man fell to the floor and the life drained out of his body. For a moment the guard watched impassively, then he reached over the dead body to extinguish the flame, removed the candle from the crevice, and put it in his pocket. Glaring around the darkened barrack, he leered at the bunks where the frightened prisoners lay shivering beneath their blankets, then turned and strode from the room.

The guard thought he had dealt with the matter and that the incident was over. But that night, in the crevice in the barrack wall, a light burned. All that night and for each of the next seven nights, a light burned. It filled the niche where the young man had put his candle, glowing steadfast for the full eight nights of Chanukah.

And nothing that anyone did could put the light out.

GO FISHING
Jay Brand

Jay Brand *was born in New Britain, Connecticut, and raised on the sunshine along the coast of Long Island Sound. He attended college in Ohio, receiving his master's degree at Ohio State University. Presently, Jay teaches drama for Arts Impact in the Columbus schools, is a teacher for the gifted summer program at Ohio Wesleyan University, works as a performing artist for Days of Creation Arts camps, and serves as president of Central Ohio Storytellers. Jay spends his free time performing and giving workshops on storytelling and drama around the country.*

Allen Zak, Days of Creation

Memories are very strong. For me, the strongest trigger for memories is smell. For example, the smell of chocolate cookies instantaneously takes me back to my mother's kitchen where, slamming the screen door behind me, I come rushing in to grab a soft and still-warm cookie. She made them with lots of love for me.

Sight is also a strong trigger for memory. For years I was frightened of large ocean waves; a reminder of my near drowning in the North Atlantic off the coast of Portugal. I overcame my fear by going back to the sea and its pounding surf. I've written this story so that I might be able to touch and trigger memories in those who wish to read it; to connect with others whose memories are just as vivid and real as mine.

or Jankel, age fourteen, it was joy and utter bliss to be fishing for carp with his father. They would sit on the banks of the river near their village—a village where time seemed to have stood still for a hundred years. The houses were old and crumbling and built so close together that the sun cast great shadows in the narrow winding lanes; it was a village of smokey chimneys and crowds of dirty, dusty people, where anything old and unusable could be bought or sold. Jankel and his father would sit on the banks of the river near their village and laugh and cry and dream—dream of owning their own land, having a home without the fear that the walls would fall down around them, and even going to the market to buy something brand-new.

All these fond delights and other memories were shattered and swept away at the Buchenwald concentration camp. Standing in line with hundreds of other Jewish men, women, and children, Jankel could hear the rough voice of a camp officer call out, "Left, left, left . . . right." Left meant certain death for the very young, infirm, and old. If you were young, healthy, strong, or had an occupation that the Nazis could exploit, you went right. There were many more lefts than rights. And Jankel was only fourteen. In order to save his own life during the "selection," Jankel lied.

"I can cut meat. I am very good."

He was not very good but he went right and worked for three years as a butcher for his captors. It took only a few days for Jankel to lose his laughter, his dreams, and his tears.

Jankel survived the camp. He immigrated to the United States and married the lovely and strong Zenia Belcovitch. He worked each day for a local butcher, came home, ate his meals, and rested in front of the television. While he was watching TV one evening, Zenia told him, "Go out. You watch too much. Go fishing."

Surprisingly, he went. That night, Jankel brought home a carp, a carp like from a dream, a carp as long as a bathtub. Jankel decided that this wonderful carp would be eaten on Sunday. For on Sunday, Paul, a boyhood friend who had spent the war in a Russian prison camp, would come to visit. They would eat carp with thick black bread and drink glasses of vodka.

But today was only Tuesday. Five days till Sunday. How could the carp be kept fresh for Paul's dinner? With a stroke of genius, Jankel proclaimed, "We will not bathe for five days. The carp will live in the bathtub."

So who could argue with genius? Zenia thought, "The caring for the carp will keep him busy and maybe he won't watch so much television." And she loved him. So she nodded her approval. And Jankel smiled.

For the next four days Jankel came home from work and cared for his carp in the bathtub, changing its water and feeding it table scraps and soggy balls of Wheaties (this was what he had used to catch him in the first place).

Sunday, after breakfast, Jankel went outside and, with a long sharp-bladed knife, he descaled the carp. Soon the whole backyard was covered with shimmering fish scales. They sparkled like sequins on a sea of green grass. And Jankel cried. He cried for the carp. He cried for his youth. And he laughed, too. But he didn't know why.

"Paul's here. Give me the fish," yelled Zenia from the back porch.

Paul had brought with him a large, uncut loaf of black bread and an American friend, who had two bottles of vodka. That afternoon all four friends ate large chunks of black bread that Zenia had cut the old way—holding the bread across her breast to slice heavy pieces for all. They drank and ate and drank. The friend was given the head of the carp so he could suck out the brain. It was an honor for the guest to be given such a gift—an honor to be remembered and never, never forgotten.

That afternoon they ate and drank and laughed—and, of course, told stories. And Jankel sang. Zenia had not remembered him ever singing, but that Sunday afternoon he did. And this is the song he sang:

The copyright for "Belz Mein Shtetele Belz" is held by J. J. Kammen Music. The English translation of the song is by Dr. Allan Blair.

The following week, Jankel quit his job as a butcher. He has his own business now. Jankel has become a greengrocer. He sells fruits and vegetables and is very, very happy.

You may ask, where did I hear such a story? I was witness on that Sunday afternoon with my friend Paul. I visited Jankel and Zenia—I tasted the black bread. I drank the strong vodka—I heard Jankel sing the old songs. I didn't know the Yiddish words, but I hummed along. And I knew that something important was happening around that table.

RIDING WITH THE MOON
Roslyn Bresnick-Perry

Roslyn Bresnick-Perry, *who was born in the Belorussian town of Wysokie Litewskie, came to America with her mother in 1929. All the people of her town per-ished in the Holocaust. Suffering from dyslexia, she was finally able to enter Fordham University at age fifty-four, graduating summa cum laude. Her master's degree in cultural history is from New York University. A storyteller, teacher, and writer, her audiotape,* Holi-day Memories of a Shtetl Childhood, *was honored by the American Library Asso-ciation. She has also pub-lished a children's book,* Leaving for America. *Roslyn resides in New York City.*

The story of Riding with the Moon is one of the last of many warm and tender memories I have carried with me from my shtetl child-hood home of Wysokie-Litewskie in Byelorussia. It is based on true happenings, although the dream sequence in the story has been drawn in greater detail than the actual dream. This memory has taken on more meaning for me with the passing years. It holds for me a prophetic content, as I have often heard Zisl calling me to save her and felt the guilt of being alive while she, my friend and cousin, is no more.

This story personifies, in a strange way, the new and the old worlds coming together in a society that was not only on the cusp of change but would, in a few short years after our leaving, be completely destroyed. There are times, even now, when I close my eyes and still see the figures of those bobbing prayer-shawled old men standing out of doors in front of the old synagogue, hon-oring the new full moon of Rosh Chodesh in the month of Hadar, with blessings and prayer.

And oh, how many times have I thought of the magic and en-chantment of being wrapped in fur blankets, tucked in warm and secure between people I loved, riding through a star-bright, frosty night in a sleigh. The tinkling bells of a frisky horse would add a musical accompaniment to the sound of hoofs on the frozen snow, while we rode with the moon on a never-to-be-forgotten night.

My family and the people of my shtetl are gone, but for me they live, and I am warmed by their glow, which I share with you.

---

y aunt Faygl was not one of my favorite people. She was the prettiest of all my mother's sisters. She was also proud, stubborn, definitely snippy, and not at all interested in entertaining me, a little girl who was used to a lot of attention.

My father had gone to America, and my mother and I lived alone in our own small apartment in a little house in a Jewish shtetl, a small village in White Russia, where I was born. We were waiting for my father to become an American citizen so he could send for us to join him.

Somehow, I always found myself in my maternal grandparents' house among my three young aunts and one uncle. It was a lively household, usually filled with talk, laughter, and the comings and goings of many friends of my aunts and uncle.

My mother was very involved with her family inasmuch as she was the oldest. She was in many ways a second mother to her sisters and brother and a right hand to her mother and father. She spent most of her time doing things for them, attending to all kinds of important business, which sometimes took her away for a few days. I had an ample supply of baby-sitters, who stayed with me in our small apartment, not far from my grandparents' home, where they overindulged me and kept me in a continued state of excitement.

Not, however, my aunt Faygl. She was not at all thrilled about taking care of me. She was busy with herself, her own friends, and the chores she had to do. She had no patience for me.

Therefore, I was not at all pleased when Faygl insisted that she wanted to stay with me while my mother took my grandfather to another town where there was a hospital. I wanted my aunt Shushke, who used to tell me the most wonderful stories, to stay with me, but Faygl insisted. She said she would also tell me stories and play games with me, and even take me for some great walks, so I reluctantly agreed. (Everyone was very upset about grandfather, but he got well quickly and my mother returned home with him in a few days.)

Faygl really tried to be nice to me, but she was very strict. She made me go to bed much earlier than even my mother did. And though she read me a story when I went to bed, it didn't sound as good as when my other aunts and uncle read to me because Faygl seemed to be in a hurry. When she finished reading and closed the door of the bedroom, I had to go to sleep by myself in the dark.

One night, just as I was falling asleep, I thought I heard voices and other kinds of strange noises in the other room. So I got out of bed and quietly opened the door, just a crack, to see what was going on.

Imagine my surprise when I saw my aunt Faygl hugging and kissing a young man whose name was Srolke. I knew that this wasn't right because young girls were not allowed to kiss young men or be with them when no one else was around. I knew my grandfather and grandmother and even my mother would be angry if they found out. But I quietly closed the door and went back to bed, smiling to myself because I now had a secret.

Having a secret is no fun if you can't share it with someone. So, the next day, I told my cousin Zisl, who lived next door to us. Zisl was the child of my Uncle Borakh, who was my father's brother. Zisl was both my best and worst friend. Zisl and I always played together, yet we were constantly fighting with each other. That was because Zisl always had so many ideas about what we should do, and sometimes I didn't want to go along.

Well, Zisl was very surprised when I told her what I had seen. She also knew the rule about not kissing boys. She asked me if Faygl or Srolke had seen me and if I was going to tell anyone about it. I said they hadn't—and I wasn't. But I did wish that Faygl wouldn't make me go to bed so early.

Then a peculiar gleam came into Zisl's eyes. She clapped her hands and jumped around with excitement. "I've got a great idea," she said. Zisl always had great ideas. "You know what," she said. "Not only can you get Faygl not to make you go to sleep so early, you can get something much better."

"What, what?" I asked breathlessly.

"A ride in Srolke's sleigh," declared Zisl, her eyes sparkling. "He's the only one we know who has a sleigh. But you have to take me along, too. Otherwise," said my cousin in her usual bossy manner, "otherwise, I'm going to tell everyone about what your aunt was doing."

Well, now I was really in a pickle because I knew that Zisl could do just that. How was I going to get my aunt's boyfriend, Srolke, to harness his horse and sleigh just to take Zisl and me for a ride?

"How do I ask him?" I said feeling pretty awful by this time and sorry that I had ever told anything to Zisl.

"Nothing to it," said Zisl. "The next time you see him, just tell him what you saw and tell him you'll tell if he doesn't take you. My brothers always get what they want by doing that." Poor Zisl, she had three older brothers who were always bossing her around and threatening her.

I was pretty miserable the rest of the day because I couldn't figure out how and when I was going to get the opportunity to make this daring request. I also pictured what my aunt Faygl would say and do about it.

I didn't have to wait long because my mother had not yet come home and Faygl was still taking care of me. So, that night, I was unusually agreeable about going to bed so early. And anyway, there was a big snowstorm raging outside and the house was very cold. I was determined not to fall asleep just in case Srolke came to see my aunt again. Sure enough, it was not much later when I heard my aunt greet him affectionately, and in no time at all, there were these strange sounds.

This time, I opened the door wide and stood there staring at them. My aunt jumped up, scolding me for getting out of bed, but Srolke stopped her and spoke to me in a very affectionate tone. "Raizelle," he said, "no one has to know I was here. Let this be a secret between the three of us. If you act like a big girl and say nothing, I'll bring a whole bag of candy just for you."

"I don't want candy," I said with a great deal of assurance. "I want you to take me for a ride with your horse and sleigh. There's lots of snow now, and pretty soon we will be going to America. My mother said they don't have horses and sleighs with bells on them there."

My aunt and Srolke looked at each other as if they couldn't believe what they were hearing. My ready answer had surprised them. My aunt started to say something, but Srolke stopped her. "Of course," said Srolke, "of course." And he promised he would do just that if I went back to bed and held my tongue, which I did.

My mother came home and life took on its familiar pattern. Somehow, the whole incident slipped from my mind because there was a lot of excitement in the family. Faygl and Srolke announced that they wanted to be married and my grandfather and grandmother agreed to the match, even though they hadn't had a matchmaker arrange the whole thing between the two families. My grandfather, however, grumbled about the out-rageous behavior of modern children.

Then, quite late, one cold night a few weeks later, there is a knock on our door and in walk Faygl and Srolke. They are all bundled up in their warmest clothes, their faces red from the cold. They tell my mother to help me get dressed again, as I was just about ready to go to bed.

"Come on," says Srolke, with a big grin on his face. "I've come to give you a ride in my sleigh, the one with the horse and bells. Remember the bargain we made," he says, laughing a big belly laugh. My mother doesn't know what is going on, but my aunt joins in the laughter.

"Come," she says to my mother, "this will be the last winter before you go to America. It's a beautiful night with a full moon. Come for a sleigh ride."

My mother can't resist the high spirits of my aunt and soon-to-be uncle. I am now being plied with sweaters, hats, shawls, gloves, and boots. I can hardly move I have so much clothing on; then, outside we go into the cold moonlit night.

It is a white world, completely snow covered, with a full moon hanging in a dark blue sky that is surprisingly bright. The little houses all around us look like so many snowy mounds with tiny twinkling lights coming from their small, glass windows. Icicles hanging from exposed boards glitter in the moonlight, and the stars seem like so many silver dots. The horse, sleigh, and driver stand waiting silently in front of our house. A frosty hush has enveloped the night, with only the crisp crackle of our footsteps on the frozen snow breaking the stillness.

I stop midway to the sleigh; I have just remembered my promise to Zisl. I turn to my uncle Srolke to tell him that we must knock on Zisl's door because we have to take her with us. All of a sudden, I hear a loud wail, then another and another, and then a whole chorus of these same sounds. I turn to where the cries are coming from and see a cluster of large white forms, completely covered in white prayer shawls, bobbing up and down in the moonlight.

"Ghosts and demons!" I scream with dread and fright. "Ghosts and demons and goblins are standing in front of the synagogue, wailing at the moon." I join the wails with my own hysterical cries.

"Narrele, foolish one," says my mother, as she grabs me in her arms. "Little foolish one, it's Rosh Chodesh Adar, the first day of the new month. Those are not ghosts or demons or goblins—they are pious, devout Jews saying the blessings for the new moon. Come, come into the sleigh. As we ride along I will tell you what the blessings say."

With that, my mother and aunt put me between the two of them for warmth and cover all three of us with a large, fur blanket. My Uncle Srolke and the driver sit up front. The driver pulls on the reins and the horse and sleigh start a glorious gliding on the hard packed snow.

I'm still sobbing, but the rhythm of the sleigh, the soft jingle of the sleigh bells, and my mother's voice reciting the blessing calm me.

"Praise the Lord," says my mother. "Praise the Lord from the heavens, praise Him in the heights. Praise Him and all His hosts and angels. Praise Him, sun and moon and all you stars of light. Praise Him, highest heaven and waters that are above the heavens, for He commanded and they were created. He fixed them fast, forever and ever. He gave a law that none transgress. He ordered the moon to renew itself as a glorious crown over those He sustains from birth, who likewise will be regenerated in the future and will worship their Creator for His glorious majesty. Blessed art thou, O Lord who renewest the months."

I watch the moon ride with us. I see the twinkling stars dance along, keeping time to the ringing of the sleigh bells. I am now warm and quiet, and as we glide along, I suddenly feel the sleigh start to rise up. Up, up we fly, straight for the moon. I catch my breath. I can't believe this is really happening. I am scared and excited. Imagine flying straight up to the moon. Then, without warning, we land right up there, on the moon.

I look around and see the moon all covered with snow. No houses, no trees, nothing, only snow.

Now I know why the moon is so white in the winter; it's because of the snow. "I want to get out," I say. "I want to walk on the moon."

My mother says, "No, it's too cold." As we argue about my going, I suddenly hear a voice calling. It's calling me.

"Raizelle," it calls, "Raizelle, come and get me out, come quickly."

"It's Zisl," I cry. "Zisl is up here on the moon. I must go to her."

"No," says my mother, "no." But I tear myself out of her grip and start running toward the voice. I run and glide on the icy snow. It feels like the lake near our house when it is frozen. I glide faster and faster, with the wind in my face. Then I see her, my cousin Zisl. She is enclosed in a round cage of ice with icicle bars completely shutting her in.

"Help me out of here," cries Zisl, "please."

"How can I break the icicle bars?" I cry with anguish.

"With your hands," Zisl shrieks, "use your hands!" I try, but the bars are so strong, so cold. I kick them with my feet. I bite them and claw at them, but they won't budge. My hands are bleeding. I see the red drops of blood sinking into the white snow, making a kind of pink flower.

"Zisl," I sob, "I'll get you out. I won't leave until I do. I'll never leave you, never."

And then I feel my mother shaking me. "Raizelle," I hear her saying, again and again. "Raizelle, wake up. You fell asleep and you started crying in your sleep. Were you dreaming?"

"Zisl," I sob, "Zisl is up there on the moon, imprisoned in a house of ice. We must get her out."

My mother and aunt start to laugh. "No," they say, "Zisl is home in her bed, fast asleep."

"But we didn't take her with us on the sleigh ride. It was her idea about the sleigh ride and I didn't even take her with me." My mother doesn't know what I am talking about, but she and my aunt Faygl and my new uncle, Srolke, assure me that the next time we go sleigh riding, we will definitely take Zisl with us.

We never did take her because lots of things happened and we didn't go on another sleigh ride that winter. The following spring, my mother and I left for America to join my father.

We left without knowing we would never see our family members again, and I didn't realize I would leave part of my heart with them.

TELLING JOKES FOR THE SAKE OF GOD

Yitzhak Buxbaum

Yitzhak Buxbaum *is a* maggid (*a teacher of Judaism and a storyteller*), *who specializes in mysticism, Hasidism, and hasidic stories. He teaches and tells stories at synagogues, community centers, and colleges. He is also an author of Jewish religious books, including* Jewish Spiritual Practices, The Life and Teachings of Hillel, *and* Storytelling and Spirituality in Judaism.

How does the famous Jewish sense of humor jibe with Judaism? The Talmud (*Taanit* 22a) tells that a mystic named Rabbi Beroka strolled through the market of Be Lepet with Elijah the prophet (who appears in visions to teach adepts mystic secrets). Rabbi Beroka asked Elijah, "Who here will attain the World-to-Come?" When Elijah indicated a pair of individuals, Rabbi Beroka asked them, "What is your occupation?" "We are *badhanim* (comedians)," they replied, "who cheer up sad people." So Elijah the prophet certifies that Jewish comedians have a special entrance to the World-to-Come.

For centuries in Eastern Europe, *badhanim* specialized in merry-making at weddings, telling rhymed jokes based on Torah or Talmud verses and poking fun at prominent guests. These European *badhanim* are the ancestors of today's Jewish comedians. They mixed Torah and jokes and were knowledgeable in both fields. So, in Judaism being a rabbi and a comedian are not mutually exclusive positions. A rabbi is even required to be funny, since the Talmud says that before a study session, a good teacher tells a joke to expand his pupils' minds (*Shabbat* 30b). But religion often makes people overly serious. We have to be reminded, as Rabbi Beroka was, that Judaism should cheer people up.

Hasidism began as a religious reform movement in the 1700s

and not only revived religious singing, dancing, and storytelling, but also Jewish humor and laughter. Due to terrible persecutions, the Jewish people were desperately sad and in danger of losing their collective sense of humor. Rabbi Israel Baal Shem Tov (the Besht), the founder of Hasidism and an accomplished mystic, had an active sense of humor. Since jokes and laughter expand the mind, humor and mysticism naturally go together. In referring to Rabbi Beroka's encounter with Elijah, the Besht said that the two holy jesters who cheered up the downcast befriended people through jokes and humor and elevated them spiritually. Through humor and laughter for the sake of heaven, he said, you can elevate your own childishness and raise it to spiritual heights. The Besht was a master teller of stories and jokes. It is said he once made a humorous remark that caused angels in the highest heavens to smile.

Some hasidic rebbes even had a *badhan*, as would a king at court. Rabbi Mordechai Rackover, the *badhan* of the holy Seer of Lublin (Rabbi Yaakov Yosef) appears in our story. The *badhanim* of rebbes were not simple shleppers. They were usually rabbis and disciples of the rebbe. One of the Seer's most famous disciples, Rabbi Naftali of Ropshitz, who was renowned for his wisdom and his hyperactive wit, also appears in our story. Before he became a rebbe he sometimes performed as a *badhan* at weddings and, appropriately, in the story he defends the Seer's *badhan*. Some stern rabbis protested the "sacrilegious" performances of *badhanim* at weddings. The following story, which contains the hasidic viewpoint, explains the custom of *badhanut* and promotes the concept of what I like to call "holy fun."

he great hasidic rebbe, Rabbi Hayim of Chernovitz (called the Be'er Mayim Hayim after his famous book, "The Fountain of Living Waters"), made a *shidduch* for his son with the Seer of Lublin's daughter and traveled to Lublin for the wedding. The Shabbos before the wedding, when he made *Kiddush*, he was swaying, turning, and contorting himself, his limbs flying all over. The Polish hasidim were amazed; they had never seen anything like this. (The Be'er Mayim Hayim was from an offshoot branch of Hasidism, from the Zlotchover Maggid [preacher], which had different customs from the main Mezritcher Maggid branch. Although the Polish rebbes were also fervent in making *Kiddush*, it was more "inward.")

Later, at the wedding feast, the Seer of Lublin's jester (*badhan*), Rabbi Mordechai Rackover, jumped up on the table to entertain and started to imitate the Be'er Mayim Hayim's *Kiddush*. He did it perfectly, and everyone was hysterical. They were rolling on the floor laughing. The one laughing the most was—the Be'er Mayim Hayim himself! He had no idea what he was doing or what he looked like when making *Kiddush*; he was in another world then. He said, "Where did he get this incredible routine from?" No one dared tell him that the jester was imitating him. But one *chutzpadik* (brazen) fellow did tell him. He said, "Rebbe, he's imitating you!"

On hearing this, the Be'er Mayim Hayim was very hurt and felt humiliated. He was sincerely trying to serve God, and now he had been made a public laughingstock. He was too humble to blame the *badhan*, but nevertheless, when a tzaddik's feelings are hurt, there are consequences. The jester immediately became seriously ill, collapsed, and was taken into the *Beit Midrash*. He was actually dying. They said to the Be'er Mayim Hayim, "Rebbe, forgive him. How can you let this happen to him?" The Be'er Mayim Hayim said: "How can *I* forgive him? This is not my doing. I have nothing against him. But he made fun of a Jew saying *Kiddush* for God alone. He is being punished by heaven, not by me!"

Rabbi Naftali of Ropshitz (the Ropshitzer), the cleverest of the Seer's disciples, was there, and he answered, "Rebbe, just as much as *you* say *Kiddush* for God alone, he tells jokes to make Jews happy, for God alone." The Be'er Mayim Hayim raised his eyebrows. Was it possible? He had never heard of such a thing. Then the Ropshitzer said to him, "Rebbe, we'll make a test. If he's telling jokes till the last minute before he's leaving this world, we'll know he's doing it only to serve God."

So they went to the *Beit Midrash*. When they arrived, they found the holy jester lying on a bench, surrounded by his friends and the *Hevra Kadisha* (burial society), who were caring for him in his last moments.

Now you have to know that in Yiddish, when you go to the bathroom, you say, "*Antshuldikt, ikh darf aroysgeyn* (Excuse me, I have to exit)."

Well, Rabbi Mordechai was about to leave this world. As the Ropshitzer and the Be'er Mayim Hayim stood there, they heard him, in his final minutes, joke to those around him, saying, "Excuse me, I have to exit."

Hearing this, the Be'er Mayim Hayim looked over at the Ropshitzer and smiled from ear to ear. Then he laughed as he walked over to the *badhan*. He extended his hand to the jester, lifted him up, and as he did so, the jester was restored completely to health.

THE GHETTO REBBE AND HIS "KINGDOM OF CHILDREN"

Shlomo Carlebach

Shlomo Carlebach, z'l, *a world-renowned hasidic folksinger and storyteller, was the rabbi of Congregation Tehilath Jacob (known as the Carlebach Synagogue) in New York City. Having studied at prestigious yeshivot in the United States, including Lakewood, Lubavitch, and Torah V'daas, he received his rabbinical ordination from Rabbi Isaac Hutner. He spent a great deal of time on tour and in Israel. Reb Shlomo has composed thousands of melodies and recorded over twenty albums and cassettes and two songbooks. He produced* The Best of Shlomo Carlebach (*songs and stories*) *in five double-cassette packages, which includes the story of the Ghetto Rebbe on Volume 1. Reb Shlomo died on October 20, 1994.*

You have all heard about the Holocaust. You have all heard what happened to the six million, but it's not just the number, the six million. We lost so many holy people that until the Messiah will come, our hearts will be so broken, so broken.

One of the greatest who perished in a concentration camp was Rabbi Kaloinimus Kalman Shapira of Piacezna, the great-grandson of the holy maggid of Kozhnitz. Piacezna is just outside of Warsaw. Reb Kaloinimus Kalman became rebbe when he was eighteen years old, and to become a rebbe at eighteen in those years before World War II, you had to be someone special. He established a hasidic court in Warsaw after World War I.

But his specialty was his belief that when children are five years old, they already need a rebbe. They need somebody to connect their souls to the highest place in heaven. He had a "kingdom of

70

children." Imagine an old Jew comes to the Piacezner and also a little boy or girl of five. To the man of eighty he would talk for two minutes, but with a child of five or six, seven or ten or twelve, he would talk all night. He had a yeshiva with thousands of children. He was their father, their mother, their best friend.

In 1939, when the Warsaw Ghetto was set up, Reb Kaloinimus Kalman became known as the Rebbe of the Warsaw Ghetto. In the Ghetto, the rebbe's young followers arranged work for him at the Shultz Shoe Factory, where boots were produced for the Nazi troops. The relatively easy, indoor work helped keep him alive through the years of persecution and allowed him to teach the students who surrounded him.

He taught these young people that they would have to "get physical" to bring about the redemption. He interpreted the sentence from the Exodus story, "Our cattle shall also go with us," to mean that "from the animal that is within man, we shall also make use to serve God. . . ." Even as things around them got worse, he told the young people: "God's salvation can come in the blink of an eye. Even if the sword is at your throat, do not give up the hope of God's mercy."

While he was in the Warsaw Ghetto, the rebbe wrote a book called *Hachshurat Huavriechim* הכשרת האברכים (*Young People Prepare Yourselves*) and another titled *Aish Kodesh* (*The Holy Fire*).[1] *The Holy Fire* contained his Torah teachings, which he gave over on Shabbos in the Ghetto, while *Hachshurat Huavriechim* was written to prepare young people for the ultimate redemption.

This is a story about a special teaching of Reb Kaloinimus Kalman that I promised to teach all over the world. This story can be heard on the audiocassette *The Best of Shlomo Carlebach*, Volume 1 (1960–1990), as "The Holy Hunchback" and "Rav Kaloinimus Kalman."

Note

1. Nehemiah Polen, *The Holy Fire* (Northvale, NJ: Jason Aronson Inc., 1994).

eb Kaloinimus Kalman Shapira, the Piacezna
Rebbe, remained in the Warsaw Ghetto until the
end, all the time teaching the young people how to
live, how to act, how to keep their faith in God. He
was one of the last Jews remaining in the Ghetto.
After the uprising was crushed, he was sent to a concentration
camp, where he died several months later. But while he was in
the Ghetto, he wrote down his Shabbos teachings and called
them *The Holy Fire*. Shortly before he was put in a cattle car, he
managed to bury this manuscript in the rubble of a bombed-
out house. After the war, a little Polish boy who had happened
to find the manuscript walked up to an American soldier and
said, "I have some papers here. Would you like to buy them for
a dollar?" The soldier gave the boy the money and, when he
looked through the papers, he realized it was Hebrew writing
and he took it to the chaplain who, at that time, was Rabbi
Hollander. The chaplain printed the book. At the beginning of
the manuscript, Reb Kaloinimus Kalman wrote:

> When you find this book, there may be no more Jews in Poland.
> There may be no more Jews in Europe. There may be no more
> Jews in the world. But in Jerusalem, in Yerushalayim, there will
> always be Jews because Yerushalayim cannot live without Jews.
> Please find the first Jew and beg him in my name to print this
> manuscript. And I swear to you that whoever will learn my book,
> whoever will print this manuscript, I will pray for them before
> God's holy throne.

When I first read this book, it pierced my heart, and I knew it
would pierce your heart, too. I began asking everyone about
those children who had studied with Reb Kaloinimus Kalman.
Where are those children? Are any of them alive? I would love
to speak with them. But I was told that there was nobody left.

One day, a few years ago, I walked down the Yarkon, the street
where the beach is in Tel Aviv. And here I saw a hunchback, so
broken, so broken. His face was beautiful and so handsome,
but his whole body was completely disfigured. He was sweeping the streets. I had a feeling that this person was special.

I said to him, "*Shalom lekha*, peace unto you."

He answered back in very heavy Polish-Yiddish-Hebrew, "Alaichem shulem."

I asked, "Are you from Poland?"

He answered, "Yes, from Piecezna."

I couldn't believe it! From *Piecezna*! I said to him, "Have you ever seen the holy Reb Koloinimus Kalman?"

"What do you mean have I ever seen him? I learned in his yeshiva, in his school, from the age of five until I was eleven. When I was eleven I came to Auschwitz. I was so strong they thought I was seventeen. I was whipped and kicked and hit. I never healed and that's why I look like this now. I have nobody in the world. I'm all alone." He kept on sweeping the street.

"My sweetest friend, my whole life I have been waiting to see you, the person who studied with Reb Koloinimus Kalman, who was one of his children. Please give me over one of his teachings?" I pleaded.

He looked at me and said, "Do you think I can be in Auschwitz for five years and still remember teachings?"

I said, "Yes, I'm sure. The holy Reb Koloinimus Kalman's teachings? How could you forget them?"

He was a real *hasidishe yid*, and he said, "I can't wait any longer." And he went to wash his hands at a nearby fountain, fixed his tie, and put on his jacket. And he said to me, one more time, "Do you really want to hear it?"

I replied, "I swear to you I'll give over your teaching over all the world."

The street sweeper began to cry. I had never seen such big tears in all my life. The man said, "I want you to know that until the Moshiach is coming there'll never be such a Shabbos again. Can you imagine the *heilige rebbe*, the holy master, dancing with hundreds, maybe thousands, of children? Can you imagine the holy rebbe singing on Friday night amidst holy angels, '*Sholem Aleichem, Malakhey Hasholem*,' greeting the holy angels? I want you to know that the rebbe taught Torah between the fish and the soup, between the soup and the chicken, and then between the chicken and the dessert."

Here the sweeper said, "Open your heart." It pierced my soul, as if he was about to give me over the deepest, deepest depths of his soul. And he continued, "I want you to know, after every teaching, this is what the rebbe said: '*Kinderlakh, taiereh kinderlakh, gedenkshe, d'greste zakh in der velt iz tzu teen emetzen ah toive* (Children, precious children, remember, the greatest thing in the world is to do somebody else a favor).'

"I came to Auschwitz. I knew my parents were dead. My whole family doesn't exist anymore. I wanted to commit suicide. But at the last moment, I heard the rebbe's voice say, '*Kinderlakh, gedenkshe*, the greatest thing in the world is to do somebody else a favor.' Do you know how many favors you can do in Auschwitz at night? People are lying on the floor crying and no one even has the strength to listen to their stories anymore. I would walk from one person to another and ask, 'Why are you crying?' They would tell me about their children, about their wives whom they would never see in this life again until Moshiach is coming. I would hold their hands and cry with them. Then I would walk to another person. It would give me strength for a few weeks. When I was at the end, I'd hear my rebbe's voice, telling us to do somebody a favor.

"Now, here in Tel Aviv, I have nobody in the world. You know there are moments when I take off my shoes and I start to go to the beach, and I'm already up to my nose in the ocean, ready to drown myself, and I can't help but hear my rebbe's voice again, saying, 'Remember, precious children, the greatest thing in the world is to do somebody else a favor!'"

The hasid looked at me for a long time. Then he asked, "Do you know how many favors you can do on the streets of the world?"

And he kept on sweeping the streets.

EPILOGUE

This incident happened just before Rosh Hashanah. I had to go back to New York. But I returned to Israel for the first night of Chanukah. The next morning, early, I went back to the Yarkon to look for my holy hunchback. I couldn't find him. I asked some people, "Have you seen the holy hunchback, the street cleaner?"

They answered, "Don't you know that on the second day of Sukkos, he left the world."

Listen to me children, the Moshiach is coming: let it be today, let it be tonight, let it be soon! Bring God to redeem the world and all the holy people will come out from their graves. And the holy hunchback, that holy street cleaner, he will come back again and he will clean the streets of the world. And you know how he will clean the streets? By teaching us that the greatest thing in the world is to do somebody else a favor.

THE SHEPHERD'S PRAYER

Susan Danoff

Susan Danoff *tells interna-*
tional folktales to children
and adults and has produced
three audiocassette tapes:
Enchantments, The Invisible
Way: Stories of Wisdom, *and*
Women of Vision. *From 1986*
to 1991 she conducted an
intensive summer storytelling
institute at Princeton Univer-
sity, and she teaches story-
telling to many adult groups
including teachers, museum
docents, and college stu-
dents. Susan lives in Prince-
ton, New Jersey, with her
husband, Neal, and son,
Jonah.

Sometimes one meets a story again and again, like an acquain-
tance one runs into in unlikely places. Over the years, "The
Shepherd's Prayer" has startled and delighted me in several versions that have crossed my path. Each time I have wanted to learn
to tell the tale I found; each time I have tried and failed.

The first version I read was Tolstoy's "The Three Hermits,"
written in 1886. His biographer, Henri Troyat, wrote that Tolstoy
loved to listen to the pilgrims tell their stories and even invited
them to his house. One man in particular is credited with telling
Tolstoy this tale, suggesting that the story had been adapted over
time as a Christian folktale.[1] Instead of a rabbi and a shepherd,
this story features three hermits who live on an island and pray
in their own way until a bishop happens along to enlighten them
about how one should really pray, or so he thinks. Tolstoy's
breathtaking ending, with the three hermits gliding across the
water to tell the bishop that they've forgotten the prayer, captures
the very essence of the story.

The Sufi poet Jalaluddin Rumi (1207–1273) wrote a version that
combines humor, mysticism, and didacticism and is titled, "Moses
and the Shepherd." After Moses hears the shepherd praying and
chastises him, God speaks directly to Moses, chiding him for
thinking there's a right and wrong way to pray. Unlike Tolstoy's
Christian version or the Jewish version, when Moses returns to
tell the shepherd he was wrong, the shepherd replies that Moses'

scolding has taken him to another plane of understanding: "Moses, Moses, I've gone beyond even that. You applied the whip and my horse shied and jumped out of itself. The Divine Nature and my human nature came together."[2]

It wasn't until I read Eric Kimmel's graceful retelling in his collection *Days of Awe* that I realized the original source was a Jewish story, the story I had been waiting to discover all along. Kimmel had been inspired by "The Prayer of the Shepherd" in *Mimekor Yisrael, Classic Jewish Folktales*, collected by the folklorist Joseph Micha bin Gorion (1865–1921). Bin Gorion lists as his Hebrew source *Sefer Hassidim*, edited by Y. H. Wistynezki and published in 1891. No doubt, the tale is much older, and the fact that Rumi uses Moses as his central character suggests that he knew the story as a Jewish folktale. That takes us back more than seven hundred years.

As in all his retellings, bin Gorion's version of "The Shepherd's Prayer" is extremely spare—just half a page—but very powerful just the same. This is the version I have used as the basis of my own adaptation, and I've tried not to change the essential elements but to add detail and write in a style suited to my own way of telling a story.

I know now that much as I love the Tolstoy, Rumi, and Kimmel versions of the story, I couldn't tell them because of what the story teaches. Just as the shepherd prays in his own way, each one of us must also tell the story in our own way.

Notes

1. Henri Troyat, *Tolstoy* (Garden City, NY: Doubleday, 1967), p. 381.
2. Jelaluddin Rumi, "Moses and the Shepherd," in *This Longing: Poetry, Teaching Stories, and Selected Letters*, trans. Coleman Barks and John Moyne (Putney, VT: Threshold Books, 1988), p. 22.

References

Bin Gorion, Micha Joseph. "The Prayer of the Shepherd." In *Mimekor Yisrael: Classic Jewish Folktales*. Vol. 3. Bloomington, IN: Indiana University Press, 1976, p. 1259.

Kimmel, Eric A. "The Shepherd." In *Days of Awe*. New York: Viking, 1991, p. 32.

Rumi, Jelaluddin. "Moses and the Shepherd." In *This Longing: Poetry, Teaching Stories, and Selected Letters*, tr. Coleman Barks and John Moyne. Putney, VT: Threshold Books, 1988.

Tolstoy, Leo. "The Three Hermits." In *What Men Live By: Russian Stories and Legends*, tr. Louise Maude and Aylmer Maude. New York: Pantheon, 1943, pp. 69-76.

Troyat, Henri. *Tolstoy*. Garden City, NY: Doubleday, 1967.

here was once a shepherd who loved God, though he had studied nothing about Him in the great scrolls. Yet in his simple love for God, this shepherd made his own prayers, and he would pray sometimes as he walked after his sheep, or as he sat in the grass as they grazed, or as the night fell and the sky filled with tiny lights.

One day as he walked after his sheep he prayed, "Dear Master of the Universe, today I shear my sheep, and their wool is soft and warm. I wish I could take the wool and weave a cloak for You and carry it up to the place where You sit. It would just be a small thank-you for the sun You send down to warm me every day of my life, for Your generosity is in every sunbeam."

Another day, as he was sitting in the grass he prayed, "Dear Great One who made all things, thank You for this mossy place You have put here like a pillow for me while I sit and watch my sheep. I wish I could gather the softest moss for as many miles as I could walk and make a pillow for Your feet, for Your generosity makes the land for us creatures to walk upon." The shepherd never said a prayer in quite the same way, for each time he prayed with only the words that came from the living feeling in his heart.

One pleasant spring afternoon, he was fishing in a small stream and he began to pray, "Master of the Universe, thank You for this water You have made so clear and for the worm wiggling on my hook and for the dinner I will catch. I wish I could cook up my fish and share it with You, for your generosity feeds all of us living creatures." The stream where the shepherd was fishing ran alongside the road, and as he prayed aloud to God, a scholar passed by and heard him.

"Who are you speaking to?" asked the scholar.

"To God. To thank Him."

"That is not the way to pray to God. God doesn't eat. God doesn't need your fish, for it is He who made all fish."

"You are a learned man," said the shepherd. "I am just a shepherd. I didn't mean to pray in the wrong way to God." Immediately he felt great remorse, for he did not wish to insult the God he loved so much.

Then the scholar sat next to the shepherd and said, "All right. If you wish to pray, I will teach you how to pray with the proper words. The *Shema* is one of our most important and sacred prayers. Repeat after me: *Shema Yisrael Adonai Eloheinu, Adonai Echod.* (Hear O Israel, the Lord is our God, the Lord is one)."

The shepherd tried to repeat the strange syllables. Even though he was a Jew, he did not know Hebrew, and it was very difficult for him.

The scholar brushed himself off and left after he'd repeated the prayer five times. But the shepherd forgot the prayer. And he lost his appetite for the fish he'd caught now that he couldn't even think about telling God how he'd like to share it. What's more, he was afraid to pray to God that night as he looked at the tiny lights in the sky. He wondered if God was angry for all those silly prayers he'd been saying, day after day. The shepherd, who had once been filled with the joy of God's creation, now felt only the sadness of his own ignorance.

Up in the heavens, God can hear the clap of thunder and the sound of a butterfly's wings; He can hear the songs of whales and the footsteps of centipedes; He can hear the oceans clapping the shores and the baby bird swallowing a worm. Everything He hears at once, and everything he hears distinctly. Among all the sounds of the world, each day the prayer of the shepherd was like a little melody with wings that reached God's ear. And God loved this simple shepherd's prayers.

That night, the scholar heard a voice: "What have you done, telling a simple shepherd how to pray? The prayers in books were once living prayers, prayers with wings, but now they are old and some people say them over and over, repeating them without understanding, without care. When you say them that way, they're just words, words without wings.

"Do you realize what you have done? You have prevented the shepherd from praying a true prayer that gladdens God's heart and his. Every man must learn to pray his own way. The shepherd knows this simply and without schooling. Prayer isn't about words; it emanates from the place without words.

"Go tomorrow and seek out that shepherd. Tell him to pray as he wishes and assure him it is good, and it is enough."

In the morning, the scholar went back to the stream to find the shepherd, but he was not there. He asked along the way, describing the shepherd's appearance, hoping that someone could tell him where the man lived, but with no luck. At last, he said to an old man walking his dog along the road, "I'm looking for a man who prays aloud to God as he works," and this man replied, "Ah, that would be the shepherd," and, pointing toward the hills, added, "he tends his sheep out in those fields beyond that low hill."

There the scholar found the shepherd, silent and sad, watching his sheep. "Shepherd," he said, "I spoke to you yesterday about your prayer, and I was wrong. God does not mind that you do not speak Hebrew and read the holy books. He asks only that you pray as you always have. Forgive me, for it is I who do not know how to pray. You pray the true prayer, the prayer of the heart."

That night, as he looked up into the darkness, the shepherd prayed, "Dear Master of the Universe who knows all things, thank You for this quilt of blackness that You've embroidered with tiny white dots and lay each night across the fields. If I could, I'd weave a cloth of my best sheep's wool for You to wrap around Your feet on a chilly evening, for Your generosity is in every breath and every breeze.

"And thank You for sending the scholar and for hearing this, my simple prayer."

REST AREA
Yitzchak Etshalom

Yitzchak Etshalom *was ordained by the chief rabbi of Jerusalem in 1984 and recently earned his master's degree in education from Loyola University. Having served as associate principal of Los Angeles Hebrew High School for four years, he is currently principal of the School of Advanced Jewish Studies in Pittsburgh, Pennsylvania. As a storyteller and musician, he has produced tapes of original stories and original music, including* Rest Area: Tales of the Road. *A native of Los Angeles, California, Yitz resides now in Pittsburgh with his wife, Stefanie.*

"Rest Area" was commissioned by Rami Wernick, a division head at Camp Ramah in California, in August 1990. For the first three Shabbatot of the camp session, I had been telling stories to his ninth-grade campers at Seuda Shelisheet as the beautiful environment of Shabbat at camp ebbed away. Rami asked me for a story that would stay with these kids and would allow them to "return" to camp every Shabbat afternoon, from wherever they might be.

I knew that I had not yet done anything to keep my dear brother, Jonathan, alive and to bring his warmth and love into my own storytelling. Ever since his death at age thirty-six, I had been searching for a way to connect his gentleness and human integrity with my own art. As often happens with music and writing, the story just happened—and it has been my signature story ever since. It is the title track on my first story tape. It is an honor to share it in this anthology—I pray that we all slow down to see the beauty around us before it's gone.

've been covering a lot of road over the past four years, driving up and down from Los Angeles to Seattle and back on Interstate 5. I'm always going fast. Not speedometer-fast, but mind-fast. I'm always in a hurry to get to the place I'm going to and not paying attention to the way I'm getting there. I live in Los Angeles but prefer being "from LA" than in LA. As soon as I can get out of town, as soon as my workday is over, I hit the road. I'm in a hurry to see my friends along the road and I want to get there as quickly as possible. Every mile of road is another mile closer to where I want to get to—and a mile farther from the smog, noise, and telephones of home. I enjoy my friends' company—the singing, storytelling, and camaraderie—so much so that I always stay a little bit longer than I can afford to and I have to turn around and hustle back at the last possible minute.

There are a lot of road-tricks to help you stay awake. The simplest is music—at various levels of intensity. Start off with some Mozart and, as you get tired and night falls, move through Sinatra and Joe Pass to Springsteen and the Stones. When that isn't satisfactory, there's always coffee. And when coffee has either done too good a job or the seventeen cups you've taken in just aren't enough, there is the healthy surrender to the road. It's called a Rest Area. A Rest Area is just about the greatest blessing on an interstate. There are clean bathrooms, picnic benches (sometimes stunning views), and lots of quiet. Rest Areas are scattered about every thirty miles or so, and I always thought that a Rest Area was a place of last refuge. When the music just isn't loud enough, when the coffee isn't strong enough, and when the road stretches endlessly, that's when you need a Rest Area.

Easing into a Rest Area is like a family reunion with relatives you've never met. A Rest Area is a magnet, attracting every pickup truck with a shell in the back, and if you pull into a Rest Area any time after ten o'clock at night, you'll see a whole row of these trucks with the gate of the pickup open and two or four or six feet sticking out the back. It's an unwritten law that when you are driving on the interstate and you pull over to a Rest Area to sleep, no matter how short you are, you're supposed to sleep toward the back of the truck, open it up, and put your legs out, as if hanging out a "do not disturb" sign. There's something very trusting about that scene, as if everyone there is ready to say, "I've got to go to sleep, I have my belongings with me, we're all brother and sister travelers, we've all got to trust each other, I'm going to sleep."

I've pulled over into Rest Areas several times, parked, gotten into the back of my vehicle, and, because of my own curious inability to fall asleep without reading, opened up my traveling Rambam, turned on the light in back, and been magically transported back to Yeshiva. There's something exciting and vaguely exotic about studying the Laws of Blessings or Laws of Vows somewhere between Roseburg and Eugene at 2:00 A.M.

So I had always understood a Rest Area: it's that last stop on the road when staying awake is no longer an option and surrender to Morpheus is the only way home. Last spring, I read between the lines of the green interstate sign: "Rest Area: Next Exit."

I was at the Northwest Folklife Festival in Seattle. I'd been performing there as a storyteller; seeing all my friends, singing, storytelling, and joking with them. As I couldn't stay for the entire festival, I took off from Seattle Monday morning. I drove south and drove fast, kept an eye out for "Smoky," and was quite happy to find myself in Medford, Oregon.

It had been a long day, and even though I have driven fast on the road, I've found that there are certain places I like to be at given times of the day. For example, I enjoy being in the Central Valley of California at night. Something about combining the wide open spaces with the night gives the feeling of grandeur, of bigness, of almost being swallowed up into the black, which has a strange kind of magnetism. I always enjoy going over the Siskiyou Mountains, past Mt. Shasta toward Lake Shasta, around sunset or sunrise. It's a very beautiful place and even at 65 miles per hour, there's a lot of beauty that can be seen. I was particularly happy when I pulled into Medford, Oregon— the southernmost point of city driving, as it were—at around seven o'clock. The sun was due to set at around 8:30 that evening, and I knew that after I drank my ritual cup of coffee in

Medford, got a refill for the road, and pulled out onto Exit 32, I would have three hours until the next major city, which is Redding, California. Three hours of beautiful driving, leaving with the sun still in the sky, arriving at night—watching the sun set over Lake Shasta, if I timed it right.

I'm accustomed to the road and I've picked up a few of my own road habits. One of these is picking up hitchhikers. Although I would never consider doing this in the city, I have found that brother and sister travelers are safe to stop for.

I was listening to *Every Breath You Take*, that release with all the great singles that's solid rock 'n roll for the tough driver and the winding road, and as I pulled onto Exit 32, I saw him standing there in the breakdown lane. I knew it was a man by the way he stood. The inner voice, the one that sometimes gets us into trouble but often walks us into paradise, told me to pull over, and I slowed and then leaned over to open the door.

Yet I didn't look very carefully at who he was. If you have ever given charity on the street, been accosted by someone who's homeless, or given a ride to a hitchhiker, you know how frightening it is to gaze into the eyes of desperation. You know how sad it is to look at a face that is so needy, that has turned to you in its hour of need. And so I give charity, and when I'm on the street and meet the homeless, I give, but I find it very hard to look at the beneficiary of this mitzva (or is it the other way around?). I don't know if it's because I'm afraid that if I look into the eyes of hunger I'll see myself reflected back or because I'm afraid of embarrassing someone who has gotten to the point where they have to depend on another human being for the next cup of coffee. I have the same problem with hitchhikers. I pick them up, yet it's hard for me to look at them or sometimes even talk to them. I imagine how degrading it is to be on the road and in need of these metal machines and their protected owners to pull over, open a door, and give refuge from the cold and the road. I opened the door and the man got in and threw his stuff through the middle window that goes to the back of the truck. He didn't say anything and I didn't say anything.

I put the volume back up so that Sting could wail on about Roxanne, and we headed up into the mountains. For the next

hour and a half, I carefully watched the sun not set as I antici-
pated the magical moment that eluded our eyes. I watched my
clock and it went from 7:30 to 8:00 and to 8:15, and as we
headed up past Ashland, toward the California border, the sun
didn't move. At first I thought it had something to do with alti-
tude and being a little higher in the mountains and seeing it
from a different angle, but when the clock hit 8:45 and the sun
was still hanging over the horizon, I knew that there was something strange going on.

As we passed through Yreka, I decided there was something
eerie going on. Just to break the ice, I turned the volume down
on the tape and said to my faceless companion: "It seems like
the sun just doesn't want to set." Something admittedly banal.
And then a voice that I hadn't heard for over ten years responded,
"The sun is waiting for you, Yitz, the day is waiting for you."

Ever since the last time I had seen my brother alive in 1980,
I had seen him walking through the streets of New York, or
Jerusalem, or Los Angeles, always from the back. Whenever he
would turn around in response to my footfalls, it was always
somebody else. Many times I had heard Jonathan's voice, until
the second or third syllable proved the illusion. But there was
no mistaking this voice or its owner.

Gripping the steering wheel with ferocious panic, I felt his
strong left hand on my right shoulder. My brother pointed with
his right hand and said, "Yitz, get off at the next exit." The next
exit was Turntable Bay Road. I'd seen it many times, but I had
never used this particular exit. It was a way to turn back on to
go to I-5 North. I was not in a position, nor did I have the where-
withal, to make my own decision to follow directions. I got off at
the exit and intuitively completed the loop onto the northbound
side. As soon as I had gunned my Toyota pickup to 65 miles
per hour, he told me, "Pull over here"—and I saw that the sign
said "Rest Area: Next Exit."

His hand was still on my shoulder, and as I pulled into the
Rest Area and slowed down to 50, 30, 10, and stopped, a flood-
gate of memories opened up.

When I was ten years old, my family and I had just moved
from a small town to the Los Angeles suburbs. I entered my new

school and tried, with marginal success, to become a regular member of the fifth-grade gang. (I might add, parenthetically, that a fifth-grade gang in 1966 was more concerned with cooties and Sandy Koufax's tendonitis than with guns and drugs.)

I quickly learned that the most important activity of the year was Little League, which was going to start in the spring. Throughout the fall and winter (such as it is in Southern California), we played catch and talked about Little League. My new potential friends reminded me, "You gotta join our Little League team; the school sponsors it, it's a great thing. C'mon, join the team, you'll be an outfielder, it'll be great." The most important thing for any fifth-grade boy was to be good at his position. I wanted to be the best outfielder, the next Willie Mays, and be on the Little League team. The day after winter vacation, I took the application and insurance forms that our physical education coach handed out, came home, and showed them to my mother. She filled out all the insurance information and I took it to my father who, without paying much attention, gave me a check for twenty-five dollars. By the end of physical education class the next day, I was all signed up and ready to make headlines.

My birthday's in April, but that year we celebrated a little early. I told my folks that what I really wanted for my birthday was a baseball mitt (I even told them that it had to be a "Rawlings Willie Mays")—and would they be kind enough to give it to me a month early so that I could have it for Little League?

Then came the second Saturday in March, the day of Little League tryouts. This was it: I'd find out if my future as an All-Star outfielder was really going to happen. I put on my sneakers, jeans, T-shirt, and a windbreaker, and got on my Stingray bike with the banana seat and the butterfly handlebars. With my newly oiled and broken-in mitt hung over the left handlebar of my bike, I was ready to go. As I got on my bike in the patio near the kitchen, my father was reading his Shabbos-book (that's what he used to call it) in the kitchen.

He looked up from his reading, waved out the window, and said, "Where are you off to on this fine Shabbos afternoon?" and I answered, ever so quietly: "Little League tryouts—they start today." He grew immediately angry and said, "Never on Shabbos—no son of mine is going to play baseball on Shabbos." "But Abba, you promised me, you signed the forms, you said it was okay, all the boys will be there!" But even with every ten-year-old's argument I could muster, there was no budging him. "No son of mine will play baseball on Shabbos." In anger, I took that mitt, which was my early birthday present from the most important man in my world, walked into the house, and threw it onto the table in front of him. "Damn you and damn your Shabbos!"

I got back on my bike and tore off like the wind. I rode oblivious to directions and speed or traffic signals. Growing legs pumped the pedals and propelled me and my wheels to North Hollywood Park. To my almost ten-year-old eyes, the paths were a thousand miles long and the trees five hundred miles high.

I tore around the track on my bike a few dozen times, fueled by a tremendous anger. When the anger was spent and I was riding along quietly, feeling empty and a little tired, I felt a hand on my shoulder. My brother had followed me to the park. I got off my bike and wheeled it, and we walked together with his hand around my shoulder.

I told him how much I detested my father and Shabbos and a whole list of other grievances, and he just let me pour it out. When I was finished, he walked me over to a park bench. We sat down—and this time I was really emptied out. We sat there with his hand on my shoulder, my bike parked securely next to the bench, and we looked up at the trees as the day began to fade. As we looked up through the trees into the final glory of a beautiful day, I noticed that each inch of the spectrum was a different color. There was the gold that shone through, the bright red reflecting through the leaves, different colors of the bark off the birch trees, and the glorious scent, almost as if a light show had come on just for my benefit. At this, I began crying. "Little brother, why are you crying?" I responded: "In fifteen minutes the sun is going to be down and all of this will be gone." He closed his eyes for a minute, as if trying to remember something from a forgotten lifetime. Jonathan looked back to me and said, "See it, love it, remember it, and it will never disappear."

I swore I would never forget that lesson. But when you're ten and you make an oath, it's pretty much forgotten by the time you're eleven. And indeed, I not only forgot the lesson, I forgot the entire episode until August of 1982, when I drove back from Jerusalem to my home on the Mediterannean and got the message to call my parents back in North Hollywood. For the first seven days of mourning for my brother, as mourners came to my house around sunset time to say Mincha and waited for the sun to go down to say Maariv, people sat and tried to talk to me, but I just looked out the window and saw the sun swallowed by the Mediterranean.

I thought about all the things that I had seen but hadn't taken time to love or couldn't remember, and all the things I didn't even take the time to see. Then I remembered. I remembered the park—I remembered that warm, strong hand on my shoulder—and again I swore I would never forget.

With time comes forgetting, the blessed absence of painful memories that allows us to move on. I forgot, and I'd been spending the last four years driving very fast up and down the highway blindly. I hadn't been seeing a thing—just where I was trying to get to and how to avoid getting back. I didn't see all of the beauty in God's world along the way. And as we pulled into the Rest Area and parked, got out of the truck, and walked hand in hand, my brother led me to a park bench. As we sat down, he pointed to the right to a corner of Lake Shasta. As we looked at it, I started crying. And as I started crying, I could see that my brother was crying, too. And I looked up and I saw that the sun had finally begun to set. My dear brother looked at me and said: "Little brother, I'm crying because I have to go back. Why are you crying?" "In fifteen minutes it's going to be dark and all of this will be gone." The echo of a response chilled and warmed me: *"See it, love it, remember it, and it will never disappear."*

I spent the rest of that drive doing some remembering, some loving, and a lot of forgiving. I don't know when he entered my truck or when he got out. The one thing I know is that the next exit is always my "Rest Area."

NETTIE BLUMENTHAL
Gerald Fierst

Gerald Fierst, *playwright, actor, teacher, and story- teller, has performed his stories from Zuni Pueblo to Oxford, England. He is artistic director of the Jewish Storytelling Center at the 92nd Street Y in New York City, founding director of the New Jersey Storytelling Guild, a board member of the New York Storytelling Center, and codirector of the Gather- ing of Mid-Atlantic Story- tellers. He is a recipient of a New Jersey State Council on the Arts Fellowship in Playwriting and his innova- tive work in schools with story and theater has been*

documented for public television on WNET's "ArtEffects." He has recorded two audiotapes, Jewish Tales of Magic and Mysticism *and* Tikkun Olam: Stories to Heal the World. *Gerald resides in Montclair, New Jersey, with his wife and son.*

I like to tell mystical stories, powerful tales that crack open real- ity so that we can perceive a world that we always knew was there in our subconscious but rarely get to see in our daily lives. Some- times these stories come from the imagination and gain their power from archetypal imagery, but often, these stories come from oral history, real events that prove again and again that stories only imitate life. During the Holocaust, every moment of life had to be lived with such intensity that any survivor who will talk can tell stories that defy the imagination. Each person who survived is both a miracle and a witness to the destruction of a thousand- year-old civilization. Yet I believe the final lesson of the Holocaust must not be the image of Jews as victims. For the Jews to have survived Hitler's war against them, both as individuals and as a culture, called for a strength of spirit and a sense of community that should be an inspiration and an example for all the world. Yom HaShoah has become the newest addition to the Jewish lit- urgy for good reason; not only was the destruction awesome, but the rebirth from the ashes has been a testament to the power of faith to create life. The story I share in this book is a talisman for me. I cannot explain how it happened or why one person was blessed and not all, but the story is true and reminds me, over and over again, that we must balance the cynicism of our scientific age with the innocence of our belief.

---

n the summer of 1984, I was writing *Dancing With Miracles*, a musical theater adaptation of Yaffa Eliach's *Hasidic Tales of the Holocaust*. As part of my research, I was interviewing survivors of the Shoah. One June weekend, I received a call from a friend, the child of survivors. "My parents," she said, "are having guests over. Would you like to come and listen?" So, with a couple of pounds of ruggelach and a notebook, I set out for Budd Lake, New Jersey, where I heard this story from Nettie Blumenthal.

Nettie Blumenthal was a small child who lived in a town outside of Budapest when World War II engulfed the Jewish communities of Europe. At first, King Karol of Hungary saw his Jews as Hungarians and would not permit his German allies to take Hungarian nationals out of the country. Thus, although the Jews of Hungary faced anti-Semitic laws and slave labor, for a time they were spared transportation to the terrible death camps beyond their borders. However, when the war started to turn against the Axis powers, when the allies began to advance across North Africa and up into Italy, and when rumors spread that the Hungarians were wavering in their loyalty and might go over to the Allies, Berlin arranged a putsch. King Karol was deposed and the Green Arrow Fascist party took control of the government. Within twenty-four hours, Adolf Eichman was on the train from Berlin to Budapest and the deportation of the Jews of Hungary began. Within six months, 400,000 Hungarian Jews would die in the gas chambers of Auschwitz.

When the soldiers marched into the village where Nettie Blumenthal lived, she and her mother and her little sister hid in an attic with a half dozen other Jews. All day long, they heard the trucks and boots, the shots and screams, the crashing of glass, the breaking of furniture. All day long, they trembled in the attic, fearing discovery. They couldn't shift their weight; they barely dared to breathe lest a sound make someone below look up and discover the outline of the trap door that led to their hiding place. At last, as darkness fell, the terrible sounds from the streets faded, to be replaced by the distant singing of the soldiers and peasants celebrating that the town was now *judenfrei*, free of Jews.

At last, one of the Jews in the attic dared to whisper, "What shall we do?" There was a rope in the attic and a small vent window. The group decided that they would lower themselves down to the ground and then run across a meadow to the forest where, with luck, they might find a band of partisans who would protect them for the rest of the war. But a mother with two small girls couldn't fend for herself; she would slow everyone down. All agreed. It was too dangerous to bring along Nettie Blumenthal, her mother, and her sister. The mother looked at the other Jews and said, "What kind of men are you? What kind of Jews? At least help me and my children to the earth. Then we will go on by ourselves." And so it was agreed.

Nettie Blumenthal, her mother, and her sister entered the forest in the middle of the night. This was a forest like you read about in old stories, with bears and wolves, thickets that tore one's clothes, and brambles that ripped the skin. The family wandered for three days without food or water. The mother cried so hard that her eyes swelled up and she had to be led by her two children. At last, they came to a road. The mother felt the pavement beneath her feet and said, "What's the use? Whatever waits for us back in town can be no worse than what will happen to us here. Let us follow the road back to town." The children began to lead their mother along the highway.

Already in her young life, Nettie Blumenthal had heard of the terrors of the Russian pogroms, of how White Russian soldiers had swept through Jewish towns, killing left and right. Now, she was leading her mother back to another army of soldiers who wanted to kill the Jews. Suddenly, the little girl looked up and saw soldiers, white soldiers, just as she had heard about in the stories, an army of white soldiers, a soldier behind every tree. "Mutti, Mutti," Nettie Blumenthal screamed, "an army, an army, an army of soldiers—the white soldiers are here in the trees." The mother, hearing her daughter's fear, yelled, "Run, run!" And all three turned and ran in the opposite direction around a bend in the road, where stood a band of partisans who took them in and protected them for the rest of the war.

Mrs. Blumenthal finished her story that afternoon and looked at me. "Do you understand, Gerald? Do you see? At that time, in that place, there were no armies; no soldiers wore white uniforms. No. What I saw were angels, an army of angels, sending us back to life."

FEATHERS

Heather Forest

Heather Forest *is a professional storyteller, recording artist, and author. For the past twenty years, she has toured her performance repertoire of world folktales to theaters, schools, storytelling festivals, and reading conferences throughout the United States. She has published two children's picture books and six audiorecordings of storytelling. Her tapes have won an American Library Association Notable Record Award and a Parents' Choice Gold Classic Award. Heather lives on a tree farm in Huntington, Long Island, New York, with her husband, Larry, and their two children, Lucas and Laurel.*

The tale of "Feathers" is an Eastern European Jewish folktale that has been used over the centuries by both teachers and modern storytellers to celebrate the power of the spoken word. It is a cautionary tale that, through simple yet graphic imagery, points out how carefully we must consider our words. Once freed from the lips, words cannot be swallowed up again.

As a storyteller, I am attracted to the subject matter of this tale, for words are my palette, a colorful tool with which I create images in the imagination of my listeners. Words paint pictures. Words can be a healing wind or, when misused, a hurtful blow. Careless words can be a cruel weapon, as anyone who has ever been the victim of a rumor knows. This tale about careless words simply but poignantly makes its point as the central character learns her lesson about spreading rumors, not by a rabbi's admonition, but through self-discovery. The rabbi, in the best tradition of fine teaching, sets forth a task that allows the student to come to a realization of truth and wisdom through her own experience.

This is also a hasidic tale attributed to Rabbi Levi Yitzhak of Berditchev. Another variation of this folktale can be found in Molly Cone's book *Who Knows Ten* (New York: UAHC, 1965).

Words like feathers fly,
In the wind, in the wind.
Reaching far and wide,
In the wind, in the wind.
Careless words, tossed about,
Cannot again be swallowed up,
Tongues like swords can cut the heart,
Words fly out . . .
The rumors start. . . .

Cruel words like feathers fly,
Cruel words reach far and wide . . .
Try and try to gather them again,
But they fly away in the wind. . . .

A woman whose tongue was sharp and unkind was accused of
    starting a rumor.
She was brought before the village rabbi protesting,
"What I said was in jest . . . just humor!
My words were carried forth by others.
I am not to blame."

But the victim cried for justice, saying,
"You've soiled my own good name!"

"I can make amends," said the woman accused,
"I'll just take back my words and assume I'm excused."

The rabbi listened to what she said,
And sadly thought as he shook his head,
"This woman does not comprehend her crime.
She shall do it again and again in time."

And so he said to the woman accused,
"Your careless words cannot be excused until . . .
You bring my feather pillow to the market square.
Cut it and let the feathers fly through the air.
When this task is done,
bring me back the feathers . . .
every one."

The woman reluctantly agreed.
She thought, "The wise old rabbi's gone mad indeed!"
But to humor him, she took his pillow to the village square.
She cut it and feathers filled the air.

She tried to catch. She tried to snatch.
She tried to collect each one.
But weary with effort she clearly discovered,
the task could not be done.

She returned with very few of the feathers in hand.
"I couldn't get them back, they've scattered over the land!
I suppose," she sighed as she lowered her head,
"Like the words I can't take back,
from the rumor I spread."

Cruel words like feathers fly . . .
Cruel words reach far and wide . . .
They leave the mouth a bitter rind,
May all your words, my friend, be kind.

Words and Music   Feathers   Music Transcription
by Heather Forest   by Elise Sobel

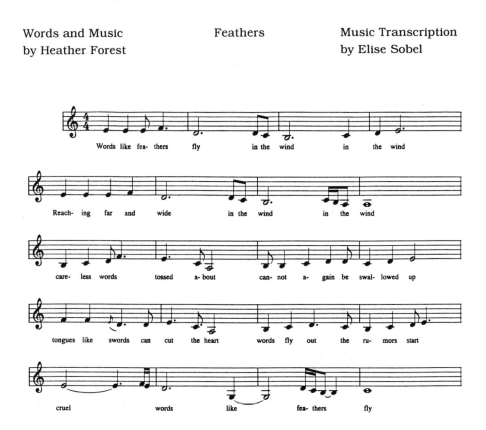

Words like fea- thers fly in the wind in the wind

Reach- ing far and wide in the wind in the wind

care- less words tossed a- bout can- not a- gain be swal- lowed up

tongues like swords can cut the heart words fly out the ru- mors start

cruel words like fea- thers fly

REVIVAL OF THE DEAD
Ellen Frankel

Ellen Frankel *is the editor-in-chief of the Jewish Publication Society as well as a free-lance writer and professional storyteller. She received her Ph.D. in comparative literature from Princeton University in 1978 and has taught writing and literature at several colleges and universities. Her previous works include* The Classic Tales: 4,000 Years of Jewish Lore *and the coauthored* Encyclopedia of Jewish Symbols. *Ellen lives in Philadelphia with her husband and two children.*

Imagery

Why is this story important to me?

Let me suggest several reasons: first, I love the "shape" of the tale. It has all the elements of a classical fairy tale—an only son born to elderly parents, a magical disappearance, an eagle sent by God (or fate or a spirit), romance, star-crossed love, and rescue through sacrifice. One can find this plot in countless stories from many cultures, which makes this tale universal.

On the other hand, this is a very Jewish story in so many ways: Solomon's father leaves home to solicit charity for the Jewish community in Jerusalem. Solomon is kidnapped while studying Torah and lands in Spain, where the king knows of his holy books and special dietary needs. The princess wants to become a Jew because she is attracted to the beauties of the tradition; she converts by immersion, assuming a new name, Sarah; she then rescues the lifeless Solomon by reciting the Jewish prayer about resurrection of the dead. This blending of Jewish particularism and universalism is a hallmark of Jewish lore, and something I especially value.

Second, I love the fact that the hero of this tale is a young woman. She desires to learn Torah even before she learns to desire her teacher. She decides to leave her faith, her land, her parents, her culture, her language, and her name to follow the young Jewish stranger from Jerusalem. And she offers her life in exchange for her beloved's, embarrassing God into reviving the dead Solomon. This Sarah, unlike Abraham's wife, parallels Abraham's daring act of faith and reenacts his story.

Finally, I love the effect the tale has on listeners. It's so romantic—until the very end, when Solomon dies just as Sarah crosses the threshold. Every time I tell this tale, there are gasps and groans in the audience when I tell of his death and a sigh of relief when he comes back to life. It's as if the listener herself has died as her hope has vanished and then come back to life as the tale ends happily ever after.

But after all, that is the magic of fairy tales. . . .

The source of the story is *Osseh Pele* by Y. S. Farhi with an English version in *Mimekor Yisrael* by Bin Gorion. This version of the story is in my collection *The Classic Tales: 4,000 Years of Jewish Lore*.

---

 n Jerusalem there once lived a poor scholar and his wife, who were childless. At that time there was a terrible famine in Israel, and the scholars of the city drew lots to choose one among them to go abroad to seek help from their fellow Jews in the Diaspora. The lot fell upon the poor childless scholar.

When his wife heard of it, she wept bitterly. "How can you leave me alone in my old age? For I have no child to comfort me, and who knows when you shall return!"

"Let us pray to God," said her husband. "Perhaps we will have a child in our old age."

So it happened. The old woman conceived, but the husband could not delay his departure any longer and so set sail before the child was born.

A few months later, the wife gave birth to a handsome boy whom she named Solomon. So wise was the child that he soon learned the whole Torah, and after that the Mishnah and Talmud. Every day he would study with his companions upon the roof of his house, where it was cool. Twice a day his mother would bring him his meals there and visit with him.

One afternoon as he strolled upon the roof awaiting his mother's visit, an eagle suddenly swooped down upon him, seized him in its strong talons, and carried him off, leaving only his shoes behind. Swiftly it bore him over the sea until they reached Spain. Then it dropped him into the king's garden and flew away.

When the king's guards found a strange youth lying on the ground, still as death, they summoned physicians, who attended to him until he recovered.

When at last he opened his eyes, he asked, "Where am I?"

"You are in Spain," they told him, "in the king's palace." And they brought him meat and wine to revive his spirits.

But the boy refused to eat or drink. "I am a Jew," he told them. "The Torah has forbidden these foods to me."

"What then can we bring you?" they asked.

"Honey, nuts, and fruits," he told them. So they brought these to him.

When the boy had regained much of his strength, he spent his days wandering in the garden, reciting all the Torah and holy words that he remembered. But he often wept, wishing that he had his books with him. The king learned of his unhappiness and sent messengers throughout his kingdom to buy him the books he wanted. And he built for the boy a beautiful house in the garden in which to study.

Meanwhile, the boy's mother, having discovered her son's empty shoes on the rooftop and presuming him dead, mourned him day after day, bitterly lamenting her lonely fate.

One night the king's daughter found herself unable to sleep and went into the garden to walk among the trees and flowers there. She knew nothing of the strange boy in the garden, for her father wished to protect her since she was but a young girl. She saw a light in the window of the little house where Solomon lived and drew closer to investigate.

Hearing her footsteps, Solomon looked up and saw in the window the most beautiful face he had ever seen. Instantly, fear seized his heart, for he imagined that this was a demon come to distract him from his studies. So he bent over his holy books and tried to banish the beautiful face from his mind.

Then the king's daughter spoke to him, but he pretended to hear nothing. She returned to the palace, bewildered by what she had seen.

A short time later she returned with an interpreter, thinking that the boy had not understood her words. But this time he answered her questions in her own language. So she sent the interpreter away and began to converse with the stranger herself.

"What are you studying?" she asked him.

"I am a Jew," he told her. "These are the books of my faith."

"Tell me what is in them," she said.

So he told her about the Torah and the ways of his people. And they conversed until it was almost dawn. Then she returned to the palace, her heart filled with a strange new happiness.

The next night she returned to Solomon's house, and he taught her more words of Torah. Night after night, the two young people studied and conversed together until the princess came to love this stranger and his teachings.

One night she said to him, "I wish to become a Jew."

"It will be too difficult for you," said Solomon.

But the more he tried to dissuade her, the more she insisted, until he had to yield. "If that is your wish," he told her, "then you must keep it a secret."

"I will," she promised.

"Tomorrow night when you come here," Solomon instructed her, "bring with you clean garments. Take off the clothing you are wearing and immerse yourself completely in the garden pool. Then put on the new garments."

The next night the princess did as Solomon had instructed her. When she emerged from the water, she said the blessing he had taught her and put on the new garments.

Then Solomon said to her, "You are now a new person and you need a new name. No longer will you be called Mary but Sarah. You must be careful not to eat impure foods or to transgress God's holy laws."

After that she asked him to teach her the *aleph-bet*, and then the prayers and blessings, and he did. With each meeting their love grew stronger until they vowed to marry. They exchanged signet rings as a sign of their everlasting love.

But the next night, as Solomon awaited his beloved by the garden pool, the eagle came and bore him off again in its talons, carrying him over the sea and dropping him back upon his rooftop. A servant found him there the next morning and summoned his mother, who rejoiced to find her lost son returned to her. In time the physicians healed him and he returned to his friends in the House of Study. But not for one moment could he banish the memory of his beloved Sarah from his thoughts, and he would frequently break off his studies to sigh, "Oh, Sarah!" His friends and family worried greatly about him, thinking that his terrible experiences must have confused his mind.

Meanwhile, Sarah returned to the garden, only to find her beloved Solomon gone without a trace. Night after night she wandered along the garden paths seeking him, until at last she gave up hope and took to her bed. The worried king and queen called in the court physicians, but they were unable to cure her.

Soon after this, the poor scholar returned home from his travels. How great was his joy to find a son so handsome and wise within his house. But he soon saw that Solomon was greatly troubled, and he questioned the boy until he finally learned the secret of his distress.

"I will go to Spain and find this Sarah of yours," he told his son. "And with God's help, I will bring her back to you."

Solomon gave his father the ring Sarah had given him so that she would believe his father's words. The next day, the old man set sail for Spain.

Disguising himself as a physician, he came to the king's palace and announced that he could cure the ailing princess. When the king's men brought him in to Sarah, he asked them all to leave so that he could consider her case without distraction. So they left him alone.

He approached her bed and whispered to her, "Sarah, my daughter, I am the father of your beloved Solomon."

At first she did not hear him, so great was the sleep brought on by her illness. But at last she opened her eyes and saw the old man by her side.

Again he whispered, "Sarah, my daughter, I am the father of your beloved Solomon. He has sent me here to find you."

Suddenly her cheeks flushed with life, and she sat up in her bed, her eyes wide with astonishment. "Is it possible? Is Solomon still alive?"

"Yes, my daughter," he said, "and here is his ring." And he showed her the signet ring she had once given to Solomon to seal their love. Then she knew that he spoke the truth.

The father then went out of the room and announced to the king and queen that he had cured the princess. They gave her food and drink, and in a few weeks she was restored to health, looking even more beautiful than before.

Then he appeared before the king and queen and said, "Your daughter needs a change of climate to complete her cure. Let me take her on a sea voyage, and then she will fully regain her health."

"She is in your hands," they answered. So the princess gathered all her jewels and gold and kissed her parents good-bye. Then they set sail for Israel.

As they neared the end of their voyage, Solomon became gravely ill, for he feared that his father's efforts would fail and that he would never see his beloved Sarah again. Just as Sarah and his father reached the gates of Jerusalem, Solomon breathed his last breath and died.

When they arrived at the poor scholar's house, they found everyone weeping. Sarah ran to Solomon's room and found his lifeless body on the bed.

"Leave me, all of you!" she cried. "Leave me alone with my love!"

So they left her and she lifted up her voice to heaven and prayed, "Dear God, Master of Life! I have abandoned my father and mother and the land of my birth to come here and seek shelter under Your wings. It was this youth who first opened my eyes to the joys of Your Torah and commandments. Have pity upon him and restore him to life so that all the world may know that You are a God who restores the dead to life. If not, then take my life, too, for I have no wish to live without my beloved. Blessed be the Lord who listens to our prayers!"

Then she stretched out her body over the dead youth's lifeless form and placed her mouth upon his mouth and her eyes upon his eyes.

"Solomon!" she cried. "Solomon, do not abandon me! I shall not move until my spirit joins with yours!"

Suddenly the form beneath her shuddered. She rose up and looked upon Solomon's ashen face. Then his eyes opened and he looked around.

"I am Sarah," she told him. "I have come to you, my love." And she kissed him. But he was still unable to speak, so she gave him water to drink and food to revive his strength, and at last he sat up. She called in his parents, who rejoiced greatly to find him restored to life.

"Blessed be God who revives the dead!" they cried.

Then they set up the marriage canopy, and the couple was married with great joy and singing.

THE PATH
Nancy R. Ginsberg

Nancy R. Ginsberg *is a graduate of Hebrew Union College's School of Sacred Music and Indiana University. She became an invested cantor in 1987. She has studied voice and opera in Milan, Italy, on a Fulbright Hayes Scholarship, as well as at La Scala Opera. She also completed a master of social work degree at the University of Pennsylvania. She currently serves as cantor at Temple Beth-El in Providence, Rhode Island. She has been a volunteer chaplain at a prison and was the founding president of the Delaware Valley Cantor's Council. An avid athlete, she completed the New York Marathon.*

A version of this story was originally published in *Good Housekeeping* magazine in 1934. However, I heard this story many years ago from a young, energetic woman rabbi. It was before I became a cantor, and the impression it made on me stuck. I often recall the line, "The end will be better than the beginning."

I think of this line each year as I prepare for the awesome task of the High Holy Days. As I reflect on the past year, I can indeed say that no matter what has occurred, be it bad or good, that I am a better person, a stronger person, because of the events of the past year. This line and this story help me take stock and count my blessings. I am able to pause and thank God for all that are in my life—for friends, family, my health, my gifts that come from God, and the energy to greet each new day, each new challenge with confidence and anticipation.

Life for all of us is a journey, and hopefully, just like the young woman in the story, as we set our feet on the path of life, we can grow from the lessons learned, be open to life's experiences, renew and refresh ourselves, share ourselves with others, and continue to travel on with blessings, hope, and love.

This is a parable about a woman who teaches us one of life's eternal messages. It is a story that deals with the prevalent themes throughout our High Holy Day liturgy. But it is a story for the entire year.

---

he young woman set her foot on the path of life. "Is the way long?" she asked.

And her guide said, "Yes, and the way is hard, and you will be old before you reach the end of it. But the end will be better than the beginning."

But the young woman was happy and she would not believe that anything could be better than these years. So she played with her children and gathered flowers for them along the way—and bathed with them in the clear stream; and the sun shone on them and life was good. The young woman exclaimed, "Nothing will ever be lovelier than this!"

Then night came, and with it, storms. The path was dark, and the children shook with fear and cold. The woman drew them close and covered them with her mantle—and the children said, "We are not afraid, for you are near and no harm can come." And the woman said, "This is better than the brightness of day, for I have taught my children courage."

The morning came, and they came to a hill, and the children climbed and grew weary, and the woman was weary. But at all times she said to the children, "A little patience and we are there." So the children climbed, and when they reached the top they said, "We could not have done it without you." And the woman, when she laid down that night, looked up at the stars and said, "This is a better day than the last, for my children have learned fortitude in the face of hardship. Yesterday I gave them courage—today I have given them strength."

And when they rose up, the children looked at the never-ending horizon, and they became filled with despair. But the mother took them by the hand and turned them to look back across the long road they had traveled. Together they recalled the joy they had shared and their many accomplishments along the way. And at the end of the day the woman felt deep peace in her heart—for she knew she had taught them of hope.

The next day came strange clouds that darkened the earth—clouds of war and hate and evil. The children groped and stumbled, and the woman said, "Look up, lift your eyes to the light." And the children looked and saw above the clouds an everlasting glory, and it guided them and brought them beyond the darkness. That night, the mother said, "This is the best day of all, for I have showed my children God and given them faith."

The days went on, and the weeks, the months, and the years, and the woman grew old, and she became little and bent. But her children were tall and strong and walked with courage. When the way was hard, they helped their mother. When the way was rough, they lifted her, for she was light as a feather. At last they came to a hill. Beyond the hill they could see a shining road and golden gates flung wide.

The woman said, "I have reached the end of my journey. Now I know that the end *is* better than the beginning, for my children can walk alone, and their children after them."

The children all gathered around their mother and said, "You will always walk with us, even when you have gone through the gates." They stood and watched her as she went on alone. The gates closed after her, and her children said, "We cannot see her, but she is with us still. She is more than a memory; she is a living presence."

THE STORYTELLER

Howard Schwartz

In memory of Reuven Gold

Marilyn L. Schrut

Reuven Gold, z'l, *was a storyteller from Chicago who earned his M.A. degree in human development at the University of Chicago. Beginning in January 1969 he told stories as recreational and cultural events and also as a leader of seminars and workshops in staff development, human relations, and community problems. He wrote: "I love to tell stories of the hasidim and of the* hasiday umos haolam, *the compassionate sages of the peoples of the world. By telling these stories, I nourish my listeners' hearts, minds, and spirits together with my own." Reuven Gold died in January 1988.*

See page 301 for bio and photo of Howard Schwartz.
See page 265 for bio and photo of Zalman M. Schachter-Shalomi.

here once was a Hasid who was a wonderful story-teller. It was said that he had begun to tell stories after hearing tales told by Reb Zalman. About this Reb Reuven used to say: "I was a baby getting ready to be born. Reb Zalman was the midwife." At first he did not think of himself as a storyteller, merely as one who told stories. Little by little people began to seek him out to hear his tales. They invited him to dinner just to hear the tales he would tell afterward. And eventually the day came when he gave up his daily work and set out into the world as a storyteller.

The name of this storyteller was Reb Reuven ben Shimon. Except when he was telling tales, he was the shyest of men, who even stuttered when he spoke. But when he began to tell a tale, the shyness and the stuttering disappeared. Each word he spoke was a rope that drew the listener into another world, the world of the tale. And it was said that none who entered that world left it unchanged.

Now, if the truth be known, Reb Reuven did not tell a great many tales. While some storytellers had as many tales to tell as there are drops in the ocean or sand on the shore, Reb Reuven only told a few tales. When asked about this, he always explained that he only told tales that made his heart dance. And anyone who heard him tell a tale could well understand this, for Reb Reuven became as entranced in the tale as any listener hearing it for the first time. And more often than not the tale would move him to tears and joyous laughter.

Once it happened that Reb Reuven told the tale of young Mordecai, who was brought to the Rabbi of Karlin because no matter what his parents did, they could not bring him to take his studies seriously. The rabbi bellowed that he would teach the child to study and had the parents leave the terrified child with him. But as soon as they departed, the rabbi embraced the child, holding him gently to his heart for the longest time, silently. When the parents returned, the rabbi again bellowed that the boy had been taught his lesson. That child grew up to be a wise and compassionate teacher of the Torah, and many was the time he said that he had first learned how to teach Torah when the rabbi had held him to his breast.

Now there was a young woman who heard this tale and was deeply moved by it, and she made the strange request that Reb Reuven tell it once again. While many a storyteller might have refused that request, Reb Reuven did not. Instead he told the story over again, almost word for word as he had the first time. And yet all of those who had heard the first telling could not dispute that while the words had been the same, the story was completely different. How was this possible?

Reb Hayim Elya asked Reb Zalman about this paradox, and added: "And this, Rebbe, is strangest of all: the first time I heard this story it was as if I was held in the embrace of my father. But the second time I heard Reb Reuven as if he were speaking with the voice of my mother." Reb Zalman said: "For Reb Reuven the words are like the notes by which music is read. They serve only as guideposts and not as an end in themselves. And the request to repeat the tale opened Reb Reuven to a new music by which the tale could be told. Just as we chant the Torah in Major and the Prophets in Minor, so too did the ears of the young woman open the mouth of Reb Reuven, for, as Reb Avraham Yitzhak ha-Cohen said, 'There are ears that have the power to open mouths.' For Reb Reuven always comes back to the symphony of the tale as if for the first time and rediscovers its music anew. It is the spirit that stands behind the words that concerns him, and not the words themselves."

Note

This story is taken from Howard Schwartz, *The Dream Assembly: Tales of Rabbi Zalman Schachter-Shalomi* (Nevada City, CA: Gateways, 1989).

Two stories from Reuven Gold
An Introduction and a Remembering by Gioia Timpanelli

Reuven Gold was a marvelous storyteller, and like all things marvelous, when he told his stories he made us feel wonder, experience joy, and suddenly smile because we were astonished. He told the stories of the early hasidic Rebbes with a voice full of music, the rhythms and phrases transporting us to Yiddish, the language of the stories, a language and culture he knew from within. He was also an American storyteller from Chicago, and this blessed combination gave us the chance of bridging two cultures, of remembering and learning at the same time. When he told stories, he'd put his head to one side as though he was listening for the right words to say—and then he'd begin, sometimes talking simply, sometimes chanting. He was a guide who each time felt the great joy of the treasures he was showing. No matter how many times he had seen these treasures himself, he always saw them for the first time with us. His stories gave the great comfort of the communal life and the great wisdom of the teachings; Reuven was always their humble servant. Sometimes in the story he would help us to understand a Yiddish word in case someone didn't know it, or the contextual significance of a phrase. He always began respectfully, pensively, as though listening for those special words that would put him in the right place to tell the stories.

When Zusya   was getting old,   he used to say to his disciples, "After I die and I go to the heavenly courts to be judged, they will not say to me there,   *'Zusya, why weren't you Moses!'* Instead, they will say to me, 'Zusya, it was fully in your power to have been Zusya   no one on heaven and earth could have stopped you   so why, so why, weren't you Zusya?

Once, at the end of telling this story, he laughed, and once he looked out with tears in his eyes, saying . . . "And so?"

His voice rose and fell, was soft and loud; he repeated phrases so that they became song, and at the end of the story he often had tears of joy in his eyes. Even in the middle of a story, at some revelation, or miracle where the heart is opened to the true living of the Teachings, Reuven could cry and then continue unstopped —as though tears are also essential words in the telling.

Here's another re-telling from Reuven:

The Rebbes   used to send   their disciples out   to the outlying villages where there weren't any teachers   there weren't any scholars   where Jews didn't   have any   real source of spiritual inspiration—of course other than the glory of creation itself—to share with them the tradition, the holy teachings, and so Dov Baer sent Zusya and   Elimelach, and they in their turn sent their disciples   and some   disciples of Zusya and Elimelach were once on the banks of the Volga River and they remembered that their Masters always spoke (and here Reuven has tears—for he must have *heard* them speaking) about eating, in a certain kretchma, a certain lentil soup that, they said,   was the most fantastic, de- licious lentil soup that they   ever had. And they came upon just such a kretchma   and they were wondering   if this could be the very same one.

And they came in, and they asked for some lentil soup, and the old woman who was running it   made them some lentil soup and it was really delicious   and she said, "You know, you two re- mind me of the time many, many years ago when there were two young men here whose faces shined with the light of Torah   like yours do   and   in those days we were also very poor. They came in and they wanted some food and we didn't really have anything to give them all we had were some   lentils and I made them some lentil soup   and I didn't even have any spices to put in it   so while I made the lentil soup   I prayed to G-d that He Himself should put in it, spices from the Garden of Eden and they told me how delicious it was and they enjoyed it just as much as you are   and I didn't have any spices today either   and again I prayed that God should put in it spices from the Garden of Eden. And I see that you two are enjoying it."

And now they knew why this was such an unusual lentil soup.

Reuven had the gift of telling. With him we were listening to a humble man, a seeker like ourselves, but because he had been given the talent to be a master teller, this seeker could show us again the treasures that have been given us, treasures that we had forgotten or had not seen. His tears were for himself and for us. I knew that he was transmitting these stories with the passion, the wonder, and the yearning of those first hearers. Through this gift, hearing the stories with Reuven brought us the experience of these great stories that open our hearts.

Thanks to Robert Bly for having saved and treasured Reuven Gold's tape, *Tales of the Hasidic Rebbes* (original chants by Rabbi Shlomo Carlebach), which was produced in 1977. The two stories in Gioia's introduction are transcribed from that tape. The spaces in the text are an attempt to capture Reuven's phrasing and style of telling.

Reuven Gold and Gioia Timpanelli were among the early and central figures in the revival of storytelling. They always met as *lantzmen,* which is what they called each other, feeling that the basic substance of their stories, although culturally different, came from the same source.

Gioia Timpanelli, a storyteller and poet, comes from a Sicilian family background. However, she grew up in a Jewish neighborhood in Gravesend, Brooklyn, New York, where she lived so close a life with her neighbors and friends that they were extended family. Gioia was considered then, and still feels, part of the *mishpukha.*

THE BURNING PIANO
Karen Golden

Karen Golden *began telling stories at the dinner table at age three and playing the saxophone at eight. Today her table is the size of North America! She is a profes- sional storyteller, musician, writer, and workshop leader. She has been featured in the* Los Angeles Times, *on* National Public Radio, *and on the Jewish Television Net- work. In 1993, she released her audiotape* Tales and Scales: Stories of Jewish Wisdom. *Karen lives in Los Angeles with her husband, Steve.*

I have often heard the statement, "Storytellers do not find sto- ries, stories find storytellers." The following stories found me in 1984 during my five-year stay in Jerusalem. They are two com- pletely separate tales that are joined together by extraordinary circumstances. Equally extraordinary is the fact that I heard both of these stories, I believe, in order to share them with others.

They bring to my mind an old Jewish folktale, which was adapted by I. L. Peretz into his story "The Case against the Wind." In this tale, a poor woman gives two loaves of bread to the hun- gry, only to lose her last remaining loaf to the wind. Meanwhile, a merchant ship sinking at sea is saved after the merchants pray to God to rescue them and a great wind whirls the loaf into the boat and it plugs up the leak. The woman and the merchants go to King Solomon for advice and he helps them to uncover the story of what happened to the loaf. The woman walks away with riches that the merchants are only too pleased to be able to give away. Their lives could have ended in tragedy had they not been joined by the loaf of bread. In my two stories entitled "The Burning Piano," the piano serves a function similar to that of the loaf of bread: it somehow transforms the lives of two individuals from tragedy to hope.

The historical context for "The Burning Piano" is complex and leaves many unanswered questions. It begins with a swell of right- wing Arab nationalism in Iraq in the 1930s, which forced Iraq's

Jewish community to enter its darkest hour. The government subjected the nation's 130,000 Jews to organized persecution, searchings, and arrests. By 1955, 113,000 Iraqi Jews had been transported to Israel. Because of the mass emigration, many were forced to live in tent camps set up throughout Israel to provide temporary shelter until enough permanent structures could be built.

On November 29, 1947, United Nations delegates from fifty-six countries met to decide on a partition plan for the tiny strip of land known at that time as Palestine. The plan was approved by a two-thirds vote, and Israel's War of Independence began the following day. Skirmishes between Arabs and Jews were bloody and devastating to both populations. By the end of the war, more than half a million Arabs had left Israeli-controlled territories. Some of the many questions that remain unanswered are: Why did so many Arabs flee their homes? Who told them to leave? Did they leave because of Jewish pressure or because of pressure from their own leaders? No order for evacuation was ever found in any historical documentation from either side. The evidence in the Arab press and radio of the time was to the contrary: Arab civilians were ordered to stay where they were. In spite of this warning, over 80,000 Arab rooms were left vacant in Jerusalem, Haifa, Jaffa, Safed, Ramle, Lydda, and smaller towns and villages. Both during and following the war, close to 200,000 new Jewish immigrants moved into these abandoned Arab dwellings due to their poor housing conditions. The Arab families never returned.

---

 hen I lived in Jerusalem, I played my saxophone in a concert band every Wednesday night. One night after practice, a group of us was sitting at the back of the band room packing up our instruments when the conversation turned to Israel's War of Independence in 1948. It seemed like every Israeli over age fifty who was sitting in our little gathering had a story of battle or heroism except for Avraham. He just sat quietly swabbing out his clarinet. "What about you Avraham?"—all faces were on him. "You must have a story or two." He was such a quiet man. I had never heard him speak before. He adjusted his shirt collar, stroked his graying black hair a few times, and pulled out a stray thread from his sweater before talking in a slow, deliberate manner. "I was only a boy during the war, not much of a hero. I don't even like war. Oh, I'm sorry, that was silly of me to say. None of us like war—what I meant was, I knew very little about the war. I arrived in Palestine shortly before the war began. It was all so new." Avraham made no eye contact; he just looked down at his clarinet. But then he looked up, and there was a quivering smile on his face. "I guess I do have a story to tell you. It's the story of why I decided to become a music teacher."

We all sat silently and watched him, not knowing how he would link his love of music to the war. The rest of the band members went home except for those of us who were huddled together in the corner trying to hear. Avraham spoke haltingly, in a low, raspy voice. "I was born in Bagdad, Iraq, and lived in a big house with my family, and what a house it was. We had a large, silver vase in the entranceway, many worn books on the bookshelf, and brightly woven carpets on the stone floors. My parents liked nice things. We even had a piano in the big room. I was learning to play when suddenly, we had to leave every-thing behind, just before my Bar Mitzvah. Life for the Jews wasn't good in Bagdad. We took a few small suitcases and flew to Pal-estine. It was my first plane ride! When we arrived, they told us there wasn't enough housing and we would have to live in a temporary camp in Jerusalem. It was a tent village. We lived in a tent! They said they would build more houses—stone ones. So we lived in the tent and waited. We had three metal beds and a few wooden chairs.

"There wasn't much to do there. No work for my father or school for me, just a lot of waiting around, trying to learn He-brew. One night, I was lying in bed when we heard a loud noise outside. It was louder than anything I had ever heard. I knew this was the sound of gunfire. My father pulled me from my bed, and we started running along with my mother and brother. We ran from the tent village and just kept running toward some permanent houses which were not far from our tents. Then we saw an opened door and we ran into a house. I don't think we knew where we were running; we just ran. My father said it would be safer inside. There was no one home, but there was a meal on the table—pita bread and salad. We left the door open thinking the people would return any minute. At first we waited for them before eating their food, but we were so hungry that we ate everything. There was even a grand piano in the main room, and that night, while we heard the loud noises outside I played the piano softly inside.

"The next day we went out, and in the daylight we saw that we had run into an Arab village and were in an Arab home. From the inside, we had had no idea it was an Arab house. There were books in Arabic, just like those we read in Iraq. But on the outside of the house was painted a small, black square, which means the family were Moslems and had made the pilgrimage to Mecca. We decided we would stay until the owners came back, even though it gave us a funny feeling to be inside an Arab home. We were afraid to return to the tent because there was no protection. We felt we had no choice but to stay. All of our neighbors were our friends from the tent village. They had all run into open homes.

"The weather kept getting colder and colder. My father couldn't find work, and we had no money. There was very little firewood, and because the house was so big, we burned it all in a few days. We had to burn the furniture to keep warm. We burned all the chairs and tables, but we were still cold. One day, my father came to me with very sad eyes and told me we would have to burn the piano. It was good wood and we would have to burn it if we were to survive the winter. First he burned the bench, then the legs and the top. I could still play it until he burned the body. Then there were just strings laying on the floor, which wouldn't burn. They were useless strings, not good for anything but to serve as a painful reminder of how vulnerable we really were. It hurt me to think that our lives had come to this: using a piano as firewood. I felt as if a part of myself had been destroyed. I decided at that moment that I would become a music teacher to bring music out of wounded hearts once again. I would teach people that the purpose of a piano is for warming the heart, not the house. This is my story of the war. By the way, the people never came back to their houses. I guess I wasn't a hero, but I do have this story. It has lived within me every day of my life."

When Avraham finished, we sat there silently. No one could think of anything to say. We just picked up our instruments and went home.

When I lived in Jerusalem I used to love going to the old city, especially to the Shuk (market) to experience "sensory overload." First, there were the smells; baking bread, spices, and sewage. Then there were all the bright colors, from Persian rugs to shiny brass coffee trays, and finally there was the symphony of sounds: people talking, mezzuins calling the Moslems to prayer, and church bells ringing. I never felt afraid to walk anywhere in the old city—even the Moslem quarter felt safe. Perhaps it's because I'm an American that I felt I could cross into this world without fear.

I had a favorite shop, not far from the Damascus gate, which was owned by an Arab man named Ibrahim. His store was like a tiny cave peeking out from under the street. It was filled with artifacts that he collected from the wandering Bedouin peoples; brightly colored pink and purple embroidered dresses, carpets, hangings, even camel saddles! Ibrahim always had a smile on his face, with two gold teeth sparkling in the front. He was a small, balding man who moved with childlike agility through the nooks and crannies of his little shop. Whenever I went to visit him he would brew up a pot of strong tea over a small, open fire, which he lit inside a metal pot. We sat on handmade wicker stools, and he always told me stories about his customers from all over the world. He was proud of the fact that he knew people from almost every country, and he would point admiringly at the many photographs of his international customers that were all over his shop—even on the dress hangers.

After the first few sips of tea, Ibrahim would pull out a huge scrapbook, at least a foot thick, filled with smiling photos, letters, quotes cut out of different kinds of documents, and newspaper clippings. On one such visit we were looking at the scrapbook when he said, "Blease, read this letter. It is filled with much Beace." He couldn't pronounce his "p's," and his English was filled with many mistakes, but he always spoke without hesitation. "You mean 'Peace'?" He laughed. "Yes, beace, I mean peace." I unfolded a well-worn sheet of blue stationery and read out loud: "Dear Ibrahim, we love our Bedouin carpet, it reminds us of your little shop and our visit with you. We have enclosed our five favorite poems about peace for your scrapbook, as promised.

We also told our neighbor Nelly, and her poems and picture will be in the mail next week. We wish you much strength. Love, Hans and Ingrid." Next to the letter were five short poems written out longhand on white paper and a picture of Hans and Ingrid standing with Ibrahim.

He flipped through the pages. There were letters written in languages I couldn't read, and many poems and quotes, such as "Peace begins with me" and "Peace, not war." The scrapbook was overflowing and loose papers kept slipping out onto the floor. One letter was from 1953! "When did you start your peace scrapbook?" I asked.

"After the war," he said. Then he laughed. "I wish after the war—it is still going on. I mean after the big one in 1948, when I was a child. I started my scrapbook when we lived in the little houses, the refugee camp. At first everyone was very angry and people said bad things all the time. The word *hate* was in almost every sentence. Once I heard my friend say something about being peaceful. I was so happy I said, 'Mohammed, will you write what you said on paper? I want to keep it.' He thought I was joking so he just wrote it and laughed.

"I kept the paper in a little notebook and thereafter, anytime anyone said something nice, I told them to write it down. My book was quite thin for a long time because people didn't say nice things very often. But then it started to grow. Whenever my friends found a poem or quote about peace, they copied it and gave it to me. I showed my book to all the people in my village who were especially angry about our move. They called me the dreamer, but at least they laughed!"

"Move—what move?" I asked.

"The move from the village of my birth in Jerusalem . . . not really a move . . . we all ran away out of fear. It was a warm spring day. The sun had gone down and we were waiting for my father to come home from work. It was getting so late that we were worried. My mother put the dinner on the table, pita bread and salad. . . . I was helping her roast a chicken in the outside stove when we heard a very loud noise and saw flames in the sky. My mother screamed, and then my father came running toward us. I don't know to this day who told us to leave or why—

they just kept yelling, 'Run, run!' So we started running—we ran from our beautiful house.

"And what a house! It was made of stone, not like the little houses we ran to, which were made of old boxes and tin. Our house was so big we even had our own yard, filled with olive trees and grapevines. Our house was so big that when the piano played in the main room, it rang out like what I imagine the voice of Allah to sound like. Did I ever tell you about our piano? I used to play the piano, but after we moved I never played again. We never went back—all gone, all gone. This is why I started my scrapbook, to make music with words and people's hearts. When I read these words of beace, I hear music in my heart."

Ibrahim showed me one final letter that day. It was in Yiddish, from an old friend of his father. "My father spoke Yiddish with an Arab accent. He had many Jewish friends before the war. He wrote to these friends until he died, but he never saw them after the war. He just couldn't. . . . But I saved the letters as proof that we can all be friends." I finished my tea and thanked him for a lovely afternoon. Ibrahim kissed me on both cheeks and said, "May Allah be with you."

I heard both of these stories within a year of each other, but I never thought of them as a single story until l came back to the United States to live. One sunny afternoon, I was thinking about my life in Israel and the many people who had crossed my path. Somehow, I thought about Avraham and Ibrahim. Perhaps it was because they both have the same name. I was awestruck when I realized that their lives may have been connected by the same house and the same piano, as well as the same war, the same sorrow, and thc same redemption. These two Abrahams have fulfilled God's prophecy by making their lives a blessing.

And the Lord said to Avram, get out of your country and from your kindred and from your father's house and go to a land that I will show you. And I will make of you a great nation and I will bless you and make your name great and you will be a blessing. (Genesis 12:1–2)

References

Peretz, I. L. *The Case Against the Wind and Other Stories.* New York: Macmillan Publishing, 1975.
Robinson, Donald. *Under Fire: Israel's 20 Year Fight for Survival.* New York: W. W. Norton and Company, 1968.
Sachar, Howard M. *A History of Israel: From the Rise of Zionism to Our Time.* New York: Alfred A. Knopf, 1979.

LEON'S PLAN FOR PEACE
James Stone Goodman

James Stone Goodman *is founding rabbi of Congregation Neve Shalom, in St. Louis, Missouri. He is also a musician and the leader of the Zambra Mediterranean Jam, performing original music, stories, and traditional music on spiritual themes. He is the founding director of the St. Louis Information Committee and Hotline on Addiction (SLICHA). He writes and lectures frequently on the problems associated with addiction. In addition, he is the founder of the Oasis of Peace, a series of teachings exploring the new paradigm linking spirituality and health. Jim is married to Rabbi Susan Talve and they have three children, Jacob, Sarika, and Adina.*

There are a number of events, recollections, and teachings that occasioned this story. I wrote this story the day I witnessed the historic handshake between Yitzhak Rabin and Yassir Arafat on television, on September 13, 1993. One of my teachers had quoted to me a teaching from the Baal Shem Tov about teshuvah (repentance) that had stayed with me throughout the High Holiday season that year. The Baal Shem Tov used to quote the Rashi to Exodus 3:3 when discussing the concept of teshuvah and whether or not a tzaddik could make teshuvah. Exodus 3:3 is the story of Moses and the burning bush. "And Moses said, 'I will turn aside now, and see this great sight, why the bush is not burnt.'" What does "turn aside" mean at this moment in the story? The Rashi reads, "to turn aside from here to approach there." To me, it was a powerful teaching, then as now: to understand teshuvah with this simple insight, to move from one's place.

As I was watching Rabin and Arafat on television that day, I was thinking how many justified reasons each party had to maintain their place. What I was hoping I saw that day was two cultures making teshuvah, moving from their place toward another place. A courageous peace movement. Is that what I witnessed? That is the question that occasioned the story.

I also thought about the ultimate dream of peace: the days of the Messiah. What would it feel like, would it be radically different than the way it is now, or "it's like this"?

In the Midrash, Abraham is granted a vision into the future, in which he sees and understands everything. The whole drama becomes clear to him in a moment when the worlds converge and the opacity of the future opens up to him. I settled for a story with all the questions intact.

I want to beg you as much as you can . . . to be patient toward all that is unsolved in your heart and to try to love the questions themselves. . . . Do not seek the answers which cannot be given you (by another) because you would not be able to live them. And the point is to live everything. Live the questions now. Perhaps, you will then gradually without noticing it, live along some distant day into the answer.

—Reinhold Maria Rilke

n Monday, September 13, 1993, I watched the foreign ministers of Israel and the Palestine Liberation Organization sign a peace agreement and saw Yassir Arafat and Yitzhak Rabin shake hands. It was two days before Rosh Hashana, 5754.

I watched Mr. Rabin hesitate just a little, then accept Mr. Arafat's hand. For a moment, Mr. Arafat and Mr. Rabin stepped out of the Sony Trinitron and into cyberspace where they stood between worlds, frozen in a gesture that transcended the common handshake. I didn't want to miss a moment of the economy of movement that contributed to the most beautiful handshake I had ever seen. I wanted to see it again. Then I heard clapping and realized that the two men had returned to the television, and the crowd was standing and applauding their handshake, and my wife and I were crying.

That night I dreamed about Leon. I hadn't thought about him in years. Leon was the old rabbi at the synagogue my parents attended. It was a long time ago, and Leon was old then. Everybody used to talk about Leon's predictions. On Rosh Hashana, Leon made predictions about what was going to happen in the coming year. They were mostly political predictions, and everybody would hang on them, and some people would even keep track of what he said. He looked as old as God to me when I was a kid, but he lived for many more years. He was probably close to a hundred when he died.

In my dream, I was talking to Leon in a park. We were both sitting on a bench in front of a pool where children played with wooden boats. It was a beautiful day, sunny and cool. Leon was dressed in black robes, the way I remember him on the pulpit, pushing the billowing sleeves back as he spoke. I asked him what his predictions were, what was going to happen—would there be a real peace, can they be trusted, does this mark the beginning of a new era? He sat with his face resting on his hand, as if he were thinking, but he did not respond. In my dream, I knew he was dead, and I asked him if, from his perspective, he could see the future. "Is there a future for you?" I asked. "Do you travel through time?" I asked. "What is it like in the next world?" He sat there deep in thought. He answered with only one sentence. "It's like this," he said. Then I awoke.

I remember thinking in the dream, does he mean it's like *this*— this park, this pool, this day, this world, this life? What does he mean, "it's like this"? Does he mean "it's like this": and I awakened before he could finish the description? Does he mean "it's like this"—a dream, as opposed to this—waking reality? What did he mean?

I looked at my watch, oops, I was late for an appointment not far from my home. I dressed quickly and dashed out of my house, wondering still about the future of the peace agreement, Leon on my mind—wondering what he meant, wondering what he saw, and wondering how in the world he came up with those predictions every year at Rosh Hashana. I had new respect for Leon and a sense of mystery that I had never before connected with him.

I ran out the front door, across the street, and to a walking bridge that spans the Parkway below and leads to town. The bridge is not just a walking bridge, though I call it a walking bridge because from the direction of my house, all you can do is walk over the bridge. There is no road that goes into town over the bridge from my side. There is only a concrete sidewalk that runs next to a railing that oversees the Parkway below. However, coming the other way, from town, is an access ramp for cars to the Parkway down below, going east. The access road curves downward to the Parkway. There is no walkway on the other side of that access ramp. That's why I was stunned to see someone walking toward me from the access side of the ramp next to the walking concrete sidewalk of the bridge that I take virtually every day of my life to walk into town.

I was stunned because there is never anyone walking toward me from that side of the access road because there is no place for pedestrians there, only the access road; there is nowhere for someone to come from as it isn't even connected to a street where people walk. There was simply no reason for a person to be walking toward me on that access road as I was walking into town over that bridge. For a pedestrian, it's a road from nowhere. And yet here came someone walking toward me over that access road.

That's the first reason I was stunned. The second reason I was stunned is that the person was Leon.

It was Leon as a young man, not much older than myself. He was looking right at me, carrying a big load under his arm wrapped in a plastic bag that I recognized as the bag that the bookstore, which is only a couple of blocks away, gives you when you buy books there. It was a big load, too big to carry like a bag, but he carried it under his arm, like a sack of potatoes.

He was wearing a light gray suit and a bow tie. He had on those "retro" glasses with metal temples and wire rims that are popular again. I have a pair myself. In other words, he could have been dressed for 1950 as well as for 1993.

It all happened so fast. I said, "Leon! What's going to happen?" The words tumbled out of my mouth.

If it wasn't Leon, he didn't look away. He was not scared. He didn't correct his name. As a matter of fact, he looked straight at me, and he answered me, I think. "It's like this," he said, and he walked on as if he had somewhere to go. I stood on the bridge, wondering if it was day or not, whether I had just seen Leon or not—whether I should fall on my face—when I heard him call out to me, like an afterthought, as he was walking off the bridge, "Exodus chapter three, verse three." And he was gone.

Was it Leon on the bridge? Did he really answer me or was he just going somewhere? If it was Leon, didn't he come to tell me what was going to happen? What was he carrying under his arm? The secret to the future? The secret story of the peace? His predictions? If it wasn't Leon, why didn't he correct me? Why did he talk to me at all? He left me on the bridge, the way he had encountered me, all my questions intact. And what about Exodus 3:3?

I went home and looked at Exodus 3:3. It's Moses at the burning bush. "And Moses said, 'I will turn aside and see this great sight, why the bush is not burnt.'" The language is strange here, especially the word for "turn aside." Why would Moses turn aside when he is granted this vision? I was stumped. I read the Rashi. The Rashi reads, *asura mikan l'hitkarev sham*—"to turn aside from here to come close to there."—To go away from here and go over there. That was it.

That was Leon's message: what I had witnessed on television that day was two peoples moving from their places, from the places they've been defending each of them for the last hundred years, each with their reasonable revenge. What they did that day was they moved from their place, each of them, and came to a new place. They left here to go there. They each moved to a different place.

I wanted an answer, but what I am left with is a question. I want to know what's going to happen. I want to know if this peace agreement marks the beginning of a new era. I want to know if that was Leon on the bridge. If it was Leon, why didn't he tell me his predictions? If it wasn't Leon, why didn't he tell me it wasn't? If it was Leon, what did he come here for? What was he carrying in that bag under his arm? Was it the secret to the future, all bound up in yellow papers and manila folders snatched away from the stinginess of time? Was it Leon's own plan for peace, brought from the future or the past to save the world? If it was Leon, where did he come from? Where was he going? If it was Leon, did he come to see me, or was he on his way to the house of Rabbi M., who also lives in my neighborhood? Did he tell him his predictions? Did Rabbi M. stand in front of his shul that night telling everyone his predictions for the future? If so, why didn't Leon tell them to me? Was he punishing me for not taking him seriously when I was eight years old?

How can anyone know the future? Is this the nature of this courageous and extraordinary peace—not that it's the right action thing to do but that it's the risky, hard, and extraordinary thing to do? Isn't that the nature of this kind of peace—the risk, the courage, not knowing the future—not the right action but the extraordinary action—the courage, the risk of it, in not knowing the future but abandoning the past for that impassioned possibility, the possibility of peace? Moving out of your place to another place?

I walk to town the same way every day. Never again will I be surprised if someone comes toward me from the side of the access road where no one walks. Someone may come walking that way again, some distant day, and I will greet him as I greeted Leon. Perhaps it will be Leon, and perhaps not, but I will ask the same questions: what does the future look like? And—what are you carrying in that bag?

THE JOURNEY OF THE LOST PRINCESS

Debra Gordon-Zaslow

Debra Gordon-Zaslow
*travels nationwide as a
storyteller, speaker, and
workshop leader. She
teaches storytelling at Southern Oregon State College,
runs a storytelling program
for at-risk students at
Ashland Middle School, and
is the coauthor of* Creative
Dramatics for Children.
*Debra lives in Ashland,
Oregon, with her husband,
David, and their two children.*

A few years ago, I was searching for a story to tell at Rosh Hashana. Nothing seemed right. When a friend suggested that I create my own story, I began my first adventure in blending traditional themes with personal themes to develop something unique. I had encountered many New Year's stories with the motif of return—most of them symbolized by a prince straying from and forgetting his father, the king. I decided to work with that theme but changed the main character into a princess. Why not? I was drawn to Zalman Schachter-Shalomi's story of two friends who each had a shofar from the head of the same ram ("The Tale of the Shofar," from *The Dream Assembly*) and I included a variation of that tale as the "story within a story" that the princess tells. I was struck by the words in a prayer book: "We cry out to God. . . . Even if you don't recognize our faces, hear our voices," and it reminded me of a time when my own voice had failed me. I blended these elements, and the story seemed to take on a life of its own. My connections to the characters stayed vibrant throughout, in a way that I had not experienced in telling a traditional tale.

I was a bit worried that the story might be too personal and so its appeal would be limited. But my fears were put to rest when

I told it to my congregation on Rosh Hashana. The story seemed to cast its own spell, and I could feel it touching people on a deep level. Since then I have told it many times, to Jewish groups, church groups, women's groups, and mixed audiences—always with success. And so I offer it to you to tell in your own way.

---

nce there was a king whose only child was a daughter. He doted on his daughter and took her with him wherever he went. They would eat together and walk together and do many things, but their favorite thing to do together was to tell stories. The king would tell the princess stories with witches and fairies and demons and magic—every kind of story imaginable. The princess would simply say, "Papa, tell me a story," and it seemed that almost no matter what the king was doing, he would stop and launch into a tale. The princess's favorite story was a story about a brother and sister who each had a shofar from the head of the same ram. When one shofar was blown, the other shofar would vibrate and hum. She would beg her father, over and over, "Papa, tell me the shofar story again!" And he would tell it again and again.

It happened that one evening, the princess and the king were in the royal carriage returning from an occasion. They were riding on a narrow road that wound through the forest on the edge of a steep ravine. It began to rain, and gusts of wind started to blow. The carriage swayed and the horses whinnied. The storm grew heavier, the rain louder, and the road muddier. Thunder sounded and lightning streaked across the sky. The horses bolted and the royal carriage toppled over. The king was thrown out and knocked unconscious not far from the road. But the princess was thrown far down into the steep ravine.

The next day, when the king awoke in his bed, he demanded to see the princess immediately, but he was told she had not been found. The king bellowed, "Send out all my men! Comb every inch of the forest! You must find my daughter!" And so they searched the forest for days, but the ground was slick and muddy, and the rains had washed away any tracks. After two weeks, the men returned and the king was told that the princess must surely be dead. The king withdrew into his chambers. He refused to eat, he couldn't sleep, and he would speak to no one.

But the princess was not dead. She had fallen over the side of the ravine and landed in a crevice between two rocks. She lay unmoving for two days. When she woke up she was stiff, aching, bleeding, and hungry. She looked around her and recognized nothing. She wandered through the forest all day, crying pitifully. When she could go no further, she found an empty cave, where she lay down and cried herself to sleep.

When she woke she was staring into the faces of a band of thieves. They peered at her in surprise. "Who is this in our hideout?"

"It's a little girl—I've never seen her before?"

"She's bleeding and ragged, and she's hurt!"

"Who are you? Where did you come from?"

But the princess could not remember who she was or where she had come from. She could only stare back at them and cry. The thieves took pity on her and fed and cared for her. Eventually, they took her in and raised her as one of their own.

Time went on and the princess grew strong and healthy. Her adopted family was delighted with her. She was clever and charming, and she entertained them with all kinds of stories—stories of witches and fairies and demons and magic. They would take her with them into the marketplace and she would engage the shopkeepers in conversation while the thieves stuffed their pockets with fruits and vegetables and anything else they needed.

Sometimes the princess would question if it was right to steal. "Is this the only way to live?" she asked. But the thieves answered, "This is all we know. It's good enough for us." So the princess didn't say any more.

One day she was walking along the same road on the edge of the forest that she had tumbled from so many years before, and she happened to see the king's carriage go by. Suddenly she was filled with a longing, deep, deep inside of her. She felt that she had to be in the presence of the king. She walked all day until she came to the palace and then stood in front of the palace gates for hours, hoping to catch a glimpse of the king. But he did not come out.

When she returned, she told her adopted brothers and sisters what she had done. "I don't know why, I just felt I had to be near the king, to be in the palace!"

They laughed at her. "You had to be near the king! In the palace! You're beginning to live in one of your fairy stories!"

So the princess said no more. But every chance she got, she would steal away and stand outside the palace. Still, she never saw the king.

Though years had passed, the king had never gotten over the loss of his daughter. He remained inconsolable. He didn't go out unless he had to, and he spoke as little as possible. His advisors had tried everything to cheer him up. They brought in royal magicians and clowns and the best musicians, but the king hardly noticed. One of the advisors recalled that long ago, the king had loved stories. They decided to hold a storytelling contest; whoever could tell the best story and gain the king's approval would become the royal storyteller and come to live in the palace.

Word traveled fast about the storytelling contest, and of course the princess heard about it. She was determined to enter the contest, and she went into a frenzy, practicing stories over and over. Again, the thieves laughed at her. "The Royal Storyteller! You're dreaming of living in the palace again! Why can't you stop living in your dream world?" But the princess did not care. She went into the forest alone and tried out all her stories, polishing every line, until she was exhausted.

When the first day of the contest arrived, the princess walked all the way to the palace. Her heart raced in her throat as she waited. When her turn came, she walked slowly up to the podium. From there she could see the king, but he was slumped over in his chair, not looking at her. She took a deep breath and began, "Once there was . . ." but her voice did not ring out. Only a rough whisper emerged. She cleared her throat and began again: "Once there was . . . ahem . . . once . . . once." Try as she might, she could not speak. Someone yelled "Next!" and she was pulled off the stage.

The next day she tried again. Again she walked to the palace, and again her heart pounded as she waited her turn. Again she tried, "Once there . . . once . . . ahem . . . once," and again her voice failed her. But the princess could not give up. She continued to practice her stories, working even harder than before, and on the third and last day of the contest, she returned and walked up to the podium again. She could see the king in his chair, staring into space, unseeing. Her hands shook, and her throat burned. She opened her mouth, "Once," but only the whisper escaped again. Someone in the crowd yelled, "Her again! Get her off the stage!" And someone else shouted: "I've seen her in the marketplace with the band of thieves! Grab her!" The king glanced up at the commotion, and for an instant, the princess met his eyes. Again she began, "Once there was," and this time her voice emerged clear and true. The guards ran to seize her, but the king raised his hand. "Let her speak," he said. The princess continued slowly, as if remembering something long forgotten, and the crowd was silent.

"Once there was a brother and a sister who each had a shofar from the head of the same ram. When one of the shofars was blown, the other shofar would vibrate and hum. The two children would play with the shofars all the time, blowing them back and forth. One day, the boy was playing in the woods with his friends and it began to get dark. His friends ran back home, but the little boy stayed, absorbed in his game. Soon it became quite dark, and he realized he was alone and could not find his way home. He wandered for a while, but eventually he knew he would have to spend the night in the woods. He was cold and frightened, and he sat down under a tree to rest. He opened up his knapsack to see if he had anything to eat, and he found that he had his shofar. He knew then that he was saved. He picked up the shofar and blew a long, low blast. Far away, in the house, his sister heard her shofar hum. She knew her brother was in trouble, and she picked up her shofar and blew back at him. They blew back and forth through the night until she guided her brother all the way back to their home."

When the princess had finished the story, the king rose from his throne. Tears flowed down his cheeks as he opened up his arms. He drew his daughter gently to his heart and welcomed her back to her true home, the place where she belonged.

And whenever we hear the sound of the shofar, something stirs deep, deep, within us, and we long to return to our true home . . . the home of the soul. And we cry out to God, "Even if you don't recognize our faces . . . hear our voices. Hear our voices."

MARIA RAEL:
A JEWISH STORY
FROM NEW MEXICO
Lynn Gottlieb

Lynn Gottlieb, *one of the first women to become a rabbi, has been storytelling all her life. She combines rabbinic scholarship, dance, sign language, drumming, and theater to create stories from Jewish tradition. She has performed her work throughout the United States, Canada, Europe, and Israel since 1976. "Telling Stories, Saving Lives" is the most recent collection of tales in performance and deals with Queen Esther and other women in myth and folklore who tell stories to save lives. Lynn currently serves as rabbi to Congregation Nahalat Shalom in Albuquerque, New Mexico. She is the author of* She Who Dwells Within: A New Vision of Women in Judaism.

"Lynn, I think I'm Jewish." Maria de la Cruz took me by surprise. We had become friends due to our mutual interest in feminist theology and now spent much time together sipping coffee at an Old Town cafe while reading and writing in our journals, discussing the patriarchal aspects of our respective religions and sharing the internal contours of our lives. I had heard rumors that Jews who escaped the Inquisition nearly five hundred years ago had eventually fled to northern Mexico and that remnants of those families still populated remote regions of the state. I never expected my Catholic friend to tell me she thought she was Jewish. (I hesitate to bring up this history and relate this intriguing tale because too many hungry writers and filmmakers from the East and the West Coast come to this enchanted place to plunder stories and artifacts for their own profit. Now, as then, the people of this story choose to remain hidden in order to protect themselves

132

from a careless public. Therefore, if you, the reader, call or write asking for names, I will not answer your questions.)

Maria repeated herself: "I think I'm Jewish." I realized I had stopped chewing on the bran muffin in my mouth and swallowed. "Do you want to talk about it?" I asked. The beautiful woman who sat before me began relating her dreams: a dream of a golden room with an altar inscribed with four Hebrew letters, a dream of an old woman in a coffin, a feeling of dislocation that haunted her every time her grandmother spoke about "the Jews" as the chosen people, and a memory of an aunt's tombstone that bore no cross but was decorated with a six-pointed lily. I listened. Eventually I met another "crypto Jewish" woman who was related to Maria through this same aunt. That family took me one Saturday to the ancestral graveyard and wanted me to communicate with the dead underfoot. I brought some earth from the Western Wall in Israel and buried it in the ground by the tombstones. Then I placed my face and hands on the earth and opened myself to messages from the otherworld. The aged grandparents watched closely. What I told them met with their approval and they, in return, revealed a remarkable history. Past and present fused. A door opened and more people began to reveal family secrets. A woman called me at eight in the morning to tell me she suspected she was Jewish, another wonders why her family recites the ten commandments with daily devotion, another refuses to eat pork, another lights candles to the patron saint on Friday evening, and yet another shows me a four-sided top he used to play with around solstice. Gradually, these loose threads form a pattern. I am amazed.

Stan Hordes, who once served as state historian of New Mexico, began researching the presence of hidden Jews in the state several decades ago, when people began to show up in his office, close the door, and whisper strange tales about women who lit candles in their closets on Friday night. It is clear that here there is a previously unknown history concerning a people who have tenaciously maintained their faith in an isolated wilderness. Recently, many of those who tenuously identified themselves as Jews or Jewish Catholics have surfaced to explore their heritage with other Jews. Their courageous resilience caused me to reflect on the fragile nature of personal identity and the parts of ourselves we keep hidden so that we can feel accepted by the "majority" or dominant culture. What is underneath the surface, however, manifests itself in strange ways.

On Yom Kippur, the Day of At-one-ment, the Sephardic communities of New Mexico gather to hear Kol Nidre, to be released from vows and secrets that oppress the spirit and divide the self into discrete fragments. Yom Kippur is one day in the year when many hidden Jews can feel at peace with Jewish tradition. I remember inviting Maria de la Cruz to hold the Torah as we took it out of the ark before reciting Kol Nidre in Aramaic and Spanish.

The darkened sanctuary was softly illumined by the flames of *Yahrzeit* candles, which filled the room. Everyone was dressed in white. Maria moved slowly through the congregation as we chanted a Sephardic melody, tears rolling down her cheeks and a glow on her face as she rose to embrace the Torah and a long forgotten fragment of herself.

The following story, Maria Rael, was inspired by the secret Jews of New Mexico. I began exploring the phenomenon of hidden Jews over twenty years ago when Paul Cowan, may his memory be a blessing, shared his research about the hidden Jews of Portugal with the New York Havurah. At that time I wrote a theater piece based on the theme of Queen Esther, called *Secret Jew*. This piece, "Maria Rael," is a continuation of my interest in Sephardic heritage and appeared as part of a larger work called *Women on the Edge: Folktales and Contemporary Stories about Jewish Women*. This story may be retold, but not performed, without permission of the author.

(Maria sits on a chair in center stage. Slowly, she raises her hand looking at herself, as if her hand were a mirror. She is chanting a melody. She glances at her face in the mirror, puts her hand down, and begins a conversation.)

Mi abuelita used to stare at me,
her black eyes looking over my face in dismay.
"Why do you have to look so much like your mother's side
of the family? Why couldn't you look more like your father's
side of the family?"
Y no me dijas nada mas.
She wouldn't say anything more about it.

One time, I was picking plums
with mi papa in the garden.
We were standing on a ladder.
"Maria, listen to what I'm going to tell you.
You must love all people, because God created all people.
But you must especially love the Jews, because they are
God's chosen people."
Y no me dijas nada mas.
He didn't say anything more about it.

Another time, mi prima, my cousin Demetria
came back from a visit to Portugal.
"Maria, guess what? Something very strange happened.
I told the people, my family is from Portugal.
They said, 'No, you are not Portuguese.' I said, 'Yes
I am.' They said, 'No. We know what the Portuguese look like
and you are not Portuguese.'"

Once, I was waiting for a bus to Santa Fe
and these two touristas were staring at me.
Finally they came over and started talking to me
in a language I had never heard. I didn't know what
they were talking about, so I said, "Que?"
They said, "Oh, we're sorry, we were speaking to you
in Hebrew, we thought you were Israeli."
You thought I was Israeli?

(Maria looks at her hand as if it were a mirror once again. Then
she rises and walks downstage to a votive candle of Guadeloupe.
She lights it, drawing the light toward her with her hands.)

Every Friday evening mi abuelita
lights candles to Guadeloupe.
I like this Catholic custom even better
than going to the church in Old Town.
It reminds me of the other family customs we practice,
Like the Catholic custom of not eating pork,
the Catholic custom of reciting the ten commandments,
the Catholic custom of dieta,
And of touching the door frame when you go into the house.
One Friday the priest was walking through Old Town and
Mi abuelita lit the candles to Guadeloupe in the closet.
Abuelita, why are you lighting the candles to Guadeloupe
in the closet? Pero, no me dijas nada.

That night I had a dream. I dreamt I was in
a room with a golden ceiling and golden walls.
I was wearing a white dress and I thought,
I'm getting married. But there was no
bridegroom and this was not a church.
I looked and saw an old woman sitting

in a coffin. She held out her hand
and called me. She was holding a key.[1]
"Take this key, mija, it is your destiny.
Take this key." I took the key and it
burned my hand. I woke up. Abuelita
was standing over me. "Abuelita, I had a strange dream,"
and I told her, but she said, "Get in the car,
we're driving to Las Lunas."
Every Saturday morning Abuelita drives me
to Las Lunas to visit the family graveyard.
She weeds around the graves, prays in her sudario,
and tells me stories about the old ones buried there.
This one is my tia, Maria Rael, the one I'm named after.
They used to call her La Paloma, the dove, but I don't
know why. That day the sky was gray and the air moist
with rain. I wanted to touch the grave of mi tia Maria Rael,
and I bent down and put my cheek on the stone above her name.
Suddenly the earth opened up and I was swallowed by the grave.
I called, "Abuelita, Abuelita," but she didn't answer me.
I was lying on top of the old woman in the coffin; a
key was in her hand and I took it—it burned my skin.

(Maria takes the key and follows a small opening through the
earth toward a light, which seems to be coming from under a
door. She reaches the door and her key opens the lock. She is
standing by a small table with Sabbath candles, and she draws
the light of the flame toward her, in the traditional movement.
Suddenly, she is confronted by soldiers, who burst through the
door.)

Are you Maria Rael?
Yes, I am Maria Rael. Who wants to know?
Maria Rael, we accuse you of lighting candles on Friday night.
We accuse you of not lighting fires on the Sabbath.
We accuse you of fasting on Yom Kippur.
We accuse you of not eating pig.
We accuse you of following the dieta.
We accuse you of following the Law of Moses.
We accuse you of mocking the virgin and spitting on the cross.
Maria Rael, we accuse you of being a Jew.

(Maria begins keening the chant that she sang at the beginning of the story, and looking at her hand as if it were a mirror. She falls back on the gravesite of her aunt and, after a moment, she wakes up as if she had been dreaming and sees her abuelita motioning her to return to the car.)

Mi abuelita called me. "Get in the car, Maria,
we're going home."
We rode home in silence.
When we pulled in front of the house, mi abuelita
took my face in her hand and said, "Maria Rael,
What is deep in the heart survives.
Maria Rael," she whispered, "somos Israelites."
Y no mi dijas nada mas.

Note

1. There are legends that the fleeing exiles took the keys to their houses with them to the new land, in remembrance.

THE CHICKEN'S TALE

Daniel T. Grossman

Daniel T. Grossman *is the rabbi of Adath Israel Congregation in Lawrenceville, New Jersey, and is a member of the Special Education Committee of the United Synagogue. He was ordained at the Reconstructionist Rabbinical College. He cowrote and participated in the video* Some One is Listening. *With his wife, Elayne, he performs "Simon Tov," a program that uses sign language, mime, music, and storytelling to bring the audience closer to the world of the Jewish Deaf. He is also active in addiction counseling and exit counseling for former cult members.*
Dan and Elayne have two children, Miriam Levia and Samuel Aaron.

Arden Photographers

"The Chicken's Tale" represents for me one of those events that brings together good-hearted, well-meaning people, a clash of cultures, and the joy of storytelling. Never had a couple (Tom and Meg) worked so hard to "do the right thing." Never can I remember being so ill at ease and out of place while trying to say thank you. Even as these events unfolded in England and at the Coalition for the Advancement of Jewish Education (CAJE), I could feel a story coming on.

I believe that although the story represents actual events that focused on myself and my wife, as a retold tale, it allows for various characters, a theme of misplaced good intentions, and some great visuals. As it is a tale written to be told, I tried to bring together the colors and flavors of the moment along with my own images of England, castles, and executions.

The story really focuses on misplaced expectations, some stereotyping, and how easy it is to feel "at home" one moment and "outside looking in" the next. The story works both in the first and third person. The second ending (at CAJE) adds a flavor, but it can be omitted.

Enjoy "The Chicken's Tale."

t was the summer of 1983. I was with forty singers from America. Forty singers of Jewish music—and me. I don't sing or play an instrument or even hum very well. I do get to travel with the group because I'm married to the conductor. I am also a Rabbi. In the summer of '83, all these elements found a common meeting ground in Shrewsberry, England.

Shrewsberry—a picture postcard of an English town. Imagine a town atop a hill, tea shops, town square, and rolling fields. At the base of the hill, white sheep graze in green meadows against a backdrop of a blue, blue sky. There it was, at the top of the hill, the top of the town, the top of the sky—Shrewsberry Castle. No Hollywood images, no Disney wonderland—this was the real article—this was England, a town, a castle, and a meadow. The one thing this town had lacked for 500 years was a Jew.

Now in 1983, Shrewsberry Castle was the home of the Shrewsberry International Music Festival. For one week, French folksingers, American marching bands, Druise sword dancers, and many more gathered together to make music. Among the music makers were forty Americans making Jewish music, and me.

The people of Shrewsberry took a particular pride in the fact that they would house all of the festival participants. This was no easy task—language differences, cultural differences, and food. There, in a small pamphlet—I think it was labeled "The Care and Feeding of Jews" or something like that—the basic rules of Kashrut were laid out. By prior arrangement, the forty American singers of Jewish music had agreed to a vegetarian or fish diet.

It was Friday morning and the bus rolled into the parking area just on the edge of town. Signs everywhere, Swedes there, Americans here, Druise here, French there. Laughter, commotion, directions, confusion—a calliope of sounds and sights. My wife and I were escorted to meet our hosts. A young husband and wife, an eight-year-old daughter with golden blonde pigtails, and a four-year-old son with a reddish carrot top. I'm sure families were selected for how well they would look in snapshots or on postcards.

After a short drive we pulled up to a perfectly quaint cottage, and yes, it had a white picket fence. The only thing that appeared a bit strange was the large number of children gathered on the lawn. As we entered the house, my eyes were drawn to a stack of books piled on the dining room table: *Customs of the Jewish People, Guide to the Jewish Homemaker, Everyday Problems of Kashrut*, and perhaps a dozen more books all about Judaism.

It was then that our host, Meg, spoke. "I was so excited that we were given the chance to host a family. A Jewish family, a Jewish Rabbi—imagine. I went to the university library in Sterling, about two hours away, and I just had to study on how to keep Jews happy." I looked at my wife and we both smiled. We were about to experience the care and feeding of Jews. Meg and her husband, Tom, began speaking rapidly about how they read the advance material on vegetarian and fish meals and then all the books on Kashrut.

It was Friday and Shabbat was coming so, still speaking rapidly, Meg said, "Fish is all right, I suppose. The books all say that Jews eat chicken on Friday night and that only Rabbis know how to kill the chickens in a Jewish way. Just think of it—we are having a Rabbi for dinner! Rabbis kill chickens and. . . ." With that, we rushed into the backyard to be greeted by the following scene:

One chicken clucking loudly.

A long-handled ax resting on a tree stump.

All the kids in the neighborhood, now in the backyard, chanting:

"Kill the chicken! Kill the chicken! Kill the chicken!"

Meekly I began, "I am a reading-and-preaching Rabbi, not a chicken-killing Rabbi. It takes special training and special tools and. . . ."

"No, no, on pages 175, 34, and 291 it says that Rabbis kill chickens." As Tom pedaled the grinding wheel, sparks flew from the ax head. It was very hard to carry on a conversation about the diverse professional duties of a Rabbi to the cadenced chant of, "Kill the chicken, kill the chicken, kill the chicken," with sparks flying and chickens squawking.

My wife suggested I treat the whole matter as *kapporis*—swing the chicken around a couple of times and then slip and release and watch it fly—and yet something else had changed. Where once I saw angelic boys and girls in the picture of the English countryside, now I saw a seething, boisterous mob in the court-yard of the Tower of London, calling for blood. The children were the bloodthirsty peasants, henny penny played Anne Boleyn, and I was cast as the Lord High Executioner, complete with leather mask and bulging muscles.

"Kill the chicken, kill the chicken!" The cries grew louder and louder until—"All right! All right! I admit I am a Rabbi, but I flunked 'kill the chicken.' I'm a failure. Worse yet—I like to eat fish. I'm so sorry."

The crowd dispersed, muttering, "He's a fake." "My priest could kill a chicken—maybe a goose." "Maybe you could wack at it till it just dies."

Meg and Tom felt cheated; their kids forgot their interest in the care and feeding of Jews. We all ate fish.

One week later, my wife and I were in San Antonio, Texas, at the CAJE conference. Jews from every land gathered together to study. There we were in line, stuffing packets of information, when we overheard the following from the British delegation:

"Can you imagine! I got a letter from my sister yesterday, and it seems some American Rabbi is traveling through England slaughtering chickens in public while he gets the crowd in a frenzy, shouting, 'Kill the chicken! Kill the chicken!'" "I cannot imagine!"

"HABERES BUENOS"
Naftali Haleva

Naftali Haleva *was born in Istanbul, the third of four sons. He attends Yeshiva University for his B.A. degree, combined with graduate degrees at the Rabbi Isaac Elchanan Theological Seminary and the David Azrieli Graduate Institute in Jewish Education and Administration. After his ordination, he plans to return to Turkey to fill a rabbinical post. His father, Rabbi Isaac Haleva, is currently the assistant chief rabbi of Turkey. Naftali has started collecting Sephardic stories from his family.*

Sephardim have a strong sense of pride in themselves, their families, their Jewishness, and their history. This pride is reflected in all their folklore. The stories, songs, proverbs, and customs paint a portrait of the Sephardim and our heritage.

When the Jews left Spain in 1492, they went to many countries in the Middle East and other places. My family came to Turkey, where Jews were welcomed and treated most hospitably all through these centuries. My family still lives in Istanbul.

There is a story about those Jews who kept the keys to their houses in Spain, thinking that if they did not go back, maybe their children, or perhaps their grandchildren, would return. But those families waited a long time, because the expulsion was not rescinded until 1968. Along with the keys, Jews brought their love of their Jewish languages, Hebrew (the sacred tongue) and Ladino (Judeo-Spanish). Most of the people of Turkey grew up speaking Ladino. In Turkish, this language is known as *musevice*, which means "Jewish language." This story "*Haberes Buenos*" was told to me both in Ladino and Turkish. When I compared both versions, I felt Ladino was the one that gave a stronger sense of my Sephardic heritage. When telling the story in Turkish at various times, I always felt that something was missing because it was lost in the translation. This has proven to me that a story not in its original language will lose some of its meaning and message. A story will always be more powerful in the original language.

My grandmother Julya Sason, who was born in Izmir but lives in Istanbul, told me this story. As with most of the older generation, she speaks Ladino. When she told me the story in Ladino, it felt as though she was reliving it. She told it with more expressive body language and more excitement in her voice than when she told me the same story in Turkish.

The story has brought me to the conclusion that we young people do not know enough of our culture or the importance of our folklore, including the old stories that have been carried from generation to generation. We really do not treat the folktales fairly when we are not interested in transmitting our many valuable stories to the next generation.

I started collecting some of these stories while I was taking a graduate course on storytelling and the Jewish oral tradition taught at Yeshiva University by Peninnah Schram. It was then that this story, and others I heard from my parents and my grandmother, helped me understand that this treasure should not be lost. Rather, it should be passed on to the next generation. I am studying to perfect my Ladino so that I can teach these powerful stories that guide us through our life and teach us to be proud of our Jewish heritage. This is why I know I have a big responsibility. I feel that this is an important turning point in our history, for we have an opportunity to capture and to know firsthand something that will soon be lost. Yes, the fear of loss has given me a strong motivation to research and learn more of our stories still remaining in the oral tradition, and especially told by my family.

---

 n Turkey, when a woman sees a bird landing on a windowsill or standing near her house, she says, "*Haberes buenos*," which means the bird is bringing good news. *Haberes* means "news" in Turkish, and *buenos* is Ladino for "good." I have always wondered, how did this tradition start? My grandmother told me this story.

Once upon a time, the women asked King Solomon why men are allowed to marry more than one woman (after all, Solomon had a thousand wives, they say) but a woman cannot marry more than one man.

King Solomon answered, "I do not know the answer, but the only thing I know is that there has to be a reason from God and this is why we have to obey it." But Solomon realized that the women were not happy with this answer, so he wanted to give them a different answer to satisfy them. Finally, he said, "Let's ask God Himself for the answer."

Solomon wrote the question on a piece of parchment and tied it to the leg of a bird. Then Solomon said to the women, "I am sending this bird as a messenger to God so it will bring us the answer." Unfortunately, the bird did not return, and so women are still waiting for the answer.

That is why, whenever a bird stands next to the window or a house, all the women say, "*Haberes buenos*—maybe this bird is bringing us good news!"

Editor's Note

In Eastern European folklore, there is a parallel tale. In Yiddish, *Skotsl kumt* ("Skotsl's here") is an expression used by a hostess as she greets a woman guest. "Skotsl's here" expresses a woman's hope that Skotsl, who had climbed onto the very top of a pyramid of village women, actually got to reach heaven. It seemed that she went there to complain to God about why the world seemed to belong more to men than to women. Since she has never returned, women are still waiting for her report. This humorous tale, "Skotsl Kumt: Skotsl's Here," is in Beatrice Weinreich's *Yiddish Folktales* (New York: Pantheon Books, 1988).

PENNIES FROM HEAVEN

Annette Harrison

Annette Harrison, *a story-teller, educator, and author, travels throughout the United States teaching and perform-ing. She has written two storytelling resources,* Story-telling Activities Kit, *with Jerilynn Changar, Ph.D., and the award-winning* Easy-to-Tell Stories for Young Chil-dren. *She also hosts "Gator Tales," a weekly children's storytelling television pro-gram. She looks forward to her trips to Baltimore to visit her mother, sisters, and their families each year. Annette lives in St. Louis, Missouri, with her husband and family.*

A few years ago, I noticed a new trend in storytelling. Folktales, legends, myths, and spiritual tales were still very much a part of a storyteller's repertoire, but personal and family stories were gaining in popularity. I was already using anecdotal family re-membrances to connect the stories in my performance, but I had not yet found the story from my family lore that I wanted to share with my audiences.

Then, one sunny December day in 1988, I had lunch with my mother. It was during my yearly pilgrimage to Baltimore to visit my family. I ordered my usual chicken salad sandwich on rye at Manny's Delicatessen, and as we were eating, I asked my mother questions about her childhood. At first she seemed reluctant to talk about it—and then it happened! Golden nuggets of family history fell from her lips.

"My Bubbe Tobey was quite a character . . ." she began. "Did I ever tell you about the time she climbed up to the roof and sent pennies down?"

With a sparkle in her eyes and a loving heart, her words began to flow. I gently prodded her with questions. My mother took me back to the 1930s in Baltimore, Maryland, on Pennsylvania Avenue—and *there she was*—Bubbe Tobey standing in front of Brown's Five-and-Ten-Cent store. She emerged as well-defined, strong, and creative; and I knew instantly that she had been a remarkable woman. When my mother spoke about the time she helped her grandson, Sidney, in a most unusual way, I knew I had my story! And "Pennies from Heaven" was born.

y mother's brother, Sidney, looked like a Ross Perot clone. My family lived in Baltimore in 1931 when Sidney was twelve years old. He was small and skinny, with a large nose, huge ears, and short blond hair. Sidney *hated* school. He had trouble learning, acted up in class, and was picked on by the bullies. He was *miserable*!

To add to his misery, he was now at the age to become a Bar Mitzvah. His mother, my Bubbe Fanny, hired a Rabbi to come to the house twice a week to teach him Torah. Each time the Rabbi came around the corner of Pennsylvania Avenue, with his curly bright red hair and beard flashing in the sunlight, looking like the devil himself, Sidney would disappear. He *really* disappeared. No one could find him. My mother told me they never *ever* found his secret hiding place. Sidney may have had trouble learning in school, but he was very clever.

His mother would have "talks" with him about the importance of Torah and being a Bar Mitzvah. All the uncles would also have heart-to-heart or man-to-man talks with him, but to no avail. Sidney continued to play hide-and-seek, and the Rabbi was ready to give up.

The family lived in the apartment above Brown's Five-and-Ten-Cent store. Fanny Brown, who was my Bubbe, owned and operated the store. She lived upstairs with her two children— her son Sidney and her fifteen-year-old daughter Elva (who was my mother)—*and* Bubbe Tobey, her mother.

Bubbe Tobey had immigrated from Rumania. She was steeped in the old ways, but she was not immune to the charms of modern American society of the 1930s. She loved the picture shows and had fallen head over heels in love with opera singer Lawrence Tibbit. She was short, about the same size as her grandson Sidney, but round and robust; and she knew more about creative problem-solving than most professional negotiators today, who could have learned a thing or two from Bubbe Tobey.

She wore long black skirts that rustled, simple white shirts, and always, a brooch at her neck. She wore a sheitel over her long, curly gray hair, and she wore Bubbe shoes. You know what I mean: clumpy, lace-up black shoes with thick, sensible heels that went clump, clump, clump as she walked across the hardwood floors. She walked a lot because she was running the household while her daughter ran the business.

One day she said to her daughter, "Fanny, you go to work—you run your business and don't worry. I'll take care of Sidney and his Bar Mitzvah."

That afternoon, she was waiting for Sidney when he came home from school. Bubbe had some of her famous apple strudel and a nice glass of milk waiting for him on the kitchen table. As he stuffed himself and his pockets, she looked him in the eye and said,"So Sidney, you don't like school, do you?"

Sidney's eyes lost their light and the smile fell from his face. "No, Bubbe, I *hate* school!"

"So Sidney, you've lived almost twelve years. Look at you! You're as tall as I am. You're almost a man."

"No Bubbe . . . everyone at school makes fun of me because I'm so little. . . . I'm short, skinny, and stupid."

"No, Sidney," said Bubbe Tobey, "not stupid—clever. Who else could find a hiding place that even your Bubbe couldn't find? You just learn different from other children. Don't listen to them—you're special, and someday even *you* will know it!"

She paused for a moment and then continued, "Sidney, did you know that when you study Torah, God smiles down from the heavens?"

"No, Bubbe."

Sidney had been sitting and listening long enough; he was ready to escape. He was halfway out of the chair when Bubbe Tobey said, "When God smiles down on you, he sends pennies from heaven."

Sidney sat back down on his chair. *Now* he was interested. His big blue eyes looked at her in amazement. "Is that true, Bubbe?"

"Would your Bubbe Tobey lie to you? Why don't you see for yourself? The next time the Rabbi comes, study Torah with him. See if God's paying attention. God is everywhere and sees everything. A few pennies wouldn't be so bad, huh, Sidney?"

Sidney decided to test Bubbe's theory. Pennies could buy a lot of candy. So the next afternoon, when the Rabbi came around the corner with his hair and beard on fire in the afternoon sun, Sidney was waiting for him in front of the store. The Rabbi was very surprised. "Sidney, is that you?"

"Yes, Rabbi."

"So what changed your mind?"

"God smiles down on you when you study Torah."

"Yes, Sidney." The Rabbi was smiling, too.

"And when God smiles down," continued Sidney, "he sends pennies from heaven."

The Rabbi looked a little surprised but he recovered quickly, shrugged his shoulders and said, "Who knows? Stranger things have happened! Come, let's study."

The unlikely pair walked through the store past Sidney's sister Elva, who was helping a customer. She was wearing most of the jewelry on sale in the store, as usual. She couldn't believe her eyes—Sidney with the Rabbi. She ran to tell her mother.

Bubbe Tobey had set up the card table in a spot of sun in the courtyard behind the store. The Rabbi was speaking and Sidney was trying hard to listen, but he found himself looking up into the heavens. Each time he looked up, the Rabbi would stop and look up, too.

Bubbe Tobey knew she had work to do. She filled her apron pocket with pennies and climbed up to the third floor, into the secret closet that led to the roof. She hid behind the eaves and threw a penny down into the courtyard. Her aim was perfect! The penny landed right on the card table.

The Rabbi and Sidney froze. In unison they looked at each other, looked up into the heavens, and looked at the penny. The Rabbi smiled, Sidney quickly pocketed the penny, and they continued to study together in earnest.

Sidney continued his studies all spring, summer, and fall. Bubbe Tobey continued as God's helper, sending pennies from heaven—some days only one penny and other days as many as two or three.

The day of the Bar Mitzvah finally arrived. The whole family was there. They were so proud of Sidney. The Rabbi beamed, Sidney's mother beamed, but the proudest of all was my great-grandmother, Bubbe Tobey. She wore her black beaded hat and her diamond brooch in honor of the occasion.

Bubbe Tobey joined God in the heavens a long time ago, but she's still helping with his work. There's a lot of evidence. I'm still finding pennies on the ground, aren't you?

A TASTE OF HONEY, A TASTE FOR LOVE

Lynn Hazan

Lynn Hazan, *a storyteller and teacher, combines drama and story, Judaica and entrepreneurship. As Artist-in-Residence at North Shore Congregation Israel in Glencoe, Illinois, she directs children's theater and facilitates workshops on creative Jewish expression. She has performed for the Coalition for the Advancement of Jewish Education (CAJE), the Greater Chicago Jewish Folk Arts Festival, and the First International Jewish Women's Conference in Kiev, FSU. In addition to folktales, she also tells her Sephardic family stories. Lynn regularly*

barters stories for stays at health spas in America and Mexico.

Stories for telling or reading are derived from many sources. Personal stories that reflect the human experience touch my heart. Long after historical dates, statistics, or numbers are forgotten, it's the human story that continues to spark my interest. Hence, I remember it.

"A Taste of Honey, a Taste for Love" is a true story that recaptures the sense of excitement at a chance meeting and the deep feelings of love that I felt when I was reunited with my second-grade Hebrew school teacher at the 1991 Coalition for the Advancement of Jewish Education (CAJE) conference.

I had not seen or spoken to Geveret Henia in years. Yet her impact on my life as a Jewish woman, teacher, and performing artist was unmistakable. She helped to provide the foundations for creative Jewish expression that inspire and motivate me on a daily basis.

My quilt of Jewish experiences has also been highly influenced by my family. I grew up, the daughter of immigrants, in Montreal. My mother and father were born in Cairo, Egypt, and Damascus, Syria, respectively. My Jewish identity was strongly shaped by

150

my Sephardic heritage, with its religious, cultural, linguistic, and culinary interpretations of Jewish life.

Memory can trigger both positive and negative experiences. Luckily, my early Jewish memories were joyous, celebratory, and participatory. They reflected what I call the "PJE," Positive Jewish Experience. Although I later rebelled against Hebrew school, synagogue, and other institutions and authority figures (my parents included), my love for the Jewish people and culture was always constant. As I returned to Jewish learning and expression, I did so with increased commitment, intellectual vigor, and curiosity.

As storytelling and drama became my vehicles for creative expression, I realized that my gift for touching people's souls could ignite the Jewish passions of children and adults, much as Henya did for me.

Henya was one of my earliest role models. She communicated what was exciting about being Jewish. She projected warmth, sincerity, and a devotion to the creative teaching process, virtues she still personifies today. She teaches and instills a richness of the Jewish experience.

The Jewish world today is a reflection of a changing world. The memories of the Holocaust, the establishment of the State of Israel, and the immigrant acculturation process are for many only stories, not firsthand experiences. Yet, there remain many witnesses. Their stories need to be told, to be recorded and documented.

As a student, I have taken on this challenge, first and foremost with my own family, to record these stories. In the process, I have rediscovered the richness of my own family traditions and honored the elders with my "listening."

New traditions have emerged as well. A feminist rendition of Dayenu raised eyebrows at my relative's Seder table. Now, the "new" Dayenu accompanies the traditional, both welcome at my Seder table.

The new generation of Jews will not share my upbringing. They will respond to new challenges of what it means to be a Jew and develop their own interpretations. The richness of Jewish tradition, with its symbols, history, and language will continue to inspire Jews and add to their repertoire of Jewish experiences.

These events provide material for the teacher and storyteller to tell and retell. They provide the foundations to connect the generations, to fill in where grandparents' stories no longer exist, and to add new rituals and interpretations.

These are my challenges as a teacher and storyteller—to learn from the past, respect the present, and plan for the future. I have been blessed with my family and teachers like Henia, who have been powerful mentors. I hope that I, too, can be a Geveret Henia for Jews with a sense of wonder and curiosity.

eshert (fate) is a word that I have often thought of with reference to my participation at the 1991 Coalition for the Advancement of Jewish Education (CAJE) conference at Hofstra University on Long Island, New York. My initial introduction to the conference had occurred in 1979, when I participated as an eager graduate student while attending Brandeis University. After an absence of eleven years, I was yearning to return for nurturing, spiritual uplifting, and an opportunity to learn from my master teachers.

Was I in for the surprise of my life! It has often been said that magic occurs at these conferences. Never before did I feel those magic sparks as intensely as on Friday night. In the true spirit of a CAJE attendee, I started the evening in one workshop and ended up in another, this time Danny Siegel's. (Danny is renowned as an inspirational workshop leader and especially for his talks about Tzedakah.) That night, Danny was to read from his latest book.

Was it beshert that drew me to Danny's session? Although it was after 11:00 P.M. when I entered the room, it was filled with eager participants. They were fully engaged in a give-and-take exploration of the evolution of Jewish to American names. Audience members called out their original family names and then the shortened or changed versions for Danny's commentary. I was sitting in the back, feeling a sense of sadness at what was lost yet fascinated by the stories being revealed. In the front row, a blond-haired, petite woman related that her name had been changed from Wisgardisky to Wise. Danny, in his own inimitable style, commented on how unusual that name was; he hadn't even heard of Wisgardisky before!

I responded immediately (I've never been shy!), "That name can't be too uncommon, because when I was growing up in Montreal, Quebec, my Hebrew school teacher's name was Wisgardisky. She thought that her name would be too difficult to pronounce, so we were allowed to call her Geveret Henia."

A gasp from the front row could be heard. "That was me!" exclaimed the voice of Henny Lewin, a Burlington, Vermont, Hebrew teacher.

I sat in my seat, disbelief ringing in my ears. With tears welling in my eyes, I sat frozen, then jumped up and ran to see my Kita Bet teacher from Congregation Beth-El in Montreal. Was she really Geveret Henia, the *love* and *source* of my childhood encounter with Hebrew school? Was this really the teacher who had loved me so completely and thoroughly, who had held me on her lap? Was this diminutive woman the same person who had shaped my passion for Yiddishkeit, who made Beth-El my second home?

I sat before Henny, searching her eyes and face for the sign of recognition. Then, it came to me—all the memories—the positive memories of Hebrew school came flooding back. In that instant they flashed: Yom Ha'atzmaut parades around the synagogue parking lot, bags of Tu B'shvat fruit, movies of Israel, and Purim shpiels.

"Yes, yes; it's me!" she repeated excitedly. Tears now streamed down my face. I hugged my teacher. The room was filled with gasps and applause. CAJE members had witnessed a miracle; they had helped to create it! People were repeatedly asking, "How long has it been since you've seen each other?"

"I don't know, I don't know," I blurted. By this time, the room was in a complete uproar. I kept crying and laughing. The tears that flowed from my eyes flowed to everyone in the room. Finally, I was able to reconstruct the number of years. I had indeed found my beloved Geveret Henia after a twenty-seven-year absence!

The other miracle was the incredible sense of timing. Had I entered the room five minutes later, I would have missed the entire dialogue; our reunion would have been a lost opportunity.

Back at the workshop, poor Danny's presentation had completely lost its focus (or had it?). Henny and I retreated to a corner of the room to reconnect twenty-seven years of stories and life experiences.

I was amazed to discover that Henia had been a Hidden Child in Europe during World War II. (In the 1960s, discussions about the Holocaust were whispered. No one talked about survivors, let alone their children.)

After the war, Henia's family was reunited. They eventually settled in Montreal, where her father ran a greengrocer store.

Henia had attended a Hebrew teacher college and taught Hebrew at a local day school. To supplement the family income, she taught after school and on Sundays at Beth-El. Geveret Henia was a remarkable teacher. Not only was she inventive in designing lesson plans, she was also very pretty. Who ever had had attractive Hebrew school teachers?

That Friday night at CAJE, the relationship between Morah and Talmida was rekindled and infused with a new sense of connection. We could now share on a different level. Yet I could still return to the sense of being that eager eight-year-old girl.

And so began the story of the student-teacher reunion. The dialogue, which started on Shabbat, continued throughout the conference. We ate meals together, met each other's friends and colleagues, and shared our challenges (and successes) as Jewish educators.

What a gift you have given me, Henia. I shall always carry you in my heart. May you be blessed to continue to touch the souls of other children (and children at heart).

I now know from personal experience that miracles are opportunities waiting to happen. They can never be planned, but holy sparks are always in the air . . . waiting . . . for the sign. Maybe Elijah came early to CAJE!

THE WISDOM
OF SOLOMON

Merna Ann Hecht

Merna Ann Hecht *is a
storyteller, dramatist, poet,
and arts educator whose
repertoire includes tales from
Eastern Europe and many
other cultures. She has
pioneered work in multi-
cultural education and with
special populations. She also
teaches for Pacific Oaks
College and in elderhostel
programs, is a guest lecturerer
for the University of Washington, and teaches Jewish
storytelling for her community
chavurah. She is a founding
member of the Seattle Storytellers' Guild. Merna lives on
Vashon Island in Washington
with her husband.*

I chose this story in honor of my grandfather. He was a master
gardener and lived close to the wisdom of nature. When I was a
young girl, he brought many Old Testament stories to life for me
with his own rich, lyrical, and often humorous tellings. To this
day it is my beloved grandfather to whom I attribute my having
chosen storytelling as a profession. He was a great admirer of King
Solomon's wisdom, and for much of my girlhood I imagined my
grandfather to have a direct connection with the wise king. Like
the legendary Solomon, my grandfather also seemed to have the
uncanny ability to listen to and understand the language of the
animals and the flowers. My grandfather retired at the age of forty-
eight. He spent the next fifty years of his life (until his death at
ninety-eight) growing, among other things, orchids, roses, and
gardenias and perfecting his skills as a botanist, gardener, and
neighborhood tzaddik. As a child, it seemed to me that King
Solomon and my grandfather were, if not one and the same, at
least cut from the same cloth. Now, years later, I find myself wondering if perhaps my childhood notions about him did hold some
vague and distant truth.

When my grandfather turned ninety I wrote nine verses for him. One of the verses was entitled "Flowers." I wrote:

Hewn by the nourishing sun
scents more potent than King Solomon's eye
the gardenia, the velvet orchid listen
as rose petals unfold their story
only the gardener hears,
only the bees reach the center.

At the time I wrote the poem and until last year I was not familiar with this story of King Solomon and the bee, although it is an old and well-loved folktale of the Holy Land. In some variations it appears as a longer and more complex tale.

It wasn't until autumn of 1992, when I was asked to participate in a National Public Radio (NPR) program on bedtime stories, that I found this simple version. I knew that for the NPR program I wanted to tell a story my grandfather had told me, since when I think of safety and comfort at bedtime, it is my grandfather and his stories that always come to mind. I could remember many snatches of his stories and songs, some in Yiddish and some in English—snippets of tales of the birds and flowers of the Bible, vivid images of King Solomon and the Queen of Sheba—they came to me like threads from the strands of long forgotten dreams. But even though I pored through Jewish folktale sources, the "right" story was not coming to me. Then I happened upon Pleasant DeSpain's collection, *Twenty-two Splendid Tales to Tell From Around the World* (Seattle: Merrill Court, 1990), and knew I had found a bedtime story, not only similar to what my grandfather had told me, but in a significant way about my grandfather.

When I think of my dear grandfather, I can almost see him standing in his garden, his pride in his flowers and his love of nature visible in the blackberry shine and earnestness of his eyes. I see him caught in a moment of bright sun, in the quiet act of taking my hand and leaning down to tell me a story. He would have loved this tale—it is what he taught me

Often, after telling me his "original" biblical and Jewish stories, just before I would go to sleep, my grandfather would lean down and whisper a short poem in my ear. He would say;

"The wise old owl, it sat on the oak
The more it heard, the less it spoke
The less it spoke, the more it heard,
Why can't you be like that wise old bird?

Now go to sleep and listen carefully, for the night has many things to tell you." Although this is not a Jewish poem, it is Jewish in my mind and heart because my grandfather told it to me. He taught me that listening, even to the smallest creatures, is a sacred act.

Incidentally, I recorded this story for NPR at the Nordic Heritage Museum in Seattle, Washington, just minutes after participating in a storytelling workshop given by Peninnah Schram.

I have reworked the story from Pleasant DeSpain's retelling. In order to make it my own story, I used language and images that I know would have delighted my grandfather. Because my grandfather was a great lover and teller of riddles and wordplay, I have added several riddles to my retelling. Of course, King Solomon is ever famous and beloved for his wisdom in solving riddles and there are many folktale variants wherein, upon her famed arrival to his court, the Queen of Sheba presents Solomon with riddles. Most of the legends in which the Queen of Sheba comes to test King Solomon's wisdom describe her as arriving laden with gifts, often with a camel train bearing spices, gold, and precious stones. However, in the majority of the variants it is usually the Queen of Sheba who, in spite of her retinue and dazzling gifts, is amazed and "completely overwhelmed" by King Solomon and his elaborate palace and riches. I thought it more fitting, and certainly more compatible with my grandfather's sensibilities and my own, to place the two on equal ground.

The riddles I have included are from the "Solomon and the Queen Of Sheba" story found in *The Book of Legends*, ed. Hayim Bialik and Yehoshua Ravnitzky, tr. William Braude (New York: Schocken Books, 1992), pp. 127–129. They can also be found in Louis Ginzberg's *Legends of the Jews*.

Finally, in choosing to contribute a folktale about the legendary King Solomon, a great and wise man who understood the language of the animals, the birds, and the flowers, I am directly celebrating the spirit of my grandfather, David.

---

t was a dazzling sight when the Queen of Sheba and her vast retinue of artisans, dancers, musicians, and attendants came to visit King Solomon the Wise. In anticipation of her visit, even the doors of his palace had been polished until the copper and brass on them shone like the sun. Many precious stones sparkled from the walls. On either side of Solomon's great throne stood tall candlesticks made of pure silver and blazing with light. Yet brighter still were the rows and rows of gold and silver ornaments circling the Queen's wrists, forearms, and ankles. They chimed, almost like bells, when she bowed gracefully before the great king. Behind her, her drummers played their African drums. The loud, steady beat of the drums and the dizzying motion of the Queen of Sheba's dancers distracted King Solomon from his usual composure.

King Solomon, for all his greatness and wealth, had not been prepared to receive such an extraordinary guest. Indeed, the Queen of Sheba was the most beautiful woman he had ever seen. He could see that the strength of her bearing was equal to his, and this took his breath away.

The Queen of Sheba arrived in Solomon's court with many rare and wondrous gifts. She ordered that they be placed before King Solomon one at a time. With each one, the king and everyone in his court gasped in amazement. Sheba had heard that Solomon the Wise possessed a magic ring that enabled him to understand animal languages, especially that of the birds. She placed before him ten glorious peacocks with huge, fan-shaped tails. The tail feathers were embellished with azure, emerald, and indigo. When Solomon looked into the dark eye of each tail feather, he saw with astonishment that he could see into the past and the future! No one in the court had ever imagined such rare birds. Next came a nest as large as that of an eagle. The queen's artisans had woven it from strands of silk and feather down and attached wings of pure gold to it. The wondrous nest could carry the king and lift itself up to the highest perch of the eagle. Even King Solomon was stunned with amazement. There was also an apple tree that bore golden apples every day of the year.

The queen clapped her hands three times. Her dancers and musicians stopped and stood still, like marble statues draped in silk. There was a hush over everyone present as the Queen of Sheba spoke to King Solomon: "Oh, great King Solomon, your wisdom is known throughout the world. I bring you these gifts from my own land to pay respect to your wisdom, in order that our two kingdoms may be on peaceful terms. I hope my offerings delight you. May they bring joy to your heart whenever it is heavy or burdened."

King Solomon nodded his head and the queen continued: "You are known as having the power to understand the speech of the animals and the secrets of every living plant. It is told throughout the land, King Solomon, that you delight in revealing that which is hidden to most other mortals."

Now Solomon nodded his head and smiled. "Then," said Sheba, "you surely will not object to guessing a few riddles. I have come all this way to find out if your wisdom is as great as people proclaim. May I present you with three riddles?"

Solomon nodded his head a third time. "You may ask them," he said.

The Queen of Sheba began: "It grows in the fields with its head hung down like reeds. It enhances the distinction of the rich but is the disgrace of the poor, an adornment for the dead yet a threat to the living. It brings delight to the birds but is a cause of mourning for the fish."

Without hesitation Solomon replied, "It is flax. Exquisite linen robes enhance the distinction of the rich, linen rags are the shame of the poor. The dead are wrapped in a linen shroud, but the flaxen noose on the gallows is a threat to the living. The birds delight in finding flax, for they eat its seeds, but the fish hate it, for they are caught in flaxen nets."

A murmur of amazement and approval swept through the crowded court. "A good answer and a correct one," said the Queen of Sheba. "Now tell me what water comes neither from Heaven nor the flowing mountain streams? Though it can be sweet as honey or bitter as aloe, it always flows from the same source."

Again, King Solomon had a ready reply. "Tears. For a tear upon the cheek comes neither from Heaven nor flows from the mountain streams. When a man or woman is joyful, their tears are sweet, but tears of sorrow are indeed bitter."

"Your second answer is also correct," said the Queen of Sheba. All the members of the court stood quietly transfixed. Then the queen called upon several attendants, who placed two identical vases of flowers in front of King Solomon, and she said, "Only one of these vases holds blossoms from nature's garden. The other vase contains flowers that have been made by my skilled artisans with elaborately colored enamels. But, King Solomon, the flowers are not real because they are made by human hands. I set the task before you, the wisest of men, to choose between these two vases of flowers. Which one is real and which is but a copy?"

King Solomon realized that this was neither riddle nor game but a serious test of his wisdom. He knew that if he failed to recognize the flowers cast from nature's mysterious workmanship, he would lose his noble standing as the wisest king in the world. King Solomon's glory and reputation were at stake as he stood before the two vases of flowers. He looked upon their exquisite beauty, seeking the subtle flaws that might reveal the false bouquet. But each green stem and bright bloom, each ivory gardenia and velvety rose petal, was perfectly matched.

Finally, after gazing at the flowers for a long time, he noticed a tiny dewdrop on one of the red rose petals. But just in that moment when he began to feel certain he had found the vase of flowers from nature's garden, Solomon saw an identical droplet on the same petal in the second vase.

With patience and humility, the king continued to examine the flowers. Looking intently at the two vases, Solomon was deeply puzzled with the third riddle that the Queen of Sheba had set before him. Everyone in the court quietly awaited his answer. The great room was filled with stillness and the hushed breath of expectation. Just then, a bee from Solomon's garden flew in through one of the open windows. A guard started after it, but King Solomon stopped him and quickly said, "We must not harm the bee. It will dance its way to where it needs to go."

Instinctively, the bee headed toward the two vases of flowers. King Solomon began to smile, knowing that the bee would not be fooled by the artisan's skill no matter how perfectly it imitated nature's artistry. Without hesitation, the bee landed in the center of the garden rose. Then Solomon raised his hand and pointed to the vase holding the fragrant blooms on which the bee was poised.

The Queen of Sheba bowed respectfully before him, for she, too, realized that nature is the wisest of teachers. King Solomon's wisdom endured because he knew that even if it is just a tiny bee sent to instruct, it is the wise who listen.

THE MOUNTAIN AND THE CLIFF
David Holtz

David Holtz, *a graduate of Hebrew Union College– Jewish Institute of Religion, is the rabbi of Temple Beth Abraham in Tarrytown, New York. In addition, he teaches communitywide adult educa- tion courses on a variety of topics in Jewish literature and is frequently a guest speaker on Jewish folktales and storytelling. His interest in Jewish folklore began while he was a staff member at Jewish summer camps. Intrigued by the power of stories told in place of ser- mons, he began to explore the art of storytelling, studying with master storytellers. David and his wife, Renée, live in White Plains, New York.*

Morton

Just before the beginning of my second year of rabbinical school, I spent the summer at the Union of American Hebrew Congrega- tions' (UAHC) Camp Harlam, one of the Reform movement's sum- mer camps. Although I didn't know it when the summer began, camp was an ideal place to hear stories. Visiting rabbis, in camp to teach and to celebrate Shabbat, were given the opportunity to speak during the morning tefillot. Occasionally, one would launch into a sermon, but most of the time they were able to restrain themselves, and instead they would give a short *drasha*, high- lighted by a story. I was fascinated by the fact that by the time Shabbat ended, the sermons were almost universally forgotten while the stories continued to resonate in the souls of camper and counselor alike.

During that summer, a rabbi whose name I did not know told a story that I could not forget. Unaware of the etiquette of story- telling, I began to retell his story, making changes here and there and adapting it for a variety of audiences, until it felt like my own. I sometimes wondered who the rabbi was who had given me, unknowingly, such a wonderful gift. But I did not pursue it. Five years later, now myself a visiting rabbi at Camp Harlam, I was given the opportunity to speak during morning tefillot. What else could I do? I told the story of the story—that I had first heard it sitting in this very chapel, that it continued to echo within me, and that I wished I knew from whence it came. And then I told the story.

So the circle was closed. Or so I thought. But revelations beget revelations, and after tefillot, a counselor approached me to say that her father, a longtime camp rabbi, told this story all the time. Perhaps he was the source?

As it happened, her father, Rabbi Fred Neulander, was indeed the one from whom I had heard this story. And with his permission, I continue to retell it. But there is more to the story of the story than that.

For me, "The Mountain and the Cliff," immediately spoke of childhood; of the need for youngsters to attempt to be independent and the important lesson that their parents will support them when necessary. That was the meaning I had in mind when I told that story to parents and children. But when I finally found Fred Neulander, I was surprised to learn that he usually tells the story in an entirely different setting—a house of mourning. He tells it to those who grieve as a way of illustrating that they should not try to bear their grief alone, that they should reach out to those around them, family and community, for help. Same story, different context. When I learned this, I understood why my teacher, Peninnah Schram, counsels her students to resist the urge to tell people what a story means. Explanations are limiting. When you tell a story freely, with no explanations, you permit your audience to hear it as they will. You allow it to strike the most responsive chord in each individual. As a rabbi, who often uses a story to emphasize a specific point, the temptation to explain, to limit, is very difficult to resist. And yet, when I am able to resist, my storytelling has more power, for it can take listeners in directions I have not even imagined.

That is what I have learned from the story of the story. And as for what the story itself really means . . .

---

nce upon a time, in the Old Country (where all the best stories took place), there lived a man and his young son. The man was a merchant, someone who sold a little of this and a little of that just to keep food on his family's table. Usually he sold his merchandise to his neighbors in the town in which he lived. But once each month he would bring out his sturdy wagon, load it up with a little of this and a little of that, hitch his horse to the traces, and head off on a trip to sell his goods to the people living in other towns. And when he went on these trips, his son always went along.

Now generally nothing very exciting happened on these trips, but to the boy they were always great adventure. That was because the town in which he and his family lived was nestled in a beautiful valley, surrounded by tall mountains. And to get to any other town, you had to cross the mountains. And that was the adventure! For the only road out of the valley wound up and around the tallest of the mountains, and it was just barely wide enough for the horse and the sturdy wagon. And as the man and his young son rode up and around, they always had the mountain on one side of the road and a steep cliff on the other.

On this particular day, their trip started out like any other. Early in the morning, the father loaded his wagon with a little of this and a little of that. Then he hitched up the horse, he and his son climbed onto the wagon, and with a soft cluck of his tongue and a gentle shake of the reins, they were on their way.

All morning long they followed the only road out of the valley, as it wound up and around, and always they had the mountain on one side of the wagon and the cliff on the other.

It was almost noon when they came to the top of the mountain, where the road turned to begin winding back down the other side. The sun stood high overhead as they came around the last bend. And there, at the very highest point, the horse suddenly stopped! The father and son looked ahead, and saw in front of them a tremendous pile of rocks, which had rolled off the top of the mountain, right into the middle of the road. Rocks of all sizes! The horse had stopped because it didn't know what to do. If they had been on a road in the valley, it would have been a simple matter to pull off into a field and go around the pile of rocks. But here, on this road, they couldn't go around, because they had the mountain on one side and the cliff on the other! It seemed as though they would have to go back.

But the boy turned and said quickly, "Don't worry father, I'll get rid of all those rocks, and then we'll be on our way." And with that he jumped down from the wagon and began to work.

He pushed rocks, he pulled rocks, he rolled rocks over the cliff.
He worked for two hours, and when he was done all of the rocks
were gone—except one. After all the boy's hard work, the big-
gest rock, the one that had been at the bottom of the pile, was
still sitting in the middle of the road. No matter how much he
tried, he could not move it. And even though he had been at it
for two hours, and even though he had removed every other rock,
they were still stuck. For with the large rock in the center of the
road, and the mountain on one side and the cliff on the other,
the horse and wagon still couldn't get past.

The boy walked wearily back to the wagon, wiping his arm
across his forehead. He looked up and said, "I'm sorry father,
but I can't move that last rock, and we can't get around it. I'm
afraid we'll have to go back."

His father looked down and asked, "Have you really done
everything you could?"

Surprised by the question, the boy thought for a moment.
Then his face lit up with inspiration, and he ran to the back of
the wagon and got out a long piece of cloth, for they sold fabric.
He went to the rock, wrapped the cloth around it, took a deep
breath, and began to pull. He pulled until his muscles bulged,
but the rock didn't budge.

Disappointed, he walked back, slumped against the wagon,
and said, "I'm sorry father, it's no use. We'll have to go back."

His father tilted his head to one side as he looked at his son
and asked again, "Have you really done everything you could?"

Though he was very tired, the boy thought for a moment.
Suddenly, his shoulders straightened as an idea came to him.
He ran to the back of the wagon and took out a long piece of
wood, for they sold lumber. He went to the rock, placed one end
of the board underneath it, and began to lean on the other end.
He pushed down with all his weight, he pushed until his eyes
bulged, but the rock didn't budge.

He stared at the rock for a moment more, then turned slowly
and trudged back to the wagon. Once more he said: "I'm sorry
father, I just can't move that rock. We'll have to go back."

And once again his father looked at him and asked, "Have you
really done everything you could?"

This time the boy got angry. "Yes! Yes I have! I have been pushing and pulling and rolling and throwing rocks for two hours. I've used the cloth, I've used the lumber. I really have done everything I could!"

His father shook his head, and said quietly, "No, you haven't, because you haven't asked me to help you." With that he climbed down from the wagon, and then he and his son walked to the rock. Together, they rolled it off the road and over the cliff. Then they climbed onto the wagon, and with a soft cluck of the father's tongue and a gentle shake of the reins, they were on their way.

A TALE OF REB NAHUM CHERNOBLER — AND A *TIKKUN*

Eve Penner Ilsen

Eve Penner Ilsen *is a psychologist, teacher, storyteller, and singer who has pioneered work weaving body, mind, and spirit for the last 25 years. Her life and work have taken her to interesting places, from rural Alaska to Brazil and Israel. Presently, she conducts seminars, in subjects ranging from mythology and mysticism to healing, and frequently coteaches with her husband, Rabbi Zalman Schachter. She also collects stories for retelling. Eve resides in Philadelphia.*

The man who first told me this story was completely dumfounded when, at its conclusion, I burst into tears. I have since read it myself, both in Zevin's collection *Stories of the Hasidim* and in Dr. Abraham Twerski's *Generation to Generation*, and have heard it in various forms, some a bit more benign than this version. It has also been told of Reb Michele Zlotchover, so it is more or less public domain. The story is one of many that polarize the spiritual and the material, assigning the former domain to the male and the latter to the female, and denigrating the value of material life. The result is a story that, while making what might be a very worthwhile point, has a strong misogynist cast. While the example of a much-respected rebbe embracing poverty is an important one in our time, an age of excess and waste in which more of us might well consider living in voluntary simplicity, I still felt that this story called for a *tikkun*—a repair. (It is interesting to me that I've heard several different "traditional" endings to this story from various people. Evidently, I am not the only one who felt uncomfortable with this rendition.)

Now, when a story involves such a well-known rebbe, I cannot take the liberty of presenting a revised version in place of the original. Nor do I wish to suppress the subtleties of the story, polarizing male and female further and reducing it to caricature. This is a story that evokes a rich complexity of reactions and associations—the signature, in my opinion, of a good story. My solution has been to hold close to the version of the story as I first heard it, and as you will read it. Then, I have proposed an alternative ending, my own version of a *tikkun*. You, the reader, are invited to participate in your own dialogue with this story.

I submit this with full respect for the memory of R. Nahum Chernobler, *z'l*, and with thanks to those of his family with whom I have spoken, who have given me their help, graciously and with good cheer.

---

 eb Nahum of Chernobl and his family lived in the direst poverty. While he was intensely engaged in a holy life of prayer and learning, ministering to the needs of his community, it fell to his wife, the Rebbetzin Sarah, to do everything else. She cared for the house, the cleaning and shopping and cooking, the washing and mending. She bore and raised the children, keeping them safe and as healthy as she could and teaching them the ways of *menschlichkeit*, of becoming good human beings. And what meager living sustained them, she made. Often, the pillows, candlesticks, and other household items had to be pawned just to put food on the table for Shabbos. Often, these items stayed at the pawnshop longer than expected. Sometimes they never came back home at all.

Reb Nahum's poverty was voluntary. When his hasidim would offer gifts to make his life easier and more comfortable, the rebbe would refuse. He did not want to be distracted from essentials and become attached to the material things of this world; and he had a positive dislike for owning money. He preferred to attach himself to things he considered of permanent value: Torah and *mitzvos*; and for these he was willing to make sacrifices. For instance, the joy he felt in fulfilling the *mitzvah* of putting on *tefillin* in the morning was enhanced by a very special pair of *tefillin* that he owned. They were the only items of any real monetary value in the whole house. The small scrolls had been written by a very holy scribe, each letter fashioned with intense *kavannah* (inner purpose) in a unique script. Reb Nahum treasured these *tefillin* and held them in high regard. When he bound them to himself he felt he could fly in his prayers far above his physical surroundings.

Other pious Jews knew about the *tefillin* as well, and several of the better-off householders had asked to buy them. In fact, one man had offered Reb Nahum <u>four hundred rubles</u>! That was enough to marry off a daughter, from the expense of a match-maker and a respectable dowry through the wedding celebration with musicians, new clothes for the bride and groom, and enough to feed all the poor of the town plus the honored guests, with even a little left over. This was an enormous sum. And all this while, Rebbetzin Sarah continued struggling to make ends meet. When times were so hard that she did not know where the next meal would come from, when the children were hungry and there was nothing left to pawn, she would approach her husband and plead with him to sell the *tefillin*. "My husband," she would say, "if you sell your *tefillin* and replace them with a more ordinary pair—no small expense—still, what would remain, if I managed carefully, could free us from worry for a long time. After all, isn't the *meaning* of the verses written in the *tefillin* what is really important? And isn't that the same in every pair of *tefillin*? And isn't it the *kavannah*, the intent, that counts most when you *davven* your own?"

But Reb Nahum wouldn't hear of it. "Don't worry," he told her. "The Holy One will help us." And somehow, they continued to squeak by from day to day, from Shabbos to Shabbos, from season to season, from festival to festival.

One autumn, it was almost the eve of Succos and Reb Nahum had still not found an *esrog* (citron) to make the blessing in the *succah*. *Esrogim* were always imported with cost and difficulty from the warm countries to the East, since they would not grow in the colder climates of Russia. This year there was scarcely an *esrog* to be found in all of Chernobl. As the last afternoon leading to Succos deepened, Reb Nahum was beginning to wonder seriously how he would be able to fulfill the *mitzvah* of blessing the *lulav* and the *esrog* as commanded for the festival, when he had a stroke of extraordinary good luck. He came upon a traveler rushing through Chernobl on his way home for Succos; and among his other possessions, he was carrying—an *esrog!* Without thinking for one moment of cost, Reb Nahum begged him to sell him the *esrog*. At first the traveler was unwilling to part with it at any price. But, when faced with Reb Nahum's entreaties, the traveler told himself that if the *esrog* was so important to the rebbe, the money was equally important to his family, and he owed it to them to consider selling the *esrog*— but only for a stiff price: 400 rubles. It was exactly the sum that Reb Nahum had been offered for his *tefillin*.

Reb Nahum stood in thought: on the one hand, he wouldn't need his *tefillin* for the next eight days, since on Succos one isn't obligated to wear them. And on the other hand, this was the only time in the whole year that he could fulfill the *mitzvah* of blessing the *esrog*. So he quickly came to a decision. He asked the traveler to wait a short time while he ran to complete a business transaction and return with the money. He ran home, took his *tefillin,* and rushed to the house of the buyer who had offered him four hundred rubles before, and who now happily paid the high price and considered himself lucky. Reb Nahum took possession of the rare *esrog*, and he sent the traveler off with the four hundred rubles and a blessing. He wrapped the *esrog* in its protective coverings and put it carefully in its box. Once home, he put it in a special place so that nothing would damage the delicate fruit and spoil it, for the fruit had to be whole and perfect in order to be used for the blessing in the *succah*.

As Rebbetzin Sarah was making the last preparations for greeting the holiday—making the food and the house and the *succah* as neat and festive as possible on next to no money— she caught a faint whiff of the sweet scent of *esrog*. She knew it wasn't possible; even if an *esrog* were to be found in Chernobl, *they* hadn't the money to buy it. So she smiled to herself, thinking that the very thought of Succos was strong enough to draw down the vivid memory of the fragrance. Then she caught sight of the box, unmistakable in its safe place. Such a box, such a fragrance—it had to be an *esrog*. She didn't believe her eyes.

Just then, Reb Nahum entered the room.

"My husband, that couldn't be—an *esrog*?"

"Yes!" Seeing her look of disbelief, he took down the box, opened it, and unwrapped the fruit to show her.

"How wonderful! But—how did you ever manage to buy it?" she asked.

And he told her what he had done.

ONE TRADITIONAL ENDING

Something in her snapped, after all those years of hardship and privation.

"The *tefillin*?" she gasped. "Your precious *tefillin*, which could have supported the whole family for so long, which I have been begging you for years to sell and you refused—you *sold* them today, to buy from a passing traveler an *esrog* that we will use for only seven days?"

The rebbetzin was beside herself with fury.

She seized the *esrog* and bit off the *pitom* end.

Now the *esrog* could not be used for the festival.

Reb Nahum was silent for a long moment. Then he said: "My precious *tefillin* are gone. And now, the *esrog* is lost to me. Satan would now like me to lose one last thing to make his victory complete: my temper. *And that I will not do*." And Reb Nahum left the room.

ONE POSSIBLE *TIKKUN*

Something in her snapped, after all those years of hardship and privation.

The rebbetzin was beside herself with fury.

She seized the *esrog*, bit off the *pitom* end, and burst into a high, keening wail.

Reb Nahum stood frozen in shock. He had, by a near miracle, managed to acquire an *esrog* in time for Succos, the only time in the whole year that he would have the opportunity to perform this *mitzvah*. Now they couldn't use it. And his wife was crying as if her heart would break.

"Sarah, Sarah, what is it? Why did you do this? Please, talk to me!" He stood by helplessly while she rocked herself to and fro, convulsed by sobs, almost retching. He had never seen her so distraught. A long time passed before she could breathe easily again, and it was longer before she could speak.

"My husband," she whispered, "for years you have been *davennen*, learning, teaching, and caring for the needs of the community." He looked at her, head to one side, puzzled. "For those same years," she said, "I have barely been able to snatch a moment to pray at length, not on the run, let alone to learn a little. Because I have spent every waking moment of every hour keeping worry from you, making it possible for you to do what you do, and eking a life out for ourselves and our children." She was trembling.

"And it's barely a life. Sometimes our sons can hardly keep their minds on their learning because of the rumblings of their empty bellies. We shiver and our noses run for over half the year because we can't afford more wood for heat." Her voice, soft and intense, began to gain strength. "Our daughter is almost of an age to marry, and all of her few rags of clothing are threadbare. When it comes time for her wedding, will she even have a dowry?"

She continued: "When I asked you to sell your *tefillin*, it was not for the sake of luxuries, but in order to buy bare necessities. Did you think that I would ask you to part with your treasured *tefillin* for the sake of a frivolity? Each time I asked, and you told me God would provide, God *did* provide—something. Then you would tell me not to worry: didn't I see, God had provided? But I *live* in worry: in what form will God's help come? Of course our sustenance comes from Him; but every evening, it is *me* that you and the children ask for dinner. It is my task to see that it gets from God to the table. I use all my heart and all my strength trying to patch it together so we can survive. It is my job to persuade the shopkeepers to wait just a little longer until we can pay our bills. Whatever comes, I am the one who counts each *kopek* (penny) and makes it stretch to last."

Rebbetzin Sarah's voice lowered to just above a whisper. "My husband, do you really think it is right that *we* all pay such a high price for your attachment to poverty?"

Reb Nahum sat in shocked silence. His eyes filled.

For the first time, Rebbetzin Sarah had found her voice.

And now, for the first time, Reb Nahum found his ears: he heard her deeply.

He moved closer to her, and they looked deep into each other's eyes.

Cradling the ruined esrog between them, the couple stood and cried together, the salt of their tears sweetened by the fragrance of the fruit.

And we are told that the joy of Succos had never been sweeter in their house than in that year.

EPILOGUE

It happened that my partner was recently talking to a descendant of the Chernobler and the subject of the *tefillin* came up. (Reb Nahum's hasidim bought the *tefillin* back for him, and they are in the family to this day.) Did my partner know the story of the Chernobler's *tefillin* and the *esrog*? Yes, my partner said, he did; and he had also heard a new alternative ending (this one), which he then recounted.

The Chernobler's descendant smiled and said: "And if it didn't happen that way—it should have."

THE NEVER-ENDING SONG
Nina Jaffe

Nina Jaffe *is on the graduate faculty of the Bank Street College of Education. A professional storyteller who performs and speaks nation-ally, she is the author of several books of Jewish folklore for children, including* In the Month of Kislev: A Story for Hanukkah *and* The Uninvited Guest and Other Jewish Holiday Tales, *which received the Sydney Taylor Award, and the coauthor of* While Standing on One Foot: Puzzle Stories and Wisdom Tales from the Jewish Tradition. *She is also a musician. Nina lives with her husband and son in New York City.*

"The Never-Ending Song" is my adaptation of a midrash that I included as the Rosh Hashanah story for my book *The Uninvited Guest and Other Jewish Holiday Tales* (New York: Scholastic, Inc., 1993). Midrashim—the word is from Hebrew and literally means "to draw out"—are parables, stories, and legends from rabbinic literature that were told in order to explain or elaborate on pas-sages from the Torah. This midrash brings together images of strange and marvelous creatures, many of whom were known, by different names, throughout the ancient cosmologies of the Near East. Mention of these creatures, Ziz, Leviathan, and Behe-moth, can be found in the poetry and narratives in the Book of Genesis, Psalms, the Book of Job, and other texts dating back to the first century. In this legend, the rabbinic storytellers trans-formed these themes and images into a story that touches on a deep moral and ethical sensibility. From a Jewish perspective, the story seems to be saying that essential values are not only for the world of humans, they are also the matrix out of which the universe itself is held together and maintained.

I first told a version of this story in 1990 for the 92nd Street Y Oral Tradition Series in New York City. I was developing the pro-gram on the theme of creation in Jewish folklore. In researching material, I came across this midrash in Louis Ginzberg's *Legends of the Bible* (Philadelphia: Jewish Publication Society, 1956). I think I wept when I first read it—it seemed to touch such a deep chord. As a storyteller, it has been a growing source of revelation to me that the Jewish tradition, too, has a "mythology." Most Jewish stories that I had grown up with or was familiar with focused on human-to-human relationships. Only when I began to research and tell stories did I come to realize that our tradition is also rich in fantasy, magic, and tales of wonder. What if, as a child, I had been told these stories—the fairy tales and the folktales—along with the "canon" of European-based fairy tales that are familiar territory for most American children? How would that have shaped my Jewish identity? This finding of not only "the child" but "the Jewish child" in myself has been an ongoing process since I have become familiar with the depth of this literature as an adult. And so, to discover in the midrash these images of mythical beasts—of Leviathan, the cosmic dragon and sea monster; of Ziz, the great bird whose wings can enfold the earth; of Behemoth, who laps up the waters of the rivers and consumes the grass on a mountaintop in a single day—was profoundly nourishing to my own sense of the roots and history of the Jewish imagination.

---

ong, long ago, before the day human beings were created, all the creatures of the world were beginning to populate the earth and the sky. The greatest of all the birds was the Ziz. Her wings were as wide as the sky itself. When she stretched them out to fly, she could reach from one end of the earth to the other. It was the Ziz who, with her shining golden feathers, protected the earth from the hot winds of the south. Once, the egg of a Ziz broke and it flooded the forest and even the mountaintops!

Of the beasts of the field, the largest of all was Behemoth. His bones were as strong as brass. His legs were like great iron bars. He could drink the Jordan River with a single gulp and every day he grazed in the pastures of a magic mountain. When he finished eating in the evening, there was not a single blade of grass left to be seen, and yet, in the morning the meadows were lush and green again. His tail was as strong as a great cedar tree, and when he walked about, the earth trembled beneath him. Behemoth kept his home in a cave in the magic mountain, near the nesting place of his friend, the Ziz.

In the swirling waters of the sea lived the greatest sea mon-ster of all time—Leviathan. He had as many eyes as the year has days, and scales that shone brighter than the sun itself. When Leviathan roamed the deep, one swish of his tail would cause huge tidal waves. Smoke poured from his nostrils and the water boiled and bubbled in his wake.

These were the great creatures of the sky and sea and earth, and they kept to themselves. At night, Leviathan would curl his tail around the ocean and sleep by the shores of the magic mountain, near his friends, Ziz and Behemoth, while up in the heavens, the angels sang them sweet lullabies.

But the Holy One had also put many other kinds of flying and creeping things in the world, large and small, and they were all trying to get used to their new homes. The small creatures were not having an easy time of it. The robins and sparrows were constantly being chased down by the great birds of prey—the eagles, hawks, owls, and condors. Day after day, they found that their nests had been robbed, and many of them were carried away by sharp talons, never to return.

The great sharks and barracudas never stopped feasting on the little fish. Wherever they turned, minnows and goldfish, guppies and trout were being hunted down in every corner of the ocean, in every lake, and in every river. On land, the lions and tigers, the great wolves and panthers were always at the heels of the mice and rabbits. The deer, the zebra, and the gentle giraffes never had a moment to rest from their running. In all the earth, there was no place to hide. The very world itself was being disturbed by the antics of small spirits and demons who ran about, hither and thither, turning mountains upside down and twisting the rivers out of shape.

Finally, all of the small creatures met to talk over their prob-lems together. Something had to be done about this! Chittering and squawking, meowing and squeaking, they came to a spot that they all agreed might be safe, at least for a little while—by the roots of a great tree that stood near a gently flowing stream.

The rabbit spoke first. "We can't go on like this!" he cried. "There is no rest for me or my family. We are always running from some big animal!"

"You are right," croaked the frog. "Surely the Holy One did not create us to live like this!"

"We know that some of us must be eaten," chirped the sparrow. "After all, I myself must live on the bugs and insects. But if the hunting never stops, we will all disappear, and there will be no creatures left but the great beasts of prey!"

"You are right again," croaked the frog, "but what can we do?"

The animals, birds, and fish twittered and cheeped together for some time, but no one could come up with an idea. Finally, from the bottom of the stream, a little starfish made her way to the top. "Shhh," she whispered, "listen to me."

"Shhh," cried all the creatures. "Let us listen to the starfish."

And the starfish began: "My friends, I have been pushed by the currents of the water to many places on the earth. One day, a great wave washed me up on the shores of a shining beach. Near it stood a great mountain. I saw there three enormous creatures. None of you has ever seen creatures so great or so powerful, and as the sun went down, the angels sang them to sleep. Perhaps they could help us?"

The animals and birds agreed that each would send a representative to follow the starfish to the shores by the magic mountain. For what else could they do?

The mouse and sparrow followed the starfish as she made her way to the magic mountain. Just at sundown, Ziz and Leviathan were about to take their rest (Behemoth had already gone into his cave), when they heard three tiny voices calling to them from the sandy shore.

"Please wake up, oh, great creatures! It is only us, mouse, sparrow, and starfish, and we wish to speak with you."

Slowly, Leviathan uncurled his tail. Ziz fluttered and fluffed her wings, and Behemoth peeped out of his cave. "What do you wish, little ones?" they asked in one voice.

"Oh, great ones, if you please," cried the mouse. "We have come to ask for help."

"Yes," said the starfish, "all over the world, the beasts and birds of prey and the hungry sharks stalk us little animals without cease. Spiteful demons are turning the mountains upside down. They are twisting the streams and rivers in all directions, just to confuse us. We are afraid that our kind will never have a chance to live in this beautiful world that the Holy One has created."

"That is why we have come," cheeped the sparrow. "Isn't there anything you can do?"

Leviathan blinked his hundreds of eyes. Behemoth sniffed into the winds and Ziz curled her mighty talons. For some time, they were silent. Then, they took counsel with the angels who were looking down from the starry heavens, and there was no sound of sweet lullabies that night. "It is time for the Great Words," they whispered among themselves.

"Yes," the angels agreed, "it is time."

Finally, they turned to the little ones and spoke again, in one voice. "Yes, little friends. There is something we can do. Return to your homes now, and wait."

The mouse, the sparrow, and the starfish hurried back to give the message to all their friends.

That year, in the month of Tammuz, when the air was hot and the summer sun burned down, Behemoth stepped out of his cave.

He lifted his great head and roared so loudly that the lions stopped in their tracks. His tail hit the ground with such force that the earth shook, and the tigers and wolves, the panthers and the jaguars trembled in their skins. They hid their heads in their paws and listened to the sound of the word as it entered their very hearts.

Out of their nests and burrows, the rabbits and mice popped their heads and, for the first time, breathed the breath of freedom as the stalking beasts rested from their ceaseless hunting.

The sound of that roar echoed on through the months of Av and Elul, until the autumn month of Tishri. Then the Ziz unfurled her enormous wings and uttered a cry that pierced through the very clouds of the sky. At the sound of that great cry, the eagles and hawks, the condors and the owls stopped in their flight, stunned and afraid. For the very first time, they felt pity and stopped their hunting for a time. They joined with the Ziz and called out her word in hoots and screeches until the winter month of Tevet.

Then, Leviathan raised his shining tusks from the depths of the sea. He whipped up the waves into a foaming froth that shook the barracudas and the swordfish from their path of destruction and hummed his word into the ears of the sharks and killer whales.

Out from behind the rocks and underwater crannies swam the little fish, lighting up the waters with flashes of silver, red, and gold. They listened as the big fish passed on the word through the currents of the oceans and streams as Shevat went by, and than Adar, until the gentle spring breezes of the month of Nisan blew in. In the heavens, the angels gathered their voices together and sang their word through the spheres until the demons bowed their heads in awe. The spirits put down the hills and mountains, and let the rivers follow their own course.

Ever since that time, the creatures of the earth have lived together, taking what they needed and no more, giving each other times of rest and play as well as times of hunting and fear. For the word of Behemoth was "Peace," and the word of the Ziz was "Justice." The word of Leviathan was "Mercy," and the word of the angels was "Love."

This is the ancient chant that circles the earth, that all animals, birds, and fish listen to and obey. Of course, all this happened before the time that human beings were created. But if you ever find yourself in a quiet place, in the woods or by the sea, and you listen very carefully, you too may hear the echoes of this never-ending song.

RASPBERRIES FOR SIMA

Betty Lehrman

Betty Lehrman *has been a professional storyteller since 1978, appearing throughout the northeastern United States, across Australia, and, through the U.S. Information Service in Thailand. She holds an M.S. in educational theater from New York University and a B.S. in Theater from Northwestern University. A moving force in New England's storytelling revival, Betty produced "Rainbow Tales," a family radio show, for seven years. She has three audiotapes to her credit and is on the staff of Simmons and Lesley Colleges. She lives in Framingham, Massachusetts, with her husband and two daughters.*

Family stories serve to strengthen the chain of life from one generation to another, and across generations. As an adult I grew close to a distant cousin, Bob Lehrman, who was himself the son of first cousins. "You mean, you can have friends outside the family?" he once joked with me. He had been surrounded by a huge extended family all his life. In 1986 he and a committee of cousins arranged a reunion for over three hundred family members. We met in the Catskills (of course!) and I heard story after story. Bob and his mother even published a book, *Lehrmans in America*, with contributions from many of the cousins. I'd already been working on family stories, inspired particularly by storytellers Donald Davis and Syd Lieberman. Bob's passion about family moved me to write even more.

I was always very close to my maternal grandmother, who moved in with my family just before I was born. She was a calm presence, reading to me or making me tea and toast when I was sick, quietly cooking or sewing. In the last fifteen years of her life we made several tape recordings of her stories.

She lived through remarkable times: she saw horses replaced by cars and trucks; she lived through the Russian Revolution and the Bolsheviks taking over her house; she outlived three husbands and one of her two children. Through it all she had a kind of sweet

179

resignation, a peaceful sense that if this was what life was about . . . fine.

She lost her hearing when she was a young woman, in 1920, during the Russian civil wars. Her parents were leaving for America and, knowing she might never see them again, she contrived to make a visit to her hometown. At that time there was terrible starvation in one region of the new Soviet Union, and children were being sent to other parts of the country where food was available. These children's trains and troop transports were the only transportation running.

Having been a teacher, Sima obtained a place on a children's train. En route, she caught typhus and, by the time she reached her parents, she had a raging fever. Her mother tended her while Sima was ill, delaying her own escape across the border to Poland and, ultimately, the United States. Sima recovered, but she was left with a severe hearing loss that got worse as she grew older. Her mother died in the United States before Sima emigrated, fifteen years later. But we still have the long blue shawl that Sima's mother gave her at their last leave-taking. This is my portrait of her.

---

 always thought she was a tall woman, because she held herself so straight. She had jet-black hair and a huge shelf of a bosom, which was perfect for burying your face and crying if you were unhappy. She was my grandmother, and I loved her with that fierce determination and devotion that kids have for a relative who never disciplines them, never scolds.

She had a timelessness about her; I thought she'd never change. She always sat in the sun and read, sewed, or wrote letters; she often took walks. Sure, she turned gray—she stopped dying her hair black. Her skin got lighter and more translucent, and she shuffled more when she walked. Her majestic 5'4" frame shrank as I grew. But I still never thought of her as really *old*— she was Grandma Sima. So, somehow I was surprised when my mother told me she'd been accepted into a nursing home—she'd move in two weeks.

Oh, I knew it was coming, but before that phone call, it was never real. "She doesn't close the door all the way—she doesn't hear the click. I come home and find her sitting with the door wide open," my mother had said. "She forgets and leaves the stove turned on. I'm afraid to leave her alone all day in the house." We'd all talked about how she'd have to move into a nursing home: she couldn't live with my parents anymore. But it was a long process—my parents took her around to different homes and put her name on waiting lists: the lists were years long. Who knew how long it would take before a place would become available.

It was a small nursing home in Glen Cove that had an opening for Grandma Sima. About six miles from my parents' house, it was quiet and sunny and seemed nice. I told my parents I'd come down and help move her there. The traffic down to Long Island was terrible—and when I finally arrived, I was in a foul mood. All I wanted to do when I walked in the door was complain about what a lousy drive I'd had. But there was Grandma's chair at the kitchen table, with her worn pillow on it, and I remembered what she always said when her feet or eyes were bothering her and we'd ask how she was. "Everyt'ing is all right. Nu, I should feel better if I complained?"

She and my mother were in her room sorting things into piles. There were the clothes she would take with her to the home, the clothes she would leave in the closet, the *schmattes* she would give to charity (she never threw anything away)—and the *schmattes* she wanted to give to me. There were dresses mended with the wrong color thread, an old white sweater with a beaded collar, a green polyester pants suit that was too tight on her so she thought it would fit me—the ugliest green you've ever seen, and besides, it had stains on it. I didn't know what to say. But then, I'd never known what to say.

For twenty years she'd gone down to Florida each winter, bringing back "presents" for us. At first it was fine—stuffed alligators with real teeth that you could cut your fingers on if you tried (I always tried); chocolate-covered coconut candies so sweet they set your teeth on edge. Then in the late 1960s, she started going to flea markets there and returning with "bargains" like mustard-paisley synthetic fabric that she promised to make into a dress for me. (It was the 1960s; I wore the dress.)

Looking at my mother and my grandmother painstakingly

sorting the piles of clothes, I wanted to escape—I didn't want to help sort through my grandmother's life. Twenty-five years she'd lived with my parents. I wanted to go back to the days of the stuffed alligators, to see my grandma tall and black-haired and strong again.

My earliest memories of her are going raspberry-picking. We had a patch of raspberries out back, and they'd ripen about the fourth week in June. We would stop in the vestibule and get little cardboard boxes for the berries. And I'd crawl through the canes, not minding that I scratched my arms and legs, popping the berries in my mouth and occasionally putting one in the box. And she'd carefully bend back the canes to get at the ripest purple-red berries beneath, placing them in her box, saying, "One for Daddy, one for Mommy, one for Lyonya, one for Pavlik [my brothers], one for Betty, one for me." She'd try to get me to do this, too, thereby teaching me to save the berries—and also teaching me the pecking order of the family—but it never worked too well and I always ate most of the berries.

I wanted to go back to the times my brother Paul (Pavlik) and I would play in the yard together and there she'd be in a lawn chair, her back to us, reading the *New York Times* "Week in Review" and shaking her head over the political news. And we'd notice the telltale dangling wire: she'd taken out her hearing aid. Without it she was completely deaf. We'd sneak up on her, one on each side, and yell "Grandma!" right in her ear, and she still wouldn't move. Then I'd tap her on the shoulder and she'd jump three feet and fumble with her hearing aid, saying, "Oh, you frightened me."

Grandma Sima's accent was both charming and an embarrassment. I remember trying to explain to her that we couldn't shake out "the shits" in the laundry. "Sheets, Grandma, sheets." "Sheeeets," she'd say, laughing when she found out what the other word meant.

Everybody in the neighborhood knew her. "How's Mrs. Peterson?" they'd ask me. She took a daily walk through our housing development and must have stopped to talk to everyone on the way: they all knew her. Then, in 1967, she disappeared and, to the surprise of the whole neighborhood, she reappeared a year later with a new name: Mrs. Yaffe. She was seventy years old and had met a man in Florida. He was four years younger and six inches shorter, but after three winters of eating together at the same table in the same retirement hotel, they'd decided to give marriage a try. The children gave their blessing, and she moved in with her new husband in Boston the same year that her oldest grandchild went to college. On the couple's first anniversary, they planned a trip to the Old Country—Lithuania and Russia. But on the plane over, my new grandfather had a heart attack and died. My grandmother returned to my parents' house with some new furniture, new memories, and new sadness.

But some of my favorite times with her were in the kitchen. I'm not sure how she learned to cook—she came from a wealthy family, and although she was the only girl and had eight brothers, her mother never allowed her in the kitchen. "Go study," she'd tell her. Still, Grandma Sima always made holidays special with her dishes. Sometimes she'd make chopped liver in a wooden bowl with a hand chopper. First you chopped the onions, then you fried them, added the liver, fried it all together, then back in the bowl to chop it all up. A little salt—no fancy spices, no food processor. I always thought her chopped liver tasted so good because of the aroma of aged wood it picked up from that bowl.

Or pot roast, dripping with gravy and covered with onions and potatoes; or potato latkes. I loved helping her grate the potatoes. I'd grate them down to nothingness until my knuckles scraped on the grater and bled and she'd say, "Don't worry, a little blood, it makes it taste good."

We finished sorting through all of the clothes in the closet and came upon a brown paper bag, all tied with string. "Dis is for you," she said, handing it to me. "What is it?" I asked. "Nu—open it." I untied the string and smoothed back the paper. There was a pile of pink lace. I unfolded it. It was a pair of delicate pink lace bedspreads I'd never seen before. "Where do they come from?" I asked her. "In 1914, when I was married to your grandfather, my mother gave deze to me for a vedding present. They're from Paris. I saved them for you, my dear."

What was I going to do with a delicate pair of twin-sized, pink bedspreads? I had roommates and a big bed you threw your coat onto when you came home. Still, they were heirlooms, treasures from her wedding to my grandfather. I'd never met my mother's father; he'd died of pneumonia when my mother was a young girl. But I'd heard the stories about him—how he was kind, strong and sweet.

In 1914 my grandmother finished *gymnasium*, which was like high school or junior college; she'd taken a two-year mathematics course, which certified her to teach. She'd come home from Vilna, eighteen years old, and told her mother she wanted to go to Germany to medical college—Jews couldn't go to medical school in Russia back then. Her mother told her, "No, you've been away at *gymnasium* for two years, now you're going to settle down and get married." Sima refused, but they agreed she would spend the summer at her aunt's summer cottage, her dacha on the sea, "thinking about things."

There she was sitting on the porch one day when a young man strolled up and asked directions to her friend Mrs. Raskin's house. He seemed confused, so she got off the porch and walked him over there. The next day Mrs. Raskin came over. "Yoseph Leib likes you very much," she said. "He would like me to invite you for tea." So they had tea together.

Speaking of the man she was to marry, Grandma Sima said, "He was a young man, just four years older than I, and tall, handsome, and cultured—he went to the opera. He had dark, dark eyes—beautiful eyes." Inquiries were made, the families met, and approval was given.

"So I told him, 'I don't want to get married, I want to go to medical college.' He said to me—I don't know how he could say this but he did—he said, 'Simachka, if you marry me, I'll make sure you go to medical college.' So we got married." In those days, the wealthy families rented a hotel in a nearby town and the whole wedding party—thirty or forty people—would take the train to the hotel to spend the weekend there. "It vas a vonderful party. Dere vas singing and dancing." And the gifts, like those bedspreads. . . .

I put the package in my room. I'd find some use for the

spreads. We finished going through the closet. The next morning we brought Sima to the home in Glen Cove. We met the director and the nurses; we put her plants on the window and covered her desk with *Soviet Life* magazines and a new magnifying glass. We made sure Grandma was comfortable and oriented before saying good-bye.

Back at my parents' house, I kept expecting her to shuffle into the kitchen, see me picking at the salad before dinner, and slap my hand, scolding, "Not vit da fingerlach."

I visited her in the home whenever I went down. She'd squint at me through her glasses and ask, "How are you?" And sometimes she'd tell me stories—like about the time when she was five and she wanted to learn to write, so she took a piece of chalk and made marks all over the walls of the house. (Her parents got her a tutor in response.) Or when she was already a mother and finally got to medical school—in Russia. It was after the revolution, anti-Semitism was officially outlawed, and Jews were allowed to go to medical school. She would walk across the frozen Volga River to her brother's house, near the school. They attended classes together for half the week. Then she'd walk back home, spending the next three days cooking for her family. After the first year, she and her brother were thrown out of the school—not because they were Jewish but because their father had been a rich man before the revolution. She didn't remember much from her classes, but she still had the scissors she'd been issued. She never threw anything away.

Sometimes when I'd visit her she'd have saved some fruit or a dessert from lunch, and she'd try to give it to me. "You're too thin, you should eat more fruit," she would say. In later years, her eyes became weak and she could no longer read even the large-print *New York Times*. I'd ask, "How are you feeling?" And she'd always answer, "Everyt'ing is all right. I'd feel better if I complain?"

She was thrilled to learn I was going to get married. "You love him? He's a nice boy?" she asked. I was thirty-two years old. "Yes, Grandma, I love him. He's a nice boy." "Good. Be vell and happy always," she said. Then she took my face in both hands and kissed me three times.

She was too frail to make it to the wedding, so we had a little party for her at my parents' house. We had some relatives and friends over for dinner, and she sat at the head of the table. I put my wedding dress on to show her, and we took pictures. "And we're going to use your lace bedspreads," I told her, "for the chuppa, the wedding canopy." "*Charashaw. Awchen charashaw* (Good, very good)." It was the last time she left the home, except to go to the hospital. At age ninety-seven she died; one day, her heart and lungs just stopped working.

There's a Jewish tradition whereby you name a new child after a relative who has died. My daughter is a year old now; my husband and I named her in honor of my Grandma Sima. And I expect when she gets a little older I'll make latkes with her, and maybe chopped liver. This summer we planted some raspberry bushes in the backyard. And maybe next year, around the fourth week in June, I'll go out there with my daughter and we'll take little cardboard baskets and pick: one for Mommy, one for Daddy, and one to pop right in the mouth and savor—for my Grandma Sima.

RAPS

Walk Like an Israelite:
A Passover Adaptation
Shavuot Rap
Chanukah Rap

Suri Levow-Krieger and Eva Grayzel

Suri Levow-Krieger *is a music and drama specialist in the New York-New Jersey-Connecticut area. Her talents lie in creating and producing original songs and stories that convey a message for elementary and high school students. She does solo storytelling and also directs full-scale musical productions. She is the co-producer of an award-winning video,* The Secret in Bubbie's Attic. *Currently teaching at the Solomon Schechter Day School, Suri resides in Bergen County, New Jersey, with her husband and four children.*

Eva Grayzel, *a graduate of Barnard College/Columbia University, is a teacher and storyteller and tours nationwide. She performs her creative dramatic presentations as "Story Theater." She adapts folk tales to emphasize values and encourages her audience to join her with costume and song. She has an award-winning video,* The Secret in Bubbie's Attic, *and an audiocassette of songs,* Proud to Be Jewish. *Eva is currently residing in Easton, Pennsylvania, with her husband and two children.*

The goal in telling these stories about three Jewish holidays is to instill a deeper understanding of the historical and moral messages behind the simple plots. As Jewish educators, we are searching for ways to motivate young people who are either unaware or unenthusiastic about the origins of Jewish holidays. Moreover, as parents (we have six children between us), we are constantly challenged with the question of why our holidays are not as visible or glamorous as the non-Jewish holidays celebrated in our community. It has become an increasingly frustrating challenge to answer our children when they ask, "Why can't we celebrate Christmas or Halloween?" We have turned to "rap" storytelling as a creative way of instilling a sense of Jewish pride and heritage both within our families and in the community at large.

The stories of Chanukah and Passover are probably the most widely known of the Jewish people, and sometimes they grow stale in their annual retelling. We have recreated these stories in an upbeat rap style that will appeal to the 1990s generation. This new poetic version is fresh, infuses the stories with life, and invites active participation by the reader or audience. The stories are traditional versions of the holidays based on biblical sources, the midrash (legend), and the oral tradition. The significance of the stories lies *not* in historical details, but rather in the deeper meaning underlying the holidays with which they are associated.

In addition to storytelling, we further experimented with an experiential component. We invite group participation through costuming, choral refrains, hand motions, vocal responses, and pantomime. The audience then feels like an integral part of the storytelling process. We also incorporate singing and music as part of the experience. Our audiences are overwhelmingly receptive to these "raps," and we believe that tellers and nontellers alike will find them fun to share. We were also encouraged to produce a video using our material. A version of "The Chanukah Rap" can be found, along with five other holiday stories, on our video entitled *The Secret in Bubbie's Attic*, a forty-five-minute VHS tape, which recently won an Award of Excellence from the Film Advisory Board in Hollywood. In the video a Torah, a shofar, a Chanukah menorah, and a very special piece of cloth are woven together into the fabric of entertaining and educational holiday stories and songs.

Walk Like an Israelite:
A Passover Adaptation

The Israelites had gone to Egypt for food.
They prospered there, they multiplied, and all it was good.
Along came a new Pharaoh, a new Egyptian king.
This Pharaoh he decided to change everything.
Like an Israelite, Mi'Mitzrayim. Go out of Egypt, Mi'Mitzrayim.
Not an Egyptian, Mi'Mitzrayim. Like an Israelite, Mi'Mitzrayim.

Pharaoh, a man afraid of Hebrew power,
Announced a new decree from his pyramid's tower:
"These people are too many, they swarm about in waves.
Let us make them work the land and turn them into slaves.
With task masters over them, they'll build us pyramids.
We'll make their lives so hard, we'll do away with their kids."

The Children of Israel, once so prosperous and brave.
They were made to sweat and work and toil and slave.
Cities of Egypt they were ordered to build.
It broke up their spirit, yes it broke up their will.
Bricks and mortar they were forced to make by hand.
They mixed their salty tears with the clay and with the sand.

This Pharaoh ordered newborn boys to the Nile.
But Moses he was saved, through some beguile.
While still a wee babe his mother placed him in a basket.
And his sister hid him deep in the reeds to mask it.
He was found by none other than Pharaoh's daughter,
When she went down to bathe at the edge of the water.

By Pharaoh's daughter in a palace Moses was raised.
And as he grew he watched his people suffer as slaves.
It tore at his heart to see them treated so bad.
He couldn't take it anymore, so angry, so mad.
He killed a taskmaster for mistreating a slave.
Yes, Moses took a risk, so that a Hebrew could be saved.

Moses knew he did wrong when he lashed out to kill.
Now he was at the mercy of Pharaoh's will.
So fast and so far, he did desperately run
He ran till he came to the setting sun.

He came to Mideon, through the desert sand.
Moses tended sheep there and got to know the land.

He saw a bush on fire but it did not burn.
"How strange," he thought, "should this be of my concern?"
When from the burning bush came a mysterious voice.
"Moses, remove your sandals!" He had no choice.
"Could this be Hashem, God speaking to me?"
God ordered, "Go to Egypt. Set the Israelites free."

"Go down to Egypt, to Old Pharaoh.
You tell him that he must let my people go.
I'll be by your side, so have no fear.
You may take your brother Aaron, just to have someone near.
He'll be your spokesman if your lisp is in the way.
Confidence and leadership you must display."

"But God," Moses said "I'm not the one to do this job,"
And with a heavy heart, he began to sob.
"I'm afraid to meet with that nasty Pharaoh king!
He'll take one look, and my neck he'll wring!"
"Don't argue with me," said the Almighty God.
Moses zipped his lips, gave a respectful nod.

Moses made his way to the Egyptian king,
to demand Pharaoh face what was happening.
With his brother Aaron, he charmed his staff to snake,
Soon all of Egypt began to quake.
Then the mighty Pharaoh, they did undertake.
As Moses made himself be heard, for freedom sake.

"Set my people free, or God will send plagues."
He spelled it all out. He was not vague.
Blood, frogs, darkness, he named them all.
Ten plagues on Egypt would befall.
The locusts came, lice attacked, animals died.
Boils, vermin, wild beasts; Egyptians wailed and cried.

After each plague Pharaoh said, "Go, go!"
But then he'd change his mind and became again the foe.
Until the last plague took Pharaoh's own firstborn.
Pharaoh was mad. His heart was torn.
He ordered the Israelites, "Get out! Go free!"
The Children of Israel began to flee.

So Moses gathered up the Israelite band,
To lead them through the desert to the promised land.
With precious few belongings, fresh baked unleavened bread,
They rushed out, young and old, knowing not what lay ahead.
They marched until they came to the Sea of Reeds.
The people were frightened, but God was pleased.

With fear in their hearts, they asked, "How can we,
get across this vast, deep, and ominous sea?"
Moses raised his staff. The waters split in two!
What an awesome scene! They hurried on through.
Then Pharaoh's heart hardened once again.
He roused his troops. He roused his men.

Pharaoh followed with his chariots, thought he'd win.
But the waters (swish), they came a-rushing in!
Pharaoh and his army were dragged down below.
The Israelites rejoiced and carried on with the show.
Miriam danced with timbrel, led the people in song,
Sending praises to God all day and night long.

The Israelites, no longer slaves, they rose above their plight.
Moses stood firm. Above his head were horns of light.
He proclaimed before God with all his heart and all his might,
"Stand tall and walk like an Israelite!"
Walk like an Israelite, Mi'Mitzrayim. Go out of Egypt, Mi'Mitzrayim.
No longer Egyptian, Mi'Mitzrayim. Walk like an Israelite, Mi'Mitzrayim.

Shavuot Rap

Moses led the Jews from the Egyptian king
Now they could break out in dance and sing
So they finally felt what it was like to be free
After crossing to freedom, crossing the Red Sea.
They believed they would now live a life that was sunny
They were promised a land of milk and honey.

They began their journey with hearts full of glee
No more slavery for them, now they were free.
But on the other side was a different kind of land.
It was a desert: dirt, dry heat, and sand.

They never dreamed that it would be so hot.
Better than Egypt, this was not!

They walked and they wandered for forty years.
So miserable they were they cried real tears.
Often they got lost as they came and they went.
They got angry and cross—their energy was spent!
There was not much to eat and nothing to drink.
They couldn't take baths—Oy, did they stink!

Finally they couldn't take it any longer.
They didn't want to trudge or walk or wander.
They cried out to Moses, "Do something, do!"
They kvetched, they complained, til their faces turned blue.
This desert really was sweaty and hot.
A better kind of life, this was not!

Moses, so upset, did not know where to turn.
When suddenly a fire deep inside him did burn!
"Moses, take your sandals off. I'm sure you will find
I'm not so hard to speak to. What's on your mind?"

"Oh, God, it's your children so thirsty, so hot.
I just don't know which way to turn or not."

"Moses, see that lonely rock sitting over there?
Speak to it and water will flow for all to share."

"Which rock God, is it this one over here?
'Cause if this doesn't work, they'll lose their faith, I fear."

"With your staff in hand, speak to the rock.
Water will flow, their thirst will stop!
As for their hunger, with the morning dew
I'll send something they can dig their teeth into."

God came in a flash, in a flash God went
this was a message from heaven sent!
He returned to the people and raised his staff,
Told them of the miracle, but they started to laugh!
Moses was so angry, he *hit* that rock
Water came a-rushing, without a stop!

Next morning, miraculously, manna appeared.
The people salivated. They danced and cheered.

They found that it had the taste of anything they'd name.
Everyone had something different. Nothing was the same.
Chicken soup with matzah balls, pastrami on rye,
lox and bagels, tzimmes, give it a try.
Cheese blintzes, chopped liver, gefilte fish,
falafel in pita, or whatever you wish.
For dessert, this amazing manna could taste,
like ruggelach, hamentasch, chocolate bobka cake.

The manna came in double portions each Sabbath day,
They were satisfied and gratified. This food was O.K.!
They ate this manna till their tummies almost burst.
The people drank—they quenched their thirst.
The people were joyous—a miraculous occasion.
They sang and danced and had a celebration.

The people were happy, satisfied, for a time.
But then once again they started to whine.
They began to fight and hurt each other.
They began to steal from sister and brother.
They called names, threw things, acted very bad.
It made Moses feel so very, very, sad.

They had no laws, they had no rules.
So the people acted like complete and utter fools.
Again Moses did not know what to do.
He got so upset his face turned blue.
He shook his head, not knowing where to turn.
And once again a fire deep inside did burn.

"Moses, it's me. I'm talking to you . . ."

"Thank God, just a sec, I'll remove my shoe.
God, you've got to help me, I just can't stand it."

"Moses, what you need are the Ten Commandments."

"The Ten Commandments, what in heaven's name is that?"

"Meet me on Mount Sinai, we'll have a little chat!"

So, Moses climbed that mountain for forty days.
Came thunder and lightning, he was so amazed.
Then a voice from out there, it was heaven sent
A voice that spelled out the Ten Commandments.

ONE   The **first** of these rules goes like this, my son
          I am your God. I am the only one.
          There are no gods of stone, no gods of rain or light,
          but one God, Hashem, God of everything in sight.

TWO   Wherever in the world you may seek,
          Your God, Hashem, is number one, unique
          No idols or statues or pictures will do
          God is one, there is no number **two**.

THREE   The name of God is a holy name.
          So, don't just take the name of God in vain.
          Don't swear, don't curse, don't use a dirty word,
          Of the Ten Commandments, this is the **third**.

FOUR   God's day of rest is a holy day,
          Relax, do no work, take your family and pray.
          Whether you live east, west, south, or north
          Remember the Sabbath day, this is the **fourth**.

FIVE   Since your Mom and Dad created you,
          then they like God are holy, too
          The **fifth** commandment says loud and clear,
          honor your parents for they are very dear.

SIX   If life so quickly can be taken away,
          naturally, someone will have to pay.
          Stay away from weapons. Be of strong will.
          Commandment **six** says Thou Shalt Not Kill.

SEVEN   The wedding vows you make, you must keep;
          with another partner you shall not sleep.
          Take heed, all you husbands and all wives,
          Please, don't destroy your married lives.

EIGHT   For those who take things that are not theirs,
          or try to keep more than their own fair shares.
          Get this straight. It's not a big deal.
          Number **eight**, God says Do Not Steal.

NINE   Gossiping, bad-mouthing, telling ugly lies,
          These are no good, not in God's eyes.
          If you hear these things, it's a real bad sign.
          So, God made this commandment number **nine**.

TEN   Don't be jealous of the people that you know,
          or the things that they have or the places that they go.
          You should just be happy with what you've got;
          remember that happiness can not be bought.

Then the voice was gone. God came and then went.
Moses knew this message from heaven was sent.

The people meanwhile lost faith in the deal.
Was this God, was this Moses guy, truly for real?
So they gathered their jewels and melted them together,
to create a God they could pray to forever.
Moses came down the mountain and raised his staff.
But the people were busy with a golden calf.

"What, a golden calf, is this what I see?
A disgrace to God. A disgrace to me.
Give up this project, return, repent!
Quickly now, perhaps our God will relent.
Destroy this calf, repent, return!
I have brought Ten Commandments for you to learn."

The people cried out, some for and some against.
But in the end triumphed the Ten Commandments.
The people bowed down low in remorse.
They promised to obey, and teach their children, of course.
To study the laws of God, Hashem,
revealed on Mount Sinai and chosen for them.

So they learned the commandments and taught it to their kids.
They tried hard not to do what the Torah forbids.
When Moses challenged the people, God won the vote.
We celebrate this day and call it Shavuot.
The day when the Jews received the Torah.
It's a time to sing and dance the horah.

Chanukah Rap

Light those lights for Chanukah
Eight little candles in our chanukiah.

I suppose you know the story of this holiday
Candles, presents, and dreidels to play.
Why it happened a long, long time ago,
In the city of Jerusalem, don'tcha know.
A guy named Antiochus was the ruler of Greece.

He tried to stir up trouble and disrupt the peace.
He ordered the Jews not to study the Torah,
Not to sing to God or dance the Horah.
He destroyed the Temple and the people who prayed.
He terrorized the Israelite in every way.
He tried to break the people's spirit, this mighty Greek.
Tried to hurt all the Jews and make them weak.
It seemed that there was little hope left for a Jew.
But, there were those who kept their faith through and through.

Mattathias had five sons, brave as could be.
And the strongest of them was Judah Maccabee.
Sure you heard of him—his name means hammer—
'Cause his strength was so great it made the enemy stammer.
Well they whooped 'um good, Mattathias and his sons.
They chased the bad guys out, every one.
They reclaimed the Temple in Jerusalem,
And cleaned it all up for the the Holy One.
Got a brand-new ark and some new upholstery,
Hung a new Mezuzah and a new tapestry.
The interior designer made a proclamation:
"We are ready at last for a rededication."
Dedication of what? Why the answer's quite simple—
Dedication of the holy place called the Temple.

Now there is yet another myth attached to this story,
that adds to Judah Maccabee's fame and glory.
The problem you see, was the Eternal Light;
supposed to burn all day and then all night.
To burn for eight days you need a special oil.
But there was none to be found. The celebration was spoiled.
They searched high and low. They searched here and there
For some oil to burn, but there was none to spare.
Until Judah Maccabee, bold and brave,
Found a jar somewhere buried deep in a cave.
There was just enough oil to burn one day
But some strange miracle happened, they say:
That little jar of oil, it lasted for eight!
There was light in the Temple for eight days straight!

Well the people were joyous, it was some occasion!
For eight whole days they had a celebration.

Listen up, you hear, with some concentration:
Chanukah, it means rededication.
Rededication—dedication I say.
That's the true meaning of this holiday.
Now I don't want to spoil any of your fun.
Go out and buy your presents for every one.
But don't forget the meaning of the Chanukah light;
A time of victory, of spirit, and of might.
It was a war of the many against the few,
Fought for religious freedom as a Jew.
When Chanukah comes think again young and old;
A time to rededicate your very own soul.

Light those lights for Chanukah
Eight little candles in our chanukiah.

THE OLD MAN
Syd Lieberman

Syd Lieberman *is an award-winning professional story-teller. The American Library Association has named four of his cassettes Notable Children's Recordings, and Parents' Choice has given awards to two others. Among his six cassettes are* The Old Man and Other Stories *and* Joseph the Tailor and Other Jewish Tales. *An illustrated book of his story,* The Wise Shoemaker of Studena, *was recently published. He lives in Evanston, Illinois, with his wife, Adrienne, and their two children, Sarah and Zachary.*

At the end of my freshman year in college, I decided not to come straight home but stop off in Benton Harbor, Michigan, where my grandparents lived. They were getting up in years, and I decided to spend the day talking to them about their lives. I didn't have any plan, there wasn't any particular subject I wanted to hear about, and I didn't even have a tape recorder (I regret that now). Yet the day was special. My grandmother was out, but I sat with my grandfather for most of the day and listened to the tales of his life.

He told quite a story. For instance, the family was starving after they arrived in America. They had come over to meet my grandmother's brothers in Chicago, but they never connected, and my grandfather wound up peddling in Cuba City, Wisconsin. My grandfather wasn't making enough money to feed his family until the Jewish community in Davenport, Iowa, heard about them and rescued them. They even found my grandmother's brothers and sent the family to Chicago.

The odd thing is that none of the stories he told me that day made it into this story. But nevertheless, that day was important to its writing. The tales my grandfather told me helped me put his life in context. They color my perception of him and, I hope, add to the richness of my portrayal of him. How special it felt sitting there in his kitchen—a bowl of apples on the table—and just listening to my grandfather talk.

This story is about my grandfather and me. I realized when I began to write it that he was a very special man to me and that I had a number of wonderful anecdotes about the times we had shared. As a matter of fact, I had more anecdotes than I could use. I easily could write a Part 2 for this piece. As you'll find out, my grandfather was a character!

e was a big man, and the first thing you noticed about him was that his arms didn't seem to fit right on his body. They hung funny. One eye was half-closed. He was always working his lips as if he were chewing his cud. He had no teeth. Well, he had three sets of teeth, but they were always in a water glass. He was my grandfather—"the old man."

That's what we called him. Now in most families, that's the father. But in my family, the children and the grandchildren all called my grandfather "the old man." There was something about him—a wisdom, a strength, a twinkle in the eye. He was the patriarch of the family, and that's why I was so surprised when my uncle called from Michigan. That's where the family business was: August Pohl Auto Wreckers. My uncle was yelling into the phone, "Come on out and pick up the old man's car. He's not going to drive it anymore. He had three accidents already this month. I'm going to take him around in taxicabs. That's it! The car is yours!" Then he hung up. Well, part of me was happy. I was a teenager and this would be my first car. I thought of myself with one hand on the wheel and the other around a girl. But a part of me was scared. Had the old man really gotten old?

All the way to Benton Harbor, where my grandparents lived, I was worried. When I arrived, it seemed as if my fears had been confirmed. Norman, the man who had worked with my grandfather all his life, was out in front of the shop leaning against the old Ford wrecker. "You don't want to go in there, Syd," he said. "You don't want to go in there."

And I didn't. When I went in, it was as if my uncle had been yelling the whole time I traveled there. "He's not driving anymore. That's it. He hit a tree ten feet off the road. He tells me the tree moved. No more. Taxicabs or we'll take him around. The car's yours."

He was yelling and yelling. I couldn't stand it—I wanted to get out of there. I walked back in the wrecking yard. What I really wanted was to walk back in time. I wanted to be a kid again, when I could jump in the wrecks, pretend I was a driver in the Indianapolis 500, crash, and fall out of the window, dead. I wanted to walk from the top of one car to the other, all the way across the wrecking yard. I wanted to dig behind the seats for matchbooks from strange places or open the glove compartments looking for old letters.

I wanted to walk back in the office and find my grandfather a king again, the way he was when I was a kid. The tires piled next to the door were like two eight-foot guards. The distributor caps under the window were a pile of jewels. My grandfather would stand under a canopy of belts and hoses, the wisdom of the ages—the auto parts book—spread in front of him. He always had one answer, no matter what you came for: "Do we have it? I don't know. Go in the back and take a look. If we have it, pull it out, bring it up. I'll give you a good price."

What did my grandfather know about auto parts? He was a peasant from Kovna Gebernia, Lithuania, such a peasant that at my good-bye party for college, he took me into the kitchen, opened up the refrigerator, and took out two apples. He looked at me and said, "Boychik. When you go to school, the main important thing is you get a refrigerator and you put apples in it." Apples in the refrigerator, the most important thing for a grandson going to college. He said it with a wink—such a wink.

Every fall he would show up with a station wagon filled with apples. My mother would say, "What am I going to do with them?"

He'd reply with a wink, "Applesauce." Or I'd be sick and he'd push the door open to my room and wink. He'd say, "Boychik. Got a cold? Stuffed up? I got something for you. It's gonna open you right up. You'll see, it's good. Here. Try it. Don't tell your mama." It was good and it did open me up. It was 100-proof Jack Daniels.

But the wink I remember the best I used to call the "Old Men Never Sleep Wink." He used to sleep at our house when he'd come into town. And whenever I would get up, he'd be up already sitting at the kitchen table, smoking Pall Malls and staring off into the alley. I'd ask, "Why is that?"

He'd say, "Old men. We never sleep."

Once I woke up in the dark. It was in the middle of the winter and the house was freezing. I thought this was it. I was going to be the first one up for the first time. I was so excited. I ran into the kitchen but he was sitting there in the dark, a cigarette in his mouth, staring off into a dark alley. He never said anything to me that night, but from the glow of the tip of the cigarette, I could see that wink.

I wanted to see the wink again. I walked back into the office. I didn't know what to do. My grandfather was on one side; my uncle was on the other. I picked up the key and started out, and my grandfather followed me. Outside, there was an embarrassed silence. I didn't know what to say. He looked at me and said, "Between you and me, Boychik, that tree did move. You know the way to the big road to go home?" And when I replied that I didn't, he said, "So follow me." And out of his pocket, he pulled the keys to the big Ford wrecker. He jumped in that wrecking truck and turned the engine over. The last thing I remember was a tableau. My uncle was running out of the office, holding his head and screaming. My grandfather had one hand on the wheel and one hand out the window. He was winking and waving good-bye.

My grandfather died at seventy-eight. The day he died, they took him to the hospital but they couldn't keep him there. They told him he couldn't drink and he couldn't smoke. I think he knew he was going. He went home and he called everybody to say good-bye. I remember talking to him that day. He was laughing and crying. We rushed out to Michigan, but he was dead by the time we arrived. I never got to see him on the last day, but I know what he looked like there in his kitchen with a bowl of apples on the table . . . smoking . . . drinking . . . and, I'll bet, winking at God.

A NEW YORKER'S GUIDE TO EDEN

Lisa Lipkin

Lisa Lipkin *is a professional storyteller, writing and performing original stories that bring a myriad of Jewish subjects to life. Her performances have taken her across the country to appear in theaters and festivals, on television and radio. Her most current work, "What Mother Never Told Me . . . Reminiscences of a Child of a Holocaust Survivor," is her autobiographical exploration of life in a survivor household. She was a New Jersey State Council for the Arts Fellow, a New Jersey Historical Commission Fellow, and a recipient of the Arad Arts Project Fellowship in Israel. She lives in Weehawken, New Jersey.*

I've always been a New Yorker, even though I grew up in New Jersey. It's more a matter of attitude than location, I suspect. Bearing that in mind, the following tale is my own interpretation of the Creation myth, from a New Yorker's perspective. But I'm starting around day three. I'm like any true New Yorker—we like to jump right into the middle of things. I call it "A New Yorker's Guide to Eden."

This is part of a collection of original stories I developed called, *Who Towed Noah's Ark . . . A New Yorker's Guide to the Bible.*

nd God, being a hopeless romantic, knew life wouldn't be any fun without a moon. So he made a moon, and it glowed in the sky. But it needed something to howl at it. . . . so he made a coyote. God tried a variation on that animal and came up with a dog. And then a cat. Larger, a tiger. Larger still, a lofty lion, an enormous elephant, a dinosaur! And when he was done with the larger animals, he made the small ones. Ants, grasshoppers, bees, mosquitos. And because he knew that one day there would be a place called New York City, cockroaches. But the moon looked lonely in the sky, so God created stars to keep it company. And the stars twinkled and glistened next to the moon. But they were so beautiful, so subtle in their magic and majesty, that God wanted to create something that was special and could understand and appreciate their beauty. And that's when he created man: a handsome fellow named Adam, whose big eyes took in every drop of life. But how long could Adam swing from the trees, and feed the monkeys, and walk the dogs? He was getting bored. And he was lonely. So, one crisp night, when the sky sang with moonlight and laughed with starlight, he decided to make a wish upon the twinkling constellations. He said, "I wish for a human companion—someone with whom I can share this beautiful place. Someone with whom I can sunbathe on the beach." And that's when Eve popped into the picture.

She was lovely, and the two belonged to each other and to God. They played games like hide-and-seek, leapfrog, and Scrabble. They painted on rocks and on each other with the earth's natural colors. And they reveled in each other's company and in the beautiful paradise called Eden. And all was fine and dandy as candy (although actually, candy only came later). But one day something terrible happened.

Adam was out collecting wild beasts for dinner and Eve was soaking her toes in a clear stream and humming a joyful tune when, all of a sudden, she was interrupted by a silver, slimy, slithering snake, which slid out from behind a willow that wept with a wide reach. "Sssay there, sweetheart. What are you sssinging?"

"Oh, just a simple tune." Eve's words had barely left her tongue when she found herself being lured by a strange gust of wind, which was pulling her, pulling her behind the towering tree. There it was, the snake. It was leaning, quite casually, on a lump of lush grass and filing its nails—I mean, its scales. Next to it sat a shiny, bright green Apple computer!

"Say there sweetheart. Why don't you try this here Apple?" And he fixed her a stump beside the computer. At first Eve didn't know what to do. Her face was overcome with bewilderment, her brows furrowed, her chin crinkled in confusion. She pushed one button, then another, and then another and another and another. Faster and faster, the pace was accelerating! Within minutes she had learned how to do word processing, type a mailing list of a thousand, even send a fax! In short, Eve was obsessed.

Back in the woods, Adam was worried about Eve. He couldn't imagine where she had gone. Suddenly, he, too, was lured by the strangest mystical wind. It drew him to Eve, who was hovering over her software.

"Why Eve! It's Adam, your man. I've been worried about you. Where have you been?"

But Eve was in no mood to talk. "Quiet Adam, I'm busy. I'm trying to figure out the maximum amount of animals I can catch within the smallest given radius." And she kept typing away.

Adam didn't know what to do. But the snake did.

"Sssay there, Adam. Why don't you try this here Macintosh computer?" It was new and delicious like a ripe piece of fruit, and Adam, too, became obsessed.

And so it went. From that day on, the two worked all the time. They only saw each other on weekends. In the morning they would get dressed (in pin-striped fig leaves, on special occasions) and run through the woods to their stations—the woods that they no longer noticed. They would work all day on their computers. The sun would shine brightly on them, but they didn't stop to feel its rays. The flowers around them smelled beautiful, but they no longer reveled in their aromas. And at night, when the stars twinkled, and the moon covered them with moon glow—they were too tired to notice.

And in this way, they could never again return to the Garden in which they were born.

HOW I LEARNED
TO STUDY TORAH
Doug Lipman

Doug Lipman *is a performing storyteller and musician as well as a workshop leader who specializes in supportive coaching of storytellers and others who use oral communication. He integrates music and participation into his stories. His writings include numerous articles and contributions to anthologies, a book on using multicultural folk songs with children, and two books in press (one on coaching storytellers). His recordings include* Coaching Storytellers *(an instructional videotape) and ten audiotapes, including* Milk From the Bull's Horn: Tales of Nurturing Men, *which includes "How I Learned to Study Torah." Doug and his wife live in the Boston area.*

Susan Wilson

I never expected to be a teller of hasidic tales. Folktales of all countries? Yes. Stories of my growing up? Fine. But to tell hasidic tales, I believed, one needs to be deeply conversant with the hasidic tradition.

I still believe that.

But my definition of "deeply conversant" has broadened.

I first heard hasidic tales told by Chaim Klein, who brought them to story-sharing meetings in the Boston area in the early 1980s. I listened to them eagerly. But I never imagined telling them to others.

There were many dinners with friends, though, when I looked down at my plate, only to see it full of food while my friends' plates were empty. I had not eaten because I had just told everyone a long hasidic tale that I had heard Chaim tell the night before.

Okay, I could tell these stories to friends over dinner. But never in public.

One day, I was on the bill for a program called "Stories of Peace." As the first six storytellers made their contributions, I tried to decide what story of mine would fit in.

To my horror, the only story I could think of was a hasidic tale I had heard Chaim tell the month before. But I couldn't tell that in public!

In panic, I grabbed a Jewish storyteller, a serious student of Jewish mysticism, at intermission. "Please," I said, "listen to this story. Tell me if I'm betraying the tradition in any way."

After my hurried telling she said, "I think you should tell it."

When the concert was over, I singled her out again. "How did I do?"

She smiled at me. "You never have to apologize for telling that story."

In the years that followed, hasidic stories continued to take over my performances from time to time. I would stand up to tell a story, only to find the image of a hasidic tale crowding out the story I had carefully prepared to tell. Invariably, on the occasions when I dared tell the hasidic tale, at least one audience member would come up to me and say, "Thank you. That was the story I needed to hear."

As years went by, I heard more tellers of hasidic tales. Some of their stories stuck with me as Chaim's had. In Tennessee at the National Storytelling Conference, I heard the late Reuven Gold tell the following story (which also appears as "Conversion" in Martin Buber's *Tales of the Hassidim*, Volume 1). The moment he told it, I knew I wanted to tell my version of it, too.

In time, I came to trust the stories to let me know when I should share them. I also began to read and ask about hasidic tradition, to add to my factual knowledge. Over the years, I started to follow my friend's advice—at last—to stop apologizing for not knowing the tradition well enough.

I still do not know hasidic tradition the way it deserves to be known. Yet, as the following story indicates so sweetly, this tradition can grow from the heart outward.

I first learned to tell hasidic tales . . . when a story held me to its breast . . . when an audience drew from me what caused my heart to beat as it did . . . when a Jewish storyteller convinced me to follow my connection to the story, no matter how terrifying my obvious inadequacy. I first learned to tell hasidic tales . . . when I began to view the tradition not only as something to be learned, but as something as primal and powerful as a shared heartbeat.

---

n Eastern Europe, there was a couple whose ten-year-old son did not want to study the Torah. This was a terrible problem. Admittedly, learning the Torah takes long hours of concentrated study. Admittedly, too, what their little boy wanted was to be out running in the fields, roaming the woods and discovering the ways of animals. But everyone knows that Torah is the key to happiness. Not only that, all the other little boys were studying Torah, so why shouldn't their son?

The unhappy parents went to the Rabbi. Obediently, they took his advice, but the little boy still refused to study the Law. In fact, where he had once been merely bored, he now became defiant.

More desperate now, the parents asked their neighbors for help. When the aid of neighbors failed, they wrote to relatives in distant cities. They followed everyone's advice in turn. The best of it had no effect, and the worst made their son resist them more than ever.

They began to despair.

Just then, word came that the greatest hasidic rebbe of their generation, Aaron of Karlin, was coming to visit their little stetl.

On the day that Aaron of Karlin visited their village, a long line of people waited for his blessing: the childless, the crippled, those who had failed in business—in short, nearly everyone in that shtetl stood in line, with their life's greatest problem foremost in their minds. And there among them was our couple, with their ten-year-old boy.

When at last they were ushered into the great rebbe's presence, they told him the whole story. After hearing it, the rebbe arose from behind his desk and stood looking at the little boy. The boy stood defiantly, his gaze down, his arms folded. The rebbe's eyes turned to the parents. They looked nervously from their son to the rebbe to each other.

Suddenly, like thunder, the rebbe spoke. "So—he won't study Torah!" he growled, so ferociously that the parents unconsciously took a step toward each other. "You leave him here with me for two hours. I'll give him a talking-to that he'll never forget!"

The parents looked at each other in fear. Should they leave their son with such a fierce man? But the advice of everyone else had already failed. He was their last chance.

As soon as the parents had left, the great rebbe approached their defiant son. Slowly, tenderly, he put his arms around the boy. The boy was stiff at first, but then, by degrees, he allowed himself to be hugged. He dropped his arms to his sides, relaxed the pout of his mouth, and finally let the great man pull him against his breast. He stood there, hearing the rebbe's heart beat. By the end of the second hour, their hearts beat together.

When the parents returned after two hours, they said, "Did it work?"

"Did it work!" He was nearly shouting. "You just wait and see!"

All the way home, the parents looked at their little boy. Was there any change? Could there be any change?

They stopped at the butcher's. The butcher slapped a piece of meat on the counter.

"Mama, the butcher is angry, isn't he?"

"Oh, I guess he is."

"Mama, what happened to him—to make him feel that way?"

Over the days that followed, the parents noticed that their son was somehow more in touch with people, more attuned to their feelings, more interested in their stories. When he heard others discussing the Torah that week, he suddenly realized: these were stories of people! He became curious about them. What made the people act that way? Within a month, he asked to be allowed to learn to read the stories for himself. Within a year, his teachers saw him as their most talented student. In one way after another, the fire of talmudic tradition began to glow brightly inside him.

One day, two neighbors were arguing over the purchase of a calf. The boy went up to them: "Wait! There's a way for both of you to get what you really want." To the amazement of the neighbors, the boy showed them both how to be satisfied with the transaction.

Before long, adult villagers were bringing their quarrels to the boy. He pointed out to each of them the solutions that had been

there in their hearts, but that they—over the roar of their fear
and anger—could not hear.

When it was time for the boy to choose a profession, what else
could he do? He became a rebbe himself.

Years later, when he was known as the greatest rebbe of his
generation, his disciples sat around him and asked, "You are
such a great scholar. How did you get your deep insight into
the Torah?"

And he said to them, "When did I learn to study Torah?" He
smiled, then sighed. "I first learned to study the Torah when
the great rebbe, Aaron of Karlin, held me silently against his
breast."

THE BOOKSELLER FROM GEHENNA

Lennie Major

Lennie Major *began telling Jewish stories as a Sunday school teacher at Mt. Zion Temple in St. Paul, Minnesota. He soon found that there was an interest in Jewish tales in the greater community, and he began to perform and give workshops on Jewish oral tradition in religious and cultural settings throughout the Twin Cities area. When not storytelling, he works as a kindergarten teacher. Lennie and his wife and their two children live in St. Paul, Minnesota.*

As a storyteller, I can leave to the theologians the question of whether demons were created by God or us humans. What matters is their value to us. Without their attempts to challenge our progress toward realizing our full humanity, it would probably take us a great deal longer to learn all of our lessons. So we must view their challenges with respect.

The story of the "Bookseller from Gehenna" took shape in my mind several years ago, when I was asked to participate as a Jewish storyteller in a multicultural peace festival for children. I wanted to find a story depicting what a Jewish community living in peace with itself and God looked like. Not finding one with the resources near at hand, I began to imagine it, and from there it was a natural step to suppose that such a community would not be allowed to go merrily on its way toward fulfillment in Torah without a challenge from the demonic world. Starting from that premise, the story shaped itself.

Since its inception, I have told this story dozens of times, and of course, that means that it already has had dozens of variants before being written down. For those of you who wish to tell the story (and I hope you are many), I give you my blessing to take any liberties with it you wish. Embellish, alter, elongate, delete, or reframe, as the inspiration calls you. I ask only that you check to see that your new variant of the story is consistent with its underlying intent as described above. For younger audiences, I have turned this story into a Chanukah tale and changed the main character, Yosuf, into a young boy or girl, who received the "Demon Book" as a present from the old bookseller. Of course, then you have to change how the resolution takes place. This story also fits well as a tale to accompany Yom Kippur, with its theme of repentance. When told in that vein, I have made the ending occur on the day of Yom Kippur itself.

One final note. The role and character of the Rabbi are worth contemplating. Just how much did he understand of what he was doing? In your variant of the story, what would *your* Rabbi have done?

---

n a valley nestled between high mountains, there was once a small Jewish village that time seemed to have left alone. The remarkable thing about this village was that over the years, it had gradually become a place where the Torah lived in the hearts of the people. While the rest of the world ignored this little village, the local band of demons from the mountains nearby were angered and concerned over its existence. Try as they might, they could not make any mischief or cause the villagers to treat each other badly. They sent sickness, doubts, and temptations of all kinds, made things disappear, ruined crops—nothing seemed to work. Finally, they sent a messenger to Ashmodai, King of all the Demons, to tell him of the danger represented by this village, and ask for his help. Knowing full well the threat posed to his minions when humans grow strong in the ways of peace, Ashmodai flew from Gehenna at once to the demons in the mountains surrounding the tiny village.

"Now watch and learn from your master. I will show you how to destroy the peace and tranquillity of even the most resistant humans," boasted the huge King of the Demons. "First, they must be studied carefully." Ashmodai made himself invisible and went down into the village. He spent some time observing the daily lives of the villagers. At last, he found what he thought was a weakness. He noticed that like Jews everywhere, these Jews had a great love of books. Because they were so isolated, it was rare when new books came along, and the few they owned were precious. With this knowledge, Ashmodai set his plan. "Now watch, and see how it is done," he told the local demons, and before their eyes he vanished. In his place appeared an old man with a donkey and a cart full of books.

Soon, an old bookseller came up the single track into the village, stopped his donkey in the marketplace, and set out his books. All work stopped and everyone in the village gathered around him. A bookseller coming into town was an event not to be missed. One by one, he began to sell his books to the villagers, books with stories of the prophets and sages, commentaries on the Torah and Talmud, adventure stories, and collections of old tales that had been passed down through the generations.

Then he stopped, looked out over all the people, and said, "My friends, I've never seen such devotion and care for the good books I bring. Your love of books has touched me. Something tells me that this is the place I've been waiting for all my life. When I was a young man, a special book was entrusted to me by my grandfather. He told me that a day would come many years in the future when I would be moved to part with it, but only to the right person. I believe that person is here in this village."

The old man took out an ordinary-looking book bound in black leather. He casually flipped through the pages, stopped, and read a few paragraphs aloud. Everyone in the village heard something different from the lips of the bookseller, something that spoke to their innermost desires. For some, the book spoke of the nearness of the Messiah, while others had visions of the Garden of Eden. Some found themselves inside the Holy Temple with King Solomon, others in great yeshivas of learning. Some knew that this book would inspire them to great artistic work, while others were caught up in a rapture of divine poetry rivaling the psalms of King David. Within moments, everyone began clamoring for the book.

"Ten dinars for that book," one shouted.

"I'll pay you fifteen."

"Twenty-five!"

"*Thirty-five!*"

"*Fifty dinars* for the book!" shouted another.

"One Hundred Fifty dinars!" came a shout from back of the crowd. Suddenly everyone grew silent. That was the savings of a lifetime.

"Sold!" cried the bookseller. "Come forward, my good man. Yes! Yes! I can see that you are the one, the one for whom this book was meant. Come walk with me."

Out from the crowd stepped Yosuf, one of the quieter men of the village. The old bookseller put his arm around Yosuf and walked with him back to his house. There Yosuf got out the 150 dinars, which was indeed his life's savings, and paid for the book.

"Now Yosuf," said the bookseller, "you understand, don't you, that this is no ordinary book. Before you share anything from the book with anyone else, make sure that you read all of it carefully. And I would advise you not to share its contents with just anybody who is curious about it."

When the bookseller left, Yosuf went into his room, shut the door, and began to read. He spent the rest of the day reading. When his wife tried to talk to him about the book, and what he had done, he told her to leave him alone. "This is nothing you could understand," he said sharply. He had never talked to her like this before. Every day after that, Yosuf spent every spare moment of his time pouring over the book alone in his room. He refused to talk to anyone in the village about the book. To his friends it seemed as if Yosuf had left them and was living in a world of his own. First the villagers were mostly curious about the book, for none could forget the magnificent visions it had brought them. Then they became resentful of Yosuf and angry that he was hiding its secrets from them.

And Yosuf? What *was* he reading? As he turned page after page, it seemed to Yosuf that he was seeing deeper and deeper into the mysteries of creation. Realm upon realm unfolded before his mind, each one more vast and closer to the ultimate grandeur of God. He felt attuned to the angels and stood with them as God designed the universe. Slowly he realized that hidden in the book were keys that he could take hold of to influence and change the nature of creation itself. How small and limited was the life he had known before he had received the book. Now his true destiny was about to begin. He had been given the book to bring a new teaching to the world. After he mastered the powers promised by the book, he would transform the lives of millions around the world. So went the thoughts of Yosuf.

As it became clear that Yosuf was never going to share anything from the book, the people of the village finally went to the Rabbi and complained about his selfishness. The Rabbi decided it was time to pay a visit. He went to Yosuf's house and called for him to come out from his room. "Tell me about the book you are reading, Yosuf," asked the Rabbi. "I am not asking this out of curiosity, you understand. I know something terribly important has happened to you and I was wondering if you needed to share it with someone else."

Yosuf felt that if anybody could understand it was the Rabbi. Soon he was describing the power and grandeur of what was happening to him through the book. The Rabbi listened and encouraged Yosuf to go on.

"Rabbi, I believe that what I have to do is to take this wisdom, this knowledge, this new Torah, and teach it throughout the lands. I know I have the power to make people listen to me, and they will change, they will see Truth as they never have before!"

"Well then, Yosuf, what better place to start than right here? If this is the new Torah, as you say, then would you honor us by reading from your book instead of the usual Torah reading this next Shabbat?"

"Yes, Rabbi, yes! And you will see. You all will see as you never have before."

Soon the whole village was abuzz with the news. The Rabbi had invited Yosuf to read from his book in place of the Torah on the next Shabbat. Arguments began and sides were taken. Had the Rabbi gone mad? Was this blasphemy? The Rabbi knows what he is doing. Don't you remember what you already heard from the book? And don't you want to hear more?

From the nearby mountains, Ashmodai and the other demons laughed.

That Shabbat, the synagogue was filled with the entire village, from the youngest to the oldest. Everyone could hardly wait to get through the Shabbat prayers. Finally, it was time to read from the Torah. The Rabbi addressed the congregation.

"As you all know, I have asked Yosuf to read to us from his book in place of our regular Torah portion. Yosuf, would you come up now and read to us."

Yosuf went up to the *bimah*, placed his book on the reader's table where the Torah is always placed, and, to the dismay of many, sang the blessing before the reading of the Torah. Before Yosuf began to read, the Rabbi told him to wait, and went to get the *yod*, the pointer, that he used to read from the Torah. This *yod* had been in the Rabbi's family for generations, since before the destruction of the Holy Temple, and it had always pointed to the truth. The Rabbi gave Yosuf the *yod*, and Yosuf put the wooden finger of the *yod* to the first page of the Demon Book. He opened his mouth to begin to read—but then he saw a thin column of smoke rise from the book, right where the *yod* touched it. The words on that page began to disappear up into the column of smoke. The column became thicker and thicker. Soon, billows of smoke began pouring out of the book. It stank of sulfur and pitch. The villagers were frightened and began rushing to get outside. The Rabbi grabbed Yosuf's arm and pulled him from the book and the synagogue.

After a few awful moments, the whole congregation stood outside gasping for fresh air. Children were still whimpering and being comforted by parents. Then the smoke billowed out of the doors, heading straight toward them. The smoke gathered above their heads and formed into a massive, threatening shape, the shape of King Ashmodai himself. The people all cowered in terror as the shape came closer and seemed to reach out for them. Then a strong wind came from the east and blew the smoke, along with Ashmodai and the other demons, all the way back to Gehenna.

As the last of the smoke left them, Yosuf looked over the people of his village. Tears filled his eyes and he cried out, "My friends, how I've been blinded by that Demon Book. Can you find it in your hearts to forgive me for how I've treated you? I see now that you are the real treasure of my life. All the mystery and awe of God's creation is right here among us, and the Torah that we have is all that we need. Rabbi, could we go back and finish our Shabbat service with reading from the Torah?"

When they returned to the synagogue, they found that the Demon Book had vanished, and where it had been set down upon the reader's table, there was nothing left but its shape burned into the wood. From that day onward, the story of the Demon Book was told in that village, and the mark on the reader's table was left there to be seen by each generation.

And as for Ashmodai—he and his demons continue to tempt and torment us, but there is one small village on this earth that they all avoid like the plague.

THE FOURTH CANDLE
Mara

Adapted from a story by Curt Leviant

Mara *is a storyteller and singer who has performed nationally on stage, television, and radio. She has released two cassettes,* Storysong *and* Seeing with My Ears, *and has had a variety of stories published in magazines and newspapers. She is on the rosters of Young Audiences of San Jose and the Wolf Trap Institute for Early Learning. As an actress, she was nominated for a Drama Desk Award for her portrayal of the title role in the off-Broadway musical,* Charlotte Sweet, *and can be heard on the Original Cast Recording. Mara lives with her husband and daughter in San Jose, California.*

I grew up in New York City. I was brought up by parents who had let go of their religion and of their heritage. And so . . . though my heritage is Jewish, I was not. What's amazing about New York City, though, is that you don't have to be Jewish to be Jewish. Everyone in New York City is Jewish.

When I met my husband, I began to explore and study Judaism for the first time. I was surprised to discover there was much that I liked. I even began to occasionally think of myself as Jewish. But I never realized just how Jewish I was until I moved out of New York City to an area where there were few Jewish families. What an alien experience to meet people who would say, "You're Jewish? Wow, I've heard of people like you." There I was, at the point of openly accepting my heritage, when suddenly I was being told indirectly that I was a sort of oddity. I must admit with a reception like that, I began to feel a little uncomfortable about letting people know I was Jewish. It was during that time that I found the story, "The Extra Flame," by Curt Leviant. Here was a story that spoke to me. I rewrote it so that it would better express my own personal feelings and discoveries and began to perform it for Jewish audiences. The story spoke to them as well.

Recently, I decided it was important to perform the story for non-Jewish audiences as well as Jewish audiences. I was amazed to see that, once again, it did not fail to touch something deep inside the listeners. These experiences tell me that "The Fourth Candle" is a story that speaks to all people. It is a story that cries out and needs to be heard. But I had one thing I needed to do first. I needed to procure permission from the original source author—Curt Leviant. Mr. Leviant has authored many stories and novels, including *The Yemenite Girl* and *The Man Who Thought He Was Messiah*. I must admit I was quite nervous about contacting him. What if he hated the idea of someone rewriting his story? I called him—and he did *not* jump with joy. Instead, he wanted to hear the story. I sent him a taped copy of my telling and waited for his response, all the while saying to myself, "Mara, you should have gotten permission *before* you did any work on the story, not after!" Finally I received a letter back:

> Dear Mara, . . . I was very impressed and moved by your beautiful reading. You have a lyrical and dramatic voice. I like your addition of the youngsters. When I heard it, I felt as if I were hearing (reading) it for the first time. Good Luck with it. Happy Hanukkah, Curt.

Dear Curt, Thank you.
Dear Reader, Enjoy.

---

achel's father walked over to the dining room cabinet. He opened it up, took out the Menorah, and began to walk toward the kitchen. "Where are you going?" Rachel asked. She was eleven years old. Her father looked at her mother as if to say, "You explain it to her."

"Rachel dear," her mother began, "we're going to light the candles in the kitchen this year."

"Why?" asked Rachel.

"Well dear," her mother began, "we don't live in New York City anymore, and there aren't any other Jewish people in this town. It would be strange and even odd to light a Menorah out front. So we're going to light the candles in the kitchen. Okay?" Her mother smiled, a little too cheerily, and hoped her daughter would understand.

"But Mom . . . Dad . . . I thought you always said it was im-

portant to light the candles out front. You said it was important to remember the courage and strength of the Maccabees.
That it was a message. You said it was like a light in the darkness . . . or something like that. I . . . I thought you said it was
important to light them out front," Rachel blurted out in anger
and confusion.

Her parents looked at each other and then finally her mother
said, "Well, perhaps we could light the first night's candles out
front." And with that Rachel took the Menorah and walked toward the front room. She did not hear her mother say to her
father, "It's only two candles. Maybe people will think it's a
Christmas decoration."

Rachel walked to the front window and parted the curtains.
She placed the Menorah in the middle of the window. "Oh," she
thought to herself, "it is going to be so beautiful. And surely
someone in my class will see it and say something to me." Or at
least she hoped that would happen.

It just seemed that ever since she began attending this new
school a few months ago, none of the kids had any time for her.
They all had other friends and family. No one seemed interested
in getting to know Rachel. There were even a few kids who lived
on her block. One of them was Brad Brown. His father was the
fire chief. Sometimes Rachel would try to start a conversation
as they walked home, but he would always look at her strangely
and then walk across the street.

Well, she was certain that someone would see her Menorah
and say something to her the next day. And so, with that certainty, she lit the shamash and then the first night's candle.
Her parents stood behind her with uneasy expressions.

She went to school the next day and, at the very end of the
day, someone did say something to her. It was Brad Brown, the
boy from across the street.

"Hi," Brad said gruffly. "My dad wants to know where you got
those candles."

"Oh, you saw my Menorah? Did you like it?" Rachel was so
excited. "Actually, we had to get them about twenty miles out
of town because there aren't any other Jewish families in this
town. But you saw my Menorah? Did you like it?"

"Um," Brad stammered, "you know, my father is the fire chief. Well, he needs to know if they're fireproof." Then, as suddenly as he had appeared, he turned and walked away, leaving Rachel alone. For the first time in her life, Rachel began to feel a knot in the pit of her stomach.

She walked home with that knot and told her parents what had happened. Her parents asked if she still wanted to light the candles. "Yes, yes I do!" she responded without hesitation.

And so that night she lit the second night's candles, and then she went to school the next day. No one said anything. She lit the third night's candles and went to school the next day, and still no one said anything. At least if someone would say it was inappropriate or that she was not allowed to—but *no one* said *anything.* And that knot in her stomach kept growing and growing. Finally, she became so uncomfortable that she decided to light the fourth night's candles out front, but no more after that.

That night she walked to the front window and again parted the curtains. She lit the shamash, and then the four candles for that night. She thought to herself how beautiful the Menorah looked. Then the phone rang. Her father answered it and called to her, "Rachel, it's the Brown boy from across the street."

Rachel walked over and took the phone from her father. "Hello?" she said. In an abrupt and harsh voice, Brad said, "My father wants to know if it's important that you put it out in *full view*?"

Rachel was startled but blurted out, "Yes, yes, it is important. There's a message being conveyed. A message about the courage and strength of the Maccabees. There's a . . ." But Brad cut in and said, "The message has been delivered." There was a click and the phone went dead.

Rachel's legs began to shake beneath her as she slowly sat down and hung up the phone. She quietly told her parents what had happened. And then in a resigned voice she said, "Mom, Dad, I guess you were right. I am going to take the Menorah out of the window now." She slowly stood up and walked out of the kitchen to the front room.

Silently, she looked at the Menorah in the front window for the last time. Two of the candles had already burned down, but two were still burning brightly. It was so beautiful. She noticed how the candles were being reflected in the window directly in front of it. That brought her attention to the outside and she could see some of her neighbors had already put up their Christmas lights.

Then she saw something that made her smile. Her Menorah was being reflected in the window across the street. And it reminded her of what it was like in New York when there were Menorahs on all the streets . . . in all the windows. "It was nice then," she thought sadly.

And then she noticed something else. Her Menorah had two candles burning, but the Menorah across the street had . . . three candles burning. "Mom! Dad!" she called out.

Her parents rushed into the room, and the three of them stood huddled together as they silently watched Brad Brown and his parents light the fourth night's candle. Rachel's mother held her family close and said, "Yes, Rachel, it is like a light in the darkness."

THE PEKL STORY
Helen Mintz

Helen Mintz, *as a story-teller, brings the rich Yiddish tradition to an English speaking audience. She wants to repair the link with the culture of Eastern European Jewish life that was so traumatically destroyed by the Holocaust. She has performed across Canada and the United States and has been on national radio and television. She gives workshops on developing our Jewish identity through our Jewish stories. An anthology of the stories she tells is soon to be published. Helen comes from Vancouver, Canada.*

Dorothy Elias

As I have grown to adulthood, many decades after the death of all my grandparents. I hunger for the sounds of Yiddish. I want to reconnect with the culture of Eastern European Jews as it existed before it was so traumatically destroyed. I want to be nourished by the strength and wisdom of this culture, to know its contradictions and foibles.

One of my favorite places to find Jewish stories is at Jewish seniors programs. And actually, that's my favorite place to perform. Because invariably, I meet women and men there who lived in Eastern Europe, who speak Yiddish fluently, and who are delighted—no, more than delighted—deeply moved by my interest in their lives. And with great generosity and enthusiasm, they share their stories with me.

One morning, I was telling stories at a seniors program in a synagogue. And I had just finished talking—I mean, I had barely shut my mouth—when there was a stampede out of the hall like you wouldn't believe. I stood back and watched, and I thought to myself, "Where is everyone going? Where is the fire? These are seniors? I'd have to go into training to move that quickly."

Well, I later found out that at the end of the program there was a free kosher lunch. And the people who supplied the lunches had the bad habit of not sending quite enough food. Well, along with the stampede to lunch was a woman who stampeded right up to me. And, I mean, she was right in my face. She spoke up loud and clear. "I have a story you've got to hear. This story," she said, "was given to me by my mother in Europe. And it has gotten me through all the difficulties of my life. Including," she added, "raising two teenage sons."

Well, I have two adorable little boys, and I know that adorable little boys become teenagers—and teenagers can be pretty trying. So I thought I'd better listen closely to her story. Which I did. And you know, it has provided me with inspiration in many difficult times in my life. I hope it does the same for you.

אַז מען זאָל אויפֿהענגען אויף דער
וואַנט אַלע פּעקלעך צרות וואָלט זיך
איטלעכער געכאַפּט איר אייגנס:

If you could hang on the wall all
the world's packs of troubles,
everyone would grab for his own.

Az men zol oyfhengen oyf der vant
ale peklekh tsores volt zikh itlekher
gekhapt ir eygns.
　　　　　　　　　　—*Words Like Arrows*[1]

ne morning Rivke arrived at the rebbetzin's house completely distraught. "Rebbetzin, Rebbetzin," she cried, "my life, it's too much for me. My eldest children, they're filled with modern ideas. If I say, do this, they do that. And then, just when I've gotten adjusted to that, they're doing something else. And my two babies, they just scream all day. Sometimes I don't know where they get the breath. And me, I work all day long in the marketplace. My ankles are as big as an elephant's, my back hurts, I'm freezing. And still there isn't enough food to put on the table. My children are hungry. Rebbetzin, I can't go on with this day after day. Please, you've got to help me."

Well, the rebbetzin was used to giving advice. She was known as the town's khakhome, or wise woman, and women came to her often with their problems. She immediately sat Rivke down and offered her some warm tea. Rivke drank gratefully, warming her stiff fingers on the cup.

From across the rough wooden table, the rebbetzin looked intently at Rivke. Then she gazed long and hard at a spot on the wall. Then she looked back at Rivke. And then she looked again at the spot on the wall. Back to Rivke. Back to the spot on the wall. Back and forth, back and forth. But finally, she looked at Rivke and she spoke. "Rivke," she said, "I know that your life is difficult. That you have a heavy load to carry. But I have a plan. I want you to go home and put all your troubles in a bundle. In a pekl. And then come back here."

Well, that very afternoon, Rivke returned to the rebbetzin's house, huffing and puffing under the enormous weight of the pekl of problems that she carried on her back. As soon as she turned the corner to the rebbetzin's house, Rivke could see that things were not as they had been that morning. From the house Rivke could hear the loud, excited chatter of many women. And when Rivke entered, she saw, crowded tightly together, all the other women of the shtetl, each with her own pekl.

With great difficulty, the rebbetzin quieted the women. And then she spoke. "Rivke," she said, "You will have the opportunity to exchange your pekl for any other pekl here."

Well, Rivke was ecstatic. She knew her life would improve by at least a thousand percent. She quickly ran to the smallest pekl. But you know, when she went to lift it, it was heavy. It weighed more than her own huge pekl. When she opened it she saw that it contained only one problem: the death of a tiny infant child. Well, Rivke immediately tied up that pekl. She knew that this tragedy was one she would never want in her own life. Though her children drove her crazy, she would not want to be without them; they were her lifeblood. She quickly moved to the next pekl.

Realizing that the smallest peklekh were not necessarily the best, Rivke went from one pekl to the next, lifting them and putting them down to search for the lightest one. Eventually, she found a pekl that, though larger than her own, weighed almost nothing. Rivke quickly opened it up only to find it filled with the large emptiness of loneliness.

This time, Rivke paused for a moment to think. She thought of sleeping through the night, and then arising in the morning with no screaming children demanding food that wasn't there. She thought about how much less she'd have to sell at the market. She imagined the quiet in the evenings, with no neighbors telling her their problems or borrowing food.

But then, she had to admit that she wouldn't want to be without the people in her life. Though none of them was good enough and she wanted them all to improve, she couldn't live without other people. And so, glancing over her shoulder as she moved, she left that pekl behind and walked to the next pekl. But you know what, it also had problems she wouldn't want. And so did the fourth.

Rivke was just heading over to the fifth pekl—as you can imagine, her pace had slowed considerably by this time—when she noticed that her own pekl had mysteriously shrunk by half. Rivke realized she might well be seeing things, and she was not one to be taken for a fool. And so, very slowly and tentatively, she walked back to her own pekl. And sure enough, it was only half as big as when she'd arrived. She easily hoisted it over her shoulders. With a smile on her face and a jaunty step, and without looking back at anyone, she left the rebbetzin's house on her way home.

Note

1. The opening quote, "If you could hang . . .", was taken from *Words Like Arrows*, compiled by Shirley Kumove (New York: Schocken, 1985).

GRANDMA'S CHALLAH
Marilyn Price

Marilyn Price *has been a puppeteer, storyteller, educator, and author since 1974. Specializing in Jewish stories and imagination stretching, she creates all her puppets with several things in mind: to illustrate the story, to help in the imaginative process and to recycle! (Nothing is safe!) She travels telling stories (with and without her puppets) across the United States, appearing at libraries and schools, major corporations, and synagogues. She has also appeared as a storyteller and puppeteer in* Puppets and Paradigms, *an educational video. Marilyn lives in Evanston, Illinois, with her husband, Roger. They have two grown children, Matt and Sarah.*

Stuart•Rogers•Ltd.

A story should be like a good friend, someone you wish to be with repeatedly and have all your other friends meet, someone you can learn from and someone you never get bored with. To tell a story that is like a good friend is a gift for the giver and the receiver. I share this with you as I introduce a good friend—"Grandma's Challah."

This particular story has many ancestors. It is a combination of a variety of folktales dealing with the special flavors of Shabbat. Even the journey of the king from his palatial home to the young girl's grandma's humble home recalls the words of the Talmud, "The Shabbat transforms the poorest home into a palace" (Shabbat 119a). It is also extremely flexible, as you can tell it over the course of the year, changing "challah" to suit the food choice of the holiday. It works remarkably well with latkes on Chanukah, hamentaschen for Purim, and so forth. However, for me it is rich with memories from my childhood of visits to my grandparents. Hopefully, someday it will remind my children by recreating their memories from the kitchens of their growing up.

My grandfather, Alex Berger, retired early to take care of my grandmother, Mabel, who had Parkinson's disease for as long as I can remember. At least twice a week, my brother David and I would walk to their apartment after school and end up in their kitchen. As often as not, Grandpa made cookies. My Grandpa Alex, who was a great teller of his own tales, was not a great cook. As a matter of fact, his cookies generally became one cookie, as he usually was talking and forgot to leave room between them. But oatmeal cookies have never been the same as that giant cookie of Grandpa's. And the smell of any cookie baking to this date always makes me smile, remembering the warmth of that kitchen, his devotion to my grandma, and most especially, how he taught me the gift of telling stories.

Now, my paternal grandparents, the Leibovitzes, were Rumanian, and the style of their cooking was quite different from my "American" grandparents (all of whom were first-generation American-born). They also lived at least three bus transfers away (as opposed to my Berger grandparents, to whose apartment we walked). But travel we did, and when we entered their apartment (on the West Side of Chicago—as notorious a place as the Lower East Side of New York), we were assailed with the smell of garlic. Grandma Libby was always—no exaggeration—always in the kitchen, and Grandpa David was always standing at the front window. To my grandma, with her very soft skin and ample bosom, who wrapped her arms around me but had little to say to me but "Eat," to her I owe my affection for the things in life that are strong and simply made, that get to the point and that do their job well.

Now of course, I had no idea of any of this while growing up in Chicago. All of it was pleasant, and none of it pertinent. I had no idea that my mind was being fed at the same time as my body. That is not unlike what many of us think about if we think at all about Jewish foods that are relevant to the holidays. The warmth and affection of their preparatory acts are not the major significance of their being. There is so much more that takes place in the kitchen than just cooking.

When I started to tell this story, to my own children and others, I put it into the "kitchen" of my storytelling house by using puppets made with kitchen objects. The king is a large fork; the chef, a bread board; and a potpourri of the others help to stretch the imaginations of my audiences and encourage them to make these objects and tell their own stories. The story works with or without puppets.

"Grandma's Challah" is not just Jewish because the bread is a symbol of Shabbat. "Grandma's Challah" teaches us of the "recipes" we hand down from generation to generation: the lessons of our Judaism, the warmth of the home. When I tell "Grandma's Challah," I remember my grandparents, cooking and loving and telling me stories; I remember Shabbat and holidays with them and my immediate family now; and I *smile in the telling.*

nce upon a time there was a little boy, not unlike some of you. He lived with his mom and dad, his grandma and his grandpa, six brothers, four sisters, twelve cousins, six aunts, four uncles, and a large quantity of servants (who could count that high?) in a very large building that they called "home" and others called "the castle." For you see, his daddy was the king; his mom, the queen; and, most especially, his grandma was in charge of making challah. And she was good at it. Thinking of that challah made him shiver with excitement and quiver with delight. Making challah with Grandma on a Friday afternoon before Shabbat was a magical time for him. He said that when he grew up to be king, no other challah except Grandma's would do! But alas and alack, when he became king, Grandma had died and all he had left was her recipe.

So, early one morning, he called out to his royal chef, "Royal chef, royal chef, come here." And the royal chef came running. "Yes, your Majesty, what would you like?" "Why Grandma's challah, of course," replied the king. "But sir, I am not your Grandma. I, however, would love to make you my challah," said the chef (who, by the way, was the finest baker in the kingdom). "Nonsense," said the king, "only Grandma's will do. So you must use her recipe and please, don't leave anything out. It must taste just like Grandma's."

And so the royal chef raced all over the kingdom, buying only the finest ingredients. He read the recipe once, and then twice, and then again. He measured thoroughly and checked everything twice. Then he added, stirred, kneaded, braided the dough, let it rise once and then again, and gently placed it into the oven. When the timer went off, he carefully removed the challah, set it before the king, and smiled. "Here it is Your Majesty, just like Grandma's."

The king nodded wisely, took a royal sniff, ripped off one piece, said the *motzi* (the blessing over the bread) and popped it, still warm from the oven, into his royal mouth. He chewed it with his royal teeth and swallowed it down his royal throat. Then he turned to the chef and said, "Now I do wish to be polite, because it isn't the worst challah I have ever eaten but . . . it is definitely not my grandma's recipe. Are you sure you did not leave anything out?" "Absolutely, your majesty. I followed the recipe exactly," said the chef. "But it isn't my grandma's challah; I'll have to ask another chef," the king said sadly.

The very next day, the king called in another chef. Although he was excited to try his luck, he was very nervous. Anxious to please the king and win his favor, he did exactly as the chef before him, only more so. He bought the finest ingredients and measured them once, twice, and then again. He added, he stirred, he kneaded, he braided the dough, he let it rise once and then again, and then he put it in the oven and set the timer. When the timer went off, he brought the bread before the king. The king took a royal sniff, and then he smiled, saying, "It smells just like Grandma's." He again pulled off a piece of the challah, said the blessing, lifted the bread to his royal lips, chewed it with his royal teeth, swallowed it down his royal throat, and said, with the saddest expression on his face, "I know that you tried ever so hard, and I want it to be ever so perfect, but this is not anything like my Grandma's challah."

And so it went. Everyone in the castle tried the recipe but failed, so the king went to the people. He came to your house, and mine, and the home of the people next door. Everyone tried, and everyone failed. The king became quite depressed; he thought he would never experience Shabbat with Grandma's challah again.

And then one day, walking through the kingdom came a young girl who was not unlike some of you. She was on her way to her grandma's house. When she saw the very sad-looking king, she stopped and expressed her concern. "Why Majesty, whatever is the trouble?" "The trouble," replied the king, "is the challah." "Oh Majesty, challah is not trouble, challah is wonderful. Why, my grandma's challah makes me quiver with excitement and shiver with delight!" "It does? My grandma's challah did the same," said the king, "but Grandma is gone and now all I have left is her recipe, and that makes me miss her even more. No one seems to be able to make it just like she did." Well, of course the young girl invited the king to visit her grandma with her that very afternoon. And of course he went.

When they arrived at Grandma's, she flung open the door, hugged her granddaughter, and was amazed at the sight of a king at her front door. "Why Majesty, what a treat! What brings you here besides my granddaughter?" The king told her of his wish to have a challah just like the challah that his grandma had made for him, and how everyone else had tried but failed (even his finest chefs), and how he feared that he would never taste challah like his grandma had made, and how very much he missed her.

The girl's grandma asked to see the recipe and then, without one further word, she sat the king at her table while she measured and added and stirred and kneaded and braided, letting the dough rise twice before she put it in the oven and set the timer. Naturally, while the challah was baking, they all cleaned up, and when the timer went off, Grandma removed the bread from the oven and set it before the king. Together, they said the *motzi*. The king chewed, swallowed and . . . smiled! "Now that's challah like my grandma made! But how did you do it—why does your challah taste just right when even my finest chefs' efforts failed?"

With a smile on her face (it was as big as the king's smile), Grandma said, "Why, dear Majesty, that's easy. When I made challah for you, I made it like I make it for my granddaughter: I made it with love. You see, Majesty, it's love that's the secret ingredient."

And that's the truth!

HOW I LOST
MY DIAMOND RING
Leslie Robbins

Leslie Robbins, *founder of Jewish Storytelling Arts (Ontario), has been a professional storyteller since 1983. She tells a variety of stories with a special love of Jewish tales. She tells in theaters and on radio, as well as in schools, in libraries, and at community events. She also uses life-size puppets, masks, clowning, and music. Her shows include "The Golem of Toronto," "Fried Onions and Garlic," and "The Singing Shtetl." Leslie lives in Toronto with her husband and children.*

The story of "How I Lost My Diamond Ring" is a totally true personal tale. I originally shaped and told this story for the Cabaret Evening of the 1988 Toronto Festival of Storytelling and I have since told it at our temple and on many other occasions. I love to tell this story for several reasons.

First of all, who is there on earth who has not lost something of value? Yet often, we take such events too seriously. We criticize ourselves for being foolish and careless when we are simply being human. It is reassuring to know that we can be foolish yet still end up living "happily ever after."

Second, this story is a reminder that there are many good and honest people living in the world, people who will always return a lost wallet full of money or a misplaced diamond ring!

And last, the fact that the ring keeps finding its way back to me is an example of a true miracle. It had been gone from my house for nearly two years, traveling more than a hundred miles, and yet, through fate and circumstance, it ended up back on my dresser. I took it as a sign from the heavens that I am eternally linked, not only to my husband but also to my beloved in-laws, who originally bought me that ring.

I should tell you that I have worn that ring face up from 1980 until now. It never left my finger until one day a few weeks ago,

231

when I was telling a story to some young girls. The story involved a diamond ring, and one of the girls asked to try on my diamond ring. I obliged, but only with great difficulty. You see, as I am getting older, my knuckles are somewhat swollen with arthritis. Then, after she handed it back to me, there was no way the ring of my youth would fit back on my finger. I do intend to have it enlarged. But meanwhile, the ring is sitting in my grandmother's silver ring case, wrapped in a cloth, at the back of the middle part of my top dresser drawer. It's a very good hiding place!

---

 lost my diamond ring! Of course, anyone can lose a diamond ring, if they have one. But I lost my diamond ring three times, and that takes a special kind of mind. Well, I am not going to tell you about the first time, and I am not going to tell you about the last time. But I will share with you the story of how I lost my diamond ring the second time.

You must understand that my parents raised me to be a modest girl, not showy or ostentatious. It was no surprise when I chose a very modest young man to be my husband. When we became engaged, he bought me an engagement present, but not the traditional ring. He bought me a chess set, $39.95 it was, and that was not cheap in 1968. Now maybe my in-laws thought that their son was remiss in not supplying the ring for the finger. Or maybe they wanted insurance that I really would marry their son. But whatever the reason, in the summer of 1968, my generous in-laws gave me a beautiful one-carat, brilliant-cut diamond set in a twenty-four-carat gold ring.

Now, think back to the 1960s: the sit-ins and marches against everything from the Vietnam War to the cruel treatment of rats in the university psychology labs. I was a part of that generation—the nonmaterialistic reaction to the overconsumption of the postwar boom. How could I wear a huge diamond "rock" to a protest rally? Yet I felt obliged to wear this gift that was a token of so much.

So, for those first few years, I always wore the ring face down, turned under so that no one could see the diamond. Back in those days, I was a kindergarten teacher and wearing the ring turned under got in my way. When I played my autoharp or when I drew pictures, it scratched things.

Then one day I asked myself, "What is the point of wearing a diamond ring turned under so that no one can see the diamond?" That was the moment when I made the decision to wear the diamond ring turned up, *but only* on special occasions, at family *simchas*. That way, I would not be embarrassed by wearing a big, showy diamond in my ordinary day-to-day life. I would safely save it for special occasions when appreciative family could enjoy its flash.

So I carefully stashed the ring in one of my jewelry boxes. I had so many beautiful boxes. One was of engraved sterling silver with little wooden sections inside. Then there were the two black lacquered boxes hand-painted in India, one with orange figures sitting in the lotus position on cushions and the other covered with red and gold flowers with tiny blue stems. I also had two alabaster boxes with mother-of-pearl and other cut stones inlaid to form lovely flowers. I was sure that my ring would be safe in one of these boxes.

Then, in 1975, my husband and I had our first baby and bought our first home. Painters and other workers were constantly wandering through the house, and I got to thinking that you never can tell what one of these workers might put their hands on and slip into their pockets.

So, I began hiding the ring in more creative places. For example, I wrapped it in tissue paper and put it in my little sewing kit, which I hid behind my sweaters. Sometimes, I put it in a little felt bag with a drawstring and rolled it in a brassiere that I also wore only on special occasions. Or else I would put it in the tiny, tarnished silver ring case that my grandmother had given me. Along would come a family celebration, a *simcha*, and out would come the precious little one. Then, after the affair, it would go back to its secret hiding place.

Life went on until one night in 1977. Dressed in his overcoat, my husband was waiting for me at the front door. We were on our way to a cousin's wedding. I called out, "I'll be right down. I just have to grab the diamond ring!" But I could not find the ring. Well, a husband can't wait forever! So we went to that *simcha* without the ring. To tell the truth, when the event passed, so did my thinking about the ring—until the next *simcha*. This time, I began looking for the ring when the invitation arrived. I searched my husband's drawers as well as my own; I even looked in my night table. I was somewhat concerned that I could not find this extremely valuable item. I was even more upset when my mother-in-law asked me about it at the affair. "So where's your diamond? I thought you always wore it on special occasions." I was stricken with guilt and began an extensive room-to-room search. I searched every drawer, every cupboard, every shelf, and every corner—high and low. But I could not find the ring. I was very annoyed.

Now, by 1978, our little baby had grown into a mischievous little boy who could have carried off the ring to heaven knows where. Who knows, he may have even flushed it down the toilet! Still I continued my unsuccessful search. Where in the world was my ring? How could I lose such a valuable diamond ring—especially one that I had been hiding so well for all those years? There could only be one explanation. Someone had stolen the ring. Our home was a constant stream of visitors: baby-sitters, repairmen, political activists, and just about anyone who sings. I became increasingly convinced that somebody had stolen my diamond ring.

So, in 1979, we initiated proceedings with the insurance company as I continued the futile search. The ring itself had already been appraised, but my grandmother's silver ring case had not, and I was certain that the ring was in that case. The insurance company asked me to find out the value of such a ring case. After that, they did not foresee any problems with our claim.

Now, it happened that our son was in a nursery school car pool with the son of a jeweler. So naturally, I went to him, at Fraleigh's Jewelry Store, for the evaluation. The afternoon of my visit, the jeweler's wife happened to drop by the store just as her husband was helping me uncover the value of the ring case. I told her the whole sad story of my stolen ring and the grandiose plans we had to spend the insurance money—a European holiday or maybe a small addition to the house.

A few days later, we were sitting around the dinner table when the telephone rang. I answered, and a man's voice asked for me, Leslie Robbins, and then said, "This is David Fisher of Temple Sinai. We have something here that may be of interest to you."

I thought, "Who is this David Fisher and what could he have of interest to me?" I asked, "What do you have of interest to me?" He answered, "I cannot divulge that information over the telephone, but let's just say that it's a matter of considerable worth." Suddenly, it hit me like a lead pipe. "You can't possibly have my missing diamond ring!" Oh no! Our great plans to spend the insurance money were instantly crushed to smithereens. I didn't even finish my dinner but instead got in the car and drove the five minutes to Temple Sinai.

When I entered the office, Mr. Fisher asked if I could describe the ring. Imagine asking a storyteller to describe something! I began telling him of the swirled gold band with the four little claws that hold the round stone. Then I went on to describe the tarnished silver ring case with the torn and faded bit of purple velvet inside. Possibly in an attempt to shut me up, David Fisher took something out of his desk and asked, "Does this look familiar?" There was my missing diamond ring! I could not believe my eyes. After all that searching and all that time, how odd for my ring to turn up here at temple. How was it possible?

Together we figured out the journey that the ring had taken after leaving our home. You may remember that in 1978, many churches and synagogues sponsored Vietnamese boat people who were immigrating to North America. Our temple had adopted a family and collected clothing to offer to them. Knowing that the family had a baby boy, I donated my son's little blue socks, unaware that they were my latest creative hiding place for the diamond ring. So, buried in a plastic garbage bag of clothes, off went the ring. Why the Vietnamese family did not take the little blue socks, I don't know, but the rejects were shipped off to someone else's garage to await the next temple rummage sale in the spring of 1980. Can you imagine the surprise of the woman who bought her son a pair of socks for twenty-five cents and found a diamond ring? The good woman gave the ring back to David Fisher at the temple, who thought he should have it appraised. Naturally, he took it to a temple member who was a jeweler—Ron Fraleigh. When Ron told his wife about the diamond ring found in the silver case at the rummage sale, she recalled my story. And that is how it was that David Fisher phoned me during that memorable dinner.

So, dear readers, I want to publicly thank the Fraleighs, David Fisher, the good woman who returned my ring, and also my in-laws, all of whom gave me cause for a new story.

IF YOU THINK YOU ARE A CHICKEN

Steven M. Rosman

Steven M. Rosman *is a
rabbi who serves the Jewish
Family Congregation in South
Salem, New York. He was
ordained at the Hebrew
Union College–Jewish Institute of Religion and received
his Ph.D. in education from
New York University with
specializations in developmental theory and the uses
of story and imagery in
educational and religious
settings. He is also an international storyteller and
author of six books, including*
Sidrah Stories: A Torah
Companion *and* The Twenty-
Two Gates to the Garden,
and coauthor of Eight Tales for Eight Nights: Stories for
Chanukah. *Steven resides in Ridgefield, Connecticut, with his
wife and two children.*

Deborah K. O'Brien

"If You Think You Are a Chicken" is my version of a parable that
I have heard from many different teachers, from many different
religious traditions, and in a variety of styles. What follows is the
way I tell it. Despite its appeal to people from different religious
backgrounds, I consider this tale to be reflective of Jewish teachings regarding the various types or levels of souls; specifically,
the animal nature of our beings, the *nefesh*, or least spiritually
connected soul; and the divine nature of our beings, the *neshamah*, or essential spiritual nature of our beings. Also, it illustrates
the Jewish mystical notion that dreams are significant sources
of wisdom and enlightenment.

Rabbi Abraham Joshua Heschel, the great contemporary Jewish spiritual master and social activist, observed that "there is
always a correspondence between what man is and what he knows
about God." We human beings are alone among God's creatures
and creations to be fashioned *b'tzelem Elohim* or "in the likeness
of the Infinite One." As we examine ourselves we notice ten fingers and ten toes, two eyes, one nose, skin and hair, arms and

legs, but with which sense do we apprehend that part of ourselves that carries the spark of the Infinite One? I am convinced that it is not with any of our conventional five senses. *Kabbalah*, or the Jewish mystical tradition, introduces us to less known senses which enable us to glimpse the *b'tzelem Elohim* that is personally ours.

Most people live the years allotted to them without discovering the particular, unique, and very personal blessing, what kabbalists refer to as our *tikkun*, which the Infinite One has implanted within us. Sadly, for most people, this divine seed will remain *in potentia*, throughout our earthly existence. Yet there are some fortunate ones who are granted the gift of such a blessed discovery. Since the Infinite One has infinite ways to live uniquely in each of us who lives, has lived, and will yet live, the *b'tzelem Elohim* implanted in our souls is not the same as our neighbors, our ancestors, or our progeny. Our great teachers of an earlier age have taught us that "a human being stamps many coins in one mold and they are all alike; but the King who is king over all kings, the Holy One, blessed be He, stamped every person in the mold of the first person, yet not one of them resembles the other."

My tale, which I received orally from other teachers, who, I suppose, received it in the same way from theirs—after all, "to receive" is the meaning of *kabbalah*—is a path to understanding that we each have the freedom to recognize the *b'tzelem Elohim* that is ours. Consequently, we can be lifted by such a blessed discovery to the heights of spiritual bliss and a life of spiritual service in the name of the Infinite One, or we can fall prey to the flock of naysayers who, oblivious to their own divine birthrights, attempt to persuade us to "go along with the crowd" and join them in their utterly vain and mundane existence.

Rather than the age-old dilemma about the chicken and the egg, this tale allegorizes the spiritual identity crisis that asks us to choose: the chicken or the eagle.

---

ne night, a young boy crossed the threshold of the Waking World and entered the World of Dreams. At first, all the boy could do was see what there was to see in this other world, and he saw the garden outside his home. How different it was. It was much larger than he knew it to be. It was so enormous that a mountain stood within its walls, a mountain that was so high its peak could not be seen.

At first only visual, the dream was now audible, too. The boy heard thunder echoing through the garden. Its rumble came in rolls and seemed to be coming from the mountain.

The child looked upon the mountain expecting to see the source of the thunder. But what he saw surprised him. Not an avalanche . . . or a herd of wild goats, it was a single egg that caught a ray of the sun as it rolled and sent the ray gleaming across the garden and to the eyes of the boy.

An egg! How could an egg cause such thunder? But things in dreams do not have to be reasonable. They do not have to make sense. The precious child was just discovering this truth about dreams for the first time.

The egg gathered speed as it escaped the grip of the mountain and wobbled over the garden grass until it came to rest at the boy's feet. Ovoid as any usual egg, but golden as something extraordinary, the egg aroused his curiosity.

Bending over and grabbing it with his two hands, the boy lifted the egg and proceeded to examine it. First, he shook it. Then he held it high above his head and searched its surface for clues, any clues of what might be inside. What else could one do with an egg?

Then he sniffed it. He placed it to his ear and listened for signs of life. Stumped for the moment, but still curious, he put it down on the ground and sat before it. Waiting.

In his dream, the child saw himself wait until dark, through the night, and into the next day. The egg did not move, and neither did he.

As the sun rose the next morning, it drew the veil of darkness from over the garden and revealed a chicken coop just yards from where boy and the egg sat.

A chicken coop! There had never been a chicken coop within the walls of the garden before. Well, there certainly was one there now, and it was filled with chickens, and chicks, and roosters. The noise was enough to wake the world, let alone the household. However, no one else stirred. No one else entered the child's dream. It was just him, the egg, and the chickens for now.

What should he do with the egg? The chicken coop seemed like a reasonable place to put it until he figured this one out. And that is what he did. He lifted the egg, opened the coop, and placed the egg among the feathered flock inside.

A long time seemed to pass, but it was hard to tell how long. Dreams do not take place in Waking World time.

The eggshell cracked, sending zigged and zagged lines over its oval surface. Soon the tip of a beak appeared, followed some time later by the creature to which it was attached. There, emerging with feathers dampened by the amniotic fluid that sustained it in the egg, was a bird of sorts. It most certainly was not a chicken. And it was not a rooster. It was not even a turkey, a duck, a goose, or a cygnet. The child was not sure what it was. He was certain only that it was a bird.

In his dream he decided that the coop was the place it should be, for now. He hoped that the birds inside that coop would know more about taking care of another bird, whatever kind it was, than he did.

Again, dream time passed. The child observed the bird grow, and he finally figured out that it was an eagle. Yet, it was being raised as a chicken by its adopted family. The eagle learned to peck at the ground with all of the other chicks. It learned to flap its wings, but never fly very far, like all the other chicks. It even learned to cluck like the other chicks.

As the child watched, the little eagle became a mature eagle. It was much larger than the other chickens. It was even larger and more powerful in appearance than the roosters. But it behaved like a chicken, because that was all it knew to do. It was raised to be a chicken and nothing more.

The eagle believed it was a chicken.

Then, later, a shadow fell upon the birds in the coop. The birds looked up and gasped at the awesome sight they beheld. Above them, a majestic bird glided through the air. Its wingspan was large enough to erase the sun from the sky for an instant.

Immediately the child recognized this winged ruler of the heavens. It was an eagle. Unlike the eagle looking up from the chicken coop, this was an eagle that was raised to be an eagle, that knew he was an eagle, and that behaved like an eagle.

The eagle that believed he was a chicken would never fly like that, would never soar upon the thrust of the wind or rise above the clouds. Just then, the child understood that those who never realize their true natures never attain such things.

AYNENI YODAYA
Donald B. Rossoff

Donald B. Rossoff *serves as rabbi at Temple B'nai Or in Morristown, New Jersey. A native of St. Paul, Minnesota, he studied at Northwestern University, Spertus College of Judaica, the Hebrew University, and the Hebrew Union College–Jewish Institute of Religion, from which he was ordained in 1981. He has played the flute since 1962 and is a member of the Jewish folk-rock group Kol Sasson. Don and his wife, Fran, have four children— Marc, Jenna, Ilana, and Nathaniel—who hear many of the stories before anyone else.*

Daily Record

In the annals of the Jewish People, there are many stories of disputations between Jews and non-Jewish persons or regimes. Those that describe the actual historic encounters between Jewish scholars and non-Jewish scholars are filled with highly intellectual debates on the interpretation of Sacred Scripture and the meaning of history. Through the ages, Jewish scholars have matched wits with the most learned of pagans, Christians, Moslems, and those representing the world of philosophy, and they have invariably emerged victorious, at least when Jews have written the histories. Perhaps the most famous of these is the series of disputations between the great Jewish scholar Rabbi Moses ben Nachman (Nachmanides) and the former Jew-turned– Christian scholar Pablo Christiani.

The story at hand does not fall into this category.

Instead, it takes its modest place among the fictitious stories in which a Jew is set against a non-Jew in some sort of theological or intellectual contest. In these tales, the saving power of Jewish wisdom always prevails, whether it deserves to or not. A number of these stories hinge on the Jewish disputant's Chelmesque naiveté. He does not really know what is going on, and yet his own flawed reasoning helps him prevail.

I love to tell this story in part because it offers a small peek into the structure and dynamics of a traditional Jewish community and conveys a sense of the tension that historically existed between many Jewish communities and their "hosts."

I love to tell this story in part because it teaches a bit of Hebrew and at the same time affords us Jews a healthy laugh at ourselves.

I love to tell this story because it tells of the saving power of Jewish wit and wisdom, assuming a few assists from an unseen helping Hand.

But I really love telling it because it is funny. It has been said that Jewish humor can best be described as a guffaw followed by a sigh. Such is the humor of "*Ayneni Yodaya.*" (A warning: This version of the story is not easily told in Hebrew.)

---

nce there was a king. He was a very smart king. He wasn't very wise, but he was very smart. And because he was so very smart, he wanted to know all there was to know about his kingdom and the people who lived there.

One day, he heard about a group of people who lived in his kingdom—"Jews" they were called. These Jews had their own laws and their own customs, which were quite different from the laws and customs of his other subjects. "I must learn about these Jews," thought the king. So he decided that he would live among them for a time to study their holy books and learn of their ways.

The Jews welcomed the king with open arms and eagerly taught him what he wanted to know. At first, he sat in the *heder* and learned with the children. "Kawmetz aleph—'aw.' Kawmetz beis—'baw.'" It was not long before he had graduated to the Yeshiva. Because he was so smart, he mastered the Talmud and all the commentaries as well as any of the rabbis. And then, having learned all he wanted to learn, he returned to his palace.

Well, it was not long before things started going badly for the kingdom. Enemies were threatening from all around, and there was not enough food for the people, who grew hungrier and angrier each day. They wanted someone to blame for all their problems.

Now the king thought to himself, "If they start blaming me

for all their problems, perhaps they will stop paying their taxes. They may even rebel against me." But then the king, who was not very wise but was very smart, remembered something that he had learned when he was with the Jews. Every time a ruler needed someone else to blame all his troubles on, he could always use the Jews as scapegoats. "All of our problems are due to the Jews," declared the king. "I hereby order that all the Jews be expelled from our kingdom!"

Well, the Jews were in a panic. They sent their wisest scholars, the very rabbis who had been the king's teachers, to plead with him for mercy. "How could you do this to us?" they asked. "Why, we took you in and treated you like one of our own. We deserve better than this! We taught you everything and you became almost as learned as we are."

"*Almost* as learned?" asked the king. "Why, I believe that I became *more* learned than any of you. I will tell you what. I will give you an opportunity to save yourselves. I will pit my knowledge against the greatest of your scholars. If my learning proves less than his, then you may stay and I will double your wealth. But if my learning proves greater than his, all of your scholars will be put to death!" The Jews protested even more, but the king's mind was made up. "Go back and choose that man who will match his learning to mine!" he said.

Back in the synagogue, there was great weeping and tearing of garments. "We are doomed," said the rabbis, for they knew how great was the king's knowledge. No one would come forward to face him. No one wanted the fate of the Jews on his shoulders. Finally, a mouselike voice was heard from the back: "I'll go. I'll face the king."

Everyone turned around to see who had uttered these words. "Oh no," they all cried, "now we are doomed for sure!" For the voice in the back belonged to none other than Shloime the Beadle. Shloime had been the slowest student in the history of the *heder* and had never made it to the Yeshiva. But since no one else would go, with shaking hands and trembling hearts, they took Shloime to go against the king.

"Here are the rules of the contest," declared the king. "We will present each other with questions. Whoever fails to answer a question instantly loses. My trusted bishop will be the judge and his decision will be final!"

Shloime was led to a chair directly facing the king's throne. "I will flip a coin to determine who asks the first question," announced the bishop. "Heads," yelled the king as the coin spun in the air. "Tails it is," said the bishop. "Let the Jews ask the first question."

All eyes were on Shloime. Shloime looked sheepishly at the king and said in a low voice, "Your highness, what do the words *ayneni yodaya* mean?"

"I do not know," said the king.

"The king does not know," declared the bishop, "and so the Jews win!"

All the Jews surrounded Shloime, smothering him with hugs and kisses. They lifted him onto their shoulders and carried him back to the synagogue like a king. They poured the schnaps and made endless toasts to Shloime's brilliance.

Finally, when things began to settle down, the head of the community went up to Shloime and said, "Reb Shloime, we will forever be in your debt. But tell us, if you will, how did you think of such a clever question?"

"Well," said Shloime, "it is like this. When I was still in *heder*, my grandfather, of blessed memory, used to take me with him to hear the great Rebbe. The Rebbe would teach and then he would answer questions. One day, a student in the back of the shul raised his hand and said, 'Rebbe, what do the words *ayneni yodaya* mean?'

"'I do not know,' said the Rebbe. And so I figured, if the *Rebbe* didn't know, the king wouldn't know either!"

I ALREADY HAVE WHAT I WANT AND NEED

Charles Roth

Charles Roth *was schooled in New York yeshivas. He served as executive editor of the* National Jewish Post and Opinion *for twenty-nine years and also worked as a broadcaster for ABC news. He is currently doing research on growth and change through Torah. He is a reteller of hasidic tales and songs. Charles lives in Woodstock, New York.*

I have loved telling hasidic tales since 1974.

I was raised hasidic and attended New York Yeshivas. I first heard hasidic tales being put to bed by my father. As I grew I heard them often at his guest-laden Shabbat table and the hasidic sh'tibles where my family davvened. Culminating with an exclusively Yeshiva education and for a few years teaching at Orthodox day schools, I left Orthodoxy and joined the agnostic multitude.

A new/old love affair with Hasidism was rekindled by the works of Martin Buber—odd as that may sound. His writing, particularly the Tales, some cogent new methods of prayer that I developed, and my earlier Jewish studies burst forth dynamically in the early 1970s to bring me to a clarity of Torah and God that I had never experienced before. I reached levels of prayer and ecstacy that I knew of only theoretically in my earlier studies. My love for telling hasidic tales grew out of this Teshuvah (return) experience.

In the past twenty years I've told hundreds of hasidic tales. Mostly, I have told them to relate a point of Torah to daily living. I have also used hasidic tales as introductions to mental processes designed to create insights or awarenesses regarding negative

245

personality traits and their amelioration. These processes have served me and others as a form of meditation and prayer.

If told with good Kavana (cogent frame of mind), then the tale being told will carry both the energy of the teller as well as that of the Rebbe. The hasidic tale takes me to a place within myself that feels like the essence of my spirit. So I relate Buber's Tales at every opportunity that comes along.

The story submitted here is based on two Buber tales. When I returned to the book to read them a few years ago I found that, without realizing it, I had changed the ending of the first story. I had always known that I added to and embellished the tales. This, I believe, grew from the response of my love for the Rebbe in the tale and from the love of the message I received. I felt over the years that the ending I was relating was the one I had read back in 1974. In presenting the story here I have offered both endings. The latter is the one found in Buber's book.

In the 1970s, when I related these two tales of Reb Yechiel Michel of Zlotchov, invariably yet seldom at the same point within the story, I would become overwhelmed and cry. As I would begin the tales, I would wonder if it would happen. And I would never know until the overwhelming moment was there. I felt as though I was having an experience, yet watching myself at the same time.

In the last few years I have not cried when telling these tales. However, I am pleased to tell that while I have lost the overwhelming feeling when telling these tales, I have found it in others.

---

 ne time after a Shabbat, the Balshem called a Hasid, who had been his guest for Shabbat, and told him, "On your way back home I want you to stop off in a small town called Yampol and give my regards to a wonderful disciple of mine, Reb Mechaleh." (This man was later known as Reb Yechiel Michel of Zlotchov.) The Hasid was overjoyed. Spending the Shabbat with the Balshem was a rejuvenation. For him, the Balshem talked in such a way that it reached directly to his soul and moved it to ecstasy. The Balshem related Torah in a way that made his soul soar from his body and into the heavens. So now he was elated that, halfway home, he would be able to meet one to whom the Balshem referred as a wonderful disciple.

So he set off eagerly, and when he came to Yampol he ran to the Synagogue and asked people there where he would find

Rabbi Mechaleh. One person responded, saying, "We don't have a Reb Mechaleh in our town; our Rabbi's name is Reb Yankev. Not only that, but there's no one in our town called Mechaleh except for one who takes the children to Cheder, and they call him the 'crazy person.'" Well, thought the Hasid, the Balshem used to take small children to Cheder, and his heart leaped and beat a little faster. The Hasid asked, "Why do the children call him crazy?" The man responded, "What would you call a person who bangs his head against the wall during prayer and reads books that we've never seen, and still further, never speaks to anybody?" Now the man's heart beat even faster, and he asked to be told where to find him. "What's the point in that since he never speaks to anybody? But I'll tell you a trick—if you tap him on the shoulder and say you're hungry, he will close his book and feed you, and then you can talk to him."

The Hasid now joyously hurried to where he was directed and found Reb Mechaleh studying over a large book, swaying gently back and forth. He tapped him on the shoulder and said, "I'm hungry." Reb Mechaleh closed his book, searched for a coin, went out and bought herring and bread, brought it back, and put it before the guest. Then Reb Mechaleh sat opposite the Hasid and quietly looked at him while he ate. After a while, the Hasid said, "I bring you a regards from the Holy Balshem." Reb Mechaleh's eyes lit up and excitedly he asked, "Were you with the Balshem during this past Shabbat?" The Hasid nodded. Reb Mechaleh's eyes lit up even brighter and he said, "You have to tell me every word that the Balshem uttered from before Shabbat until after Havdalah."

So the Hasid began to relate everything he had heard from the Balshem. As he did so, Reb Mechaleh's face shone with exhilaration. With each word the Hasid uttered, Reb Mechaleh seemed to bloom, and a shining aura seemed to surround his body. The Hasid felt that he was the carrier of secret wisdom, of words laden with deeper meaning. He related everything to Reb Mechaleh that he heard during Shabbat. By this time, Reb Mechaleh was in ecstasy, and while he still sat in front of the Hasid, his soul was transported to another reality. "Tell me," said the Hasid, "I've seen by the way you grasp and respond to the Balshem's teaching that you are exceedingly steeped in learning to say the least. Yet the people here think you're crazy. From my meager knowledge of Torah, I know that in practice, you could have anything you want. You could leave here and do anything you pleased. How is it, then, that you remain here in poverty, ridiculed and thought to be a crazy person?" Reb Mechaleh looked at him with sparkling and shining eyes and replied quietly, "If you understand the power of Torah so deeply, and you understand that I could have everything I want, how is it then that you don't understand that I already have everything I need *and* everything I want."

Other Hasidim claim that Reb Mechaleh responded with a parable. He related that there was once a king who invited all his subjects to the festive marriage of his daughter, the princess, whom he loved dearly. The invitation sent by the king promised an extensive multicourse dinner to celebrate the event. But before the date set for the wedding, the princess suddenly died. The king grieved, as did nearly all of his subjects except one, who showed up on the wedding date, invitation in hand, demanding to be served the sumptuous dinner in every detail. Then said Reb Mechaleh to the Hasid, "Should I behave as crassly as the invitation holder and demand my due while the *Shechina* is in exile, separated from her lover?"

Word quickly spread about Reb Mechaleh. People heard about him and a delegation came to the Balshem from a small town and requested that he appoint Reb Mechaleh as their Rabbi. "Good," said the Balshem, "I agree. Go and tell him that it's time for him to leave his studies and become your Rabbi." Joyfully they approached Reb Mechaleh and informed him that the Balshem had designated him as their Rabbi. Reb Mechaleh replied: "There must be some mistake. My job is to sit here and learn and I will continue to do that."

So, regretfully and sadly, they returned to the Balshem and told him of Reb Mechaleh's refusal. The Balshem sternly said, "I want you to tell him that I insist that he become your Rabbi." They returned once more and told Reb Mechaleh that the Balshem insisted he become their Rabbi. Reb Mechaleh thought and thought. It wasn't like him to countermand the Balshem's instructions. He thought and then finally said: "It's not my place to be a Rabbi, and again I must refuse." Regretfully, they returned to the Balshem and told of Reb Mechaleh's continued refusal. The Balshem ordered the delegation to bring Reb Mechaleh before him, which they did.

The Balshem looked at Reb Mechaleh and said, "I've ordered you before, and now I'm ordering you again, to assume the role of Rabbi of this congregation." Reb Mechaleh quickly responded: "Tell me to walk off a cliff and I will gladly do it; tell me to jump into the ocean and I will jump unhesitatingly. Anything the Rebbe would tell me to do would be carried out instantly, but I cannot assume this role of Rabbi. I have to continue to study." The Balshem responded angrily, saying, "If you don't accept this position I will take away your *Olam Hazeh* and *Olam Haba*" (meaning, "I will remove from you this world and you will also lose the world to come"). Reb Mechaleh grew pale and ashen white. He trembled, and tears welled up his eyes. He thought for a long time and, with tears streaming down his pale cheeks, said, "I will jump into the fire if the Rebbe so ordered, as Abraham did, but I cannot fulfill this role." The Balshem's stern face softened to a smile. He looked squarely into the eyes of Reb Mechaleh and said, "Return to your study, my friend. You have passed the temptation."

THE DAY THE RABBI STOPPED THE SUN

Robert E. Rubinstein

Robert E. Rubinstein *has recorded three storytelling cassettes. His* The Rooster Who Would Be King & Other Healing Tales *received a Parents' Choice Seal of Approval. He directs the nationally known Troupe of Tellers from Roosevelt Middle School, as well as "Eugene's Multicultural Storytelling Festival." He has published two young-adult novels, over a hundred articles, and* Hints for Teaching Success in Middle School, *which was based on his years of teaching. Robert lives with his wife and three teenage children in Eugene, Oregon.*

The past twenty-three years of my working life has largely focused on teaching—teaching middle school. As a parent of three teenagers who must survive and who, hopefully, will live happily as adults in tomorrow's world, I also try to teach them—but how do you teach? How do you make learning meaningful and relevant, a life experience for young people, including for your own children?

In our Jewish life and tradition, the rebbe or rabbi is the teacher from whom we seek to learn and understand life as a Jew, both religious and secular, through the Torah, the Talmud, and the rabbi's wisdom and perception. It's not enough, though, just to learn facts and verses and to discuss ideas. For learning to truly have meaning, what is learned must relate to life, to living life in the present time. A rabbi, or any teacher, cannot command a student to learn, but can only provide the opportunities, the atmosphere, and the encouragement to learn. To do this, the rabbi-teacher must understand each student—the student's needs and the student's heart.

This story is about such a relationship: about a rabbi who understands the heart of his student and what the student needs to make learning part of life.

The source of this story is a local legend concerning "The Wonderful Rabbi of Rivington Street" and collected in *The Sidewalks of America*, edited by B. A. Botkin. I have recorded this story on my audiocassette, *The Day the Rabbi Stopped the Sun and Other Jewish Tales*.

---

 riday morning came. It was a bright, clear morning on Rivington Street in the Lower East Side. The sun had already begun to warm the hard squares of cement sidewalk.

After he finished leading the morning prayers, the Rabbi walked out from the small synagogue. He stretched and turned his face to the sun's full rays. He smiled—a warm smile. His full, red beard seemed to glow and sparkle in the light. And this Rabbi of Rivington Street laughed—the laughter of life.

The Rabbi then walked slowly down the streets of the neighborhood, where many of the members of his congregation lived. He nodded and smiled and waved to those he met. Often he would stop and chat with someone or bend down to talk quietly to a child.

Today, behind the Rabbi walked his best student. This student wore glasses, stood tall and thin, and walked rigidly, filled with his own self-importance. After all, he thought, "I should walk this way! The famous Rabbi has chosen *me* to accompany him today. An honor! It's a special privilege to be with the Rabbi and to listen to his wise words. Others will see me, too, and will treat me with respect." And so he looked down solemnly as the famous Rabbi bent to take a small child's hand in his own.

The Rabbi continued on. "Yussel, my friend, how is business with your fruits and vegetables?"

"Shalom, Rabbi. A fine day!" greeted Yussel the grocer. "Since you blessed my business when it opened, Rabbi, it has done very well. Thank you."

The Rabbi smiled and nodded . . . and walked on.

"Rabbi, Rabbi!" called Mrs. Horowitz as she looked down from her third floor apartment window.

The Rabbi stopped and looked up, shading his eyes from the

glare of the sun's light. The student frowned. "No one should yell from their apartment at the famous Rabbi like this."

"Rabbi, I want to thank you so much. My rheumatism, my aching bones, they feel so much better now since you came to see me. What a miracle you have performed!"

Again, the Rabbi smiled and nodded . . . and walked on.

The student continued to follow behind, never daring to say a word to the great Rabbi. He only spoke to the Rabbi if the Rabbi happened to speak to him first. Now the cantor, the one who sang the service in the small synagogue on Rivington Street, came to the Rabbi. "Shalom, Rabbi. Did you know, Rabbi, that Jacob, who moved to the Bronx, is very ill? He told me he would like to see you if that were possible."

The Rabbi remained silent, remembering his good friend Jacob. "No, I did not know he was ill. I must visit him immediately."

The Rabbi, with the student following behind, hurried to the nearest subway train entrance and boarded a train to travel to see Jacob. But the Rabbi had not traveled to the Bronx very often. He got off the train at the wrong stop. So the two walked down strange city streets toward Jacob's home in the Bronx.

Perhaps they walked a mile, twisting down this street, crossing over to the next, and peering into dark, narrow, garbage-strewn alleys between tall apartment houses. They asked directions. The student grew weary and his legs ached. But the Rabbi did not slow his pace, and the student would not speak to the Rabbi.

In one of these alleys was a girl. She was a child of eight or ten, and not one of the Rabbi's congregation. But the Rabbi of Rivington Street heard her crying. He went into the alley to see what was wrong.

The girl sat against the alley wall, hunched over and clasping her knees. She looked dirty, with her face tear-stained and her dress thin and ragged. The Rabbi walked up to her. "What is wrong, my child?" he asked in a soft, gentle voice. Her crying continued. She did not answer.

The Rabbi bent down, placing his hands on her thin, bony shoulders, and slowly raised her to her feet. "What has happened, my child?" But the child would not speak—would not raise her head.

Then, the Rabbi tenderly raised her head with his hand to see her face. He saw upon her face—on her cheek—a large, purple bruise. "How did this happen, child? . . . Did someone do this to you?"

The warmth of the Rabbi's touch, the gentleness of his touch and his words, caused her to answer. She nodded her head once and whispered, "Yes."

"Who—who would do such a thing?"

"My—my uncle," she whispered.

The Rabbi of Rivington Street placed his arm about the shoulders of the girl. He bent and kissed her lightly on the top of her head. "Show me where this uncle lives."

The girl led the Rabbi, followed by the student, out from the alleyway and down the street. They stopped before an old, run-down apartment house and climbed the steps to the front door.

Inside the apartment house, the halls held only shadows and darkness. Voices of unseen people and noises invaded the stained hallways. The three began to climb up the stairs. The Rabbi followed the girl, but the student, feeling afraid of this place, trailed far behind.

After climbing up three flights of the splintered wooden steps, the girl stopped in front of an apartment door. The Rabbi moved in front of the girl and knocked firmly on the wood of the door. Grumbling and heavy footsteps sounded from inside the apartment. The student stood a good distance from the girl and the Rabbi. "A student," he said to himself, "should not have to do these things—to be in these places! A student should stay in the synagogue and study the Torah, the Talmud, discussing ideas with others."

A rough voice yelled, "Who is it? What do you want?" The Rabbi knocked again. Suddenly, the door shot open and a very large man filled the doorway space. He glared down at the Rabbi. "What do you want here?"

The Rabbi stood the girl by his side and together they faced this man. "Did you strike this girl, this child? Your niece? Did you make that large bruise on her face?"

"So? So what if I did? She's *my* niece and she lives here with me, don't she?" The Rabbi stared up into the man's eyes. He fixed a steady gaze on the uncle. Then, he placed one hand lightly on the uncle's arm. The uncle stopped talking, stopped glaring down at the Rabbi and the girl. The anger and strength seemed to drain from the uncle. His face softened.

"You must promise—promise God and promise me—that you will never, never strike this child again," said the Rabbi.

The student, trembling with terror, watched in amazement. It seemed that the Rabbi possessed so much more strength in the hand touching the uncle—so much more—that the uncle could do nothing but obey.

In a low voice, the uncle turned to the child and said, "I am sorry that I hurt you. I will never do it again. I will never hit you again. I promise—I promise before God."

The girl ran to her uncle and hugged him. The uncle lifted her into the air, held her gently in his arms, and kissed her cheek. And the Rabbi of Rivington Street smiled and nodded . . . and walked away.

When they stood outside the apartment house, the student dared to speak: "It is growing late, Rabbi. We must hurry home before evening comes and it is time for the Sabbath."

"We must first visit Jacob. He is very ill and has asked for me. Why else did we take the subway train all the way here? Let us go to him." So the Rabbi continued walking, soon arriving at a small, two-story house squeezed between two tall apartment buildings.

Jacob's bedroom was dark. The curtains had been drawn. Only a small light flickered near the bedside. Jacob lay in the bed, several pillows beneath his head.

"How are you, my friend?" Jacob smiled a small smile. The Rabbi sat on the edge of the bed and took the dry-skinned, wrinkled hand in his own.

"I know I will pass on shortly, Rabbi," said Jacob in a weak voice. "I could ask for nothing more than to see you again. I remember the good times we shared together. . . . With your touch, I feel no pain. The pain is all gone."

"I am glad, my friend. Rest—and find peace." For several more minutes, the Rabbi continued to sit there holding his old friend's hand. Neither one said a word.

The student stood by the bedroom doorway watching. A tear rolled from one eye down his cheek. Quickly, he took his handkerchief and wiped the tear away, and softly blew his nose. Then a second tear fell, and a third. These he did not wipe away. He had begun to understand what he could never learn from just reading books.

Jacob closed his eyes in sleep. The Rabbi gently released the hand and rose from the bed. He walked to the doorway, stopping to turn one last time to look at his friend. Then, the Rabbi left.

Once they had returned to the street, the student became increasingly concerned. "We must hurry, Rabbi! We must hurry! We will be late for the beginning of the Sabbath. We must not travel on the Sabbath. It would be a terrible sin!"

The Rabbi walked on at a steady pace until they at last reached the entrance to the subway. The train roared above the ground and then descended into the dark tunnels. The evening shadows began to cover the city.

"It is too late—too late, Rabbi," moaned the student.

"Have faith," answered the Rabbi. And then—right there on the subway—the Rabbi of Rivington Street began to pray. "God will help us if we have faith," said the Rabbi.

When the train reached the outside world once again, all was covered with night. The passengers stood in the electrically lighted darkness and walked down the streets with shadows. But all around the Rabbi of Rivington Street, and around his student also, was a warm, golden light—sunlight. When they walked from the train station, the light still surrounded them.

This Rabbi, the Rabbi of Rivington Street, had, with the help of God, performed a miracle: he had stopped the sun.

"For us," said the Rabbi, "for us it is still Friday and the Sabbath awaits." And the Rabbi smiled and nodded—his red beard glowing in the sunlight.

THE MIDWIFE'S REWARD

Barbara Rush

Barbara Rush *divides her year between Jerusalem and the United States, combining her loves of librarianship, teaching, writing, storytelling, and Jewish folklore. A retired New York librarian and a professional storyteller, she teaches storytelling and library science for Israel's Ministry of Education. She has published seven books, including the award-winning* The Diamond Tree *and* The Book of Jewish Women's Tales. *Her husband, Don, travels the continents with her.*

This is one of my very favorite stories, which I have told dozens of times: at naming ceremonies, women's programs, even Sabbath programs. And each time I tell it I feel that the story is mine and that Grandmother in the story is my grandmother. Although the story comes from Kurdistan, a place far, both in geographic miles and in cultural habits, from my own home, I can hear this first-person story being told by a Jewish woman and I feel that she is telling the story to me. So in a sense, via the words of the story, I am bound to my Jewish sisters across the world. I hope that, in my retelling, I am transmitting that same feeling to my listeners.

A version of this tale was told to me personally in the late 1970s by a Kurdish woman in her Israeli home in Maoz Zion, a *moshav* near Jerusalem that was originally founded by Kurdish immigrants. I heard the story again from a Queens, New York, resident as we sat next to each other one seemingly endless night on an El Al flight to Israel; her story was about her own Moroccan great-grandmother, the midwife. The story is known to Ashkenazi women as well. The version presented here is based on one found in the Israel Folktale Archives in Haifa University and in published sources, namely *Folktales of Israel*, by my teacher and friend, Dov Noy, and in my own books, *The Jews of Kurdistan* and *The Book of Jewish Women's Tales*.

I love this tale because it reflects the *mitzvah* of participating in the birth of a child—and what moment could be more intimate or rewarding to a woman! My own daughter, Avi, whose children were delivered by midwives, is herself a practicing midwife, having participated in many births. Midwives have, in general, had a good reputation in Jewish folklore since the extensive treatment of Shiphrah and Puah, the midwives of the Hebrews in the Book of Exodus (1:15–21), who, because they feared God, saved the males alive, thus disobeying the order of the King of Egypt. The Babylonian Talmud (Sotah 11b) comments: "It was as a reward to the righteous women who were in that generation that the Israelites were redeemed from Egypt." Could any reward be greater?

I love this tale also because, in it, a Jewish woman who believes in the power of righteousness overcomes the power of evil. And I love it because it is a Jewish woman who transmits the ethic: the reward for a good deed is the deed itself (*Pirkei Avot* or *Sayings of the Fathers* 4:2). This is the message that my mother, of blessed memory, practiced all her life, and so, in some way, when I tell this tale, I feel that my mother (and her values) are with me.

But one of the special beauties of this tale is that it contains another message, a hidden, educational one. By telling this tale, the woman narrator (the tale was traditionally told *by* women *to* women) was instructing her young female listeners how to act if a strange man approached. In that Kurdish community the message was: "Act as Grandmother did! Don't panic or show fear! Remain silent! Think of what to do!"

Do women tell such stories today? Recently, I heard an analysis of a story told by a woman in New York City about her neighbor who, unfortunately, had been raped. This woman teller inserted instructions for her female listeners: "She [my neighbor] should have looked around to see who was following her. She should have had her key ready so that she could get into the house quickly." (Men telling the same story about a neighbor or relative who was raped did not include these instructions.) When I heard this story, I thought, "Why, that's Grandmother's story, with the same catharsis in the telling of the tale, the same emulation of the heroine, and the same educational message to the listeners." The demon may have been replaced by a male rapist, and the setting may have changed from Kurdistan to New York, but yes, we are still telling the same tale.

And, finally, I love this tale because it's a fun tale to tell—and allows for a variety of time and voice changes: the whispering of the cat, the urgency of the husband, the commanding of the chief demon, and the naive voice of Grandmother. Enjoy telling it as much as I do!

y grandmother, may she rest in peace, was a mid-wife. She was always ready for a knock on the door that would call her to her work, to help at the birth of a newborn child. Grandmother worked for the love of it and never asked for any reward. She was sure that her payment would be to go straight to Heaven. Since there were neither doctors nor qualified midwives in the town of Zakho at that time, my grandmother had more work than she could handle.

One day she was sitting outside her house, embroidering. She was very tired after a hard day's work. Suddenly, she saw a beautiful cat creeping quietly into the house, sniffing in all the corners as if searching for food.

My grandmother took a liking to the cat and fed her. As she did so, she noticed that the cat was pregnant. "Ah, if only I could be this cat's midwife," Grandma said to herself.

Days passed, and one dark and stormy night my grandmother was awakened by the sounds of footsteps. There was a rap at the door. She rose quickly, dressed herself, and opened the door. There in the doorway stood a man, tired and sweating as if he had come in a great hurry. "Grandma, come with me," he said. "My wife is about to give birth and there is no one to help her."

Grandmother listened quietly and rejoiced with delight. How lucky that such a request had come to her at this time! "Why, to bring a child into the world on such a stormy night and at such a late hour," she thought to herself, "would be like doing all the 613 *mitzvot* at once."

Now, Zakho is a small town, and Grandma strode up the main street behind the man. She could not understand why she did not hear the sound of his footsteps. Suddenly she noticed that they had gone beyond the last house in the town and were now walking in an open field. Grandma trembled all over, knowing that no one lived there. She understood that the man leading her was none other than a *shed.*

"Lord, have mercy on me," she muttered to herself, but she did not utter a sound. Soon they came to a bridge made of large stones and, thereafter, they entered a huge cave. There Grandma heard a man's voice: "Grandmother, come in. You have reached the place."

Now Grandmother was really frightened. She glanced about; there inside the cave were *shedim* and *shedot,* prancing and dancing and meowing like cats.

"What dreadful company in which to find myself," Grandma thought, but she did not say a word. The *shed* with the longest horns took her aside. "If the newborn is a son," he said, "you will get everything you want, but—if it is a daughter, God forbid!"

Pale with fear, Grandma did not answer a word. She entered the room of the birth, and what did she see? The cat that had visited her a few days before was lying there.

"Dear, dear Grandmother," whispered the cat, "do not eat here or you too will be turned into a *shed.*"

My grandmother listened to the warning of the cat and did not eat anything in the cave during the whole night, even though she was offered the best and most delicious of foods and drinks. When the time for birth came, she rolled up her sleeves and set to work.

A male cat was born. What rejoicing broke out in the cave! Why, the cries of joy even reached the heavens! The chief of the *shedim* called my grandmother to him and said, "Whatever you ask, even up to half my kingdom, I will give you."

"No, no, no!" said Grandmother, "I do not want anything. The reward for a good deed is the deed itself."

"That is impossible! You must take something! This is our custom!" warned the chief.

My grandmother was aware this was a serious matter. She looked around and her eyes fell upon a bunch of garlic in the corner of the room. Grandma asked for a bit of the garlic, just to satisfy the chief of the *shedim,* and before she knew it, the sleeves of her clothes were stuffed with garlic—and the *shedim* quietly escorted her home. Tired and discouraged, Grandma threw the garlic near her door and sank into bed.

The next morning, her grandchild woke her up. "Grandma, Grandma," she called, "from where did you bring so much gold?"

Grandma looked at the door and saw that the garlic was, indeed, nothing else but pure gold. She divided the gold among her children, her grandchildren, and all of her family.

After many years Grandmother passed away. Her children and grandchildren are now scattered all over the world; my sister and I live in *Eretz Yisrael*, the Holy Land. And each of us keeps until this very day a small piece of golden garlic—to remind us of the reward of our grandmother, the midwife, and of her gift to us.

COULD THIS
BE PARADISE?

Steve Sanfield

Steve Sanfield, *a professional storyteller and recording artist, is also an award-
winning author and poet. His
books include* A Natural
Man: The True Story of John
Henry, The Adventures of
High John the Conqueror
(ALA Notable), The Feather
Merchants and Other Tales
of the Fools of Chelm *(Parents' Choice Award), and a
new collection of poems,*
American Zen by a Guy Who
Tried It. *Steve is the founder
and artistic director of the
Sierra Storytelling Festival
and lives in Nevada City,
California.*

It was my grandfather (may his memory be a blessing) who gave
me the gift of stories. He came to this country at the end of the
last century. Like so many others he was seeking a better life,
seeking freedom from pogroms and persecution.

He had been a baker's apprentice in Vilna and he continued to
follow the baker's trade here in the United States. And although
he was a fine, fine baker, what he liked to do most of all was tell
stories. He would tell a story to anyone who would listen: us children, family, friends, coworkers, customers, even strangers. He
would tell you a story even if you didn't want to hear one.

He would never, however, stand up, as many of us do, and
announce that he was going to tell a story. Rather, he would wait
for what he perceived to be the perfect moment. Much like the
Dubner Maggid, who had also grown up in Vilna (130 years earlier) and had become famous for "hitting the bull's-eye" with each
tale, my grandfather always seemed to find the right story for the
right moment.

He and I used to spend every Sunday morning together. We
would always begin by looking at the sepia photo section of
Boston's weekly Yiddish newspaper. He would give me his unique
view of each picture, which might help to explain why I became a
storyteller, and then we'd move on to other topics.

One Sunday morning I was complaining to him about my position in life, much as young people are still prone to do. Nothing was right; everything was wrong. My parents didn't even like me, to say nothing about what my teachers thought of me. Why did we have to live in this small town of Lynn? Why couldn't we live in the capital, Boston, like my cousins? Why couldn't I go to summer camp like my neighbors? Why did I have to wear the clothes my mother picked out? Why couldn't I choose my own?

I went on and on, and my grandfather listened with what now seems like infinite patience. When I finally finished, he said, "Stevela, let me tell you a story." Then he told me this tale.

I have recorded this tale on my audiocassette *Could This Be Paradise?*

---

here was once a man who was unhappy with his life. Nothing seemed to be right. He had to work much too hard for far too little. Neither his friends nor his neighbors gave him the respect he felt he deserved. His wife was always complaining, and his children were never satisfied.

Despite his hopes, his condition did not improve, so he spent most of his time dreaming about Paradise. Whether alone or with others, whether at work or at rest, the idea of Paradise filled his head. "Someday," he kept telling himself, "someday I'm going to go to Paradise."

And one day—no different from any other—he decided that this was the day he was going to set off for Paradise. Rising from his morning table, without saying a word to his wife and his two children, he went out the front door, past the gate with a broken latch, and through the open fields until he came to the edge of the marketplace. He already knew which women would buy what goods from which merchants at what price and what they would argue about. He passed a bakery opposite a butcher shop, moved on through the center of town with its synagogue and town hall, and continued out through another set of fields to the base of a long, steep hill.

He climbed the hill until he reached the beginning of a broad, flat plateau. There he paused and took one last look at his village below. He was sure he would never see it again. He was a man bound for Paradise.

All day he walked along that plateau, and when the sun was setting in the west, he decided to take shelter under a tall pine tree. Before going to sleep he removed his shoes and pointed them in the direction in which he was sure Paradise lay. But— how was he to know that in the darkest hour of the night, a demon, an imp, would come and, whether to punish him, save him, teach him a lesson, or maybe just to play a joke on him, would take his shoes and turn them around? There was no way for the man to know that.

The next morning, the man rose early, said his prayers, and stepped into his shoes, certain that they would lead him to Paradise. Off he went, his head filled with dreams. Suddenly there he was at the edge of the plateau and just below him was Paradise. He had arrived. "Strange," he thought, "it's not much bigger than my own village. Oh well."

He descended the hill and walked through the fields to the center of town. Here in Paradise there was also a synagogue and a town hall. As he stood there looking at them, the man thought, "They've been lying to me all these years—or at least exaggerating. They said that everything in Paradise would shine and gleam, but these buildings, why, they're almost as shabby as those in my own village."

When he passed a bakery that stood opposite a butcher shop, he began to suspect that when he entered the marketplace he would know which women would buy what goods from which merchants at what price and what they would argue about— and he did. Now, more out of sadness than anger, he was sure that if he continued through the fields in front of him he would come to a gate with a broken latch—and he did.

As he stood there pondering his situation, he heard a whining voice from the house. "Come in and eat your food." It was enough to drive a man mad. It sounded just like his own wife. But never having said no to his wife, and being a bit hungry, he went into the house. He sat down, ate some black bread and some herring, and had a cup of coffee.

Two children came running up to him and jumped into his lap. Playing with his beard, the youngest one asked, "You'll stay with us this time, won't you Papa?" Not wanting to say no to the children, he agreed.

And to this very day, that man sits at that table every morning, drinking his coffee, trying to figure out whether he's in Paradise or not.

WINEDROPS ON THE EYELASHES

Zalman M. Schachter-Shalomi

In honor of Howard Schwartz and
Neshamah Carlebach
(daughter of Reb Shlomo)

Zalman M. Schachter-Shalomi, *Reb Zalman, as he is affectionately called, has been at the forefront of pioneering Jewish spiritual renewal. He was ordained at the Lubavitch Yeshiva and holds graduate degrees in psychology of religion and a doctor of Hebrew letters. He is currently professor emeritus at Temple University. Through prayer and meditation, counseling and mentoring, movement, song, storytelling, and philosophical discourses, he shares the central teachings of Hasidism and Kabbalah in a manner that is at once authentic, contemporary, and compelling. In 1962 he founded P'nai Or Religious Fellowship, which has now merged with ALEPH: Alliance for Jewish Renewal.*

Somewhere I read this story, many years after I heard it, and put it into my reveries. In the book it had become flat and lifeless, mere hagiography to get us to say, "Oy, what a Tzaddik the Baal Shem Tov was." I first heard this story from Reb Berl Baumgarten as I described it. It lit a fire in me. In my imagination I stood with Chaim, the Yoshev, the Batlan, at the Besht's door and was with him in his attempts at being a merchant. With him I was in the shipwreck and on the island. With him I was teleported by the Shem back to Mezhibuzh.

There are so many inspiring turns to the story. The Yoshev's life at the Bet Hamidrash of the Baal Shem Tov. His simplicity. How he is deployed by the Besht, through a chain of vicissitudes, to get the Name of the Jumping Road, the *Shem* for *K'fitzat Had-erekh*. (This notion of quantum jump or space warp comes up in many science fiction tales; Frank Herbert's *Dune* picked it up and called the mutant the Kwitzatz Haderekh.) The island sanctuary for those loyal to the God of Israel in a time of idolatry is so reminiscent of the Jews of Djerba and Tunisia, and the purity of their loyalty to tradition, which rejected the incursions of the less traditional Alliance Israelite.

However, the notion that Shabbat on earth in a body of physical resurrection is an even more advanced state than the soul's post mortem spiritual paradisial existence—that was for me most inspiring.

When I first heard the story, I was told that Reb Chaim had said that he could not accept such an offer, no matter how tempting, without the advice of his Rebbe the Besht. Later I heard it with some differences from another source. Now the motive for returning was stressed to be that Chaim did not want to leave his wife, an *Aguna* (an "anchored" and chained-down woman who could not marry, for there was no evidence that she was a widow). And how could he enjoy such a blessed state at such a great expense to his wife and kids?

I liked this ending better and printed it that way in the *Holy Beggars' Gazette*, a journal published by the House of Love and Prayer in San Francisco, Reb Shlomo Carlebach's Bay Area Shtibl of the seventies. It was first published in the Winnipeg *Jewish Post* and later a revised and edited version in the *Yiddishe Heim* of Chabad.

I would tell it often when I conducted a retreat. It set the mood of the participants into a state altered from their everyday routine consensus reality. It provided us with our own *K'fitzat Haderekh* to the state in which miraculous quantum jumps could be made to transformative insights and theophanies. It is a pleasure to share this story in the hope that you too may experience a *K'fitzat Haderekh*. So jump ahead *gezunterheit*.

---

et me tell you a Ma'aseh!

Professor Heschel says, "A Ma'aseh is a story in which the soul surprises the mind." It is a key.

A key is a peculiar thing. You put it in the only opening remaining in a door and seemingly even stop this opening up, but when it is fitted, turned and used, it opens the door.

I heard this Ma'aseh from Reb Berel Baumgarten, who heard

it from Reb Dovid Nosson, who heard it from the Komarner Rebbe, who heard it from his father and he from his, up to Reb Eisikel, and he from the Lubliner, who heard it from the Maggid, who himself heard it from Reb Chaim.

Reb Chaim was a *Yoshev*—a sitter—at the court of the Baal Shem Tov. A sitter sits and learns Torah day and night. The Baal Shem Tov gave him a stipend on the third day of every week: the day on which God twice said, "It is good."

Reb Chaim, waiting at the Baal Shem's door, was this Tuesday not called to receive his stipend. When he came home to his wife she asked for the money and he said that the Baal Shem Tov had not called him this day—an oversight. An oversight that will *misstamme* be corrected next week.

"What should I do in the meantime?" she pressed him.

"Pawn our pillows."

Grudgingly, she did. He, Reb Chaim, studied on.

The next week Reb Chaim stood at the door, waiting, suppliant—in his heart thinking at the Rebbe—"It is I, Chaim, my stipend!—last week—this week—Rebbe!"

But he was not called.

"Chaim! Chaim! What now?" his wife demanded.

"Borrow! The candlesticks, pawn them! The Rebbe will remember. I shall stand near him at the evening service—he will not forget. Perhaps next week."

But the studies soured on him. The flavor was gone. What will be? Perhaps business—*Tachles*!

No, no! The Rebbe will remember. On the following Tuesday Chaim stands at the door and waits. His wife, she paces up and down outside and she, too, waits. Like a sentry on the post she does not leave. So he takes heart, Chaim. He knocks on the door, timidly enters and faces the Rebbe's seemingly anger-clouded face.

"What should I have done, Rebbe—how was I to know that I displeased you. I did not? So what else? You don't want me here—but my three weeks of debts! What am I to do? Business? Rebbe, I have no business sense and such bad luck all the time.

"You will give me a blessing. Amen! So be it. And something so the blessing will be able to take hold? Thank you, Rebbe. I am sure there is a purpose in this. I am resigned. Yes, Rebbe, resigned and alert to my new role."

Reb Chaim thus became a merchant. And what a merchant! The Baal Shem Tov's blessing that he—Reb Chaim—will, with God's help—find favor in the eyes of his beholders—immediately proved potent.

The money became a goose; the goose, a turkey; the turkey, a goat; the goat . . . *Bakitzur*—to make a long story a bit shorter— Reb Chaim was the proud owner of a store, a feed store, a general store. He even had a jewelry counter—a jewelry store.

His supplier of gems tells him that he buys the merchandise in Leipzig. "Leipzig? I can also go there to shop!" Some purpose drives Reb Chaim—and he is off to Leipzig. He can buy the gems direct and have all the profit. There is so much to see in the world. Jews, *Minyonim*, *Rabbonim*. But since Chaim compares them all with Mezhibuzh and the Baal Shem Tov, none of them can really measure up.

Leipzig—the fair—the tumult—the noise. "The jewels don't come from Leipzig? Where from? Amsterdam?" Reb Chaim thinks as long as he is in Leipzig he might as well go on to Amsterdam!

Our Reb Chaim finally gets to Amsterdam. "What? The diamonds come from Africa?" Then Africa! There is something in Reb Chaim that urges him on—Africa!

The journey is long and the sea is wide. Sea travel is not for the former *Yoshev*. He is ill. A storm—up—down, can I say it better than the psalmist?

> They that go down to the sea in ships,
> That do business in great waters
> These saw the works of the Lord,
> And his wonders in the deep;
> For he commanded, and raised the stormy wind,
> Which lifted up the waves thereof;
> They mounted up to the heaven, they went down to the deeps;
> Their soul melted away because of trouble;
> They rolled to and fro, and staggered like a drunken man,
> And all their wisdom was swallowed up—

A rock—a hole in the ship—it sinks. Reb Chaim holds on to a board for dear life. He is glad that he is tossed back and forth—the immediacies of preserving the bit of life drown out some anxious questions concerning the Baal Shem Tov's intentions that burrow their way into his awareness.

Tossed up—down—ahead—back—slush comes a wave over his head and carries him ahead and, with a jar, he lies on the land.

He drags himself a bit farther ahead. On the slight dune of sand he sinks exhausted into an imageless sleep.

He awakes—and looks about. "Where are my *tallis*, my *t'fillin*? Lost on an island?" He looks about and sees smoke—a fire? People—anybody? *Baruch HaShem*, blessed is the Creator who provides. Reb Chaim goes on and finds a village, he enters a house, a *Mezuzzah*! Jews! "Blessed Art Thou Who bestows such kindness on the undeserving!"

He surveys the simple furnishings on the table, a bottle of schnapps, a few pieces of Lekach cake, a *tallis*, and two pair of *t'fillin*—Rashi's and Rabbenu Tam's. He dons them, and lo and behold, the knots tie just like his own, they turn outward—just like in Mezhibuzh! And the way in which he *davvens* in them! These *tallis* and *t'fillin* really pray by themselves, and his soul wafts upward:

Thou art the Lord God all alone
Thou hast made the Heavens
The heavens of the heavens, all their hosts
The Earth and all that is upon it
The seas and all that fill them—
And thou art m'chaya—invigorating."

Ah, *M'chaya*—Reb Chaim enjoys this prayer—he waits for the impression of *t'fillin* straps on his hand to pass away and he helps himself to a *L'Chaim*. A volume of the Talmud is at hand and he studies. Soon the owner of the house will come—there is a pot of soup boiling on the stove—so when the owner will come he will surely invite him to eat. All the questions he will ask then! Has the Baal Shem Tov ever been to this island before? When he tried to go to the Holy Land?

Reb Chaim gets hungry and cannot wait any longer, so he helps himself to the soup—Ah!

No one comes. Reb Chaim impatiently visits the other houses, finds them the same as this, but not a soul to be seen. He despairs and wonders. When he feels sleep approaching he makes himself comfortable and is soon asleep.

The next day still not a soul to be seen. The bottle refilled, the Lekach replaced, the pot of soup a-boil, but not a soul around and when, on the third day, still no one can be seen Reb Chaim comfortably despairs. He saw no one, sees no one, ergo he will see no one—and with a happy naivete that is pained only for the lack of company he accepts his lot as he goes to bed on Thursday night.

To the *Shochet* with the chickens! To the sea for fish! Vegetables from the garden, and fruits! Men, women, and children, all in an eager rush to make Shabbos, awaken Reb Chaim from his troubled sleep.

Chaim turns to them. "Please tell me who you are, what you are, where are you from, what are you doing here?"

But talking to them is just like talking to people during their prayers. Engaged in a *mitzvah*, doing God's will, how can they be interrupted then?

Chaim would like to help prepare for the Sabbath, but there is no answer coming his way. So Chaim, like an orphaned shadow, wanders among the people, watches them prepare for the Sabbath while his soul aches over his isolation. How much he would like to be part of it all!

In the afternoon he repairs to the bathhouse, and there, enveloped in steam, with the other people preparing for the Sabbath, he sees their joy and still is not a part of it.

Toward sunset all of them go toward the synagogue and Chaim with them. The cantor begins to *davven* and Chaim, who has been to many places on this trip, Chaim who has been to many cities in Poland, who has been to Leipzig, who has even been to Amsterdam, who was on his way to Africa, hasn't heard such *davven*ing since he left Mezhibuzh in the home of the Baal Shem Tov. Chaim feels at home. Ah-h-h, the taste of the world to come!

The cantor begins again: "Come let us sing unto the Lord! Let us chant to the rock of our salvation!" That singing, that chanting! The ecstasy of that prayer! Oh, yes, Chaim feels at home and Chaim merges with them.

"Come, O friend, to meet the bride! Let us meet the Sabbath!" The melodies, though they are not the same, have the same lilt, the same flavor as those of Mezhibuzh, the home of the Baal Shem Tov. Before long, all too soon, the service is over.

The *shammas* approaches Chaim and asks him to be the guest of the rabbi. Chaim is only too glad. Now he will find out. Chaim follows the rabbi to his home. Seated around the table he attends as the rabbi bids the angels welcome. "*Shalom Aleichem Mal'achei Hashareth*. Peace unto you, angels of peace!" Chaim almost feels the clasp of the angel's hands in his as he, too, says, "*Shalom Aleichem*. Peace unto you."

The rabbi intones the *Eshet Chayil*. "A woman of valour who can find? Her worth is far above rubies. The heart of her husband is secure in her!" Chaim is transported into the realm where God sings this song of valour to his *Shechina*.

Then the *Kiddush*. The cup of wine glistens in the rabbi's hand. "It is evening, it is morning, the sixth day. And the heavens and the earth were finished." Chaim, before his mind's eye sees the completion of the universe, how God hallows this day and prepares to rest and Chaim stands as a witness to this sublime fact of all creation, the Sabbath. Oh, such spiritual *Ta'am Gan Eden*. It is as if the tendrils of his sensory nerves were connected to his very soul. Feeling with his *neshama* the delights of this world through the Sabbath.

Very soon, the rest of the people are gathered around the rabbi's table, the *tish*, as he begins to expound the Torah based on the portion of the week.

Chaim has heard many preachers, he has heard preachers in many parts of Poland, he has heard many other preachers. Even in Leipzig there are preachers! He has even heard preachers in Amsterdam. Chaim was on his way to Africa for diamonds, but such preaching, such fervor, such ectasy, such a feeling of hearing the *Shechina* talking through the throat of Moses, this feeling he only had at Mezhibuzh and here again. Chaim is amazed and Chaim is wondering.

It is very late when the *chevra* break up, going home, each one to his place, and Chaim to the place where he had stayed all week—and he rests. All the anxieties of the week are gone. In the back of his mind he still wonders: who, what, where, when, how, but Chaim thinks, "There will be time to ask."

Behold it is the Sabbath morning.

First to the sea for a ritual dip. Refreshed, renewed, Chaim is able to pronounce with the rest of the congregation, "The soul of the living blesses Thy name, O Lord, and the spirit of all flesh. . . ." His very flesh is enthralled at the song of his own soul to God.

The Torah is being read. The words float through the air as if they were intricate designs of fire. All the people stand erect for the reading of the Torah. No one dares to chat at the time when God speaks to each man's mind and soul through the words of the Torah, as it is being read from the reader's desk.

Then the *Haftarah*. Oh, Chaim can see the prophet on the hilltop addressing the throng surrounding him. Chaim feels even in the denunciation of the prophets the very tender mercies of God. Chaim knows at that moment that the voice of God still speaks to man in Mezhibuzh and here. "Oh," Chaim sighs, "if only in the other cities of Poland and Leipzig and Amsterdam . . ."

The *Musaf* begins and at the *K'dusha*, the sanctification of God's name, Chaim joins the rest of the congregation and feels as if he were an angel standing in the presence of the Throne of Glory, approaching that Throne and placing the Crown, wrought by Israel's prayers the world over, on the head of God.

"*Keter Yitnu Lecha* (the Crown they give unto Thee)," Chaim chants, "Holy, holy, holy . . . the Lord of Hosts." Chaim, too, feels like one of the *Seraphim* in Heaven, chanting God's praise.

When they come to the passage: "And the sacrifice of this Sabbath we shall render unto Thee in love," Chaim has a *Kavvanah*, an insight, something he had never felt before, nor fully understood. Chaim had always wondered, "How is it possible to make up the sacrifice of this Sabbath even at the time of the coming of the Messiah?" And now Chaim understands! The sacrifice of this Sabbath, this very Sabbath, which we cannot sacrifice unto you, O God, in the life of an animal, or on the altar in Jerusalem, the sacrifice of this Sabbath, O Lord, we sacrifice to you in love, by loving you.

Chaim joins in the jubilation of the *Eyn K'Elokenu*, "There is no God like our God." After the service is over Chaim goes back to his host, the rabbi, and for the first time in his life, he then fully understands the meaning of the saying that the first meal on the Sabbath was established by Abraham, the second meal of the Sabbath by Isaac and the third by Jacob. The first and the last meals Chaim could always enjoy. Somehow Isaac frightened him. It is at this moment, sitting at the rabbi's table, being in this sublime atmosphere, for the first time in his life, he is able to say to Isaac, "Thou art my father, my grandfather." Strange—Isaac became familiar to him as he mirrored his own loneliness and isolation and the sense of fellowship with the one who was lonely in this universe for God.

The Torah of the second meal was worth hearing, repeating, remembering and meditating upon. Shabbos lasted and this meal lasted until *Mincha* time, when the people again assembled in the synagogue and with tremendous joy in his heart, and with the premonition of the parting of the Sabbath, adding some tartness to the flavor he felt in his soul he said the words, "Thou art One, and Thy name is One, and who is likened unto Thy people, Israel, one nation upon the earth."

At the third meal of the Sabbath there was not much said, but the melodies that were wafting between man and man as they sat around the table in the synagogue—the melodies were of the kind he hadn't heard anywhere. Chaim had been around—been to many cities in Poland, been to Leipzig and been to Amsterdam and he was on his way to Africa for diamonds, but Chaim hadn't heard melodies of this kind since he left Mezhibuzh. Yet he knew these melodies, he recognized them. They must have been the melodies that the Levites chanted in the Holy Temple.

The Sabbath was over. The *Maariv*, the evening prayer, was being said, and the *Havdalah* was being made—and Chaim wanted to ask. His curiosity had reappeared with the new week.

Just as Chaim was about to ask the rabbi, the *Havdalah*

candle was raised and the rabbi intoned: "*Hiney E-l Y'shuati* (behold the God of my salvation)."

In his new, weekday state of mind, beholding God is a terrifying thing. Chaim stood as one paralyzed. At the end of the *Havdalah* ceremony the rabbi doused the *Havdalah* candle with the leftover wine of his *Havdalah* cup and everyone stepped forward to dip their small fingers into the wine, touching them to their eyelids. Lo and behold, as they touched them to their eyelids, they disappeared, one by one, the rabbi himself being the last. As suddenly as they had come, they had disappeared. Now Chaim knew, somehow he was sure, that all during the week he would have to be in the same loneliness as he was the week before. . . .

Although his wants were well taken care of, with his schnapps replenished and the cake there every day, as well as the soup, Chaim's wonderment, and the many theories that he spun, grew larger and larger. But he knew Friday morning he would wake up and there they would be. Again he made up his mind that, come Saturday night, he would ask the rabbi, he would prevent him if need be, from dipping his fingers into the wine before he touched his eyelids, in order to know the truth. Again the Sabbath went, and again Chaim felt as if transported into a higher world, a supernatural, more sublime world.

Again the rabbi intoned: "Behold God is my salvation, I shall trust and never fear." The way in which he said it started Chaim thinking, as if this was the answer to his own problems, as if this sentence of the Bible would tell him that he must trust and never fear. So he was caught in meditation until this time, too, all the people and the rabbi were gone.

For the next week Chaim devises a plan. He will not listen to *Havdalah*, he will make *Havdalah* beforehand, right after the service in the synagogue is over and the Sabbath is gone, before they came to the rabbi's house; he will make *Havdalah* and keep his fingers in his ears and not even listen, because he knows that were he to listen he would again be transformed by a new way of looking at this sentence. This time Chaim is prepared.

Just as the rabbi is about to dip his fingers in the wine, Chaim grabs his hands and says: "Rabbi, you must tell me! Who are you? Where are you from? What does it all mean?"

As if a cloud had dropped before the rabbi's eyes, the rabbi heaves a sigh and says: "Chaim, why did you have to ask? Chaim, you cannot remain with us any longer in the same way that you have during the past. Chaim, you must now make a choice, you must decide one way or the other.

"I will tell you our story, after which your decision must be made, a decision that will be irrevocable."

It was in the time of the first temple, in the time of the prophet Elijah, when a group of our parents approached the prophet and said to him:

"Master, Thy servants desire to leave this land, which is so full, both of holiness, but also of idolatry. We do not wish that our children and that we ourselves become polluted by the idolatry that you are so hard pressed to fight. If you grant us permission we shall leave this country and settle somewhere far away, on an island, where we can serve God according to the dictates of our conscience, according to the way in which we recognize His truth."

And the prophet agreed. Moreover, he gave them the sacred name for *K'fitzat Haderech*. *K'fitzat Haderech* means the jumping of the way. It is as if a long road was made shorter. It is as if all of space would become warped and distances no longer would remain distances and could be traversed with ease.

We sent a group of spies. They found this island on which we are now. They came back, reported to us, and we held hands, one to another, standing in a great circle and a Holy and Terrible Name was pronounced and when we opened our eyes we found ourselves on this island where we built what we built and made ourselves at home and continued to worship God.

Before every one of the three pilgrimage holidays, before Passover, before Shevuot, and before Succot, one third of our community would be delegated to go on the pilgrimage to the Holy Temple and to offer the sacrifices on our behalf and on their own behalf. Our entire community would walk with them to the edge of the sea, and there, after song and dance, and tender leave-taking, the chosen ones would hold hands, close their eyes, utter the Name and be transported. The day after the holiday we would again gather by the shore to await them. So we did, year after year.

Once the group we had sent for Succot came back and was there before our eyes, but gone were their festive garments, instead they were clothed in sackcloth and ashes, and as we wondered why, with no answer forthcoming, we knew and realized the terrible tiding.

The Temple, the House of God, the place where He Himself had chosen to dwell, was destroyed! And we wept, all of us, our youngest and our oldest. We wept until our souls could stand it no longer and separated from our bodies and we found ourselves before the great tribunal on high.

They didn't know what to do with us. Some argued that even Heaven, with Abraham, with Isaac and with Moses, was not good enough for us. Perhaps we did not think it so. Yet they were adamant and none knew where we were to be placed.

Suddenly there came a voice from the Throne of Glory saying: "What is the greatest reward I have in my treasures? The greatest reward that awaits man is that he return again to his body that his soul and his body become one. But with one important difference. That whereas now it is the body which receives its life from the soul, then the soul will receive its life and sustenance from the flesh. For the flesh is in some ways closer to the inscrutable, ineffable heights."

The rabbi explained, "Is it not so? Only the flesh can hide the light of God from the soul. Therefore the origin of the flesh is in its root much higher and much more sublime. It stems directly and immediately from the divine *Ayin*—the No-Thing, without having to become subject to innumerable transmutations and developmental steps like the soul. All the angels on high agreed, and so it was decided.

All week we were to be in Heaven and our souls were to receive their reward. The reward where the righteous sit with crowns on their heads and bask in the radiance of the *Shechina*. Before Sabbath we were to be returned to Earth, because he who does not work for the Sabbath, who does not prepare for the Sabbath, what will he eat on the Sabbath? And the Friday is as much of the Sabbath as the Sabbath itself. The more preparation, the higher the rejoicing of the Sabbath itself. The more preparation, the higher the rejoicing of the Sabbath, the deeper the draught of life that the soul will derive from the body. On the Sabbath we are granted the resurrection, the bodily resurrection here on earth. . . .

In all his amazement Chaim somehow understood.

The rabbi turned to Chaim and said: "Chaim, now you must make up your mind. Chaim, either you become one of us and join us, and then you, too, will dip your fingers in the wine and disappear like the rest of us, or else, Chaim, you must leave this island. I will see to it that you find transportation. The name of *K'fitzat Hederech* shall help you arrive where you have to arrive."

Chaim thinks and thinks very deeply. Such an opportunity— for which souls are waiting for eons and eons, for which he will have to wait if he is to return. To have all of eternity, even higher than heaven, at his fingertips. Surely Chaim wants to avail himself of this, and yet he thinks, "The body, the flesh, the soul derives from there . . . True, it is not visible during the week, but on the final Sabbath it will become palpable and become known. . . ."

Yet Chaim sees his wife, deserted, chained, never able to remarry, never finding solace, not knowing whether her husband was dead or alive and her fate being worse than one of death. Chaim thinks of the opportunity of the soul, but what were any opportunities of the soul if one would have to renege on God's *mitzvahs* to man and forget a fellow creature.

With a sigh, Chaim declares himself to the rabbi saying, "This opportunity is desirable yet my choice must be to return."

The rabbi lifts his hands and says, "Blessed art thou, Chaim, for making this choice. May the Heavenly Husband so think of his Earthly Bride, may God so think of His people Israel as thou thinkest of thy wife and become reunited with her and redeem her."

"Amen," said Chaim.

The rabbi told Chaim to open his hand and in the palm of his hand he placed the name of *K'fitzat Haderech* and he told Chaim to close his eyes and to see himself where he wanted to arrive and there he would be.

"But Chaim," he warned him, "on your arrival you must throw this terrible name of *K'fitzat Haderech* heavenward, or else you will be a child of death."

Chaim closed his eyes and naturally the place where he imagined himself to be was Mezhibuzh. As he opened his eyes he found himself in the marketplace of Mezhibuzh ready to throw up the terrible name of *K'fitzat Hederech*, when a hand took hold of his hand and, without turning, Chaim screamed, "Murderer, leave my hand."

The gentle voice of the Baal Shem Tov said to Chaim, "Chaim, it was for this Name that you were sent where you were sent."

If you want to know what happened to Chaim I can tell you. Chaim sold all his possessions and became a *Yoshev* again with the Baal Shem Tov, and the Baal Shem Tov had his name of *K'fitzat Haderech*. But what does the end of the story matter . . . ?

GOING ALONG WITH JOHA: A MEDLEY OF MIRTH

Peninnah Schram

Albert J. Winn

Peninnah Schram *is associate professor at Yeshiva University's Stern College. A storyteller, teacher, and author, her books include* Jewish Stories One Generation Tells Another *and* Tales of Elijah the Prophet. *A professional storyteller since 1970, she travels everywhere presenting workshops and programs on the Jewish oral tradition. Since 1984, she has been the founding director of the Jewish Storytelling Center at the 92nd Street Y, New York City. She lives in Yorktown Heights, New York, with her husband, Jerry.* Peninnah's two children, Rebecca and Michael, are continuing the storytelling tradition.

In Jewish folklore there are many kinds of humorous stories. Some of the more well known are the "Wise Men of Chelm" tales about the fools who live in the town of Chelm. In this case, the words *wise* and *foolish* are synonyms. Another type of simpleton in the Ashkenazi tradition is Shmerel Nar or Simple Shmerel, who is often mistaken for a Holy Man or a seer. Through his naivete and sets of coincidences, he manages to resolve problems and thus save the Jewish communities wherever he travels in the world. The humor often comes about as a result of wordplay, a valued Jewish motif.

Still another type of popular comic character is the trickster. And in the various regions where Jews have lived, there have been trickster characters called by different names, some even adopted from the surrounding culture. In Eastern Europe there is Hershele Ostropolier, a very Jewish character who was jester to a hasidic rebbe. In Turkey, Greece, and Morocco, there is Joha or Juha, a beloved character in Arab folklore whom the Jews have adopted. (*Joha* is the more Sephardic pronunciation, while *Juha* is more Arabic and Moroccan.) But all the characters share the same qualities of being an antihero in a short pithy tale that teaches an object lesson. The trickster uses ingenuity and cunning to outwit others. Sometimes these characters avenge an insult, sometimes they teach a miser a lesson, and sometimes they are fools who take words too literally. At other times, the trickster can also be a canny, mischievous character who selfishly sets out to deceive so as to gain something for himself, especially a dinner. But the audience always gets to laugh and enjoy—and also learn a lesson—at the expense of, or thanks to, this complex character known as the trickster.

Whenever I tell these kinds of stories, I often find that many people in the audience do not know what I mean by a trickster tale. It makes more sense when I refer to the animal trickster tales of coyote (Native American) and Anansi the Spider (African), or perhaps the better known Nasr-ed-Din Hodja (Turkish). But every once in a while, I'll see Sephardim in the audience suddenly break into a huge smile at the sparked memory of hearing about Joha when they were children. After the program, they are usually anxious to tell me some of their Joha stories. One man remembered that as a child, whenever he did something foolish, his mother would raise up her hand with a wave and say, "Joha!" That was all he needed to realize the foolishness of his actions.

The first of the medley, "Why Joha Never Got Married," is found in the Israel Folktale Archives (IFA 12,726) from Solonika. There are other versions of this tale in which Joha always interprets the same Hebrew phrase too literally—thus the humor.

The second story in the series is one of the most popular teaching tales in the Middle East regarding hospitality. It is found in world folklore in Syria, Turkey, Greece, and Italy with other fool/ trickster characters as the "hero," such as Hodja, Djuha, or Giufa. There are many variants in the Israel Folktale Archives including IFA 1408 and 5870 (Persia), IFA 6077 (Yemen), IFA 6784 (Afghanistan), IFA 3072 (Poland) and IFA 6645 (European Ashkinaze). A version of this story, "Welcome to Clothes," with Elijah the Prophet in an unusual trickster role, can be found in my book *Tales of Elijah the Prophet* (Northvale, NJ: Jason Aronson, 1991).

The third Joha story is adapted from a popular tale type, "A Dispute in Sign Language," IFA 505 (Iraq). However, years ago I heard an Arabic version of this tale that influenced my telling about the debate between Joha and an arrogant scholar. In this way, there is a different learned lesson and reward from the more "traditional" versions between the Jews and the king or priest.

This is a cycle of three stories that I have strung together. However, there exist whole cycles of stories about Joha (or another trickster). Because once you start telling trickster tales, it triggers other such stories. Let's go along with Joha!

oha was a trickster. At times, he was ready to teach someone a lesson in a shrewd and clever way. At other times, he would act in such a stupid way that he duped himself. Sharp and sly *or* naive and foolish; I'll leave it to you to match the description that fits him better in this medley of three stories. But going along with Joha is always an adventure!

Joha always wanted to get married, but somehow it never happened to him. You see, whenever he met a young woman of marriageable age, he would always manage to do something stupid, and that would be that! It would convince the young woman to look for a different prospect without wasting another moment.

One day, Joha was walking down the street. Who should be walking toward him but the matchmaker, the *shadkhan*. No sooner had they greeted each other when Joha began to complain.

"I want to get married, but I can't seem to find anyone who will marry me. Perhaps I am doing something wrong. Can you give me some good advice so that I can find a bride?"

The matchmaker listened, and then suddenly his face brightened. "Listen, Joha, meet me later this afternoon and come along with me to this certain house where we will meet with a young woman who is ready to be married. The father of this young woman would be delighted that I am bringing an eligible suitor. Now about the advice, listen! When you are sitting with the young woman, you must pay some attention to her. *Lizrok 'ayin*—throw her an eye! Glance at her! Be a gallant! Remember, above all, *lizrok 'ayin!*"

Joha questioned him more about this, and finally he said, "I understand." And they decided on the time and place to meet later that day. As soon as Joha left the matchmaker, he went home to change his clothes and then he went directly to the butcher and asked, "Do you have any cow's eyes?"

The butcher answered matter-of-factly, "Yes, as many as you want."

"Good! Give me a dozen and put them in a sack." Joha took the sack and went to meet the matchmaker. Then they both went to the house where they would meet the young woman.

When the father of the young woman opened the door and saw the matchmaker and a suitor for his daughter, he heartily welcomed them and invited them to sit in the best chairs. He then asked the daughter to bring the guests some drinks.

The young woman came in, bringing a large silver tray with some refreshments, which she put on the table. Then she sat in a chair near her father.

At first there was silence. Joha was thinking what to say. But then he remembered the matchmaker's advice, *lizrok 'ayin*, throw her an eye!

Joha reached into the sack, took out one of the cow's eyes, and threw it at the young woman.

"Ai!" she said, startled.

A short while later, Joha again remembered the advice. He took out a second cow's eye and threw it at the young woman. "Oi, va voi!" she cried out. And when Joha threw the third eye, the father stood up, and in a rage shouted, "This man is crazy! Get out of here, both of you!" And Joha and the matchmaker were chased out the door.

So now perhaps you can understand better why Joha was never able to find a bride!

Joha always loved a wedding, even when it couldn't be his own. And Joha also loved food. And what better place to enjoy good food than at a wedding, especially at someone else's expense!

One day, Joha was walking down the street, dressed in his usual ragged clothes, when he passed the large house of a wealthy family and noticed there was a celebration going on. He asked the guards about the occasion. They told him that a wedding was taking place and the feast was about to begin. When Joha heard the words *wedding* and *feast*, he asked to himself, "What better combination could there be? But how is it that I was not invited?" Then he said aloud, with a broad smile, "I will have to see for myself."

Since the poor people of the town were often invited to even the richest of weddings, the guards let Joha through the gates. When Joha knocked on the door of the house, the father of the bride opened the door. Seeing this beggarly looking man, he said, "You are not invited to my daughter's wedding feast."

Joha left. He went to a friend's house and borrowed some very fine clothes—even a high hat. And then he returned to the house of the wedding feast.

The guards greeted him with great courtesy, ushered him to the door of the house, and knocked on the door for him. When the father of the bride opened the door and saw this elegantly dressed stranger, he invited him in with great *kovod* and, with great honor, seated him at the head table. And the father of the bride himself began to bring the choicest foods and wines to him. Joha watched as the food was placed in front of him. Then he took the meat with the pomegranate seeds and stuffed it all down his sleeves. "Eat, sleeves!" he said with a hearty laugh. He took the other meats and rice and vegetables and salads and crammed them into all of his pockets until they were packed and over-flowing with the food. "Eat, clothes! Eat well!" he urged. Finally, with a sweeping gesture, he picked up his wine glass and slowly poured the wine down his shirt and into all of his pockets. "Drink, pockets!" he commanded. And all the while he kept re-peating, "Eat, sleeves! Eat, clothes! Drink, pockets! Enjoy the feast, my clothes!"

The guests stopped eating, stopped drinking, stopped talk-ing! All their eyes were on the stranger, watching this elaborate ritual but yet bewildered by what they saw. The father of the bride ran over to Joha and shouted, "What are you doing? How dare you do this! Explain yourself!"

And Joha, with a laugh, replied, "Sir, you turned me away when I came to the door in ragged clothes. But when I returned wearing these fine clothes, you invited me in with great honor. It is clear that you were inviting only my clothes. So they are eating the feast."

And then Joha, paying no more attention to the host, contin-ued eating. "Eat some more, sleeves! Drink heartily, pockets!"

One day, Joha was sitting in the coffeehouse eating heartily, and, at the same time, trying to figure out a way to avoid hav-ing to pay for the meal. Sitting not far from him was a scholar who was disliked by all because he thought himself superior to everyone around him. He often engaged an unsuspecting visitor in a philosophical debate (since the townspeople knew better than to become involved in any such debate). Every time, this arrogant scholar was merciless in shaming the visitor by using his disparaging display of learning with great disdain for what the other person might know. The poor visitor would then politely find an excuse to leave, and the scholar would feel as though he had won another battle.

As Joha was drinking his cup of coffee, he suddenly had an idea. He went to the owner of the coffeehouse and said, "I will teach that scholar a lesson, but if I do, then the meal I have just eaten will be free. Agreed?" The owner was happy to witness such sport, which would surely entertain his guests as well, and he agreed.

Joha then approached the scholar and said, "I will debate you in signs. What do you say?"

"Agreed!" replied the scholar. "I shall begin and make my point first."

The scholar pointed with one finger (meaning to say that there is but one God).

Joha pointed at the scholar with two fingers—and the scholar was taken aback at this response. (The scholar thought, "He is right, there is the King in Heaven and the king in our land.") The scholar conceded the point and announced, "You are right!"

Then the scholar opened his hand with his fingers separated and gestured with his palm down (thinking to say that the Jews are scattered all over the world). Joha then raised his hand and made a tight fist. Again the scholar was amazed. ("He is right," the scholar thought. "While the Jews are scattered, they will be gathered together when the Messiah comes.") The scholar called out, "You are right again."

Then the scholar took a piece of white cheese from his plate and held it up (thinking to ask, "Does this white cheese come from a white or black goat?"). Joha ran into the kitchen and returned with an egg and held it up. And the scholar turned red. ("He is right again," the scholar thought. "He is answering with the same question, 'So does this egg come from a white or brown hen?'") And now the scholar lamely answered, "You are right."

This time it was the scholar who suddenly had an appointment that he had forgotten about and slid quickly and quietly away. Everyone at the coffeehouse was laughing with satisfaction. They gathered around their new "hero," who had taught this arrogant scholar a lesson to remember. But they also were puzzled by the contest. "Joha, tell us what the debate was all about. What was the meaning of all the signs?"

Gloating, Joha sat back and answered: "It was all very simple. He is not such a great scholar as you had thought him. First, when he pointed at me with one finger, he was threatening me that he would poke out my eye. So I held up two fingers to answer, 'Try it and I'll poke out both your eyes!' Then, when he spread out his fingers with a thrust of his arm, he was saying to me that he would push me out of the coffeehouse. So I held up my fist to say: 'Oh no you won't. I'll punch you in the face.' Finally, when he held up the piece of cheese, I figured that he wanted to continue eating and end the debate, so I held up an egg to show him that I was in agreement since I was still hungry anyway."

So what did the people do? They all bought Joha more food and drink.

Note

For more Joha/Juha stories, read *Djoha, What Does He Say?: Popular Judeo-Spanish Folktales* (in Hebrew) by Matilda Koen-Sarano (Jerusalem: Kana, 1991) and also *The Treasure of Our Fathers: Judeo-Spanish Tales* (in Hebrew), edited by Tamar Alexander and Dov Noy (Jerusalem: Misgav Yerushalayim, 1989).

THE MIRACLE OF
THE BLACK PEPPER
Rebecca Schram-Zafrany

Rebecca Schram-Zafrany *is a high school English teacher and storyteller. She has performed in the United States and in Israel for various audiences and shares stories with her students as a creative teaching tool in her classroom. For several summers she served as the cultural coordinator for UJA-Federation day camps in the New York area. She was also the main translator from Hebrew to English of stories included in Peninnah* Schram's Tales of Elijah the Prophet. *Rebecca currently resides in Ashdod, Israel, with her husband, Emile, and their daughter, Dorielle Netta.*

"The Miracle of the Black Pepper" is an original and true story told to me by my mother-in-law, Mrs. Annette Zafrany. This incident occurred in Marrakesh, Morocco, to Mrs. Zafrany's grandfather, Shlomo Issan, at approximately the turn of this century, and it has been a legend in her family ever since. Shlomo Issan, born in the 1850s and died in the 1940s, worked with spices until he was seventy years old. It is believed that there is even a distant family connection to the Ben Atar family.

Rabbi Mordechai Ben Atar was a descendant of the well-known Ben Atar family of rabbis and holy men in Morocco. The most famous members of this family were Rabbi Moses Ben Haim Ben Atar and Rabbi Yehuda Ben Jacob Ben Atar, who lived toward the end of the seventeenth century and the beginning of the eighteenth century. This family produced many well-known rabbis and storytellers whose advice was often sought by kings and princes. Their words and writings are still called upon, and there are many synagogues throughout Morocco named after various members of this illustrious family.

Rabbi Mordechai Ben Atar also lived at approximately the turn of the eighteenth century and was known to perform miracles and

give sage advice to those in trouble. It is said that his staff is
embedded in the wall at the entrance to the Mellach in Marrakesh
to this day. His name is still called out by many people, when
ever they are in need of help. My husband, Emile, recalls that, as
a child still living in Marrakesh, he would kiss the arch or touch
the thick wall (which was painted green), as he was passing by,
without knowing why. He was simply following the practice of the
people around him.

The Mellach is a walled community where a large concentration of Jews lived. The first Mellach in Morocco was built in Fez
in 1552, approximately sixty years after the expulsion from Spain.
The huge gates of the Mellach were locked at night and guards
were placed there in order to protect the Jews. This was ordered
by the Muslim rulers, who often built the Mellach near their pal-
aces.

Jewish life prospered in the Mellach, both spiritually and eco-
nomically. The whole community shared in both joys and sorrows
as one. The streets of the Mellach were divided according to occupation. So, for example, if a person needed to buy spices, he
would go to a street where spices were sold (called "El Atrian,"
which means "spices" in the Moroccan Arabic dialect). The name
Atar, coming from the same root word, is a general word meaning "spice-dealer." Black pepper, a very important spice in a long
list of spices used in Moroccan cooking, is called Lebzar Ilkhil in
the Moroccan Arabic dialect.

Whenever Mrs. Zafrany would tell this story about her grandfather to the older family members, she would narrate it in the
Moroccan Judeo-Arabic dialect. However, when my mother-in-
law told the story to me, she related it in Hebrew, which she
speaks fluently. It is interesting to note that she always pronounced the name of Rabbi Mordechai Ben Atar in the Moroccan Judeo-Arabic dialect so that it sounded like *R'bi M'rdchai
B'n Atar*.

---

ong ago Shlomo, a simple spice merchant, lived in
Marrakesh. He made his living by buying spices
from different spice dealers and then selling them
to his neighbors in the Mellach (the enclosed Jewish community) in Marrakesh. Shlomo and his family lived a comfortable life and there was always enough food
on the table for everyone, especially on holidays or on Shabbat.
Even enough for the passing beggars, who were never turned
away empty-handed.

Shlomo, who was a pious and believing man, would always call out to Rabbi Mordechai Ben Atar, as was the custom, when going through the arched gates of the Mellach. Rabbi Mordechai Ben Atar was known to perform many miracles, and his name was often called out by people for protection from evil or for good luck.

Soon war broke out in Morocco and many items became scarce in the Mellach. However, nothing was more scarce than spices. Among the scarcest of the spices was black pepper. Any black pepper that was found was either sold at outrageously high prices or confiscated. The police would routinely make searches among all the spice sellers and if they found any black pepper, they took it, and then put the merchant in jail. Shlomo felt that it was important to try and find this spice because it was one of the main spices used in Moroccan cooking. He tried his best, but the only spice he could find to sell was red pepper, which was bought and sold for very little money.

Then suddenly, as if in answer to his prayers, there was a rumor of a new shipment of spices outside of the Mellach. Without much hesitation, Shlomo hired a driver with a horse and wagon and left the Mellach. As he rode through the main arch of the Mellach, he touched the side of the wall and called out to Rabbi Mordechai Ben Atar to watch over him.

When he reached the market, he saw sack after sack of spices being unloaded. He approached the supplier and asked what spices were being sold. "Only black and red pepper," answered the man in a booming voice.

"How much for the red pepper?" asked Shlomo.

"Fifty dirhams per sack."

"And how much for the black pepper?" Shlomo asked.

"A thousand dirhams per sack."

Shlomo did not know what to do. Should he buy more of the red pepper and sell it for very little, or should he buy the scarce black pepper? If he bought the black pepper, he would make more money but would also risk being arrested or losing all his expensive merchandise, and possibly his whole business.

Shlomo decided to take a chance. He bought twenty sacks of black pepper. The man in charge, however, was very greedy and decided to take advantage of Shlomo. He loaded nineteen sacks of the precious black pepper onto Shlomo's wagon and, when Shlomo was not looking, he substituted one sack of red pepper. Shlomo paid for twenty sacks of black pepper and began his return journey to the Mellach. On the way back he began to think about the money he would make when selling the black pepper since he would be the only one in the area selling this rare spice.

As he approached the gates to the Mellach he saw police everywhere. They were making a surprise inspection of everyone's wagon going in and out of the gate. As he moved closer, Shlomo began to worry. His mind raced with possibilities of what to do. But neither turning away nor going through the checkpoint seemed possible. In the end, seeing no other way to escape, Shlomo approached the police's checkpoint.

"Stop! Check the sacks in that wagon!" ordered the captain, pointing at Shlomo. Sitting on his wagon, under the arched gate of the Mellach, Shlomo called out to Rabbi Mordechai Ben Atar to help him. In a trembling voice, his driver called to the horses to stop.

One of the officers approached the wagon, opened its back door, and climbed up and over the sacks of pepper. He randomly chose one of them. He took out a knife and ripped it open. He put his hand deep in the sack in order to check its contents. Shlomo could hear the officer opening the sack and was sure the next thing he would hear would be an order for the confiscation of all the merchandise in the wagon. But the officer came up with a hand full of *red* pepper! And the only thing the officer said was, "Let this man through! He only has red pepper."

Shlomo didn't understand. He knew that he had bought black pepper and not red. When he got off his wagon well inside the Mellach, he looked at the one sack that had been opened by the officer and saw that it was indeed filled with red pepper. He then opened the other sacks, one after another, and saw that they were all filled with the expensive and illegal black pepper. He realized then that the merchant dealer must have cheated him. He thanked Rabbi Mordechai Ben Atar for watching over him and making sure that the one sack that the soldier checked was the one with the red pepper. It was truly a miracle!

Shlomo drove the rest of the way to his shop and let it be known that he had black pepper to sell at a fair price. He provided the whole community in the Mellach with this important and rare spice during the time of the shortage, and the wonderful smells of the special dishes prepared that Shabbat reminded Shlomo of the miracle of Rabbi Mordechai Ben Atar.

THREE STORIES FROM THE HEAVENS

Turning: a Midrash of the Sun and the Moon
The Sign: A Midrash of the Rainbow
Midrash of Mayim: A Water Story

Cherie Karo Schwartz

Cherie Karo Schwartz *is a full-time storyteller with over twenty years of nationwide teaching and telling for all ages in synagogues, museums, schools, and universities. Her specialities include worldwide Jewish folklore and stories recreated. She is the coordinator of the CAJE (Coalition for the Advancement of Jewish Education) Jewish Storytelling Network and cofounder of Omanim b'Yachad (Arts in Jewish Education Conference). She has produced five audiotapes, including* Worldwide Jewish Folktales . . . of Wishes and Wisdom *and* Miriam's Tambourine, *and her first book,* My Lucky Dreidel. *Cherie lives with her husband, Larry, in Denver, Colorado.*

These are three stories from the heavens. Nine years ago, when Peninnah, Seymour Rossel (a friend and publisher), and I first talked about creating a "this is my best" book of favorite stories of Jewish storytellers, we wanted tellers to submit stories that they wanted to share with the world because they had personal and spiritual attachment to them. I wondered all those years ago which story I would select. And now, as it happens, I have chosen stories that did not exist then, except in their original ancient sources: three stories with unconscious threads weaving them together.

These are stories that sing to my soul. They are stories that begin with pain and lead toward healing. They all speak of right thinking, feeling, and action. They show ways in which the world can turn away from suffering and once again be set into balance and harmony. It is as though the words that I have been sharing with my audiences and students for over twenty years have finally come home to be heard: "If you let go of the story itself, then the story will tell you." What is contained in these three stories is the gentle message that things can turn for the better, that there will be healing and that the healing brings a glimpse of heaven.

The sources for these stories are stories unto themselves. "Turning: A Midrash of the Sun and the Moon" is talmudic (B. Hullin 60b; Midrash Berashit Rabbah 6:3; and Konen BhM 2:24–27). Versions of the story include Louis Ginzberg's *Legends of the Jews* (vol. 1, pp. 23–24); Raphael Patai's *Gates to the Old City* (p. 264, 4th day), and Ellen Frankel's *The Classic Tales* (story 3, p. 7). The story tells of the moon's jealousy of the sun, and of God's response. I expanded the human aspects of teshuvah (turning), repentance, and becoming whole. The moon becomes a reminder of our ability to return, to continue to grow.

"The Sign: A Midrash of the Rainbow" comes from the story of the rainbow as covenant found in Torah (Genesis 9:13, Noach). Beginning with the idea that the waters were the tears of God, this is my setting of the scene, including the reason for the covenant: God's understanding of human behavior. I can see the hand of God forming the rainbow as a sign and a shelter. The colors are symbols; they are reminders of the colors of our lives. The story ends with the realization that all things come full circle.

"Midrash of Mayim: A Water Story" is an adaptation of a Syrian Jewish folktale, Israel Folktale Archives, gathered by M. Rabi from J. Matilya, J. Statya. The story appears in such sources as Dov Noy's *A Tale for Each Month*, Barbara Rush and Eliezer Marcus' *Seventy and One Tales for the Jewish Year* (pp. 20–22), and Ellen Frankel's *The Classic Tales* (story 183, pp. 373–374). There is a wealth of aggadic and folktales of rabbis and righteous ones who help restore rain through prayer, fasting, and good deeds. It seems to me that the nature of this story lies in the feminine closeness to the earth and the elements, so the central character became a woman. The original folktale ends with the coming of the rains and the explanation of the contents of the jar. The story felt incompletely resolved at that point. I continued the tale of the jar and added the miraculous tree.

At first, it seemed odd to me to be submitting retellings rather than my original or family stories. And then I realized that the seeds of my telling, my teaching, and what I've been trying to hear (if only I would listen) are contained in these three tales. May they help bring shalom.

May the words of my mouth
the art of my hands
the meditations of my heart
the stories of my soul
be joyful songs of blessing
be joyous dances of praise
for you
for You
Creator of the World
—(inspired by Psalm 19:15)

Turning: A Midrash of the Sun and the Moon

In the beginning, there was nothing.

No light, no sky, no earth, no sea.

Six days later . . . the Earth and all that surrounds it were created.

And it was good.

But, of course, some things were not always as they are now.

Once, the sun and the moon were the same size and cast the same radiance. This was not pleasing to the moon. "Look at that! Look at that sun!" the moon huffed. "If we are both the same size, how will everyone know that I am more important? This sky isn't big enough for the two of us!"

The moon pondered the possibilities. Hmmm . . . only the One could set things right. So the moon went to God to lodge a complaint. "There is not enough room for me *and* the sun in the sky. As you can plainly see, we do not even have space to turn around!" The moon paused before adding, "This is not good. This is not just." Proud of this speech, the moon waited for God's answer.

God listened, thought about the situation, then spoke. "You are absolutely right, moon. Justice must be done. You cannot both be the same. Thank you, moon, for bringing this to my attention."

Swelling with pride and feeling itself growing larger already, moon suddenly felt a stab of pain, and a hurt coming from deep inside. "God! God!" cried the moon, "look at what is happening to me! I am shrinking! Help me!" The moon grew smaller and smaller.

Then God spoke: "You were right, moon. It was not good that you and the sun should be the same size. You were the one who was not satisfied. You wanted justice. So, now you have your wish. One of you is greater: the sun."

The moon looked at its diminished body and began to weep. "But God! That's not what I meant!"

"Still, you must learn to be satisfied with what you are."

"What am I, anyway? A small and insignificant ball of light? Look at me!"

"For that pride, you shall give up your light as well. From this day forth, the only light that you shall shed will be reflected from the sun."

"What? My only light from that . . . that . . . sun! How could that be? I can turn from my ways. Believe me, please!"

"Moon, you will indeed turn. And so will the people who gaze at you from the Earth. They will see you turning, from darkness to light. They will see you appear to grow larger and smaller each month, and they will see that, by turning, you can once again grow whole."

The moon wept, tears of moonglow falling from the sky. "But God, I can repent. I am truly sorry, and I see the error of my ways. Please help me. I am lost in the dark sky."

Filled with compassion and mercy, God gazed into the heart of the moon and saw that moon had repented. But what has been decreed by God cannot be undone, only altered. "Moon, you shall rule in the night sky as the sun rules in the day."

"But over what shall I rule? What is there? And, what has become of me?"

"Your domain shall be the night. People will look into your night sky and be filled with wonder. The sun is too harsh, too bright to behold. Your light shall be a comfort to the traveler and the dreamer. They will gaze upon you and ponder the wonder of the universe."

"This is a comfort to me. But I will be so very lonely!"

With that, God bent down and gathered up the pieces of moonglow and placed the small pieces of light high up in the sky. "These shall keep you company," God said. "They are the sparks of what you once were. These are your tears of repentance. They shall be called the stars."

The moon looked to the night sky where tiny points of light glimmered. "But God, how will I ever regather all of the sparks?"

"There is no need to gather them all, sweet moon. Your sparks shall fill the whole sky from one end to the other. You will fill the whole sky . . . and you will remember."

The Sign: A Midrash of the Rainbow

In the beginning, there was light, the heavens and the waters, the planets, plants, animals and people, and a garden of Eden. And it was good and it was good and it was very good. And God looked upon it and saw that it was good.

But the goodness did not last, because with the thoughts and actions of people came not just kindness but also selfishness and greed and anger and hurt.

God looked upon it and saw that it was not good.

And God was sad.

So God decided to destroy this world and make a whole new world.

God thought about how much time and effort it had taken to make the first world. It had taken six whole days! And after that, God needed a whole day's rest!

So, God decided to keep the same world but just destroy whatever was on the world.

When God thought about that idea, it still did not seem just right. After all, God thought, if all of the people and animals were gone from the Earth, there would be no one from whom to learn.

So God decided to keep some people and some animals. God looked out over the Earth and found one family that could be counted as truly good in their time: the family of Noah.

Then, God called upon Noah to build an ark to hold himself and his wife and their three sons and their wives, and some animals.

But God thought about the animals. Since they had not really been part of all of the badness, God decided to save at least two of every kind.

After Noah and his family built the ark, which God sealed, the rain began to fall. The rain would not destroy the Earth, only cover and cleanse it. The waters of the rain were the tears of God, who wept because the world had not turned out to be good and whole.

God's tears fell for forty days and forty nights. On the forty-first day, the ark came to rest on top of Mount Ararat. A dove, which Noah had sent out, returned with an olive branch that had been cleansed and had survived the flood.

Noah and his family stepped out into the first sunshine they had seen in forty days and stood upon the first land seen for forty days. When they saw the clean, new Earth for the first time, Noah and his family wept for joy and God wept with them. The sky wept a sunshower of tears as God spoke to the family, saying:

"I am God who brought you forth into this new land. Look around you and see the cleansed Earth. Listen and hear the sounds of animals and trees and the wind moving through the plants. Now what do you not hear? You do not hear anger and rage. The world is once again new. I know that the world cannot always be this way. It does not seem to be human nature to be good always. But you and the generations that come after you can try.

"I will make a covenant with you, the family of Noah, the first of the world's new people. I will give you a sign that I am with you, one that reminds us that the world was created in peace and then was recreated in peace, to remain so for all time—if we remember.

"The sign will be a smile that fills the heavens, an arc of light, just as there was at the very beginning. But this will be a new light, one that shines through the waters of a flood or a rain or tears. This light will show all of the colors of beauty that can fill our lives as we live in peace, and as we remember the waters of cleansing. This promise shall be called—the rainbow.

"Listen to the silence. Remember what has happened on the Earth, and so will I. I will never again destroy the Earth. I will keep my promise. Will you?"

Then God bent toward the Earth with a mighty hand and an outstretched arm and made an arc across the sky. And just where the hand of God had been, there was a sheltering arc of every color spread out across the blue sky.

And God began to speak of the colors and of the signs of the rainbow. First comes red, for the blood that gives people life, God explained. Orange is for the flames of warmth that can comfort and surround us. Yellow is the color of the sun, the full light of day, that helps all things grow. Green is for grass and the trees, of new life for the plants. Blue is the color of the sky and the color of the sea; it connects the air and the ground. Indigo is the color that happens twice in our day: once just at dawn as the day begins and once at dusk, just as the day ends. Violet is the color of the night, when the world rests and renews itself. It shows that we come full circle, in our days and in our lives.

Why doesn't it appear that the rainbow is a full circle? All that we see is an arc that surrounds and covers us, to protect us. It shows us that not all things are yet circles; sometimes we must work toward making things come around whole.

But who is to say that the rainbow is not a full circle? The rainbow we see is just part of the story. The rest of the circle may lie deep within the earth, connecting the heavens and the Earth. Those who travel above the Earth know the truth. Only high above the ground and above all of our troubles can we see that the rainbow is actually a complete circle of beautiful light.

And how do we on Earth know that the rainbow is whole? It is. We have to believe as much in what we cannot see as we do in what we think we see. Some things are obvious and others are hidden. Our task is to believe in the hidden part of the rainbow, for there lies peace as we all touch in full circle.

Midrash of Mayim: A Water Story

It was a time of drought. There was no rain. There was no dew upon the grass. There was no water in the streams or the rivers. The earth was parched. The people were parched, and their skin had begun to wither; and the animals withered, too. Every day, those who were young and still strong enough were sent to walk miles to the muddy river far away to bring back small pails of water so the people could live.

The heavens would not open. It would not rain. There was no water, save that shed by the people as tears.

The Rabbi called his entire congregation together, and together they prayed. They prayed fervently. The Rabbi reminded them to think of anything they had done wrong as individuals or as a community in the last year, and to pray from the depths of their hearts, but still there was no rain.

They prayed all night and into the next day, sick with thirst, but still there was no rain.

In the midst of their prayers, the Rabbi thought he heard a voice ask, "Where is Rachamah?" He opened his eyes, looked around the tiny congregation, and there was no Rachamah.

Rachamah was an old, quiet woman who lived in a small hut on the edge of the town. She kept to herself, lived by herself, and people rarely saw her. "Where is Rachamah?" the Rabbi asked out loud. "Where is Rachamah?" A whisper passed through the congregation: "Where is Rachamah? And, why would the Rabbi ask?" The entire congregation stopped their prayers to listen. Everyone knew the answer: she wasn't there! She hardly ever came to the synagogue, and after years of asking, they all had let her be by herself.

The Rabbi left the *bima*, right in the middle of the prayers, walked through the congregation, and went out the door. The minutes passed, and then, through the open door came the Rabbi . . . with Rachamah.

The Rabbi and Rachamah went to the front of the congregation, and Rachamah turned to face the people. In her hands was a small clay jar. She held it in front of her, and, as the people watched, her lips began to move as if in prayer. She held the small clay jar up before her, and she spoke in a small whisper. As she continued to speak, her voice gained in power, until all could hear her prayer.

"Dear God, our land, our animals, our children are dying. The people grieve. I have been grieving for years for so many reasons, but I do not let it show. When things have been too hard for me to bear, I cry, but I do not let the tears just dry and go away. I gather the tears of my grief in this little jar. They are all here. Dear God, we are all starving. The earth is dying and so are we all. This is not right. If you will not restore the rain, then I will take this jar of my tears and smash it on the ground—smash it and let all the tears run out."

Rachamah stopped and she stood still and silent. The whole congregation watched, waiting—but for what? A sound began, far off, and no one could be sure what it was. Then there was a low rumble, soft at first, but gradually it became louder and closer. Suddenly, lightning split the sky, thunder shook the synagogue . . . and the rains came. The rain began as quietly as Rachamah's whisper, and then it grew loud enough to drown out all of the voices in the congregation and all of the pain in the people's hearts.

Rachamah just stood before the congregation. The people were whispering, talking, shouting, praying with joy. They opened the door of the synagogue and watched as the rain came down to replenish the earth.

And the rain, now steady and gentle, came in abundance.

The people sat and looked in wonder at Rachamah. They looked at the small clay jar. What a miracle! They reached for it.

But Rachamah, holding her small clay jar, moved away, walked out of the synagogue, into the blessed rain, and back to her own small house.

The next day, the people went to visit her, many for the first time, and asked to see the small clay jar. "I have returned it to the earth," was all she would say. And no one ever saw it again.

The rains came in their season, the people and the animals thrived, and the earth was restored. Months passed, and one day some children noticed a small tree growing next to the synagogue and wondered where it came from.

Years passed, and the sapling turned into a strong and beautiful tree, and red fragrant blossoms appeared on the branches. Then the flowers fell, and tiny green fruits began to grow. They grew bigger and rounder and then turned deep red. The branches of the tree had grown to touch the synagogue as though to protect it. The pomegranate tree was beautiful, and it lent its beauty to the synagogue. The children came and picked the pomegranates and they said that they were the sweetest they had ever eaten.

People came from all around to see the beautiful tree and to taste the sweet juice of its fruit.

And some people say that they know how such a tree came to grow on that spot. They say they know the source of the tree. They say that they remember the story of Rachamah and the rain, and they know the connection. For inside every pomegranate, there are hundreds of seeds. And each one is shaped like a small, wet tear.

THE COTTAGE
OF CANDLES
Howard Schwartz

Howard Schwartz, *a folklor-*
ist and anthologist, is associ-
ate professor of English at
the University of Missouri–
St. Louis. He lectures exten-
sively on the Jewish oral
tradition, telling stories as
part of his talks. He has
edited a four-volume set of
Jewish folktales: Elijah's
Violin and Other Jewish
Fairy Tales, Miriam's Tambourine: Jewish Folktales
from Around the World,
Lilith's Cave: Jewish Tales of
the Supernatural, *and*
Gabriel's Palace: Jewish
Mystical Tales. *He has also*
edited many anthologies,
including Gates to the New City: A Treasury of Modern Jewish
Tales. *Howard lives in St. Louis, Missouri, with his wife and*
three children.

"The Cottage of Candles" is an example of a divine test, similar
to the one to which God subjected Abraham when he commanded
him to sacrifice Isaac on Mount Moriah. The identity of the old
man who tends the soul-candles and conducts the test remains
a mystery, although his supernatural aspect is quite clear. As the
Keeper of the Soul-Candles he functions as an Elijah-type figure
or as one of the *Lamed-Vav Tzaddikim*, the Thirty-Six Hidden
Saints, who are said to be the pillars of the world.

The man in this tale is clearly attempting to fulfill the biblical
injunction "Justice, justice, shalt thou pursue" (Deuteronomy
16:20). One way of reading the tale is to see that in arriving at
this cottage, the man is on the verge of completing his lifelong
quest to find justice, but he is first tested to see if he himself is
just. It is interesting to note that the man's quest in this tale is
many ways parallel to that of the man from the country in Kafka's
famous parable "Before the Law" from *The Trial*, who comes seeking justice at the gates of the Law.

In this tale the man who seeks justice sins when he attempts to steal oil from the soul-candle next to his own. But there are other Jewish tales in which the reverse is true. See, for example, "The Enchanted Inn" in my book *Gabriel's Palace*, where a boy finds a candle about to burn out and pours additional oil into it as a good deed, only to later discover that it was the candle of his soul. Another variant, which is in the Israel Folktale Archives (IFA 8335), tells of a cave in which there are bottles of oil, where a person lives until the oil is exhausted. Nor is the motif of soul-candles limited to Jewish folklore. Variants are found in Latin American folklore as well as in Spanish tales, among others.

I am struck by the interesting parallel between the soul-candles, which burn as long as a person lives, and the Jewish custom of lighting *Yahrzeit* candles on the anniversary of a person's death. These memorial candles are intended to last for twenty-four hours, and remain lit until they burn out. The lighting of the candle is done to symbolize the verse "The soul of man is the lamp of God" (Proverbs 20:27). This same verse no doubt inspired the story of "The Cottage of Candles."

I was powerfully attracted to this tale the first time I read it, despite the fact that it was recounted in a rather primitive oral version, collected by the Israel Folktale Archives. Later I found that this tale exists in many versions, and was widely known throughout the Middle East. The version included here is IFA 7830, collected by Zevulon Qort from Ben Zion Asherov from Afghanistan, which demonstrates how far it has traveled.

---

here once was a Jew who went out into the world to seek justice. Somewhere, he was certain, true justice must exist. He looked in the streets and the markets of cities but could not find it. He traveled to villages and he explored distant fields and farms, but still justice eluded him. At last he came to an immense forest and he entered it, for he was certain that justice must exist somewhere. He wandered there for many years and he saw many things—the hovels of the poorest peasants, the hideaways of thieves, and the huts of witches in the darkest part of the forest. And he stopped in each of these, despite the danger, and sought clues. But no one was able to help him in his quest.

One day, just as dusk was falling, he arrived at a small clay hut that looked as if it were about to collapse. Now there was something strange about this hut, for many flickering flames could be seen through the window. The man who sought justice wondered greatly about this and knocked on the door. There was no answer. He pushed the door open and entered.

Before him was a small room crowded with many shelves. And on the shelves were a multitude of oil candles. Together their flames seemed to beat like wings, and the flickering light made him feel as if he were standing in the center of a quivering flame. He held up his hand, and it seemed to be surrounded with an aura, and all the candles were like a constellation of stars.

Stepping closer, he saw that some of the flames burned with a very pure fire, while others were dull and still others were sputtering, about to go out. So too did he now notice that some of the wicks were in golden vessels, while others were in silver or marble ones, and many burned in simple vessels of clay or tin. The plain vessels had thin wicks, which burned quickly, while those made of gold or silver had wicks that lasted much longer.

While he stood there, marveling at that forest of candles, an old man in a white robe came out of one of the corners and said: "*Shalom Aleichem*, my son, what are you looking for?"

"*Aleichem Shalom*," the man answered. "I have traveled everywhere searching for justice, but never have I seen anything like all these candles. Why are they burning?"

The old man spoke softly: "Know that these are soul-candles. Each candle is the soul of one of the living. As long as it burns, the person remains alive. But when the flame burns out, he departs from this life."

Then the man who sought justice turned to the old man and asked: "Can I see the candle of my soul?"

The old man led him deep into the cottage, which the man now saw was much larger on the inside than it appeared to be from outside. At last he showed him a line of tins on a low shelf. He pointed out a small, rusty one that had very little oil left. The wick was smoking and had tilted to one side. "This is the candle of your soul," said the old man.

A great fear fell upon the man and he started to shiver. Could it be that the end of his life was so near and he did not know it?

Then the man noticed that next to his tin there was another, filled with oil. Its wick was straight, burning with a clear, pure light.

"And this one, who does it belong to?" asked the man, trembling. "That is a secret," answered the old man. "I only reveal each man's candle to himself alone."

Soon after that the old man vanished from sight, and the room seemed empty except for the candles burning on every shelf.

While the man stood there, he saw a candle on another shelf sputter and go out. For a moment there was a wisp of smoke rising in the air, and then it was gone. One soul had just left the world.

The man's eyes returned to his own tin. He saw that only a few drops of oil remained, and he knew that the flame would soon burn out. At that instant he saw the candle of his neighbor, burning brightly, the tin full of oil.

Suddenly an evil thought entered his mind. He looked around and saw that the old man had disappeared. He looked closely in the corner from which he had come, and then in the other corners, but there was no sign of him there. At that moment he reached out and took hold of the full tin and raised it above his own. But suddenly a strong hand gripped his arm, and the old man stood beside him.

"Is this the kind of justice you are seeking?" he asked. His grip was like iron, and the pain caused the man to close his eyes.

And when the fingers released him, he opened his eyes and saw that everything had disappeared: the old man, the cottage, the shelves, and all the candles. And the man stood alone in the forest and heard the trees whispering his fate.

Y. L. PERETZ IN THE ISRAELI ARMY

Shai Schwartz

Shai Schwartz *was born on a kibbutz in the Upper Galilee and spent twelve years of his childhood in South Africa. After serving in the Israeli army, he became an actor. Today he is also a director, a writer, and a storyteller. He uses stories in workshops at the Neve Shalom School for Peace. He has performed several one-man shows in Israel and in the United States, including* A Story of a Bass Fiddle, Get Out You Naughty Boy, *and* Stories Around the Table. *Shai lives on Neve Shalom, a joint Jewish-Arab cooperative near Jerusalem, with his wife and three children.*

Israel is the land of storytellers. Step into a bank or a shop, wait for a bus or sit next to a cabdriver, and you are inviting a story. You never know when someone is going to drop their stories on you!

Of course, we Jews and Arabs who live in Israel come from a tradition of storytelling. To this day you can still find old men and women who were renowned in the Old Country as storytellers and continue to attract an audience. These storytellers are disappearing rapidly, but "Old Storytellers never die," they just come to the end of their stories.

Young storytellers are taking their place. They are appearing everywhere. Actors, librarians, writers, and teachers are learning storytelling and many have chosen this form of art as their sole profession. Thus here in Israel, as in many other countries, in this electronic-digital period we are seeing a renaissance of storytelling!

I have found in the storytelling experience values I never had in theater: freedom, intimacy, and personal contact, and very often, even a transcendental spiritual experience.

One of the more fascinating places to tell a story is in the army. The "Education Corps" of the Israeli army is responsible for moving hundreds of lecturers and artists all over the country. They deliver all the cultural and educational activities to the different units in the army, which means a lot!

I perform four times a month in the army as my army reserve duty. I travel all over and find myself in the strangest situations and telling stories in the weirdest of places: dining halls, garages, hangars, barracks, and tiny outposts in the middle of the field, high up in the mountains and out in the middle of the desert. I even found myself one day a few years ago crossing the border in a disguised car to tell a story to a group of soldiers in a tiny outpost in Lebanon.

I have a special sentiment for the story "Y. L. Peretz in the Israeli Army," for a number of reasons. This story illustrates graphically what we storytellers go through all too often, if not in reality, then in our fears and fantasies.

"The Story of a Bass Fiddle" was told to the musical accompaniment of Israel Borochov, a very talented musician who was one of the founders of the famous Natural Gathering Band. He now has his own group, called East-West Ensemble, and is invited to tour internationally most of the year. This story brought me, during most performances, to a spiritual experience and many a time when the show came to its end I would spy a tear coursing down a tanned cheek. It is truly a beautiful story, which made it all the more torturous every time we performed to a less-than-receptive audience. The incident in the army was unbearably painful. It took me quite a while to get over it, but once I started retelling the experience I found it not only healing but also immensely funny. My audience laughed and allowed me to laugh as well.

The antidote to this story was when once telling a story in a barracks to a small group of soldiers at an isolated outpost on Mt. Hermon, a bundle of bedclothes on a bed suddenly came to life and a soldier sat up in bed. It seemed I had woken him up. For a while he stared blankly, not knowing where he was or what was going on. He most likely had not slept very much in the last few days. But eventually he got caught up in the story and by the end was totally involved. "First time I have ever been woken up by a story," he mentioned afterward.

The end of "Y. L. Peretz in the Israeli Army" seems to me the epitome of the storyteller. The storyteller at the end of the show just disappears, and all that is left with the audience is his story, as with the Cheshire Cat in *Alice in Wonderland* who, when disappearing, left only its smile behind. . . .

y reserve duty in the Israeli army I do in the Education Regiment—as a storyteller. When anyone happens to ask me what I do in the army—and this is a frequent question in Israel—I say, "I tell stories." The retort is always, "You're telling me a story!" But that is what I do.

I had staged a storytelling show with the music and accompaniment of Israel Borochov, a well-known Israeli musician. The story was called "The Story of a Bass Fiddle." This was one of the shows we performed in the Educational Regiment. The story is beautiful, almost poetic, and concerns a strange young boy who appears in a shtetl called Tomashov, in Poland. He is made the laughingstock of the village until he joins the Klezmer band and, in a very dramatic ending—during a great wedding—he ascends to heaven to play there.

It is a very entertaining but low-key story, and its beautiful language, when recited in the middle of a "working" week, can sometimes fall on sleeping ears.

With the army, we stipulated that the show was good only for units of intelligent soldiers in a relatively rested condition. This usually worked. However, one day I got a phone call from the commanding officer of the Southern Command Education Regiment. She said she was planning a week of intensive culture for her units and would like us to perform for a unit of infantry in basic training. I remembered back to the days I was in basic training in the infantry: when I wasn't running, I was sleeping. Nothing in between! I refused point-blank. She was stubborn—and persuasive. It was a long conversation. The breaking point came when she said she was even parachuting the Israeli Philharmonic Orchestra into the desert. I don't know if she meant it literally; I found myself imagining the pianist playing while parachuting down to earth. Somewhere after that . . . I don't remember how or why . . . I agreed.

Borochov, the musician, didn't buy the Philharmonic gimmick. (He is a very talented, but tough, musician!) The whole army escapade wasn't to his liking, as he is a very demanding musician and he found fault with even the most successful performance. It took thirty-five minutes to calm him down on the phone. In the end I promised him that if the show was a bomb we would just get up and leave in the middle.

Two weeks later, a gigantic military truck drew up and blocked the small street where I lived. The driver knocked at my door. "I've come to take you," he said laconically.

"Where to?" I asked, alarmed.

"You've got a show on in the army—in the south—don't you know? Are you Shai Schwartz?"

"Oh my God. That show! I had completely forgotten," I exclaimed, and added, "but why in that monstrous truck?"

"You've got equipment, haven't you?"

"A guitar, a high stool and a bass fiddle," I answered. "For that you don't need a truck."

"That's what we've got," he replied. "Let's get going; we've got a long journey ahead of us." He had a hint of a smile as he said it, and I felt shivers running down my spine.

Borochov hadn't forgotten. That's why he had conveniently gone shopping. But he made the mistake of coming home too early. He took one look at the truck, shouted, "I'm not going anywhere in that thing," and disappeared upstairs to his fourth-floor apartment. By this time cars were hooting at the truck driver, who was blocking the road with his monster.

After a tedious and long summit meeting with Borochov, I managed to persuade him to come down. Soon we were on our way. Like two little stones in a gigantic tin box, we bounced to and fro in that truck, which was normally used to transport whole units to the battlefront.

Two and a half hours later we arrived in Beersheba, the last city before the desert begins. Hours later we were still traveling south . . . on and on, into the desert. Borochov had completely introverted, doing some kind of "anger meditation" peculiar to himself. The mantra was usually something like, "Why the hell did I agree to . . . ?" or "Why do I always listen to that screwball?" (meaning me, of course). Anyway, even if he had wanted to talk it would have been an impossible mission. The noise this truck was making was something between a printing machine and a cement mixer (all gone mad). I thought it would be a good idea to have secret meetings of the chief of staff on a truck like this . . . no one would ever find out anything!

Somewhere in the desert—I don't know where or why—the driver turned right, off the so-called paved road. We were then traveling on what seemed to be a dirt road, traveling on and on and on in a black hole of dust.

Suddenly we saw a soldier sitting on a beach chair. He held a rope in his hands that stretched across to the other side of the road. Why he was sitting like that in the middle of the desert, heaven only knows. The terrain was exactly the same on one side of the rope as on the other . . . but it seemed as if we were there. Somewhere in the dusk, through the dust, I managed to make out a few tents and one or two prefabricated huts.

After a twenty-minute search, I managed to find a dusty Women's Army Corps (WAC) soldier who maintained that she was the education department of the unit.

"So . . . where are the soldiers?" I asked.

"They're coming."

"What do you mean 'they're coming'?" I demanded.

"They're coming," she repeated, as if I didn't understand. "They've had a week of field maneuvers and they're on a route march back here."

"Oh," I said. "You mean they haven't been sleeping much lately?"

"Not much less than usual," she answered—which actually meant nothing at all.

"So what do we do?" I asked.

"Wait," she answered.

Borochov, it seemed, was transcending into higher spheres of his meditation, and was holding on to himself so as not to become violent.

After a period of time that seemed like an hour or two (in the desert it is very difficult to evaluate time), we noticed on the horizon a small cloud of dust. It was moving and it was approaching us. Two light-years later they arrived. They stood there, on parade, like clay statues. They each wore a heavy layer of dust. They were weighed down by all their battle equipment.

They were swaying and bowing to the "god of slumber." Every so often one of them would succumb and tumble forward, completely asleep—then stumble a few steps, wake up, and step back into line.

We entered a tent to tune our instruments. The commanding officers were there, taking off their equipment and settling down. They snickered at us.

"You came to give a show?"

"Yes."

"Well, you'd better play very loud." Everyone seemed to find this immensely funny and cracked up laughing.

The soldiers were sitting down on the bare floor in one of the small huts, surrounded by their battle equipment. We climbed over their equipment. I said, "Good evening, guys. I see that you are all pretty tired." Here and there I saw some halfhearted smiles cracking in the dust masks. "Well, do whatever you feel like, but just try, please, to keep quiet."

I started to tell my story. In the beginning I had their attention; some were even amused at parts. But, slowly and surely, eyes were closing. Bialik said it best: "One by one my stars extinguished at dawn."

I had experience with similar situations so, instead of shouting and trying to wake up the sleepers, I concentrated my attention on those who were still awake. There was a hardy core of guys in the middle, still listening to me, but they were falling fast. I was desperately telling them my story, but their eyes were fluttering and, one by one, their heads nodded and fell. I concentrated my efforts on one soldier staring out at me with red eyes. He was battling to stay awake. He looked intelligent and I knew I could depend on him. He stayed with me a way, but at a certain moment he tried to make himself more comfortable and leaned on his friend's knees . . . and he, too, was gone!

This Jewish story of Y. L. Peretz was echoing around the room, detached from me. I was three-quarters of the way through when suddenly it hit me: I was telling my story to a room of sleeping soldiers. Should I carry on or should I stop? I felt like a "midnight express" charging through the night with no brakes! One thing I did know: I wasn't going to make any pauses. If I had to stop and should hear a snore, that would really be my final humiliation. My ego couldn't stand up to that.

During all this time I didn't dare look at Borochov. I could feel his eyes boring into the side of my face. If looks could burn, by now I would have been a piece of smoldering toast.

Near the end of the story, there is a dramatic entrance of a mysterious beggar king. Then, with him opening the gates of heaven, we understand that the young boy is playing his bass fiddle with the band of the heavenly choir. When the beggar king disappears I say: "They say that man was . . ." I leave a pregnant pause and the audience usually completes the sentence silently in their minds with the words, "Elijah the Prophet." This night, during that pause, I heard a terrible, heartrending snore! Then I realized that there were a few people still awake—maybe the commanding officer at the back—because after the snore came a few giggles and guffaws.

At that moment, there was nothing I wanted more than for the earth to open and swallow me up. The earth didn't even tremble and I carried on to the bitter end.

At the end, Borochov starts playing a beautiful chasidic melody that he had composed for the show, and the two of us sing together. Sometimes the audience quietly hums with us; here and there some moist eyes appear.

Tonight there was silence, but suddenly, one of the soldiers who had been awake throughout the whole show (afterward I found out that he had just come back from being AWOL) started singing with us, clapping his hands and waking up his friends— as if we were in some rollicking sing-along. Soldiers were waking up and, not even knowing what was going on, just joined in in a grand crescendo, as though they were at a Bob Dylan concert.

A large number of the soldiers were still sleeping as we gingerly stepped over bodies and walked out into the cold desert night. A young soldier approached us and said to me: "You know, if you had given me the book of that story last year, when I was in high school, I would have taken it and thrown it to the other side of the room. But tonight I had a real spiritual experience." Well, I sighed inwardly, it seems that we traveled all the way into the desert, in that gigantic truck, to tell this story to a room full of sleeping soldiers—just so that one soldier could have a spiritual experience! God has mysterious ways of acting . . . or something.

On the way back I tried to thaw the atmosphere with Borochov by telling a joke. "Listen, Israel," I said, "you know, one day a week or a month from now, at a certain break in a maneuver, one of those sleeping soldiers will turn to his friend and, with a puzzled look on his face, ask: 'Remember the storyteller they brought us one night? What happened to him? Where in hell did he disappear to?'"

Borochov smiled. "What a profession!" I thought to myself.

MESSIAH MAN
Rami M. Shapiro

Rami M. Shapiro *is rabbi and storyteller of Temple Beth Or, Miami, Florida. A graduate of Hebrew Union College–Jewish Institute of Religion, he also holds a Ph.D. in philosophy. He is the founder and director of Rasheit Institute for Jewish Spirituality. An award-winning poet, liturgist, essayist, and author, he has published over a dozen works of fiction, nonfiction, and poetry. Rami lives in Miami with his wife, his son, two dogs, and a host of figments of his imagination.*

In every age, at any given moment, there are thirty-six righteous men and women whose spiritual energy sustains the universe. So effortlessly do these *Lamed Vavnikim* (Hebrew for "thirty-six") accomplish their task that they themselves do not know they are among the thirty-six. Indeed, the hallmark of these messiahs is that there is no hallmark. Ordinariness is both their sign and their shield. Yet, if we are lucky, we run into one of these folks now and again.

At the time we may not notice anything special, for there is nothing special to notice. But in time, when the confusion of the everyday is laid to rest in memory, the mind trips over hints of divinity, and we suddenly realize our lives have been touched by the ordinary miracles of these nobody specials.

I made just such a discovery regarding a Yemenite Jewish silversmith named Micah. I met him in Jaffa, while I was studying philosophy and hasidic thought at Tel Aviv University in 1971. I didn't start telling his story until a decade later. It took me ten years to begin to grasp the message of our irregular encounters. For too long I had made Micah someone special. It was only with his death and the softening of memory that I allowed him to become the nobody special that he always was. Then, I knew that I had met one of the Thirty-Six.

I'm certain that if Micah could hear my claim he would laugh at its absurdity. That is the difference between him and me. If someone were to suggest that I might be a *Lamed Vavnik*, I would outwardly scoff and inwardly wonder: "Could it be? Am I worthy of being nobody special?" Of course, that thought alone would make it clear that I am a *Lamed Zion* ("thirty-seven"): a somebody who aspires to be among the nobodies.

The short tales recounted here are among a cycle of stories I tell about my encounters with this simple messiah. They are both reminiscences of the man and reminders of the deeper truth he sought to impart. Each time I tell these stories I am challenged to be a little less special and a little more real. I hope something of that comes across in the reading as well.

MESSIAH MAN

 first met Micah at the Shuk Ha Pishpishim in Jaffa, Israel. The Shuk is a flea market of sorts where craftspeople come to sell their wares. The vast majority of stalls are owned by Sephardic Jews, people from Morocco, Iran, Egypt, Syria, and Yemen. It is the Yemenites who dominate the marketplace, specializing in a finely crafted silver jewelry painstakingly fashioned by wrapping tiny bits of silver fiber into traditional geometric shapes.

Micah was a jeweler. His shop was not much different from any of the others. A hut more than a store, crammed into a tight row of huts spilling out into the crudely marked footpaths that served as aisles in the shuk. The place smelled of strong coffee and tea saturated with sugar. Metal filings danced in the air like fleas.

The day I met Micah was one on which I had come to sell, not buy. I was a student at Tel Aviv University, and the money my parents had given me when I left home some eight months earlier was supposed to have lasted all year. But as summer approached I knew that my reserves had fallen dangerously low. So I had come to the shuk to sell my winter coat. American clothes went for lots of money, even used, and I was pretty confident of bringing in at least a month's supply of cash. After all, the University meal program kept me fed, so the money was used primarily for travel and books.

After some initial investigative work among the first few craftsmen I met, I found that the shuk had an informal arena set aside for the kind of freelance bargaining I had in mind. With my fleece-lined corduroy jacket tucked bulkily under my arm, I squeezed my way through the narrow aisles to the designated area. What I found upon my arrival was a Sephardic version of Filene's basement. Bodies crammed against one another in the most awkward and compromising fashion; people reaching and testing, poking and feeling, trying things on, tearing things off, all in one mass huddle of humanity. I waded in. But before I had gone more than ten feet a burly arm grabbed mine and a rough voice demanded to see the coat.

I looked at the man. He was about five-feet-eight inches tall, with dark complexion and dark matted hair, and weighed at least two hundred pounds. He looked about fifty years old.

"This coat won't fit you," I said politely.

"Then I will get it for less," came the matter-of-fact reply.

"No, I mean it is too small; if you try it on it might rip."

"Then I will get it for less."

Now, I had expected to be taken advantage of as an American, but this guy was going to tear the jacket right along the seam. I tried to move away, but he grabbed the coat and began to put it on. It was at least three sizes too small, but—thank God—it didn't tear.

"Good," he said. "I'll take it. How much?"

Before I left the university dorm I had figured out what I wanted for the coat, and then settled on the minimum I would accept given my immediate monetary needs. I looked at the man and doubled my asking price.

"Too much. This is a winter coat and it's summer now."

"But it will be winter again," I said, repeating the price.

"It may not fit next winter. Besides, it is too hot now." He halved the price.

"It doesn't fit you anyway," I said and added 25 percent to his offer.

"Look, you want to sell a winter coat when it is summer, you have to sell at summer prices. Otherwise wait until winter." He halved my compromise offer.

"I won't be here next winter," I said mentally calculating how close he was getting to what I wanted.

"Good. Then you won't need the coat at all." He cut ten percent from his offer.

"I don't need the coat, I need the money."

My throat felt tight and strained; my voice sounded even more
so. My classroom Hebrew was designed to teach me Bible and
Mishna, not bargaining. I was holding my own, but I had the
dim sense that I was speaking in the Hebrew equivalent of Eliza-
bethan English. Luckily my roommates were Israelis who delighted in teaching me the vernacular of the street.

"Listen," I continued. "The coat doesn't fit you; the season
doesn't suit you, and the price doesn't excite you. Why don't
you just give up and wait until I have a summer clearance sale?"
I offered him my final price. To my surprise he took it.

"Plus a cup of tea in my shop," he added as he handed me
the money, put his thick arm on mine, and led me away to his
store.

To tell the truth, I had no desire to spend any more time with
this guy, but you don't violate the rules of hospitality that gov-
ern the Yemenite community, or the rules of good behavior that
allow the shuk to function just one degree short of all-out an-
archy. So I went, sat down on an upturned crate that served as
a stool, and sipped the thickest sugar tea broth I had ever tasted.
I declined the baklava but engaged my host in conversation,
much to the delight of us both.

He told me his name was Micah, that he came from Yemen in
the early 1950s, and that he was the Messiah.

I bought the first two items, but balked at the third.

"It is so," he calmly replied as I made light of his holiness. "It
is so. I sit here day after day making jewelry, weaving infinitely
fine strands of silver into patterns of beauty. It is messiah work.
It moves me out of the shuk, out of Israel, out of the Middle East.
I am," he said locking my eyes with his gaze, "a planetary person."

With an effort, I willed my eyes to look around the shop. It
was crammed with Micah's work. Exquisite pieces reflecting the
traditional patterns of Yemen, yet with a subtlety all their own.
He had managed to infuse his own originality into the inheri-
tance of centuries of family jewelry crafting.

Something deep inside me shouted—"Get the hell out of here."
Something even deeper whispered, "Stay."

WATCH THE SEA

"Notice the fine subtle curves of the design," Micah was saying as he introduced me to the intricacies of Yemenite craftsmanship. "No broken pieces, no straight lines. Only circles and curves; bits and pieces bending back into themselves to create a web of silver as fine as any spider ever wove."

I looked carefully at the pieces of jewelry he had laid out on his shop counter. They were exquisite. No matter what the overall size of the piece—and they ranged from tiny earrings to pendants the size of silver dollars—each was a variation on a timeless pattern of arcs and falls.

"It reminds me of the ocean," I said, sensing that this kind of analogy would spark more of my friend's messianic musings.

"The ocean," he murmured in a voice that seemed to transport him to some private sea inundating solemnly in his memory. "Yes. It is the ocean that inspires my work. It is the ocean that informs everything I do. The ocean is the greatest teacher. That is why I choose to live here in Jaffa, to be by my teacher, the sea. Come, I will show you."

I knew better than to protest that it was mid-morning and that a field trip to the Mediterranean would probably cost him customers, but I did so anyway.

"The customers can wait. They know my work, and if they want it badly enough they will wait. If not, then I would rather not sell it to them."

I shrugged, smiled, and let him push me gently out the door. A sign in Hebrew and English noted our absence and suggested a time of return. Micah never locked the door.

"So what if they steal the pieces, the soul of my work is in my heart. I bestow it upon the buyer as a gift. The piece without my blessing is only twisted wire. It means nothing."

The city of Jaffa is situated on a craggy cliff overlooking the Mediterranean Sea. The surf mounts an endless series of attacks against the city; whitecapped warriors crashing mercilessly upon the beach's rocky armor. Kamikazes in an eternal contest of water and stone.

"Watch the sea," Micah was saying in an urgent whisper. "Watch it."

We walked out on a jetty and sat down. Micah remained silent, his eyes focused on the battle.

"Not a battle," he replied several minutes after I had made the analogy aloud. "A dance. Water and stone in harmony; each true to its nature. Deeply true, simply true. You never see a stone pretending to be a sea, nor a sea pretending to be a stone. Each is itself and thus allows for harmony within diversity. But, please, enough talk. Watch."

I moved quietly to one side to get an unobstructed view of the sea. It was magnificent: a blue no painter could mix melting effortlessly at the horizon into the slightly paler blue of the sky. Minutes passed in silence, first singly, then by fives, and finally by tens. It was an hour before Micah looked from the sea and caught my eye.

"What did you see?" he asked in a manner that precluded any obvious response.

"The dance of eternity," I replied, trying to please him by picking up on his own metaphor.

"You saw no such thing," he said with a matter-of-factness that stung me as much as if it had been a slap. "No one sees the Dance of Eternity. One dances or one dies. But there is no observation. No observation tower, no separate seer who looks down. You were watching the sea when you should have been rolling with it."

"But you told me to look," I protested. "You said watch the sea, so I watched."

Micah shook his head slightly. "It is hard to instruct in these matters. Yes, I said watch the sea, but I had thought that by watching you would become lost in the dance and slowly become a dancer as well."

He began to turn and look away, but must have caught my expression of confusion. He turned his head to face me, his eyes focused somewhere deep inside my head.

"Which comes first," he asked, "the shore or the sea? Tell me, can there be a sea with no shore or a shore with no sea? No, the one 'goes with' the other. They arise together. Without the Other the One is inconceivable. The same is true of God and Creation. Which came first? The Creator or the Creation? Can there be a creator without a creation or a creation without a creator? No. Each 'goes with' the other. Without the One the Other is inconceivable.

"How do you learn this? No book can teach you. No person, either. The teacher is the sea and the shore. They instruct by doing, by being, by involving you in them, and thus opening you to yourself. When you watch the sea, watch it deeply without thought or comment. When you let the waves swell and crest and crash into a million tiny shards upon rocks worn smooth with eons of rolling surf; when you allow this to happen you find it happening in your own soul, your own mind.

"What is it that waves? The sea, the wind, the pull of the moon? No, it is your mind that waves. Watch the sea and you will see yourself. Ebbing and flowing, rising and crashing, turning and returning in an infinite array of patterns.

"This is what my art portrays. No, this is what my art embodies. Embodies. Listen closely: embodies. All wisdom must be embodied, incarnated, animated. You are the body of all wisdom. All you need do is watch the sea, become the sea, and then the oceanic within speaks to you of time and eternity. Spirals within spirals within spirals.

"My jewelry is the ocean wrought in silver. My body is the ocean wrought in flesh. My mind is eternity wrought in consciousness. It is the same with you if you would but stop thinking of the ocean as an other and see it as your self. When you find the ocean within and merge with it, then you become the planetary patternmaker of creation, the jeweler of life-webs, the Messiah. But first you must become one with the sea."

With a grace and speed that surprised me, Micah lashed out with the heel of his right foot and sent me tumbling off the jetty into the warm waters of the Mediterranean. I hit the water so suddenly there was no time for thought. For an instant the sea and I were one, and I sensed Eternity welling inside me. A moment (or was it a lifetime) later, Micah scooped me out, flailing

my arms, sputtering saltwater, not sure whether to laugh or cry
or have him committed.

DAWN

I don't know how he found me, but one morning, early—too early
to really be called morning in polite society—I found myself being
not-so-gently shaken awake by Micah.

"What the . . . ?"

"Dawn teaches. Come and see." I wrapped a blanket around
me and followed Micah out onto my dormitory balcony. My room,
situated on the third floor of a three-story brick building, faced
the sea. I watched the dawn roll in with the tide.

"Listen to the world awaken," Micah said softly. "Can you hear
the flowers stirring, preparing to unfold?"

"Nice image, Micah," I replied thickly, my throat pasty with
the sea air. "But it is too early for a nature lesson."

"It can never be too early," Micah said, gripping my shoulder
for emphasis. "Only too late. I always arise at dawn. I get up
with the grasses. I start work with the ants."

"The ants will still be there at ten," I sighed, knowing that I
was missing the point, but caring more about missing my sleep.

"True, but by then you have missed the magic and the lesson
is stale. Come, get dressed, and let's go downstairs."

I don't know why, but I got dressed and trudged heavily down
three flights of stairs. We walked across campus and came to
rest in a small patch of garden that provided the only swatch of
color in an otherwise gray concrete metropolis.

Micah motioned for me to sit. I sat. He pointed to a small flower
dipping precariously under the weight of a beetle. I looked and
shrugged. First at the beetle, then at Micah.

"What's the point?" I asked absently.

"No point," he said slightly irritated. "There is never any point.
Points are theories, opinions, isms. I am not interested in isms,
I am interested only in what is." His voice rose and his irritabil-
ity sharpened.

"Is there a point to the damn beetle sitting on the stupid
flower? No. Is there a point to the flower supporting the dumb

bug? No. There is no point, ever!" With that Micah ripped the
flower from the earth and sent the beetle flying head over four
heels into the grass. "What's the point?" he shouted, one deci-
bel below a scream.

"I don't know what the hell you're talking about, Micah," I said
letting my irritation show as well. "You drag me out into the
middle of campus three hours before breakfast to watch a bug
on a flower, and then you rip the poor thing out by the roots.
Just tell me what it is you think is so great out here and leave
the gardening to professionals."

Micah broke into a deep and powerful laugh. He did that often.
Sometimes I got the joke, sometimes I was the joke. Most times
I felt I had missed the punch line. This was one of the latter. I
shook my head in annoyance.

"All I wanted was for you to see the thing. Just see it. As it is.
No isms, just is," Micah said through laughter's tears. "Let me
try again.

"Why do you think the Bible says, 'There was evening, there
was morning, the first day'? Why does evening come before
morning? Because night represents nothingness, and morning represents somethingness. Something arises out of nothing, always. First there is nothing then something. Then nothing again. Over and over. Emptiness to fullness to emptiness
again. But why the seeming priority of emptiness, nothingness, evening? To teach us that only when we empty ourselves
of the somethings we hold dear can we hope to have a new
dawn.

"Do you follow? No, I can see it in your eyes. Try this: cup
your hands over your eyes. That's it. Make it perfectly dark in
there. You can leave the lids open, but let no light in. Relax into
the darkness. Let your eye muscles relax. In the darkness all
the somethings of life disappear. You see nothing. Your vision
is empty. Sit that way for a minute. That's all, sixty seconds. I'll
count. . . ."

I liked this crazy jeweler from Jaffa, so I sat with my hands
cupping my eyes for one full minute, actually enjoying the rest
it gave my pupils.

"Now," Micah said when his count had reached sixty, "take

your hands away and look around. Tell me if you notice a difference."

I am a skeptic at heart, but I had to admit it—the world looked at least three shades brighter. And it wasn't that the sun had risen a bit higher, it was that my eyes had registered that much more color.

"You see, I told you," Micah said after I had reported my results. "You emptied your eyes of seeing, you made a sixty-second evening of nothingness, and then opened up to the something of morning, and the world looked newer, shinier, deeper.

"This is the point: to see each day with new eyes; eyes emptied of yesterday's knowings and assumptions and fears. You will not forget the skills you have mastered in the past, but you will free yourself of the prejudices that have mastered you. This is why I rise at dawn, to greet the world as it comes into being with eyes also just coming into being.

"By letting go of yesterday, by inviting evening and emptying the self of false knowledge, you have the gift of new sight, the promise of new dawns, the hope of surprise. Only when you let the evening happen can you hope to wake to the sweetness of morning.

"Messiahs know this. It is time you learned as well."

HEALING

The news was laden with an anxious depression. Six Israelis murdered by a terrorist bomb in Jerusalem. Four Jews, two Arabs. The speculation was that this was the start of a new wave of terrorism.

Talk in the cafeteria, in the dorms, in the classrooms was dominated by rumors of war. Old stuff to the Israeli students, most of whom had fought in at least one war themselves, but totally new to us Americans suddenly confronted with the dangerous underbelly of life in the Middle East.

I tired of the arguing and the speculation and went to clear my head by the sea. I had learned some of Micah's listening technique and sat on the jetty near his shop several times a week, letting the sea write its lessons on my soul. But this time, every wave seemed like a body crushed up against stone hearts hardened by years of false hopes and expectations.

After an hour or so I gave up and rose stiffly to walk back to the dorm. With one last nod to the sea, I turned to find Micah standing some yards away watching me.

"Listening to the Teacher?" he asked.

"Class was canceled due to war," I said. "I couldn't hear a thing except the crying of the families of those who died this morning."

"Yes, I have heard it too. You know, I fought in three wars here. I have widowed more than a few women and orphaned more than a few children. And you know what we fight over? Dirt. Just dirt somebody drew an imaginary line through and scrawled a name over on a map."

"Not dirt," I protested. "There is more here than simply nationalism. The Arabs want to throw the Jews into the sea. They want us dead. Why else attack civilians and murder children? They don't give a damn for their land, they only want revenge on those who they imagine stole it from them. If we gave them a country they would turn it into a staging ground for genocide. This is what we fight for: our very survival."

The use of the first person plural embarrassed me. I had never fought in a war. And I had no intention of doing so. Not that I would go home if war broke out—I would volunteer for a non-combatant support position. But my life would not be on the line. So what right did I have to speak of "we"? But Micah ignored my grammar and repeated his position—"Dirt."

"You know," he continued after a moment's reflection, "there is no respect for the Land by either side. To them it is only an idea: dirt made holy by history, not by nature or the spirit. The fact is that if they held the land sacred, they could not bloody it with each other's guts. So to them it is only dirt; dirt and history, dusty memories of an idealized past. Jews and Arabs both— fighting for a past at the expense of a future.

"It will only get worse. And do not think it is we alone who exercise such madness. No. You Americans are no less guilty. And the Soviets, the British, the French and the Germans. We are all battling over the past. We are making the dirt damp with the blood of our children to fulfill the nightmares of our parents. We look out upon the planet and see only dirt and lines and boundaries and privation. If we had insight into the Land, respect for the Earth, there would be no boundaries and no privation."

Micah looked at me as if to invite a reply. I had none, so he went on. "Imagine the ultimate climax to this war over dirt. Imagine a world prematurely darkened by the ash of a thousand thousand firestorms. See blind birds die of starvation and the surviving bumblebee hunt for a suddenly extinct flower. Watch the plant life fade with the blackening of the sun. Feel the cold of winter pierce what should have a been summer's heat. Hear the stone quiet of a world without life. And all because we fight over dirt and trample the Holy Land, the planet itself, under our tank treads.

"Do you know what we need in Israel? It is not security. There is no such thing. Damascus can eliminate Jerusalem in minutes. And vice versa. There can be no security behind borders. Borders are just lines in the dirt, easily scratched out with the heel of the boot. What we need is healing, not security. Healing."

Politics has never been my forte. I quickly become impatient with the jingoism of politicians and the inhumanities of armchair tacticians. But neither have I patience for the naive quietism of peace-niks. Had Micah not been so intense in his manner and his speech, I might have excused myself for home. As it was I settled down upon a rock and motioned him to continue.

"There is no solution to the Arab-Israeli conflict. If there were it would no longer be a conflict. Our language betrays us and peace is impossible. There never will be a Greater Palestine nor a Greater Israel. Both Arafat and Begin will die with their dreams. There is no hope for Palestine, but there is hope for Palestinians. There is no hope for Israel, but there is hope for Israelis.

"People, not nations, can make peace. Peace through healing. Have you ever talked with an Arab? Really dialogued with one? No, I thought not. Most of us haven't. And those that do often find the most verbal to be the most hostile. Some of my neighbors are Arabs. We are neighbors, not best friends. But when we speak, we speak as human beings. Do you know what worries them? The price of gasoline and groceries. The threat of violence, and the thought that their children might die in a terrorist attack. Do you know what worries us? The same things.

"When we talk of life and not of history we speak as human beings. We effect healing. We reveal our commonality and can better allow for our differences. We don't need peace, we need healing. We need people meeting and falling in love. We need friends risking their emotional lives for each other. We need to sit down face-to-face and scream out the pain that is consuming us and turning this Holy Land into dirt.

"But it won't happen from politicians. They live only in the past. The future to them is only a justification of the particular history to which they pledge allegiance. Their policies are determined by the past, not by the people or the planet. They have no vision and stumble blindly toward Armageddon.

"Better the engineers should run the country. They would build bridges, lay pipes for irrigation and wires for electricity. Or let the soccer players run the country and battle it all out in the playing field. Or let the women run the country and give the men a chance to know the children they so cavalierly send out to kill and be killed. Or let. . . ."

Before Micah could finish, a rock whizzed by my ear and struck him in the head. A crease of blood beaded across his right eyebrow.

We both turned to see an Arab boy picking up a second stone. From behind a donkey bearing the day's groceries an Arab woman ran screaming at the boy. She grabbed him by the ear and pulled him to the donkey. "I am sorry, Adoni," she called to Micah in a heavily accented Hebrew not unlike his own.

"I am all right, Imma," he replied, honoring the stranger with the title "Mother."

"I will see that he never does such a thing again," she said turning to the boy and her donkey and steering both for home.

"If she can do that for her son," Micah said to me as he too took his leave, "there may yet be a healing in this bowed and bloodied world."

NIGHT LIGHT

One afternoon as I gazed out over the majesty of the Mediterranean, Micah happened by (or not; did he ever just happen by?).

"The ocean is a great teacher, but not the only one. It is time for us to go to the mountains."

He said this with such calm matter-of-factness, as if incapable of imagining that I might have something else to do. He was right. Where Micah was concerned, I never had anything else to do. He made allowances for my school schedule and we set a date for a private trip into the Sinai.

We left on a Friday before sunrise, and had traveled well past Elat when first light reminded us that we had not yet eaten breakfast. Micah pulled off the road, reached for a sack he had tossed into the backseat of his much abused reparation model Mercedes, and offered me a sandwich of thick bread and chocolate butter. Typical Israeli fare. We ate quietly and took in the view.

The Negev is a stark, red desert. To our right were the mountains-of-hiding where, centuries before, the Essenes had prepared for the final battle between the Sons of Light and the Sons of Darkness. In those caves proud and rebellious Jews had staged a war of attrition against the conquering Romans. Who could tell what fragments of history still remained in the cracks of these eternal cliffs? To our left lay the Dead Sea, so-called because its salty water could sustain no life.

It was only somewhat different with the Negev. Life there depended upon fresh water, which was always in short supply. But given the moisture, the earth responded with her bounty. It was the genius of the Israelis that they could settle the Negev and bring water to its parched soil. But the settlements did not extend this far south, and we were quite alone.

Micah had finished his sandwich and a cup of hot coffee he had poured from a thermos. He left the car to stretch out on the roadside. He was staring in the direction of Jordan, just across the sea from us. There too the land was mountainous and nearly barren. With binoculars we could pick out an occasional bedouin shepherding a flock. Other than that the scene was still and silent.

"Let's walk," Micah called to me from outside the car. "I want to show you something."

I finished off the last of my sandwich, swallowed a bit of water from a canteen, and ran after Micah, who had already begun walking.

We walked away from the sea and into the foothills. At first the climb was an easy one, but after forty minutes or so it became quite steep. Micah took to the climbing like a mountain goat, leaping from rock to rock. I followed in more lizardlike fashion, sometimes leaping, more often crawling on all fours.

By the time the sun had reached its mid-morning perch, Micah had reached his destination. He sat patiently and waited for me to catch up. When I had, he patted a smooth boulder and beckoned me to sit. I did so gladly. My breathing fell back to its normal pattern within a few minutes, and I managed to keep the sweat from stinging my eyes by mopping my brow with an already too damp shirt sleeve. I noticed that Micah wasn't perspiring at all. Just sitting there like a lizard on a rock, he looked cool and confident as an actor selling deodorant to a harried America.

Following Micah's model, I found a rock cushion angled slightly so as to help me keep my knees on the ground when I sat upon it crossed-legged in yoga style. I shuckled a bit side to side and let myself settle into a comfortable sitting posture, my back relaxed but straight, my sternum up, my breathing slow and deepening. And I sat. Once my body quieted a bit, I discovered a soft breeze coming through the mountains. It was delightful. If I sat still and let my breathing find its own level, the breeze took care of my sweat and my discomfort. Freed from bodily distractions, I took in the scene that was so engrossing Micah.

The Negev was a kaleidoscope of reds and browns. Swirls of color danced around and around as if someone were perpetually turning the kaleidoscope before my eyes. The lighter browns, offset by the rich mahogany of the darker shades, looked like streaks of lightning in a dark and stormy sky. The whole place was in motion, yet as still as only a mountainscape can be.

The shadows cast by the few scrub trees that shared the cliff with us reported the time. It was early afternoon. I was startled and a bit frightened. We should have been many miles south of here by now. I turned to wake Micah from his reverie, but Micah was gone.

I stood and called to him. Mercifully, he answered immediately. I followed his voice and found him inside the face of massive rock.

"Cracks like these run throughout the mountains," he said to an unspoken question shouted by my shocked expression of finding him almost totally encased in yellow stone. "It is here that the mountain whispers her most intimate secrets. We will stay here for the night, for there is much to learn."

By "here" I thought Micah meant the flat rock plateau we had been sitting on. There was room for sleeping bags and the fire would be lovely if enough wood could be found. But Micah did not mean the flat rock. He meant the crevice of the rock face. And he was serious.

Within a couple of hours he had made the round-trip from the cliff to the car, and returned with camping supplies and several pairs of shirts and slacks. He had me put them all on at once.

"Stylish," I said, "but not conducive to rock climbing."

"They will keep you warm when night falls. And besides, you will do no more climbing today." Micah turned and motioned for me to follow. Bulky in my layers of clothes, I stiffly made my way to his side.

"Here is where you will spend the night," he said, pointing to a golden crack in the swirling rock. "Climb in at sundown, and listen to the rock as you learned to listen to the sea. You know the way." I opened my mouth to protest. This had gone too far. Who knew what dangers I faced being stuffed into a jagged crease in the mountainside? But Micah assured me he would stand guard, build a fire, and look out for my safety. We had known each other quite a while, and I trusted him as both a teacher and friend. I smiled and slipped into the rock for a test run.

The real thing came with sundown. The air cooled quickly and I was thankful for the layers of clothes that crushed against me as I crushed against the rock. The glorious colors that so dominated the rockscape faded with the light, and soon I was left with only the moon and stars to illumine my narrow berth.

The night noise of the Negev chilled me even more than the air. But I caught a glimpse of Micah's fire, and heard him singing to himself not too far away. I trusted him, and turned my attention to the mountain. I wanted to trust the rock as much as I did the man.

My body totally immobile, my eyes closed to the moonlight, my mind closed to the absurdity of my situation, I listened to the rock. . . .

The smell of tea and chocolate butter roused me. It was early morning. Micah was standing over me, arms outstretched to pull me out of the crevice. I stripped off the excess clothing and the two of us walked silently to the fire that Micah had kept burning all night. I drank the tea, savoring the sugary broth as it ate through the night-film on my teeth.

Micah handed me a chocolate butter sandwich and raised his eyebrows as if to invite my commentary on the night's experience.

"The sea taught me about change," I said between bites of my sandwich, "and the mountain spoke of eternity. I sensed that both are part of a greater truth, two sides to a coin I cannot begin to grasp."

"Can teeth bite themselves?" he asked me. "Can a finger point to itself? You cannot grasp hold of what you already are. The coin you sense is your true identity. It is Messiah. It is yourself. The sea and the stone are teachers of the greatest kind, for they point to the truth both inside and outside of you. In fact, of course, there is neither inside nor out, for each goes with the other. But the point, I trust, is clear: The light that illumines the path of truth is an everlasting light burning in your own belly. It is a night-light streaking the darkness of ignorance with the brilliance of truth."

All this Micah said distractedly, without emotion. His eyes took in the distance but ignored my presence. Then he turned to me and smiled.

"You have listened well. Come, we have much to do if we are to make Sinai by sundown."

LOVE SONG

Where the Negev is a swirl of color, the Sinai is the absence of color. White sands on white cliffs. A hard place, foreboding, brooding, and silent. Here and there a lone palm with a camel scratching against its trunk or tearing at its leaves. Here and there a bedouin checking the wooden tent stakes of a goat-hide shelter. But as I sat silently on a hilltop, no bedouin hammered and no camel spat. Nothing moved. There was no sound.

I had spent most of the night alone on this ragged overturned bowl of a rockpile. Micah had pitched camp about a mile away, but had instructed me to spend the night up here. My sleeping bag wrapped tight around my shoulders, I huddled against the chill that turned the baking sands into a frosty wasteland within minutes of the setting of the sun. I watched the stars poke holes in the pitch black of the night sky. And, as always, I listened.

But here, atop this hill of hardened sand and rock, there was no sound. Only my own breathing punctuated the silence. I was tempted to scream just to shatter the quiet. But I refrained. There was a beauty here, a power here that I could not violate with any expression of fear. So I sat, trusting that the rock would not betray me to a serpent, and that morning would find me none the worse for my experience.

And then I heard it. A hum of some sort. Like the quite dull strumming of a deep bass string, or the thick low moaning of an electric plant. I was startled, and looked around to find the source. But whenever I looked I lost the sound. Only when I remained still and quiet did the silence give birth to the hum. And then, of a sudden, the hum gave way to a symphony. The mountains seemed to play the bass line, the lower hills peaking with the melody, the sands singing out a chorus of magical incantations.

I felt as if I were in the presence of angels calling out the essence of life: holy, holy, holy is the One who Manifests the Many. Holy, holy, holy are the Many who embody the One. But soon the symphony became too sweet even for angels. Something else was happening. A singing, yes; and also a sighing; a passionate heaving sighing of love. Sky making love to earth; mountains singing the praises of sea; sands embracing stones. Everything called out to everything else. Everything embraced everything else. Everything became everything else. All in love. All was love. All is love.

And I sighed and sang with it All.

For a moment—or was it longer—I was rock and sky, stone and sand and sea. For a moment I was the All calling to Myself in love. For a moment, then I could stand it no longer and fell much too swiftly asleep.

I awoke before dawn. The symphony was over, but still the silence spoke. I heard a hiss, a whisper. It spoke to me as clearly as I am speaking to you. It used words, images, comparisons and contrasts. I took it all in and nodded motionlessly at the profound truths that were being revealed to me. And then, as soon as it had finished, I forgot it all. Only the hiss remained.

I stood up, gathered my sleeping bag up in a bundle, and started down the hill to return to Micah. My very first step brought me up short. Something was different. I stepped again and the same thought arose in me: Something had changed. No new idea possessed me. No new insight illumined my path. What was it that seemed so wondrously fresh and exhilarating that it made each step a gift of the greatest joy?

Then I knew. It was the steps themselves. The way I walked had changed. I thought of Jacob arising from his death struggle with God to find his victory had cost him his gait and that the mark of holiness would leave him with a limp forever. But I was not Jacob, nor had I spent the night wrestling with the gods. And I wasn't limping, but flying. I sensed not a loss of balance, but a renewal of balance. It was as if a new harmony had been infused in my body. A new wholeness. A sense of inner and outer balance that let me step lightly through life leaving no more tracks than does a bird in flight.

I danced and spun and twirled and leaped like a drunken gazelle. And I laughed. Powerfully, deeply, so deeply that the earth laughed with me, and the two of us rolled with the joy of just being alive.

DRUM

Micah loved drums. His small apartment was a storehouse of percussion instruments. Congas, bongos, even a small steel drum he had received from a Jamaican fellow in trade for a piece of jewelry. Micah would sit for hours and slap out rhythmic patterns on an old Indian tabla, sometimes singing the beats with a rapid jazz-talk before playing them on the taut skins.

He used to invite me to impromptu concerts with his friends. Everybody would get a drum and someone would start out hammering something or other while the rest of us waited for just the right moment to leap into the improvisation.

I marveled at the fact that I knew when to jump in as well. I am no musician, yet the rhythm was so obvious and my duty so clear that I could effortlessly play along with the best of them.

"Drums are great teachers," Micah would say.

"To you, everything is a great teacher," I replied, smiling.

"Just so. Everything teaches what it knows. That is the duty of all living things, to teach what we know. The drum is a teacher of great mysteries. For the drum articulates the hidden rhythms of life." I looked at him without responding, knowing that he was warming up to a topic.

"Where do you think these rhythms come from? Do you think we just invent them? How do we know of beats and measures and timing and such? If rhythm were external to you, you would never get it. It is internal. Each thing has its rhythm, and that allows it to open up to the rhythms of all other things."

Micah reached for a small bongo and tapped out a rapid, fiery beat. He tossed me another drum and had me imitate him. I couldn't. Then he took up his drum again and motioned with his head for me to drum along in my own way. This I could do, and our improvisation found its integrity and soul.

"Precisely my point," he said as I noted this fact aloud. "You cannot copy the beat of another and maintain its original integrity. But you can add to the rhythm with your own and create a greater integrity. Even in a symphony where the musicians are playing someone else's score, if they do not make the score their own, they cannot play it well. They can imitate, but imitation is not true and it rings false every time.

"Each of us is like a drum, capable of many rhythms. All by itself the drum is mute, only in relation to others does it come alive. It has a great range of sounds and beats, but it always remains true to its nature. You cannot get a drum to sound like a violin."

"But how do we find our range of rhythms?" I asked. "How do we know whether we are remaining true to our nature?"

"You only know by experimenting. There is no knowledge without experience. You cannot say in advance this is me or this is not. You do and then you learn. If the beat is clear and powerful then it is true. If it is strained and hesitant then it is false. When your beat is true, it blends in effortlessly with others who are themselves true. When it is not, it blends with nothing and creates only discord.

"But there is no way to know this beforehand. This is the risk of rhythm. To know the truth of who you are you must dare beat out loud the rhythm of your soul."

TOUCH

I received a letter about two weeks ago from one of Micah's friends. It was a short handwritten note in Hebrew. I had to read it over several times before I was sure I understood its contents. Maybe my Hebrew was rusty. Maybe I just didn't want to understand. The note said Micah had died.

We hadn't corresponded much over the years. It didn't seem necessary. We had linked ourselves at a level untouched by distance or time. If I were ever to see him again, we would pick up where we had left off as if we had never left off at all. But I would not see him again. There was no one left to see. Micah was dead.

My mind drifted back to Jaffa, to one particular night after I had gotten word that my grandfather had died. My family didn't have the money to fly me back to the States for the funeral, so I marked the day with quiet meditation, and spent the evening with Micah.

"Do you ever think about dying?" I asked him.

"Sometimes, when I am feeling very brave. You see, thinking about dying—I mean really thinking about it—is a frightening activity. It is frightening because it challenges our assumptions and forcibly reorients our perspectives and priorities. To think about my death is to know what I am and what is truly important to me. It is much easier not to know these things."

"Well, what do you think happens when you die? Do you believe in a soul? What about a world to come or reincarnation?"

"Yes, the world has a soul, it is God. God wears the world like a clown wears a mask. But there is no world to come. This world is still a world to come, a world coming into being. It is not stagnant, not finished. It is evolving, we are evolving. The world to come is only this world in a context as yet unrealized.

"As for reincarnation—I am reborn each moment. I die each moment as well. There is no 'me,' no core at the center of this body that shifts from form to form. There is only experience and the semblance of continuity that the mind gives to things in order to keep from going mad. But there is no eternal I. Only temporary I'ings dancing to a rhythm all their own yet part of all others. When we really investigate death, we see there are no boundaries to life. We see that the wind and the air, the bird and the tree, the dancer and the corpse—are all me."

Micah's eyes bespoke the fact that his words had given way to a vision beyond the ordinary. I knew that at such times it was useless to question him. I sat and I waited, thinking of my grandfather. After an hour or so I decided to leave, but before I reached the door Micah spoke:

"There is, in the heart of each being, a link to the Heart of All Being. There is, in the heart of your being, a center that you share with all being. This is the source of your power, your integrity, your truth. This is the pulsating source of life that animates everything you do or say or think. This is the Actor who wears your face like a mask yet who loves you as an expression of his own being. This is the place of awareness that lets you die and live in a new way: a way without boundaries, without fears, without time or expectations. This is the power that opens you to the 'is' and lets the 'ism' quietly fall aside. This is the place of truth.

"It is useless to think about death. What is useful is to die. Here and now. Die to false ego, die to isms, die to opinions of what must be and wake up to the truth of what really is.

"Your grandfather is dead. His energy now fuels something

else. His essence has returned to the source where it is to be recycled into yet another form. He is tree and earth and sky. They are now your grandfather. Welcome them as family. Love them as you loved him. See him in them, and them in yourself. Then you too can die with peace and live with integrity."

Something in his words—perhaps the feeling I had that they seemed to come from a space beyond himself—stung me. I left without saying good-bye.

I cried. Hard and long. I mourned for Grampa, and for myself. I cried and I cried and I cried. And then, slowly, perhaps at first unconsciously, I began to laugh. I remembered the funny things he did, the meaningful things he taught me; the way he lived. His being became a part of mine and an immortality was suddenly present. I laughed as long and as hard as I had cried.

After reading the note about Micah's death, I cried again. It was the same hard cry. And it too gave way to laughter. I saw him in the clouds, and in the grass. I heard him instruct me from the willows and the waves. I felt his touch and warmed to his jokes.

We walk together still, this messiah man and me. And somewhere deep inside we touch, and touching each other we embrace you all.

THE UNTOUCHED OIL
Eliezer Shore

Eliezer Shore *graduated from Sarah Lawrence College in 1982 with a degree in religious studies as well as work in the performing arts. Since then, he has been studying Torah in yeshivot, in both America and Israel. He has been an informal collector and reteller of classic chasidic tales. Since studying storytelling at Yeshiva University's Azrieli Graduate Institute, he began to write original stories for both adults and children. He publishes a small journal of chasidic thought,* Bas Ayin, *and is working on a tape of original children's stories. Eliezer now lives in Jerusalem.*

Y. Paltrowitz

There is a story behind this story. It didn't simply show up one morning as a twinkle in the author's eye. The tale has been rolling around the world for probably several centuries, and how it got from Africa to the Lower East Side of New York is a story in itself.

In the fall of 1991, I was attending a graduate course in storytelling taught by Peninnah Schram. It was my first introduction to the world of professional storytelling, and my teacher was a consummate artist. We learned all facets of the art: how to locate stories, catalog them, and tell them. It was the creation of new stories that particularly intrigued me. I remember Peninnah explaining to us how storytellers adapt stories from foreign cultures to make them their own. This is just how classic tales traveled from country to country and land to land. To illustrate this point, Peninnah used one of her own stories as an example. She told us about one of her favorite, most personal stories, "The Golden Watch," published in her book *Jewish Stories One Generation Tells Another*. The story is based upon a Liberian folktale about a hunter who goes out to the field and never returns. He leaves behind him three boys and a pregnant wife, who subsequently gives birth to a fourth son. Slowly, the father is forgotten. Years later, when the youngest son has grown up a bit, he asks about his father. This motivates the other brothers to go searching for him. They find their father's bones and magically bring him back to life. The story concludes with a happy ending and everyone returns home. Peninnah told the original story in class and concluded, "And I took this story and transplanted it to the Lower East Side as an immigration story about legacies; that remembrance is our legacy."

Those words immediately sent me into a trance. Most storytellers, as you can imagine, live only partly in this world. Much of their time is spent in a shadowy patchwork reality of images, narratives, descriptive gestures, and fanciful tales, and the slightest provocation—the suggestion of a good story—immediately sets their minds spinning. I didn't hear the rest of the class. All I kept thinking was, "How did she do it? How did she transpose the story to the Lower East Side?" I don't even remember how I got home that night, my mind was so preoccupied, but by the time I did, I had most of the details worked out. The story I created, I was sure, was exactly the one Peninnah Schram had written. Later, when I read the story "The Golden Watch," it had almost nothing in common with my story *except* in the structure—and in being set on the Lower East Side! This is a fascinating example of the diversity of storytellers' minds, even when working from the same source material.

As Peninnah pointed out, the original story had a Jewish message in it, which is why it so easily lent itself to translation. Perhaps, a long time ago, it originated as a Jewish story. There is a story about the Baal Shem Tov, who once heard a Gentile shepherd whistling a song that he immediately recognized as being a lost melody from the Beit HaMikdash—the Holy Temple in Jerusalem. The Baal Shem Tov offered to "buy" the melody from the boy. As soon as he handed him the money, the boy immediately forgot the tune, and the Baal Shem Tov returned it to its proper place among the Jewish People. Storytellers like Peninnah Schram can recognize a Jewish tale when they hear one. Perhaps she too has redeemed a lost Jewish story from exile.

---

 o say that life was hard for the residents of the Lower East Side was to do them an injustice. The streets of New York were not paved with gold, as they had been led to believe. Their stones were cold and hard. No work, no money, no opportunity. Grown men ate portions of food too small for children, and children ate much less. For every one job that opened up, fifty new immigrants streamed off Ellis Island. Life was indeed hard, but it was hardest of all for those Jews who still clung to the religion of their forefathers. Monday morning out on the streets looking for work—take what you can get—then on Friday afternoon came the inevitable question, "Are you coming in tomorrow?" "No." "Then don't come in next Monday." This is how it went, week after week. Not many held on, not even the pious.

Yaakov Cohen was one of these faithful. A descendant of a long line of distinguished rabbis, he could recite his family tree with ease. Furthermore, he was a Cohen, a Priest, which was another unending source of pride. He often dreamt of the day when the Holy Temple in Jerusalem would be rebuilt, and how he and his children would serve there. In his small town in Poland he was a prominent figure. His small grocery provided a modest living for his wife and four sons, but his real life centered around the community. He was the *gabbai* of the shul, ran a soup kitchen for the needy, gave classes to young married men, and every Friday afternoon, lit the golden candelabra in the synagogue, to welcome the oncoming Shabbos. He was a good Jew, and no one could question his faith.

But America was different. There were many Yaakov Cohens here, many other pious individuals, but they had fallen before the onslaughts of hunger, sickness, and cold winter nights. Yaakov, like the others, had come with the dream of building a better life, and like so many others, he found his dream difficult to fulfill. His problem was accentuated by his appearance— his beard and *peyos* clearly labeled him a *Shomer Shabbos*, and employers would hardly look at him.

What could poor Yaakov do? Compromise crept in slowly. The *peyos* eventually went. The beard was trimmed, shorter and shorter, until it too was gone. But as for the Holy Shabbos, that he would not touch, not even a hair.

However, the hunger of winter was the hardest of all, and Yaakov could find no work. Nothing. He walked the streets, peered into store windows, eavesdropped the conversations of well-fed businessmen on street corners. Maybe, maybe. . . . Then one day he spied a little notice beside a drugstore telephone: "Bookkeeper wanted. Inquire 11–15 Delancey St. Second floor." Yaakov pulled the note down and stuffed it into his pocket.

Moments later, he was ushered into a small office. A fat man with a noxious cigar showed him his job. "Here are the books. These are the entries. Here is what you write. This is what you add. It's a lot of work, and it must be done on time." Yaakov nodded, acceptingly. "And one more thing," the fat man added, "of course you work Saturdays." Yaakov looked down. He rubbed his dry, cracking hands, he stared at his worn, peeling shoes. He nodded, acceptingly.

Life changed after that, both for better and for worse. Yes, there was food for Yaakov's family, but now he hardly saw them. Off to work early in the morning, back late at night, and how many nights did he sleep at his desk? He found that if he worked very hard, he could silence the small nagging voice within him. Meanwhile, his sons were growing up. Without a strong father figure to guide them, their own commitment to Torah was becoming lax, and New York offered many distractions for these strong young men. Only Yaakov's youngest son, Ephraim, maintained his childish faith. Still only nine years old, he enjoyed saying *Tehilim* or studying Torah in the back rows of the corner *shteible*. Ephraim was very young when his family came to America. He did not remember Poland, and his memories of his father before his transformation were poignant but fleeting. Still, he read the *Chumash* and the *Midrashim*, and he dreamt of a Golden Temple in a holy land where Priests served the living God. One day, he and his family would be there.

Time passed. Yaakov the Cohen became thin. Leaning over his books, his eyes became weak. He did not observe much of anything these days, and he would not remember the past.

It was a cold afternoon in late November. Ephraim Cohen was searching through his parents' bedroom closet, as children often do. Perhaps he was looking for a hidden treasure, or, since Chanukah was less than a week away, he may have been searching for a little flask of pure untouched olive oil. In any case, he found something just as good.

Among some old papers, an expired passport, a birth certificate, and some tattered greeting cards, he found an old black and white photo of a young boy wearing a pair of Tefillin. The boy's face shone with strength and intelligence, and he stood with a pride undimmed in the faded print. On the back was written the date—1901.

Ephraim brought the photo to his mother. "Mother, who is this?" he asked. His mother stared at it long, she turned it over, then over again. "I believe this is your father on his Bar Mitzvah day," she sighed. "Is this father? Is this really father?" he said in disbelief. Ephraim ran down to the street, where his oldest brother was unloading a wagon. "Shimi," he said, "who is this?" He examined the photo and recognized something of that same look in his own little brother's eyes. "This is father," he said softly.

That night, the brothers sat around the kitchen table and sighed, passing the photo back and forth. "This is father. What has happened to him? What has happened to us? We must try to help."

Suddenly, Shimon, the oldest, spoke up. "I have an idea," he said. He ran to the hall closet and began shifting through the old newspapers, the yellowing tablecloths. After a moment he pulled out a faded blue cloth bag—his father's Tefillin. Long unused, they had sat there patiently waiting. He ran back to his brothers, holding up his prize.

That night, a Wednesday, as Yaakov slept at his accounting desk, his oldest son quietly entered the office and placed the Tefillin on the table before him.

When Yaakov awoke in the morning, he could not believe his eyes. It was as though a dream of the past had floated down into reality. He gently picked up the bag and smiled as he examined the gold and silver embroidery on the blue velvet. He put his hand inside and felt the smooth leather straps. What is written in Tefillin? "Hear, O Israel, the Lord is our God, the Lord is One." And what is written in God's Tefillin, the Talmud asks. "Who is like Your people, Israel, a one nation on earth." Yaakov returned to his accounting, but throughout the day, as he wrote with his right hand, his left hand rested comfortably on the Tefillin bag before him.

That night Yaakov again fell asleep at his accounting table and in the still darkness, his second son, Nachum, slipped into the room and quietly laid his father's Tallis in front of him.

When Yaakov awoke that next morning, a Friday, he blinked in disbelief. "What is going on here?" he thought. "Where did this come from? Is this real?" He rubbed the yellowing wool, he fingered the fraying *tzitzis*. It was real. He spread out the Tallis. It was worn and moth-eaten, a little like Yaakov himself. Still, there was a certain dignity to it. He remembered the High Holidays services, and how, even as a child, he would stand at the front of the synagogue, Tallis over his head and arms, and bless the people: "May God bless you and protect you. May God shine His face upon you and be gracious to you. May God lift His face to you, and bestow upon you peace." He had always meant it, as well.

"It's cold in here," he told himself. "Maybe this will keep me warm." He wrapped himself in the old Tallis and strangely, it *did* keep him warm. He bent over his work and continued, the ragged Tallis around his shoulders, his left hand resting upon the Tefillin.

Sometime toward dusk, Yaakov laid his head upon his arm and fell asleep. When he awoke it was already night. He looked up and saw what appeared to be two flaming angels hovering in the darkness before him. He blinked, rubbed his eyes, and beheld two Shabbos candles burning brightly on his desk. While he had slept, his third son had placed them there, made the blessing over the Shabbos, and left. Yaakov gave a great shudder. A flood of memories overwhelmed him. "Shabbos," he whispered to himself. "Shabbos, Shabbos."

Yaakov stared into those lights. He sat unmoving for hours as they slowly burned down. In those holy Shabbos lights he saw many things. He saw his own wife lighting Shabbos candles back in their home in Poland. He saw his mother, too, as she would pray for her family before the Shabbos lights, and his ruddy-cheeked grandmother kindling, as well. Yaakov saw the oil lamps of the Beis HaMedrash, where scholars studied the holy Torah deep into the night. And he saw the Shabbos lights of his own shul, that he, himself, once lit.

His vision went back. He saw the lights that Jews had lit for thousands of years—a million *Chanukiot* in a million homes. He saw the Cohen Godol tending the lights of the holy Menorah in the Sanctuary, and the wars of the Chashmonaim, as they fought to reclaim their religion. He saw the countless Jews whose lives had ended in flames because they had refused to abandon their Torah. And, at the very end, before the candles died out, as they flickered their last, dull, orange and blue flame, he saw the destruction of Jerusalem, the burning of the Beis HaMikdash, and the beginning of the long, dark exile.

Yaakov did not return home that night, nor Shabbos by day, nor *Motzoi* Shabbos, nor Sunday. And Sunday night was the first night of Chanukah.

In their small apartment, his four sons sat anxiously looking out the window. In their hands was a small candle that would serve as an impoverished Menorah. They watched the darkening horizon, waiting for the proper moment in which to light, but silently, their eyes scanned the streets, searching for something else. Darkness fell, and the stars would soon appear.

"We may as well begin," Shimon, the oldest, finally said. At that moment, from down below on the street, they heard a call. "Shimon, Nachum, Tzvi, Ephraim. Come down!" It was their father! Like sparks from a bonfire they flew out the door and down the steps.

Standing in front of the house was Yaakov. Beside the door, in a small glass case, was a beautiful gold tinted Menorah. "My boys, my dear boys," he said, "you saved me. You did. You were the angels who brought about my deliverance. I've made many mistakes, I'll admit them, but from now on things will be different." His eyes were wet with tears. "Now, come, who will help me light the Menorah? We have only one candle tonight."

Shimon, the oldest, spoke up first. "Me, Father, because I brought you your Tefillin, it was really my idea." "You're right, my son, and it was a beautiful idea. It's what woke me up from my sleep." Nachum stepped forward. "Father, I brought you your Tallis." "Yes, my son, that too was important. It warmed my very soul." "Father," said Tzvi, "I lit the Shabbos candles." "Tzvi, that was the most precious gift of all." He turned to Ephraim, the youngest. "What about you, Ephraim? What did you do?" "Nothing, father. Only I . . . I found an old photo of you in the closet, and I went around asking everyone, 'Is this father? Is this father?'"

His father paused. "Then to you, Ephraim, I owe the most. Because you cared enough to ask about me, and a man is never completely lost as long as someone cares for him. Your words woke up every one of us." He took Ephraim's hand. "Come boys, let us light the Menorah with your little brother, Ephraim." The brothers gathered around as Yaakov bent forward to light the Menorah, and there was joy in their hearts, because they knew their father had returned.

A TALE OF DIAMOND LISTENING

Laura Simms

Laura Simms, *a storyteller, author, teacher, and scholar, has been in the forefront of storytelling since 1968, telling traditional stories and personal narratives. She is an award-winning video and recording artist. Her newest compact disc is* Making Peace; Heart Uprising *and her most recent book is* Moon and Otter and Frog. *She is on the faculty at Naropa Institute in Boulder, Colorado, and other institutes, is in residence at the United Nations School in New York, and teaches privately. Laura resides in New York City.*

I began telling stories in 1967. It was a sunny afternoon of sudden warmth in an otherwise cold April. The first story I told was a Russian fairy tale to a group of adults and children. It came naturally to me. I sank into the world of fairy tale easily and deeply, just as one falls into much-needed sleep. Only later, after years of researching, performing, writing, and teaching, did I understand the connection I had in my bones from the beginning. I grew up, albeit in Brooklyn, in the old world of Eastern European Jewry, where the wisdom, imagination, the spiritual, the traditional was the source of joy . . . the gift of my ancestors.

Both sets of grandparents came from that old world, Poland and Romania. My father's mother, Grandma Ida, told only a few tales that I recall. It is not storytelling that I received from her but the gift of dreams, another sort of listening.

randma Ida came from Lumza in Poland, a suburb of Warsaw. "Mud. That's what I remember, Laurele. Also, there were roses in the springtime." We knew nothing more about her childhood in the old country. She fascinated and frightened me. She was beautiful and tiny. She wore diamond earrings even to sleep. When I was ten years old we were the same size. The fact that she was married to a man who was six-foot-four and was my father's mother made her big in my mind's eye. What frightened me about her was that she snored at night as loud as a man.

Her snoring awoke me. I was certain she snored my name in her Yiddish accent, LHARRHELHA! I had to be careful not to think. If I thought a word, she snored it.

When she was dying she stopped speaking English. In the hospital she spoke only Yiddish and Polish. My father and mother, my brother and I were mistaken for people in Lumza. I was thirteen and too busy discovering boys and hairdos to pay much more attention to Ida. On the day she died she became famous in the hospital. The nurse placed a bedpan beneath her. We were told she had stopped speaking. But when the nurse tapped her, asking, "Mrs. Simnowitz, are you finished?" Ida sat up suddenly and proclaimed (in her last words): "No. I am Jewish!"

I miss her today. That mystical world of Yiddish language, secret family connections to a distant past, and real Jewish food is gone. One night, I dreamed of Ida and her diamond earrings and remembered our secret connection.

Whenever Grandma Ida came to visit she slept in my room, which is why I knew about her snoring. Sometimes before sleep, we spoke. I watched her thin white hair curled like sea foam around her pale white skin. She had blue-green eyes, piercing but gentle and luminous. Many times she told me that the earrings were stars from her village in Poland.

"Meidele, when you are older, I will give you these stars. Oi, a lebn af dayn kop. Oh, a blessing on your head." That is how I heard it, over and over. I sometimes made fun of her and said, "Granny, I will not live on my head." She tried to explain the Yiddish and then gave up.

We must have been a disappointment to her. We never spoke

Yiddish, and Jewish holidays were fun for us, but not much more. I never heard her complain about it.

When Ida came to visit, she carried with her a bottle of her chicken soup, a tin of cookies, and homemade blintzes, which we had to warm up or store in the freezer. She always smelled of warm milk and distant places. When she kissed me hello, I marveled at the small red spots on her skin the size of little shirt buttons.

At the dinner table I loved to watch the stars shine in her ears. She sometimes baby-sat for me. Those were the times I most recall, partly because of the snoring. Let me tell you about one night where story and magic and Lumza entered my heart:

My brother and I ate matzoh balls the size of baseballs and cleaned our plates with fresh baked challah bread. We washed it down with seltzer and Fox's U Bet Cherry Syrup as the tale began:

"Your Grandpa Dave had a job as a trolley car driver. Kinder-lakh, don't tell anyone about this or he'll get into trouble. He went back and forth on Broadway in Manhattan. He was a night bird. Because he stayed out later than he was supposed to. He did a little extra. This is the part you shouldn't speak about."

I snuggled close to Ida. Her words rolled like grass in the wind over stones. Her accent from the old world made every story into music.

"He undid the trolley and hooked it onto another track. He wanted to make a little more money. Those were hard times. He traveled up and down another avenue collecting nickels. Half the nickels he gave to the company, and the other half he hid in the dresser in the hallway. It was his dresser, so I never looked inside. Then one morning, I hear a loud crash like thunder. What is that? I wonder. Gonifs in the house? All the nickels exploded in the drawer and fell to the floor. Kinderlakh, the truth, God willing, always comes out. There was a gonif in the house. Your grandpa." She said it smiling and proud. We loved the story.

"What did you say to him?"

"What could I say? We were laughing too much to speak about

it. And your grandpa took a handful of nickels and took me out for breakfast. Of course, he promised to never do it again."

"Did he do it again?"

"You think I married a real thief?" she answered.

In the dark I could see her earrings glimmer like stars. She lay down in the bed between us and told us to close our eyes. "In my backyard, the stars were as big as pumpkins. Heaven was filled with stars." For the first time, she described the little house she grew up in. "A wood fence surrounded it. The goats were tied to the fence so they wouldn't eat the roses."

My brother went to his room and my grandmother climbed into the folding cot in my bedroom beside my bed. I couldn't sleep. I asked her for the first time, "Grammy, how did you get stars in your ears?"

I could hear the tears in her voice. "My bubbe gave them to me."

After a long silence, Ida got up and handed me my bathrobe and slippers. We went outside, into my backyard in Brooklyn.

We stood quietly looking up at the sky. "The night world is like magic. The stars are where the angels live." Grandma Ida handed me a little glass bottle and told me to catch fireflies. Watching them flicker off and on in the dark, she whispered, "This is a little night garden."

We let the fireflies go. Then she lay down in the grass. I knew this was no ordinary evening. Grandma Ida told me another story. A story I can never forget.

"A long time ago my bubbe sat with me in a garden just like this one. I saw her reach up into the sky. Her hand reached all the way to the stars. When she brought her hand back down to Lumza, she opened her fingers and there, on the palm of her hand, were two tiny stars. She placed them in my ears and there they sit right now. She said, 'Myne sheine kleine, Meidele, my beautiful little girl, with these earrings you will never be lonely. I will come to you in your dreams. These stars are like blessings.'"

Then my own grandmother reached up and I saw her hands rise straight up to heaven. When she brought down her hands there were two tiny stars in her palm. She placed them on my ears. "Blessings from the angels," she said as she put the diamond earrings in my ears. "Tonight, and for the rest of your life, you will have dreams so beautiful like you never had before." And so it was.

Years later at my own mother's funeral I learned two things about Grandma Ida. She was the dreamer in the family. "She dreamed of those who were dying the night before their death. She would see herself in the kitchen of the house in Lumza, looking out at the garden. The one to die would walk out the wood fence, turn and wave to Ida, and vanish." I also learned that she spoke more than six languages.

I froze. My hair stood on end. I trembled with sorrow and joy. The night before my mother's death I had dreamed of her standing in our garden. I was in the kitchen when I saw her turn, waving, and vanish. I had inherited Grandma Ida's dreams. I laughed to myself about this small woman and how I had never thought to ask her how she learned six languages in that small village in Poland.

Recent dream, November 1994

I was watering green healthy plants flowered with red blossoms. I had taken them back from a woman who kept them for me for a long time. The bucket of water fell on a photo, covering the image with thick mud. I scraped the mud off with a miniature trowel and saw my Grandma Ida's face. Behind her was my mother and myself. I placed the photo in a planting box like a seed, placed it in moist soil and awoke, refreshed.

THE CANDLE MAKER OF LIGHT

Devorah Spilman

Devorah Spilman *has been creating and telling her own original stories to children since 1975. A graduate of the Del Arte School of Physical Theater, she also appears as Dillyzoozilly the Clown. She has lived and performed in Israel for five years. Currently, she is working on a new one-woman show of true stories for adults. Devorah is now living in Los Angeles with her husband, but they are preparing for their return to Israel.*

I grew up in an American Jewish home where the holidays we celebrated were wonderful but limited to Rosh HaShanah, Yom Kippur, Chanukah, and Passover. I didn't discover the wonder and joy of Shabbat until I was in my twenties. Now that I celebrate Shabbat, I can't imagine living without it. The moment of candle lighting is for me a powerfully healing transformation.

About six years ago, I was invited to tell a Shabbat story for children and adults at a Shabbaton. I wanted to share my experience of Shabbat with them. I also wanted to give them the tools to create for themselves a moment of wonder and transformation, of prayer and healing. Like one candle lighting another, I wanted them to touch this light themselves and share it with others.

This story is particularly special to me for two reasons. First, it expresses what I really experience and feel when I light candles. And second, it is a story that works for all ages. Most of the stories I create and tell are for children. They are told from the child's view of the world and reflect their struggles and victories.

Since my specialty is creating original stories, that is exactly what I did. I closed my eyes and looked inside myself. I concentrated on what I wanted the essence of the story to be and I waited to get an image. I saw a beautiful old woman, alone in her house, lighting candles and sending that light out in streams into the world and into people's hearts. I built this story around that image. I change some details as I tell it, depending on my audience. So feel free to change the story to fit your heart and the hearts of your listeners.

This story touches all ages and is about what one generation passes on to the next. But before we can pass a tradition on, we have to have something to transmit. Nothing helps us more in passing on tradition than stories and rituals. So I offer you here a little of both.

---

n a small Jewish village, many years ago, lived the first Candle Maker of Light. Her name was Hannah. She lived alone in a small house on a hill surrounded by trees. No one knew how old she was, and even she couldn't remember. On Friday evenings, if anyone had ever looked in the window, they would have seen her lighting her candles, with light filling her house and flowing out of the windows in streams of light, into the hearts and souls of the people.

Rena was an orphan who lived in the same town as Hannah. Her parents were killed tragically when she was seven. For the last five years, Rena had lived with her Aunt Bracha. Rena loved her Aunt Bracha, but she was still filled with pain and loneliness. She especially missed her mother on Friday evenings. She remembered lighting candles with her mother, and how they would gather up the light three times and stand for a long time making wishes and giving blessings. Her Aunt Bracha lit the candles, said the blessing, and quickly went on to something else. Rena tried standing at the candles alone, but it wasn't the same, and usually her Aunt Bracha told her to set the table, anyway. Soon she stopped even trying. But the empty sadness never left her.

On Thursday afternoons, it was Rena's job to buy the candles from the candle maker in the marketplace. There was nowhere else to buy candles except from Hannah, the candle maker. Rena did not like this job. She would go to the marketplace with her money in hand: "I'd like these four candles," she would say. Hannah always sat at her table, arms folded, a frown placed purposefully on her face, with her eyes sparkling. "How much money do you have?" would be Hannah's brusque reply. Rena showed her the money. "You don't have enough money for those candles," Hannah retorted. "Well, I'll take any candles you say I can afford," Rena stammered. "Oh! Now you don't care which candles you take?" Hannah replied indignantly. "No, I do care," stuttered Rena. "I just don't know which ones I can afford." Then Hannah pointed, Rena picked, and the ordeal was over until next week.

But on one particular Thursday afternoon, it didn't happen that way. Rena arrived a bit earlier than usual at the market-place. There were very few people around. When she arrived at Hannah's table, Hannah motioned for her to be quiet, and then she looked in both directions, as if making sure that nobody was nearby. Then, she did something amazing. She looked Rena directly in the eye and she began to smile, a warm, deep, gentle smile, filling her face with light. Rena gazed in amazement, her mouth hanging open. She had never seen Hannah smile. "I want to invite you to my house for Shabbat," said Hannah, her voice sweet and gentle. "Can you come tomorrow, before candle-lighting?" Rena said absolutely nothing. She could only gaze in shock, her mouth hanging open. "Rena," said Hannah, "close your mouth." Rena gasped, closed her mouth, and began to laugh.

"I'm sorry, I was just surprised. I have to ask my Aunt Bracha if I can come to your house." "Then go and ask her, and take these four candles. They are my best. They are a gift. Now hurry." Rena ran all the way home, bursting breathless into the house. "Aunt Bracha, Aunt Bracha," she shouted over and over. "Rena, what is it? What's the matter?" "Nothing's the matter. It's just that Hannah, the candle maker, invited me to her house for Shabbat. She wants me to come tomorrow, before candle-lighting. I told her I had to ask you first. Can I go?" "If Hannah invited you," replied her Aunt Bracha quietly, "then you must go. It is a great honor. She is the oldest and perhaps even the wisest person in our village. There must be a reason she has chosen to invite you."

"She gave us these candles, too, as a gift," Rena said. The

candles were Hannah's most beautiful, long and white, and seemed to shine all by themselves, even unlit. "They are beautiful," her aunt replied, and she took them gently from Rena's hands. "I have to go back and tell her that I can come," said Rena. "Then hurry up and go tell her."

When Rena arrived at Hannah's table the second time that afternoon, Hannah made her wait until they were alone. "Well?" said Hannah, smiling again at Rena. "I can come," Rena said. "Good," said Hannah, "and bring two of the candles that I gave you, and for now, do not tell anyone that you are coming to my house." Someone else came up to the table. Hannah was again brusque, her face pinched. With a wave of her hand, she brushed Rena away. "Hurry up! Now go on home, Go on. Go on." Rena turned and ran home. She wondered why Hannah didn't want anyone to know that she was really so nice.

The next day, Rena didn't know whether to be more scared or more excited. She didn't know anyone who had ever been to Hannah's house. Everyone knew where it was, but it seemed that no one had been there. She put on her best Shabbat dress. Her hair combed, the candles in her hand, she kissed her Aunt Bracha good-bye and wished her a good Shabbos. On her way to Hannah's house, she stopped to pick some wildflowers to give to Hannah as a gift. She reached the door and knocked nervously. "Come in, it's open," she heard Hannah call from inside the house. Rena walked slowly into the house. She was surprised—it was not so different from the house she lived in with her Aunt Bracha. "Come in, come in," Hannah called. "Put your candles into the candle holder over the mantlepiece, and you can put the flowers in the vase on the table."

"How did she know I brought flowers?" Rena thought, looking at the flowers in her hand. She put them in the empty vase on the table. "And don't forget the water." Hannah called. "How did she know?" thought Rena. She filled the vase with water and returned to the table. At that moment, Hannah walked into the room. Rena stared at her in amazement, her mouth hanging open. Hannah was dressed all in white in a flowing dress. Her face seemed to shine. She was beautiful.

"Good Shabbos, Rena." Rena couldn't get any words to come

out of her mouth. She just stared in wonder. Hannah looked so different. "Rena, close your mouth," Hannah said, smiling at her. "Oh!" said Rena. She quickly shut her mouth. "It's just that you're so beautiful."

"Come," said Hannah, "it is time to light the candles. When I light them, I want you to watch me closely, and you will do just what I do. When I finish you will light your two candles and gather up the light three times, and cover your eyes. Then, when you say the blessing, let every word be its own song. When you are finished, do not uncover your eyes. Wait. Look at the light within you, see what you can see. Make three wishes—prayers from your heart—one for the whole world, one for your family and friends, and one for yourself. When you feel my hand on your shoulder, you will uncover your eyes."

"But what if I make a mistake? What if I don't remember everything you said?" "Don't worry," said Hannah, "whatever you do will be right. When I am finished I will nod my head and you will begin to light your candles." Hannah struck her match, lit her candles, gathered the light and sang the blessing. When she finished she nodded her head, but she did not uncover her eyes. Rena struck her match, lit her candles, and began gathering up the light. As she gathered the light, suddenly she remembered that this was the way she used to light candles with her mother. She covered her eyes, which were now wet with tears, and began to sing the blessing over the candles. Each word was its own song that seemed to sing itself within her, and when she finished, it seemed to Rena that she could see streams of light flowing out from the candles and out from her fingers, through the windows and the walls and into the hearts of people, filling them with light. She wished that the whole world would be filled with the light of Shabbat. She wished she could see her parents again, even though she knew it was impossible. She wished that the new girl in school would want to be her friend. She felt a gentle touch on her shoulder. She opened her eyes. The room seemed to be filled with light. Hannah's face was glowing, her eyes radiating love. Rena thought of her mother, and tears welled up in her eyes. Hannah wiped her tears and held her close.

"Did you see anything?"

"I . . . I saw—this might sound funny . . ." said Rena. "Go on," said Hannah. "I saw light coming out of the candles, streams of light. It was as if they were coming out of the candles and out of my fingers. And they flowed out of the house, and it seemed to me that these streams of light split up into many, many, many streams, and each one went inside a person and filled them with light. It was very beautiful, Hannah. It made me remember when I used to light candles with my mother. We would say that we were sending Shabbat light to all of our family and friends. But I never saw the light actually going out and into people. I hope that's OK."

"It is more than OK, Rena. It is why I picked you." "Picked me for what?" asked Rena. "I picked you to take over my job," said the candle maker. "What do you mean?" "I am very old. And I will not live forever. When I die, there must be someone to take over for me." "But now that I like you, I don't want you to die," said Rena.

"Like everyone, I, too, must die," Hannah replied gently. "But before I die, I will teach you how to make the most beautiful candles in the world. But more than that, I will teach you how to be the Candle Maker of Light."

Rena couldn't move. But the moment Hannah said that, she felt a strange sensation lighting up within her. "I will teach you," continued Hannah, "not only how to make candles, but how to truly send the light of Shabbos out into the world to heal and nourish the hearts of the people." Rena gazed into Hannah's eyes and saw that it was true. "When you grow up and get married, you will come and live in this house. And you will be the new Candle Maker of Light."

Rena still could not speak. She felt a great joy filling up inside her. She had been silent for so long that Hannah finally said to her, "What do you think of all this, Rena?"

"I believe you," said Rena. "When I looked in your eyes I could see that what you were saying was true. For the first time since my parents died I feel the pain is somehow less and maybe I'll be happy again. With you, I can light candles as I did with my mother. But Hannah, there's one thing that bothers me. Why were you always so mean when you sold your candles in the marketplace? Do I have to act like that?"

"No, my dear, you do not. I am not allowed to reveal who I truly am. And so, for now, you must not tell anyone what I have told you. But by the time you are grown, this will no longer be necessary. And you will sell your candles with light and joy. For this is your way."

And so it was that it came to pass exactly as Hannah said. Throughout the rest of her childhood, Rena came monthly to spend Shabbos with Hannah. And every week she came after school to learn how to make candles. Hannah lived to see Rena married. And when she died, Rena and her husband moved into Hannah's house. Rena became the new Candle Maker of Light. By day Rena sold her beautiful candles in the marketplace. But unlike Hannah, she greeted all who came to her table with a smile of warmth and love. And all who came to her house for Shabbos learned how to gather the light and let each word of the blessing sing itself within their hearts and how to send the light of Shabbos out into the hearts of all who needed it.

And now we too can gather that light and send it out into the world, where so much light is needed.

SHOSA LAYA, THE WISE

Susan Stone

Susan Stone *is a profes-*
sional storyteller and theater
educator. In 1991 she won
the Parents' Choice Gold
Award for her audiotape of
Jewish tales for children, The
Angel's Wings. *In addition to*
performing at schools, festi-
vals, and museums, she is
on the adjunct faculty of
National–Louis University in
Evanston, Illinois, teaching
teachers how to integrate
story and drama into curricu-
lum. Susan lives in Evanston
with her husband and two
children.

My great-grandmother, Shosa Laya, was from Hungary. Her sheitel-covered visage stares at me every time I ascend my staircase; her cheekbones are my own. Although I never knew her, but because I was given her name, I began to combine her image with my own—that of a storyteller. Thus, this character was born.

I love telling stories-within-stories—perhaps that is how they were often told. In this story there is the tale of "Zalmen and the Seer of Lublin." It is adapted from "What Ten Hasidim Can Accomplish," found in *Tales of the Hasidim* by Martin Buber.

On occasion I have extracted the tale of Zalmen from this larger story and told it at bar mitzvahs and major birthday celebrations. After hearing the tale, all of the participants are asked to raise their glasses and toast the celebrant with a hearty, "L'chaim!" It is always a powerful moment.

And the other tale-within-the-tale—the dirty pastry story told at the woodcutter's house? Shosa's experience at the home of the woodcutter echoes my experience at a retirement home.

I had been sharing Jewish stories for many years at schools, festivals, synagogues, and museums. One day I was invited to appear again at a retirement home. I had been there many times before. I went with the Yetzer ha-Tov, on one hand, telling me it was a mitzva, and the Yetzer ha-Ra, on the other, darkening the good deed with greedy thoughts and an impure heart. I really didn't feel like going.

But the storytelling session was uplifting, rewarding, and filled with love. After the program some of the listeners stayed in their seats. They began to tell tales, and this time it was I who sat enthralled. One man, Mr. Goldstein, joyfully shared his Yiddish story called "Pochayente" (a Pocahontas takeoff—not exactly from the old country). Mr. Goldstein and I connected through story and laughter, and I modeled the woodcutter after him. The elderly people there never knew how I really felt and the deed transcended the intention.

The Tunisian tale about the dirty pastry was adapted from *Jewish Folktales* by Pinhas Sadeh. Other versions from Eastern Europe and Egypt can be found in the Israel Folktale Archives.

We know that the legendary maggidim were men. While women batchentes[1] did often tell stories to entertain (for instance, at weddings), most women told stories simply for the pleasure of it. Wisdom was imparted, warnings were implicit, women's roles were explored, and jokes were shared—all through story. The oral tradition—folkloric, midrashic, and biblical—was assuredly passed on by women telling stories to other women and to children. This story is my way of honoring those women.

Note

1. Beatrice Silverman Weinreich, in the introduction to her book *Yiddish Folktales* (New York: Pantheon Books, 1988), discusses the role of these women storytellers. Also refer to *The Book of Jewish Women's Tales* by Barbara Rush (Northvale, NJ: Jason Aronson Inc., 1994).

---

 n a land made salty by the tears of many, made glad by faith and laughter, lived a kind old woman named Shosa Laya. She was a teller of tales. Though her body was weary and bent with age, her mind remained sharp, her voice rang clear. She would appear in the homes of those most in need, almost like Elijah himself.

With her husband long since dead and her children moved away, Shosa Laya told tales for the price of a meal or the chance to attend a celebration. She did this, always, with a glad heart and great love. For she was a true storyteller, and that was her nature. There are many tales of Shosa Laya. Here are some of them.

Once, just before the Days of Awe, Shosa was summoned to the home of a very wealthy old grandmother. Shosa pulled her woolen shawl around her thin shoulders and brushed imaginary lint off her tattered dress. She was, as always, immaculate. With her angular chin held high, she set off down the road to visit the old woman.

Tante Esther, as she was called, lived alone in a big house. Since her husband's death she had become despondent and forlorn and took little food or drink. Her friends came to call, only to be turned away. Even her servants were dismissed. It seemed that listening to stories was the only pleasure she allowed herself.

Shosa arrived at the impressive estate. She straightened a wrinkle on her bodice, pursed her withered lips, and with determination, rapped her bony knuckles on the rich woman's door.

"Nu?" came a somber voice from within.

"It's Shosa Laya," the storyteller replied firmly.

The heavy door opened from within and, once her eyes had adjusted to the dim interior, Shosa was astonished. Books were scattered everywhere, as if some demon suddenly needed to know the secret of the universe and had searched frantically for the book that held the special clue. Opened books were strewn across tables, chairs, and windowsills. Yellowed pages glared from washbasins and parchment scrolls blocked the path of the guest. The house smelled stale. The air was as old as the gnarled face that greeted her.

"Please," said her hostess, "come in. Sit here and I will make you a glass of tea." Dressed in a long brocade gown that looked as if it had been worn for many weeks, the old wealthy woman, with much effort, brushed several volumes off a cushioned chair, shuffled into the next room, and soon returned carrying a tray with glasses of tea and a small bowl of sugar cubes.

"Now," she said, when Shosa Laya had been made comfortable and she herself had settled down, "please, ease my mind with a story and I will pay you handsomely."

At first, Shosa told her stories of the townsfolk, funny stories to lift her spirits. But the old woman only smiled wanly, her eyes still glazed and distant.

No one spoke. Shosa closed her eyes and opened her heart, waiting for the right story to come to her. Slowly she entered the world between worlds, that mystical place where the presence of the stories could be found. Then Shosa turned to the sad figure before her. "Do you remember, dear Esther, hearing stories of Rabbi Yaakov Yitzhak, the famous Seer of Lublin?" Tante Esther nodded.

The storyteller began: "A long time ago, in Poland, there lived a hasid named Zalmen. One year, Zalmen decided to leave his village and travel all the way to Lublin to spend Rosh Hashana with his old teacher, the Seer of Lublin. He put on his very best clothes and fur hat and set off for the city. Zalmen loved to be the first person in the synagogue on Rosh Hashana, and so, before the first star even appeared in the sky, he arrived at the darkened shul and entered. 'Gut Yomtov, Rabbi,' he greeted the Seer of Lublin.

"The tzaddik looked at him closely. 'Zalmen, return home immediately.'

"'But Rabbi, I've come to pray.'

"'Zalmen,' the Rabbi was emphatic, almost imploring, 'return home.' Well, Zalmen didn't know why the Rabbi wanted him to do this, but he was used to obeying his rebbe, so he turned around and began to walk home, dejected and confused.

"Just then a group of Zalmen's old Lubliner friends called to him. The hasidim were sitting in front of an old house around a table covered with small glasses and many bottles of schnapps. 'Zalmen, you look terrible,' one of them called. 'Come, have a drink to the New Year with us!'

"So Zalmen sat down. One of the hasidim raised his glass and said, 'To you Zalmen, l'chaim.' He tossed his head back and swallowed the schnapps in one gulp. Zalmen drank a glass too.

"Then another of Zalmen's friends raised his glass. 'To you, Zalmen, for a good year.' He too drank, and Zalmen drank. The black hats bobbed up and down as one man after the other, all of the ten men at the table, tossed their heads back and drank a 'l'chaim' to Zalmen. And he drank with them. After a while, as you can imagine, Zalmen was feeling a little better. He picked himself up and went back to see the Rabbi.

"'Rebbe, tell me,' Zalmen demanded. 'Why did you send me home?'

"The Seer of Lublin stared directly at him. 'Where have you been? What has happened?' And Zalmen told him. 'Zalmen,' the Rabbi explained softly, 'when you first came in I could see that the Angel of Death walked with you and I knew you had only a little time left on this earth. I thought you would want to spend it with your family, so I sent you home. But now, now that so many of your friends have wished you a "l'chaim," they have chased the Angel of Death away. So come in, Zalmen, and pray.' And Zalmen was inscribed, that year and for many years to come, in the Book of Life."

A long silence filled the room. Finally, Tante Esther stirred in her chair. Her eyes glistened. She thanked Shosa Laya, paid her, and led her to the door.

In the days that followed, the townspeople whispered that Tante Esther had appeared in the marketplace and had even made conversation with the fruit sellers. One day, she visited the shul. Another day, she was actually seen gardening. Finally, they say, she opened her shutters and invited some friends for a glass of tea. And maybe, just maybe, some schnapps.

Shosa Laya felt blessed to be able to tell her tales, but on one occasion, the Divine Presence seemed to have deserted her. It happened one erev Shabbos when Shosa was invited for a meal to the house of a poor woodcutter and his wife. The man was ailing and it was thought that Shosa might ease his mind with fantastic fables and legends. She was tired and her stomach was as empty as her purse. It was in this weakened condition that the Yetzer ha-Ra saw its chance. It slithered into what had been her pure soul.

"Why should I go to this old couple's home?" thought Shosa. After all, she reasoned, the couple was very poor. There would be no extra coins to line her pockets, no influential people to meet—people who might invite her to a celebration. She had been there before and would have to offer new and different stories. She was becoming more and more agitated. The meal, she knew, would be spare; the house would smell of old herring and schmaltz. The evil inclination was unrelenting. But still, she thought, she should go. "It is a mitzva," she sighed out loud.

So Shosa Laya went. She would do her good deed by the letter of the law but not with the spirit of it. The three sat down and the blessings began. Dutifully, after the meal, Shosa told a small, tired tale. At the end, as always, she would pat the sheitel on her head as if to make sure it had not wandered off while she was busy with her stories. Soon, though, the peace of the Sabbath settled over the small bare room and the spirit of the Sabbath Queen entered her soul. Like the Shabbos candles, a spark had been ignited inside of her and the Yetzer ha-Ra was forced to flee. The stories poured out of her like sweet wine.

Miracle-working rabbis and lost princesses shared the room with the fools of Chelm. The ailing man's cheeks seemed to glow as his spirits brightened and peace came to the eyes that had once looked frightened and wild. The old couple kvelled over Shosa and her stories, their faces radiating admiration. There was so much peace in that room that night you would think the moshiach had finally arrived!

"He will get well," thought Shosa, forgetting to pat her sheitel, "he will get well." The stories had been healing. Shosa felt happy. She felt, well—guilty! She had come, begrudgingly, to do a good deed but the peace in her soul told her that she had received more than she had given.

Again, she wrapped her shawl around her shoulders and thanked her hosts for the meal.

"It is we who should be grateful," replied the wife. "You have raised our spirits and brought joy to our home."

"But I must confess," whispered the old storyteller, "I did not come with the proper intentions."

Then the old man looked up from his chair, stroked his thin beard, and motioned for her to sit once again. He looked at her with piercing eyes. "Let me tell you a story."

"I was once a very wealthy man. I did not marry for a long time and could think of nothing but ways to make money and how to spend it on myself. And then one day I walked into a bakery shop and bought a small cake. Oy, did I love my sweets!"

At this point, the old man, who had become lost in reverie about the types of cakes and cookies he had once been able to afford, was gently nudged by his wife.

"I took one bite of the pastry," he continued, "and it fell to the ground. I looked down and saw that it was covered with dirt. What did I care? I could buy dozens more. But when I looked up I saw that a schnorrer, a beggar, was looking longingly in the bakery shop window. I picked up the dirty pastry, went outside, and handed it to the schnorrer. Then, of course, I bought another one for myself.

"That night I had a dream. I dreamt that I was sitting in a cafe. A large cafe—very crowded. Waiters were running everywhere, bringing all the customers the most delicious cakes and sweets. But my plate remained empty. When I could stand it no longer I angrily summoned a waiter and the waiter finally served me. He served me a piece of dirty pastry! 'What's the meaning of this?' I shouted. 'I am not a charity case. This pastry is covered in dirt! I'm a rich man and my money is as good as anyone's!'

"'I'm sorry, sir,' replied the waiter. 'Your money will do you no good here. You've just arrived in Eternity and all you can be served with here is what you yourself have sent ahead from the World of Mortals. This dirty pastry is all you have sent.'

"At that moment," said the old man, "I awoke." He stared at Shosa and waited until the presence of the story had drifted off. "*Metoch shelo lishmah, ba lishmah*—even without the intention, comes the intention. We're so glad you came."

Shosa Laya, too, was very glad she had come. From that time on, the Yetzer ha-Ra had to look for another home in which to rest its slimy self. Even when it did come knocking on Shosa Laya's door, she never bothered to answer it.

A LAMED VAVNIK
Arthur Strimling

Arthur Strimling *weaves the life stories of people he interviews together with traditional Jewish legends and tales. His solo performances are seen in theater, community and senior centers, synagogues, and schools throughout the country, and he leads workshops in life-storytelling for all age groups. He is the artistic director of Roots and Branches Theater, which brings old and young actors together with theater professionals to create and perform original plays. Arthur also performs his solo play,* All That Our Eyes Have Witnessed, *which describes his awakening to Judaism through the retelling of stories recorded by Barbara Myerhoff. He and his wife, Lisa, live in Brooklyn, New York.*

This story is based on a real event. There really was a Senior Center: there really was an old woman; and she really told me about her grandson and her dying husband. But I've messed with the details to get at an essence. In other words, I have "re-membered" the story. So the result is what the poet Marianne Moore called "an imaginary pushcart with real vegetables in it." (Ms. Moore wasn't Jewish, but she was from Brooklyn and a baseball fan, so I'm sure she and her pushcart fit comfortably in a Jewish anthology).

I do a lot of listening to old people, so much that I've become a sort of expert, a life stories maven. People call me to interview their grandmothers, because they don't have time (I do?). I get manuscripts in the mail with covering letters assuming I will know how to get them published (I don't); and invitations to talk on topics like "creative aging" (not that there isn't such a thing—there is, and it can be learned to some extent—but there are limits. For example, I'm often asked if it's true that age brings wisdom. No! Age brings more of what you were when you were young: if you had a bent toward wisdom when you were young, you might get wiser with age; if you were vain or misanthropic or craven, then . . .).

Some stories I hear do contain a holy spark. They draw me, and I have to re-member and tell them. The ones I most want to tell, like this one, resonate with great Jewish themes, so I try, as here, to weave the stories and the themes together.

One of the great themes (wonderfully revealed by our editor, orally and in a book) is the Elijah tales. And there are many sub-themes, my favorite being "The Unexpected Meeting That Changes a Life." All the work I do now is the result of such a meeting. My "Elijah" was the great anthropologist Barbara Myerhoff.

Barbara's book, *Number Our Days*, about old Jews at a Senior Center in Venice, California, along with her Academy Award-winning film of the same name, changed the way we think about reminiscence among the elderly. The earlier attitudes can best be characterized by my experience as a teenager listening to my grandmother in a nursing home. The social worker overheard us and took me aside to warn me off encouraging Grandma to remi-nisce because, as he put it, "Reminiscence is the high road to senility."

Barbara and others showed us that by telling us their life sto-ries the elderly are seeking to be remembered, to project them-selves into the future. They may also be trying to pass on the wisdom of a lifetime, or coming to terms with their lives as a part of coming to terms with dying. So reminiscence, far from being the "high road to senility," is one of the central tasks of aging.

I met Barbara completely by chance in 1981, at a theater fes-tival in Minnesota. I was an actor in an experimental theater company, The Talking Band, and had never heard of her or her work. But from the moment we met we started telling each other stories, and we never stopped until her death in 1985. It was she who introduced me to the joyous nourishment of listening to the old ones. And, through our passionate conversations about spiri-tual hunger and because of a last dying wish, it was she who gave me a path into my Judaism.

Shortly before she died (of cancer at age forty-nine), Barbara read me the transcripts of interviews she had done in the Fairfax neighborhood of Los Angeles. She called Fairfax a chosen ghetto, because Jews from widely varied backgrounds and nationalities have moved there in order to live in a Jewish milieu. She had planned to write a book about it, but there would be no time for that, and she asked me to "tell the stories." Eventually, I found a way of fulfilling her request by creating a solo performance called All That Our Eyes Have Witnessed, which comprises the stories within a frame of relating how telling them over and over has awakened the Pintele Yid, the hidden essence of Judaism, in me. So I dedicate this story, as I do each performance, to the memory of Barbara Myerhoff.

The event described here happened after a performance at a Senior Center, and, in a different form, it is now part of the play.

There is a Jewish tradition
that in the whole world
at any time,

there are 36
—and only 36!—
wise and just people . . .
who keep the world going.

They are called the Lamed Vavniks.

Now,
we don't necessarily know who they are
in fact,
they don't necessarily know who they are.

So . . .
anyone you meet,
anyone you talk to . . .

Perhaps the one you least expect
could be one of the thirty-six.

 want to tell you a story that was told to me by a very old woman at a Senior Center on the Upper West Side of Manhattan. Have you ever been to a Senior Center? If you have, you know what exotic places they can be, and the Senior Centers on the Upper West Side are especially exotic. So, before you can fully appreciate this woman's story, you have to have a feeling for the place where I heard it. Just as Reb Nachman of Bratslav lovingly set the scenes for his fabulous tales, I must lead you into the exotic world of a Senior Center on the Upper West Side of Manhattan.

This particular center is located mid-block between Central Park West and Columbus Avenue, two of the most elegant boulevards anywhere. Lincoln Center, Juilliard, and the main studios of ABC-TV are all within three blocks. At mid-morning, when most of the seniors are making their way to the center, the neighborhood is a barrage of activity. Businesswomen and anchormen flag cabs; stick-straight dancers heading for rehearsal cut along the sidewalk like knives; soap opera stars hide behind sunglasses and look to see who notices them, while other actors wait on tables or yell at their agents on the corner pay phone. Professional dog walkers and maids with strollers steer their charges, and stunning bodies in gorgeous workout clothes head for Central Park or cool out in front of Jack LaLanne on Broadway. The Korean grocer family on the corner water vegetables, while the panhandler who always sits in front of their store holds out his paper cup and tries to look needy but non-threatening. He is the only one not in a hurry. Even the window shoppers at the elegant shops on Columbus Avenue have an impatient, hard-edged look about them.

In all this glamour and hustle, it's easy to miss the old people of the Upper West Side. You might see a few sitting on benches in the center strip of Broadway, but mostly those have been taken over by the younger, hardier homeless. Or, you might do an end run around a couple of old ladies walking too slowly for the rhythms of this part of town. You would see them if you went to free student performances at Juilliard or movies in the afternoon or rode the bus, which you probably don't because it takes too long.

You will literally bump into them at Fairway, the famous discount vegetable market, because the aisles are too narrow and it's impossible to navigate your cart around the old women folded over bins, meticulously scrounging through the potatoes and bananas. And in line, you'll curse them for questioning the cost of every item, and myopically examining every coin they grudgingly hand over to the harassed Haitian checkout women.

These old people are not poor, not in the conventional sense. They have pensions to supplement Social Security; Medicaid makes the doctor affordable; and some can even fly away to Florida when winter in New York gets oppressive. Long ago they lived well here, as the families of mid-career stockbrokers, lawyers, and psychiatrists do now. But now almost everything the Upper West Side has to offer costs too much. They are neighborhood-poor.

But they stay! They cling to this unwelcoming environment like ancient gnarled trees to the side of a cliff. Why? It would be so much easier to join their sisters and brothers in Florida. Why don't they? Inertia, yes; friends and family, yes; and the refusal to abandon the place where at least the ghosts of their glory days reside. All of these are true, as they are for elderly everywhere.

But I think there is something special about these gnarled trees, something very New York: they cling to these cliffs *because* it's so hard. True New Yorkers that they are, they take pride in knowing that no matter how tough it gets, they can survive!

So, they stay, locked into their rent-controlled apartments; attending free concerts and discount afternoon movies; riding the buses for half price; pinching pennies at Fairway; and eating their hot meal of the day for seventy-five cents at the Senior Center.

The center is in the basement of a former synagogue, now run by the Jewish Association for Services for the Aged (everyone calls it JASA). It's a big, gloomy room, where the social workers have to struggle to create a cheerful atmosphere. The seniors come early—this is their community, their village, their shtetl. An elderly volunteer, tight-lipped and battleship-bosomed, collects seventy-five cents from each one and hands each a number, handwritten in large digits, so that even the near-blind can read it, and encased in ancient, finger-greasy plastic.

They take the number to a table, making sure to get their own seat with their own friends. This is very important to them; most live alone, far from family, and for them this daily dose of socializing may be even more important than the cheap lunch. I have seen otherwise dignified people throw plates of spaghetti at each other over a seat at a table.

Some write their number on the paper place mat and go off to paint or dance or listen to a lecture on the Middle East or the opera. Near the front, two women shmooze while they wrap plasticware in paper napkins and make neat piles beside little cups of applesauce and bread slices individually sealed in cellophane. Others talk in small groups, read, or just sit, snoozing or guarding nests of numbered place mats. They look sullen in repose—perhaps they are, or maybe it's just the droop of aged flesh.

These old folks are not cute. They don't fit the "Golden Girls" television image of old people. Nor are they the blue-haired ladies and yellow-jacketed gentlemen of the suburbs. Their clothes are not new; their bodies sag, spread, and bend; bad wigs and garish slashes of lipstick and rouge abound; and the men tend to look seedy. Some have simply stopped taking care of themselves: they don't even brush their teeth anymore. These are the ones who have lost everyone who cared how they dress or smell or if they are alone or even alive. These are the ones who spurn new friendships—perhaps the pain of chancing another loss is just too great.

Lunch starts promptly at twelve—and woe to the eager lecturer who tries to keep class a few minutes late to share one more gem. Starting at ten minutes 'til twelve, he will be speaking into an increasing shuffle of chairs and feet, until by two minutes of, even the most devoted have decamped for the lunchroom. These old ones love culture, but their priorities are clear: lunch comes first!

Given this eagerness and the well-known Jewish willingness to ignore decorum, it is essential that serving lunch follows a strict regimen. The ticket lady stands up front with a microphone calling out numbers, like the stewardess when you board a plane: "1 through 15 . . . 16 through 30," and the old ones line up. Each receives a tray with a segmented Styrofoam dish—sections for meat, vegetables, salad, and dessert. Usually there are also a small cup of canned fruit, fresh fruit, bread, a container of milk, and coffee or tea. Many take the bread, milk, and fruit home, or if they don't want something, trade or perform small acts of Tzedakah (charity). For example, Sam gives his milk to Minna, who has a cat.

The menus vary over the week: meatloaf, fish, spaghetti, stew, and the big draw, chicken. By far the most people show up on "chicken day." (There are several Senior Centers in the neighborhood, and some people actually follow the chicken from one center to another over the course of the week). Like any performer I want a big audience, so I always try to schedule my gigs on chicken day.

There was a good crowd on the day I'm telling you about. The weather was balmy and the chicken juicy, so the center members were relaxed and ready for some nice entertainment.

But I don't tell "nice" stories—entertaining, I hope, but not "nice." The stories I tell are true, told by Jews who have lived them. They can be funny or harrowing, or even profoundly disturbing, but the qualities that matter most to me, aside from that they be terrific stories, is that they have some powerful Jewish resonance and that they create a hunger in listeners to complete the cycle by telling their own stories back to me.

And they do. They rush me after performances with stories falling out of their eyes, off their clothes, their hair. They grab at my shirt, my sleeves, they shove each other aside. This day was no exception. So, to give some form to this chaos—and to protect my clothes—I bring juice and cookies, and we gather around a table and make what the old women call "a tisch mit menschen," a table with people.

At first there will be a rush of stories. Some are well worn, unfolded at every opportunity. Others, genuinely triggered by the play, are told more haltingly and with a quality of wonder, as the teller re-members what had decayed into forgottenness. Inevitably there comes a lull, and that's when I remind them of the Lamed Vavnik tale I've told that day, and I ask, "Did you ever meet someone you thought might be a Lamed Vavnik?" I get lots of stories. This is one.

Actually, this story wasn't told during the workshop. This happens a lot: they come up after, and grab me by the shirt right around the second button from the bottom, pull me close and whisper, "I didn't want to talk with all of them around, but I'll tell you special."

This time I was hooked by a tiny, vivid woman. She brought my face to hers and announced, "I am ninety-two years old," not proudly but with the certain knowledge that this simple fact would rivet my attention . . . and scatter the opposition—age takes precedence at a Senior Center.

Most of the people had already gone home. It was getting late; it was starting to rain. I had been there for hours, telling and listening. I was exhausted, and I wanted to go home too. But I said, "Tell me."

We sat down. The corner of the table was between us. Styrofoam coffee cups and plastic flowers were on the table. The kitchen help was cleaning up, banging pots and pans around behind us; the janitor was sweeping; and the social worker was doing her paperwork.

She told me her name was Anna, and she told me that her husband had died many years before. It was a lingering and painful death. The summer before he died they went to their country home, and their nine-year-old grandson came to visit.

Well, one miserably hot, muggy August afternoon, when the old man was in terrible pain and very weak, the boy came to Anna and said, "Grandma, let's take Grandpa down to the river. I'll take off his shoes and socks and put his feet in the water, and it will be cool for him, and he'll feel better."

"Oh," she said. "That's a wonderful thought, but you see, the path down to the river is steep and rocky, and Grandpa is very . . . weak, and I think it would . . . wear him out. But it's a beautiful idea. Thank you. . . ."

But the old man was listening, and he said, "No—let's go!"

So, slowly, painfully, they practically carried him down to the river. They sat him on a rock, and the boy took his grandfather's shoes and socks off and put his feet in the water, and they sat there for a while.

Now, I thought she was going to tell me that her grandson was a Lamed Vavnik, but instead she said, "You know, it didn't help my husband to go down to the river. In fact, getting back up that path nearly killed him. But he knew what it would mean to that nine-year-old boy to have done something nice for his dying grandfather. . . . He knew what a memory it would make.

"My husband," she said, "he was a Lamed Vavnik!"

THE MOST PRECIOUS THING IN THE WORLD

Joan Sutton

Joan Sutton *has been telling Jewish stories and world tales in the San Francisco Bay Area for the past twenty years. She created a radio series, "Apples and Honey," and is the featured storyteller on five holiday audiotapes for young children,* The Jewish Holidays. *She often uses puppets, masks, musical instruments, and group participation in her storytelling to communicate the excitement of the Jewish tradition. Joan lives in San Francisco, California.*

This story is based on a hasidic tale that I heard many years ago. Recently, I found a version called "The Tear of Repentance" in *Stories from Hebrew and Yiddish Sources.* The compilers are Abraham N. Franzblau, M.D., Ph.D., and his students. I also was influenced by two writers: Hans Christian Andersen ("The Angel") and Oscar Wilde ("The Happy Prince"). However, when I first wrote the story, I was not aware of all these influences and sources. Rather, the story had somehow stayed in my memory and flowed out one day when I needed a new story to tell for the High Holidays. It was my desire to explain the concept of repentance, and this tale seemed just right.

In the version titled "Tear of Repentance," the setting is Eastern Europe, so there are very different scenes from the modern ones in my story. For instance, there is a soldier dying in a battle—the angel brings a drop of his blood; the angel also catches the dying breath of a nurse who sacrificed her life to save others; and the tear of repentance comes finally from an evil man who repents when he sees a mother teaching her little son the blessings as she is putting him to sleep. However, the basic story line is the same.

The Andersen and Wilde fairy tales have this in common: a precious thing is unexpectedly found by an angel. In "The Happy

Prince," a little bird finds instances of suffering in the city and alleviates them with a jewel from the statue of the Happy Prince. At the end, God tells an angel to find the most precious things in the city: they are the melted-down leaden heart of the Happy Prince and the body of the dead bird, who together died for the sake of others. The Andersen tale is about an Angel carrying the soul of a dead child to heaven; on the way they are gathering beautiful flowers to place in God's garden. But the Angel also gathers one broken pot with a dead flower; it was this humble flower that had kept a sick little boy happy. As it turns out, this seemingly worthless object was the most important—the angel had once been that sick little boy. These stories impressed and moved me when I was a child.

When I first told this story, someone commented that angels are not female so I went home and changed all the cases of *she* to *he*. But I didn't feel comfortable with a male angel; I had always visualized her being a female, so I changed it back again. The question still remains as to whether angels can be female, but I guess they are neither *he* nor *she*. The same question applies to God. The more I think about it, the more important it becomes to me not to refer to God as *King*, *Lord*, and, in general, *He*. Therefore, I have been very careful in this story not to apply any male appellations to God.

I find the concept of repentance a difficult one, but it is central to the High Holidays; the new Union Prayerbook for these holidays is even called *The Gates of Repentance.* Where there is repentance, one must presuppose sin, but I wanted to tell a story that also emphasizes ordinary people's good qualities. An important teaching in Judaism is that you cannot request forgiveness from God before you go to the people you might have hurt, either intentionally or unintentionally, and sincerely ask them for forgiveness. We must also try to give up our own anger at those who have treated us cruelly or unjustly. Only then can God open the gates of repentance. So this story builds up to these ideas, which have special significance in the Jewish tradition.

---

nce upon a time, God spoke to an angel and said, "For this Rosh Hashana, the New Year, bring me the most precious thing in the world." The angel bowed low to God and then winged her way to earth. Searching everywhere, she visited forests, mountaintops, and soft, green meadows. But although she saw bright butterflies and flowers, nothing seemed quite right. Then, peeking through a window, she saw a mother holding her baby. As she gazed down at her child, the mother's smile was full of love and tenderness. The angel thought, "This mother's smile must be the most precious thing in the world. I will take it to God." Gently, the angel took the mother's smile, but the mother didn't even notice; she had so many smiles left that she would never miss just one! With great excitement, the angel showed the smile to God, who answered, "This is indeed wonderful—the smile of love that a mother gives her child—but it is not the very most precious thing in the world."

So the angel went back to earth and searched again everywhere. One starry night, in the midst of a deep, dark forest, she heard exquisite music: it was the song of a solitary nightingale singing among the trees. The song was so beautiful that the angel folded her wings and listened for many hours. Then she took the song to God. But, upon hearing the music, God answered, "This is indeed very special, but it is still not the most precious thing in the world!"

The angel was getting tired but she knew she could never give up, so again she flew back to earth. This time she arrived in the big city, where she saw crowds of people. They were all in a hurry to get somewhere. They pushed each other as they passed quickly in the streets. They waited impatiently in long lines at banks and supermarkets. They looked nervous and weary. Everywhere there were traffic jams and tired drivers honking angrily.

Standing at one busy intersection was an old man. He was waiting to cross the street, but there were so many cars that he didn't know when to try. People kept rushing past him, never pausing to notice his predicament. The old man felt dizzy and confused. Just then, a young girl came walking up to him. She had noticed him hesitating and looking ill and felt sorry for him. "Excuse me," she said to him shyly, "but may I help you cross the street and walk you home?" Gratefully he gazed into her kind eyes and answered, "Yes, thank you, young lady, I was feeling so tired and weak!" He took her offered arm and walked with her across the street. Slowly and steadily, they made their way to his apartment building, which was nearby.

Now the angel was watching all the time, although the old man and the young girl couldn't see her. The angel was so happy! "This really must be the most precious thing in the world—a kind deed, a mitzvah, a helping hand! It has many names, but it is the same everywhere. If we can help each other, we can have a peaceful world! So I will take the story of this kind deed to God. It must be what I have been looking for all the time!"

God heard the story of the kind deed and answered, "This is indeed important. A mitzvah is one of the most special things in the world—still, it is not quite what I have been waiting for. Go once more, dear angel. You are on the right track, and I feel sure that this time you will find what we seek. Look everywhere— in cities, forests, schools, and homes—but especially look into the hearts of people."

Sighing with disappointment, the angel again winged her way to earth. And she looked in so many places! Still, she could not find the precious thing. "Maybe I should give up! But how could I fail my God? There must be an answer or God would not have asked me to do this." Tired from her ceaseless searching, she sat dejected upon a rock, resting and thinking. As she sat there, she heard something—the sound of someone crying! It was not a little child crying, but a grown man! He was walking through the woods with tears rolling down his cheeks. "Soon the High Holy Days will come, and I am thinking that I was cruel and mean to my dear brother! We had a fight about something un-important. There were harsh words and now we haven't even spoken to each other in several weeks. Today, this very day, I will go to him and ask him to forgive me. Then I will pray to God to forgive me too, for I am truly sorry that my unthinking anger has caused so much unhappiness." Another tear rolled down the man's cheek.

The angel felt that she had found the answer. Being an angel, she was invisible, so she flew up to the grieving man and gently caught one of the tears that were falling from his eyes. The man thought to himself, "What a soft and fragrant breeze is surround-ing me! Suddenly I feel better. Perhaps this is a sign that all will be well!" The angel flew away; she flew away to God. In a small, tiny bottle she held the one tear that she had collected. She held it up to God. And God . . . smiled upon the angel. The radiance of that smile filled the whole world like the sun coming out suddenly from behind dark clouds.

Then God spoke: "My faithful angel, this is indeed the most precious thing in the whole world—the tear of someone who is truly sorry. For it is a tear from the heart, and it will bring peace into the world. The two brothers will forgive each other, and they will enjoy a loving and happy New Year. My dear angel, I bless you for your good work. And may this story be told, so all who hear it can learn from it. L'Shana Tova—a sweet and happy New Year to everyone!"

MY GRANDPARENTS

Sarika's Story

Charoset

Susan Talve

Susan Talve *is the rabbi of the Central Reform Congregation, a community that finds its meaning in the telling and retelling of the story of our people to our children, each other, and our neighbors. She was ordained from the Hebrew Union College– Jewish Institute of Religion in 1981 and is a past president of the St. Louis Rabbinical Association. In 1990 she helped to found a support group for families of children with congenital heart disease. Together with her husband, Rabbi James Stone Goodman, she parents their three children, Jacob, Sarika, and Adina Chaya.*

The first of these two tales, "Sarika's Story," was first told as part of a presentation by the Jewish Caucus of the National Women's Studies Association to a plenary meeting of the association in 1986. In an attempt to share our diversity, a few Jewish women were asked to tell "our" stories. Pregnant with my third child, I stood before a great gathering of women and told of my Sephardic heritage through stories of my grandmother, Sarika. Thanks to the taping of the session and the vision of Melanie Kaye-Kantrowitz and Irena Klepfisz, my oral story was written and included in *The Tribe of Dina*, an anthology that they edited. In 1990, the story became the narrative for a musical revue of Sephardic culture that included oriental dance, poetry, and song and was sponsored by the Jewish Community Centers Association of St. Louis. "*Charoset*" was first told when I was asked to tell "Sarika's Story" to a group of storytellers and realized that most of them had heard it before! Both stories were most recently published in volumes 1 (1991) and 2 (1992) of the *Sagarin Review*, the St. Louis literary journal edited by Howard Schwartz. Both stories are a small part of a much larger tale that I hope to

376

continue remembering and telling in order to honor the memory
of my grandparents and to bless the lives of my children.

Sarika's Story

arika saved my life when I was a baby. I loved to ask
my grandmother, "Tell me the story of when you
saved my life," because she would always answer,
"It was God who saved your life." Her humility and
strong Jewish faith became a part of me at a very
young age and shaped the life of the person that I would become.

Sarika had the most beautiful smooth olive skin one could
imagine. Her first wrinkle didn't appear until after her seventi-
eth birthday. Her granddaughters always wanted to know the
secret of her beautiful skin. When she was in a serious mood,
and when she knew that we were serious, she would say it was
because of the waters in her town outside Salonica, near Drama.
My grandmother was a Sephardic woman, and she spoke of the
well in her town and the crystal-clear, pure water with which
she began her life. Then she would look at us and say, "You
know, all beginnings are important," as if to suggest that those
waters were connected to her faith.

We would sit many hours in her apartment in Brooklyn fighting over whose turn it was to braid her long dark hair, and she
would tell us story after story of her life before she came to this
country. One of my favorite stories took place just before the
Sabbath in the small town near Drama. Sarika (a name that
means "little Sara") and a bunch of her girlfriends were collecting flowers in the village square, when a handsome cavalier
named Sabbatai came into town. All the girls were looking at
him and he was looking at all the girls. Each young girl held
out a flower for Sabbatai to smell. "Ah," she would say, and as
she reenacted the scene, the room would fill with fragrance. He
smelled each one, throwing them aside until, of course, he
reached Sarika, who held the sweetest of them all.

She took him home, and they celebrated *Shabbat* together.

Even though he was a Turk and she a Greek, their common Sephardic heritage linked them. They married and their families were happy. They had a beautiful child called Reina, after Sarika's mother. But this was right before World War I, and my grandfather was a merchant. He traveled around enough to know that it was time to leave, so he gathered what he could and raised the necessary fare to book passage for his young wife and their infant daughter to journey with so many others to America. With a pain in her heart that I'm sure she never lost for leaving her mother and her sisters, Sarika boarded the boat with Sabbatai and arrived like hundreds of thousands of others at Ellis Island.

In America they got off the boat with their clothes and one pair of *Shabbat* candlesticks that they had managed not to trade for a little more shelter for their child, or a little more clean water to bathe with. They changed their names from Sarika and Sabbatai to Sara and Sam. They birthed seven children on the kitchen table, accumulated fifteen grandchildren and fourteen (we're still counting) great-grandchildren. They were proud to be in America, but there was always that sadness in Sarika's stories because, looking back, she remembered that they were the only ones of their large extended families who survived World Wars I and II.

From Ellis Island and Eldridge Street on the Lower East Side, they made the big move to Brooklyn. My grandmother lived in the same neighborhood for sixty years and never really had to learn English because her Ladino, the Spanish language of the Sephardic Jews, was always understood at the grocery store downstairs, even as the neighborhood changed from Sephardic to Puerto Rican to Cuban. You would enter her apartment and feel like you were in a different world. The smells were different. The music was different. The movement was different. Somehow her granddaughter, this Jewish girl from the suburbs of Westchester County, felt more at home in her grandmother's apartment than anywhere else.

I don't think my grandparents ever really understood my becoming a rabbi. I was, however, the only one of all the children and grandchildren that my grandmother would call every Friday night just before the Sabbath would start. At the time I thought that this was because she knew it was also a sacred time for me, something that she and I shared. Now I think the real reason she called was to make sure that I didn't forget that it was *Shabbat*. I mean, I was a rabbi—wouldn't that be awful!

But the time she really tested me was when she was dying in a New York hospital. I lived across town. Every day I took the bus to bring her a kosher Sephardic meal because she wouldn't eat the hospital food: it was "poisoned." I cooked for her, brought her food, and fed her for more than a month. Then one night she was like a frail bird, so close to death. I really didn't want to leave. I stayed later than usual and then went home. Later the call came. "Come quickly, come quickly, she's asking for you." I ran all the way. I wanted to be with her. I wanted to hold her as she left this world. I wanted to say good-bye.

When I arrived she was sitting up in bed. All the doctors and nurses were standing around her with their mouths open in amazement. Sarika was putting red ribbons in her hair and giving orders just like the old "Nona" we all knew. "Ah, Suzika" (that's what she called me), "get me a rabbi."

I said, "Nona, I am a rabbi."

She laughed. You should have seen her. Red ribbons in her hair to keep the evil spirits away. Red, from the red of the earth of Lilith's hair.

She said, "Your grandfather, Sabbatai, he came to me during the night. Was he handsome! He was all dressed up. He said, 'Sara, I'm not ready for you yet. Get well. I'm having too good a time.'"

Whatever it was, my grandmother lived ten more years.

Just before my grandmother died, I brought my three-month-old daughter, Sarika, to meet her. They lay together side by side on a couch. My grandmother, losing her ability to move around but still with that glint in her eye, well past ninety, looked at this little Sarika lying next to her and said, "This is what I lived for." And then she said, "Remember Sara of the Bible? She was ninety when she had her child. This one is mine, anything is possible. . . ."

I do all the life-cycle events in my family. It's just easier to

call me for weddings, Bar or Bas Mitzvot, baby namings, whatever. They call me. I'm cheap. I do them. I know what to say,
what not to say. It's easy. But when it came to my grandmother's funeral, they wanted a "real" rabbi to say Kaddish.
The Kaddish prayer is a prayer we say for the dead. Traditionally a woman does not say the Kaddish prayer in public. (One
reason given is that she might humiliate the men. If a woman
is saying the Kaddish, people might think it's because no man
is able to.)

My father insisted that I do the eulogy because no one knew
my grandmother like I did. No one loved her quite the same way,
and I think everyone knew that. But when it came to the
Kaddish, they hired an Orthodox rabbi to come and do what
was really important. I gave the eulogy and stepped away for
the Orthodox rabbi to come up and read the Kaddish. Instead,
I saw that he was standing there with tears in his eyes. He nodded to me to continue. His heart had been opened by a tradition that is meant to be loving and inclusive, a tradition that is
meant to open hearts and minds, not close them. And both with
tears in our eyes, for this woman who had pushed our tradition
to its best, perhaps just for this moment, he followed as I led
the Kaddish for Sara Aruest Talve, the daughter of Yitshak and
Reina. And we cried together for this woman, who for just that
moment changed the world a little bit.

Then her children, grandchildren, and great-grandchildren—
who really are more American than anything else, I must say—
for that moment remembered not that they were the children of
Sara and Sam but that they were the *people* of Sarika and
Sabbatai. And for the very last time we all gathered around my
grandmother and sang to her together her favorite lullaby:

Duerme duerme mi alma donzella
Duerme duerme sin ansia y dolor
Duerme duerme sin ansia y dolor

Sleep, sleep my sweet soul
Sleep without worry or pain
Sleep now and be at peace.

Charoset

If you want to begin to understand the difference between the Ashkenazim and the Sephardim, look at the *charoset*. Ashkenazim make it lumpy with apples, walnuts, almonds, and sweet red wine. Sephardim make it with raisins, dates, more raisins, wine and it's smoother, very smooth. There is a midrash in the *Meam Loez*, an eighteenth-century Sephardic commentary, about the mentioning of the plagues during the seder. The Almighty hears us crying for the Egyptians as we dip our fingers into the wine, drip it onto the tablecloth, and remember the plagues. God then says that we should be crying for the hardworking Jewish wives who slave to make the *charoset* smooth!

At my seders growing up, we always had to have both, the kind with apples that you ate on a matzah and the kind with raisins that you would eat wrapped up in a big piece of romaine lettuce. My two grandfathers would both preside: Sabbetai from Turkey, speaking in Ladino and Hebrew, and Heschel from Talnoe, Russia, speaking in Russian and Hebrew. By the time the seders were held at my parents' home because the preparation had become too difficult for my grandmothers, my grandfathers were quite old.

They called themselves Sam and Harry. In fact, everyone, including their wives, called them Sam and Harry. But they called each other Sabbetai and Heschel. As different as they were, there were things they knew about each other that only they could understand. Sabbetai left his entire family to come to this country and never saw them again. Heschel returned to Russia after escaping the czar's army to free his family. His young brother Jacob was shot in his arms as they were running away. Part of them died there, and when Sam called Harry "Heschel," and when Heschel called Sam "Sabbetai," they reminded each other of who they were.

Sam and Harry sat at the head of the table with their respective bowls of *charoset*, leading the service. Sam would chant everything, and I mean everything, from start to finish, in Ladino, with the blessings and other sacred texts in Hebrew, and wearing a *kippah* on his head. Harry sat beside him, hatless, reading the Hebrew and going on in Russian about how ridiculous this whole thing was and saying (to us? to God?), "What kind of God are you anyway and, if you are God . . . who needs you!" It was an interesting harmony. The only time they were ever in unison was when they were quite old and both of them would momentarily forget where they were and break into a chorus of World War I tunes. In the middle of what seemed to be an endless drone we would all be awakened by "Johnny get your gun" and "Oh how I hate to get up in the morning." I wonder now if it was their joke to get our attention, which it always did. But, they would never try the other's *charoset*.

What I would give to have them back at my seder table. I long to tell them all I've learned and the meaning it has for me. I would love to show them how the seeds they have planted have grown and to share with Sabbetai that we use many of his melodies at the seder with our children today.

That the children of Sam and Harry fell in love was no surprise. The goal of the next generation was to assimilate, not to forget who they were but to be American as best they could. Sam's fifth child and Harry's only daughter met in a doctor's office in a poor part of Brooklyn where she worked and he came in as a patient. It was love at first sight for him, if you hear her tell it, or for her, if you hear his side. Whatever, they wanted to see more of each other and had to brave each other's families to do so. He met her family first. They took one look at his dark curls, his flashy clothes, and assumed because his family spoke only Spanish that their daughter was in love with a Puerto Rican. I would love to have been there when my mother's mother, a proper Englishwoman from Birmingham, said, "What do you mean his sister is a belly dancer and is going to dance at the wedding?"

But this was America and they were in love, so the marriage of the two cultures took place. They had much to learn about each other's traditions. A new kind of Judaism emerged from them, an American kind that was not quite enough for us, their children, so we tell their stories.

If only I could have them at my seder table just one time. Sarika and Sabbetai, Heschel and Chaya. I would listen, oh how I would listen. I would ask them to bless my children, we would chant the melodies of both traditions, and we would eat the *charoset*, and it wouldn't matter which one because the secret of *charoset* is that it's sweet. It's supposed to represent the bricks and mortar we had to use as slaves to build the Egyptian cities. But it's sweet. It's so sweet that no matter how much bitter herbs you put with it, it's still sweet. That's what they had in common, too. True to the tradition of their people, no matter how much bitterness they experienced, they too made their lives, and the lives of their children, and of their children's children full of sweetness.

If only I could, for one time, share that world with my children, I would ask my grandparents to anoint them with sweet-smelling oils and exotic spices of jasmine and cardamon. I would ask my grandmothers to enchant them as they did me with the stories and songs of our people. I would ask them to tell the tales of Torah mingled with their own journey. I would ask them to teach my children as they did me that it is by remembering who we are that we can open our hearts to theirs. By remembering who we are and where we have been, we will respect the journey and worlds of others. This is the great lesson of our journey that will ultimately take us to a place of peace, of shalom, for ourselves and for others. When we remember our grandparents we do so with the Kaddish prayer, which ends, of course, with a prayer for peace. May it come soon.

LOOK NOT
UPON THE FLASK

Hanoch Teller

Hanoch Teller, *a rabbi and teacher, is the author of sixteen books, some of which have been translated into four languages, and over one hundred published essays. His books of inspirational stories include* Above the Bottom Line, Soul Survivors, *and* Souled: Stories of Striving and Yearning. *His writings have won several awards, launching a speaking career that has taken him on lecture tours to fifteen countries and across America. He and his family reside in Jerusalem, where he studies in the Mirrer Yeshivah and teaches in numerous local seminaries.*

Karen Benzian

"Look Not upon the Flask" is based upon the true story of the match between the famous head of the Sanzer chasidim, Reb Chaim, and his wife, Rachel Faigele. Tradition has it that when the despondent groom revealed that their match had been made in Heaven, the bride caught a glimpse of herself in the mirror—and saw that her reflected image had but one leg. She then knew that he spoke the truth.

I love this story because it is true: faithful to the essence of what transpired, and illuminating in its insight on life. The message of this story has been instrumental in bringing countless couples to the bridal canopy.

The Mishna, in *Ethics of Our Fathers*, teaches, "Look not upon the flask, but at its contents." First impressions can be deceiving; externals do not always reveal the more significant internals. There is no monopoly on sound counsel, and we would do well to be receptive to wisdom no matter from which quarter it emanates. Rachel Faigele did heed the teaching, resulting in her becoming the matriarch of one of the largest chasidic dynasties.

This story appears in my book, *"Souled!" Stories of Striving and Yearning* (Book 2).

384

ince the two great Rebbes were honored guests at the *chassanah*, they could allow themselves certain liberties, and as the entertainer had thrice dropped the bottles he was juggling and was more than likely to burn the town down with the lighted paper cone he was trying to balance on his nose, they withdrew to a quiet, safer corner of the square. The waiter was signaled and a fresh quart was brought to their table.

"I have a daughter, you know," said the Amdinover as he filled his colleague's glass.

"So I've heard," the Brezhinover replied, lifting his drink in salute. "A *ba'alas chessed*. And a wonderful *balabusta*."

The Amdinover drained his glass and refilled it. "That she is," he said, "and more. You have a son, yes?"

The *klezmer* were off-key and overloud, but with the conversation taking so serious a turn, neither of the Rebbes appeared disturbed. A group of heavy-footed dancers lurched past their table bearing the white-faced *chassan* aloft in a singularly graceless pose. "Look not upon the flask," the Brezhinover remarked, "but upon its contents."

His learned companion considered this somewhat irrelevant mishnaic comment for a moment. Surely, he thought, the Rebbe had not referred to the truly vile concoction they were imbibing; neither the flask *nor* its contents were noteworthy, except perhaps for their common vulgarity. He inferred, therefore, that the remark related to the pallid *chassan*, a boy who was known to have difficulty holding his *Gemara* the right way around and who looked now, on the night of his wedding, more like a sacrificial lamb than a happy bridegroom. Perhaps, the Rebbe concluded, there was more to this young fellow than met the eye.

But this was of no interest, not when the subject at hand concerned a union between the two greatest chasidic houses in all of Europe. He steered the conversation back on course. "I've heard your son is a great *talmid chacham*," he said, "an *ilui*." He knew he was overstating the case, but the stakes were very high. The Brezhinover raised an eyebrow. With that one small word, his colleague had, perhaps knowingly, substantially raised the price of the dowry. Negotiations now began in earnest.

The level of liquor in the bottle had descended to a point just above the false bottom by the time the terms of the *shidduch* were agreed upon, and the Rebbes were both immensely pleased with the bargain they had struck. They drank a final *"le'chaim"* to seal the agreement, clapped one another heartily on the shoulder, and, offering their warmest blessings to the *mechutanim*, hastily departed for home.

In every shtetl, in every corner of Europe, the upcoming wedding between the son of the Brezhinover and the daughter of the Amdinover became front-page news, so to speak. The thought of uniting the two most esteemed courts flamed imaginations and kindled hopes for the *Geulah*. It would be the affair of a lifetime, the gossips proclaimed, nay—the affair of the century! Every member of chasidic nobility was sure to attend, and it was rumored that the *Tzaddik* of Sassov *bich'vodo u've'atzmo* would officiate.

"I heard from my cousin Mottel, the son-in-law of the baker of Amdinov," reported one of the more reliable talebearers, "that two thousand loaves of challah have been ordered, and a cake more than two meters high!"

"My great-aunt's dressmaker's assistant," pronounced another, "has been sewing pearls onto the lace of the *kallah*'s gown for two months without respite. She says there must be as many pearls on the gown as there are in the Sea of Japan!"

The grapevine relayed word that not a cow or calf would remain in all of the Austro-Hungarian empire after the *shechting* was done for the bridal feast. The most trustworthy butchers and cooks were being brought in from five major cities. Orchards were being picked clean of fruit for miles around. Trainloads of wine and whiskey were already en route from the most reputable vineyards and refineries.

"It is said," whispered an itinerant peddler from Grodsk, "that the wedding gifts thus far received are greater in value than the combined treasure houses of Franz-Josef and Tsar Nikolai! And the presents have only *begun* to arrive!"

For once, it seemed, the rumormongers had not exaggerated.

As the day of the great *chassanah* neared, excitement rose to a fevered pitch. In the shtetls, it was enough for a humble villager to have *touched* one of the honored invitees for him to be endowed with glory. "Reb Shmelke gave me a kopek to shine his boots for the wedding!" an old cobbler announced proudly. "Ooh," his audience moaned ecstatically. "Aahh," they cried, "*ah sguleh!*"

But none enjoyed more adulation than Huddel the *sheitel-macher* who had personally laid eyes on the *kallah*. "Mere words cannot describe such beauty," she gushed. "An artist could not do her justice."

"It is a match made in heaven," said Yuske the *melamed*. "The Rebbe's son was a child prodigy and has grown to become such an outstanding Torah scholar that even *misnagdim* run to ask him *shailos!*"

"The offspring of this union will be doubly blessed," predicted Yentl the midwife, whose oracular pronouncements were rarely off the mark. "They will have their mother's face and their father's brains!"

Only one cynical misanthrope dared to point out that the bride and groom had never met. "What a farce!" he chuckled derisively. "They might despise one another on sight!"

He only just escaped with his life.

Because of the great distance that separated the towns of Amdinov and Brezhinov, this not-insignificant matter had indeed been neglected. Of course the *chassan* and *kallah* were unlikely to defy their fathers' express wishes; still, it was customary—indeed, halachically mandated—for the prospective bride and groom to be introduced at some time before the solemn moment, even if only as a formality. Provision was therefore made for the two young people to meet eight days prior to the wedding.

But, as it is said, "Man toils; God foils," and the train carrying the youthful *chassan* was derailed many kilometers from Ovinsk, where a coach that was to take him to Amdinov awaited. Fortunately, there were no injuries, although the delay cost the groom and his party three days traveling time. And when the train at last pulled into the station at Ovinsk, the coach was nowhere to be found.

A wagon and driver were hired—the only available transport

in Ovinsk—and the *chassan* and his family hastily boarded, knowing full well that the ragtag conveyance would make a somewhat undignified entrance at Amdinov. Still, it couldn't be helped. Were they to await the return of the coach, they might be forced to spend Shabbos among total strangers; moreover, they could not allow any further delay. Time-honored custom forbade encounters between bride and groom during the week prior to the *chassanah*, and, as it was, they were far behind schedule.

Outside a remote village some two days' ride from Amdinov, the wagon lost a wheel and the only wheelwright in that town was a drunkard sleeping off the previous evening's bender. "Like clay beneath the potter's hand, thus man conforms to God's command," it is written, and clearly God had not intended for the groom's journey to be uneventful. By the time the wagon was roadworthy once again, yet another two days had come and gone, and the *chassan* arrived only minutes before his own *chassanah*.

The thousands of invited guests, notables and townspeople, were in a most agitated state when the driver reined in the horses in the center of the village square. Although riders had been sent on ahead to convey the message of the *chassan*'s unfortunate delay to the *kallah*'s anxious family, tension had been mounting with every passing hour. The bridegroom's arrival was therefore greeted with uninhibited cheering and jubilation.

The bride, dressed in a gown the exquisiteness of which outshone even the gossip's description, hurried to the window of the upstairs parlor. As she watched, her *chassan*'s baggage was lowered from the wagon, his family members were helped from their seats, and finally, the young man himself alit. All at once, a look of horror came over the bride's lovely features and her hand flew to her lips in dismay. She spun on her delicate heels, lifted her frothy lace skirts, and ran from the room.

Word of the *kallah*'s refusal to go through with the ceremony spread as swiftly as the wagging tongues could carry it. Delegations of sisters, cousins, and aunts were dispatched to appeal to her through her locked bedroom door, but their pleas fell on deaf ears. The bride's anguished sobbing was all the response they received. Even aging Tante Shprintza, who had traveled for the occasion all the way from Reisha, could not coax her grandniece out of the boudoir.

Down in the square, pandemonium reigned. The *mechutanim* tried desperately to bear the disgrace in a manner befitting Rebbes of their stature, but it was all too apparent that a scandal could not be avoided unless drastic measures were taken to rectify the situation. The *kallah*'s refusal to go through with the *shidduch* was unfathomable, not to mention inexcusable! Nowhere in the empire could she hope to find a young man of finer virtue or nobler character. At last, the Amdinover himself went to petition his recalcitrant daughter.

"You deceived me!" the young woman cried when her father knocked.

"Deceived you?!" the Rebbe exclaimed, genuinely surprised. "How can you say that? Is the Brezhinover's son and heir not a great *talmid chacham*? Is he not a *ba'al midos*? Is he not destined for greatness?"

"Yes, *Tatteh*, he is all those things," the bride conceded through a veil of tears, "and he is also *lame!* Nothing you could say would make me marry a *cripple!*"

Only the bridegroom, that unequaled *ben Torah*, that present *ilui* and future *gadol*, received her rebuff with equanimity. Over the raucous din of the crowd, he called for silence, "I must be allowed to speak with the *kallah* myself," he said, and several female guests swooned.

It was unheard of! That the *chassan* and *kallah* should meet during the wedding week was nearly as scandalous as the last-minute cancellation of the nuptials itself! Reputations had been destroyed over less brazen acts. Despite this, and after a lengthy consultation, the Rebbes granted their permission.

When the *kallah* unlocked the door of her room, she was thunderstruck to find her rejected suitor standing alone on the threshold. She covered her tearstained face in shame—as much at the humiliation of having been betrothed to a cripple as at her own disgraceful behavior.

"I have come to tell you something important," the *chassan* said gently, but the *kallah*'s mortification knew no bounds. She began to weep again, deep tortured cries, and the *chassan* waited patiently for her sobbing to subside.

At last, red-eyed but composed, the beautiful *kallah* lowered her hands and forced herself to look upon the boy whom she had so mercilessly spurned.

"Matches are not made on earth," the young man began, "but in the corridors of Heaven. The Talmud relates that forty days before the creation of a child, a voice from Above proclaims: 'This daughter of so-and-so shall wed so-and-so.'" The bride nodded mutely, knowing he spoke the truth.

"Forty days before the birth of my match, a vision came to me," the *chassan* continued. "In it, I learned that my *kallah* would be not only a woman of valor but the daughter of an illustrious family. She would be a *ba'alas chessed* and would raise our children to be God-fearing. And . . ." He paused to allow the impact of his next words to penetrate: "she would be lame."

"But . . . but . . ." the bride stammered in confusion. The bridegroom went on. "When I learned that my *kallah* would suffer such a fate, I cried bitter tears—not for myself, but for this unfortunate girl whose entire life would be marred by a deformity.

"I fasted and prayed with all my heart that *I* be the one to receive this decree, that the deformity should be *mine* and not hers. And *baruch Hashem*, my fervent prayers were answered."

The wedding of the House of Amdinov and the House of Brezhinov took place, *b'sha'a tova u'mutzlachas*, right on schedule.

"EXCUSE ME, I HEVE AN APPOINTMENT WITH THE PRIME MINISTER"

Dvorah Menashe Telushkin

Dvorah Menashe Telushkin *was the personal assistant, translator, and editor for Isaac Bashevis Singer from 1975 to 1988. She is a graduate of the City University of New York with a major in language and literature and also of the Uriel Weinreich Graduate Program in Yiddish Studies, Columbia University. Since 1973, she has been a storyteller and performer of tales from the Yiddish masters, enhancing her telling with mime and Jewish songs. She has written a book of memoirs about working with I. B. Singer called* The Master of Dreams. *Dvorah lives in New York City with her husband, Joseph, and their children.*

I was the personal assistant and translator for Isaac Bashevis Singer from 1975 to 1988. I first met Isaac at Bard College, where I studied creative writing with him and shortly thereafter began working for him. Initially I answered letters and organized his lecture tours. Years later, after studying Yiddish at Columbia University and at the Yivo Institute in New York City, I was able to translate his stories from the original Yiddish. My experience has long reminded me of Franz Kafka's words, to the effect that learning Yiddish is like recalling a language one once knew well, but over time had slowly forgotten.

In 1978, Isaac won the Nobel Prize for Literature. The Nobel Citation stated: "For Isaac Bashevis Singer for his impassioned narrative art which, with roots in a Polish-Jewish cultural tradition, brings universal human conditions to life." At the time, he often kibbitzed with people when they asked him again and again if he was surprised when he won the prize. His answer was, "How long can a man be surprised?" In truth, he was amazed, almost stunned at the news. On the other hand, at seventy-five years of age he wasn't about to change and suddenly become haughty. Instead, he kept telling everyone, "Yesterday I vas a Yiddish writeh. Today I'm a Nobel Prize vinner. Tomorrow, I'll be a Yiddish writeh again."

After the amazement wore off, he settled down to prepare his speech. He rented a room at the Wellington Hotel in Manhattan as an escape from all the activity and attention he was receiving. I recall how he sat at the edge of a hard chair, a notebook resting on his lap; the speech poured out of him in less than an hour. In a sense, he dedicated his speech to belief in God and to the Yiddish language:

"There are some who call Yiddish a dead language, but so was Hebrew called for two thousand years. It has been revived in our time in a most remarkable, almost miraculous, way. Aramaic was certainly a dead language for centuries, but then it brought to light the *Zohar*, a work of mysticism of sublime value. It is a fact that the classics of Yiddish literature are also the classics of modern Hebrew literature. Yiddish has not yet said its last word. It contains treasures that have not been revealed to the eyes of the world. It was the tongue of martyrs and saints, of dreamers and kabbalists, rich in humor and in memories that mankind may never forget. In a figurative way, Yiddish is the wise and humble language of us all, the idiom of frightened and hopeful humanity."

Until the end of his life, Isaac wrote for the *Forward*, one of the last remaining Yiddish newspapers in America. He always wrote the first draft of all his stories, essays, and plays in Yiddish. He believed that people must stay with their mother tongue and repeated often, "It is important for a writer to go back to his roots. One should never look down and spit on his tradition. If one cannot understand yesterday, one cannot understand today."

I am now in the process of completing a memoir based on the years during which I worked with Isaac Bashevis Singer. The book *The Master of Dreams* is due to be published in 1995 by William Morrow. This is a chapter from the memoir.

---

vill never go to them again," Isaac was saying remorsefully as he sat in a little coffee shop a few blocks from the Regency Hotel. "They are all fakers and they vant I should provide for them a little publicity. Never urge me to go to them."

Fall of 1978: Israeli Prime Minister Menachem Begin, along

with President Jimmy Carter and Egyptian President Anwar as-Sadat, had just announced that the Israeli and Egyptian leaders would meet with the American president at his retreat, Camp David. This was an extraordinary moment in Jewish life, the first time since Israel's creation in 1948 that one of its Arab adversaries had announced a willingness to meet with the leader of the Jewish state.

Begin headed from Washington to New York to meet with Jewish leaders, and just a few days after he arrived, the telephone rang in Isaac's house. "The prime minister is requesting a meeting at the Regency Hotel on Park Avenue," Begin's secretary announced. "Could Mr. Singer come at 2:00 P.M. this afternoon?"

"Vhat vould he vant vith me?" was Isaac's main concern after he hung up the phone. "OK, you come vith me and vee vill go. Vhat is the vorst that could happen?"

At the entrance of the Regency Hotel stood a row of security guards, each six feet tall and dressed in gray uniforms with silver buttons. A large crowd was milling around outside the hotel, blocking every entrance. Isaac and I were both dressed in old woolen coats: his pants cuffs were draped over his shoes. My coat, a navy cashmere, had been worn by my grandmother fifty years earlier, and my black oxford shoes stood out over my sheer stockings. Like two immigrants, we approached the doors.

"Excuse me, I heve en appointment vith the prime minister," Isaac muttered to one of the "giants" who was guarding the door. The man stared ahead and made no response. When Isaac repeated his request, "Could you help me, I heve . . ." the guard waved us away. Dejected, we stood at the glass door looking inside, staring into space, wondering what to do. Suddenly a cameraman stationed in the lobby rushed over to us. He had recognized Isaac. "Bashevis Zinger, Bashevis Zinger!" he screamed, then slapped the guard on the back and swung open the door at the same second. He led us up in a quilted elevator to a hotel suite crowded with people. Pushing and elbowing his way through, he made a passageway for Isaac and me.

In a living room graced with pale pink wallpaper sat Menachem Begin, surrounded by twenty or thirty men dressed

in dark suits, leaning over a glass coffee table, hollering in Hebrew. Mrs. Begin rushed over to us and introduced herself. I
caught a glimpse of Moshe Dayan standing quietly in the corner with a perfectly straight posture. The two leaders moved
toward Isaac, and the other men moved toward him too. They
were honored he could join them: could he please come in, sit
down. "We have so much to talk [about]. . . ."

"It vas actually a monologue," Isaac said later, "vith me as the
audience." They spoke mainly in English, partly in Hebrew. Isaac
introduced me and they asked me (in Hebrew) about my name,
about my parents and grandparents and where they were from.
Of course, I answered in Hebrew. Never before had I appreci-
ated my yeshiva background as much as I did at that moment.
What an embarrassment it would have been had I been unable
to answer them. Menachem Begin then turned to Isaac and said
with animation, "Ahh, a krasavitza!" and planted a big wet kiss
on my cheek.

A few seconds later, Isaac was also bent near the glass coffee
table seated beside Menachem Begin, with the crowd of men in
dark suits surrounding him. The prime minister continued
shouting as photographers and cameramen crowded around
them. I stood behind the men and tried to salvage Isaac's hat,
which was being crushed by people scrambling over the chairs.
Snatching his hat from being flattened at just the last moment,
I was then able to approach the group and attempt to listen.

Isaac had meekly voiced a complaint, saying, "It is a pity that
in the great land of Israel, the Jews have neglected Yiddish to
such a high degree. We could have saved treasures vith just a
small effort. You have taken the Hebrew language, which was
dead for two thousand years, and resurrected it. But vith Yiddish, you took a living language vhich vas alive for some eight
or nine hundred years and killed it."

Menachem Begin, who had himself grown up in a Yiddish-
speaking home, began pounding his fist on the glass while spittle
flew from his lips. I was astonished, since his public persona
was one of utmost courtliness.

"With Yiddish," he shouted, "we could have not created any
navy; with Yiddish, we could have no army; with Yiddish, we

could not defend ourselves with powerful jet planes, with Yiddish we would be nothing. We would be like animals!"

Isaac sat with his hands folded in his lap and shrugged his shoulders. "Nu," he said sweetly to the hushed crowd, "since I am a vegetarian, for me to be like an animal is not such a terrible thing."

THE REST OF CREATION
Arthur Waskow

Arthur Waskow *is a Path-finder of ALEPH: Alliance for Jewish Renewal and director of the Shalom Center, a division of ALEPH that draws on Jewish thought and action toward healing the earth. He has been on the faculty of the Reconstructionist Rabbinical College and helped found the National Havurah Committee. His Ph.D. in United States history is from the University of Wisconsin. He is the author of many books, including* Godwrestling, Seasons of Our Joy, Before There Was a Before *(coauthored with his children, David Waskow and Shoshana Waskow), and* Tales of Tikkun *(coauthored with Phyllis Berman). Arthur resides with his wife, Phyllis Berman, in Philadelphia.*

In the summer of 1974, I was living with my children, David and Shoshana (ten and seven years old), and a dozen other Jews at "the Floating Havurah." That was a rented house in New England where members of the nascent fellowships (*havurot*) of Jewish renewal came to relax, study Torah, watch Richard Nixon resign the presidency, and cook and eat and schmooze and write and sing and pray—to live a Jewish life—together.

One evening I started to read aloud a schoolbook with stories of the Creation. "Booooring!" said David and Shoshana. "Think we can do any better?" I asked. "Sure!" they chorused, and together we wrote a set of stories, which we titled, "Before There Was a Before." I questioned, the kids answered and dictated, I wrote it down, the kids edited, and I polished. In our stories, God started out lonely, was never a King, and became only temporarily a Parent. As the world grew more mature, it took a greater and greater part in the creative process—the Creation according to Buber.

For ten years, we sought and failed to find a publisher. Jewish publishers said the tales weren't Jewish enough, general publishers said they were too religious and too childlike, children's publishers said they were too grown-up, and schoolbook publishers said they were too well and freely written to be textbooks. Finally, in 1984, Esther Cohen of Adama Books "got it," and Adama published *Before There Was a Before*. Carol Hall, a composer of Broadway musicals, bumped into it in a bookstore and took an option on turning it into a musical, while we agonized and laughed over how God could be played onstage. As a woman or a child? As a shimmering light with a voice? Like Harvey the Invisible Talking Rabbit? But finally, she decided the market for a religious musical was too small.

Although those years were hardly a "market incentive" to keep experimenting with the form, I kept on loving it, wanting to write that way. And the very last chapter—the chapter of Shabbat, the seventh day, the day of rest, kept swirling in my head. It was the one piece about which I didn't feel "at rest."

Shabbat itself was becoming more and more important to me. I learned to see it as a healing for my workaholism, and the more I wrestled with how to think Jewishly about issues of nuclear danger and environmental disaster, the more and more interested I grew in how Shabbat is both cosmic and political. Both what the universe needs in order to seal its own continuity and creativity, and what human beings need in order to be free. (In the Exodus version of the Ten Commandments, Shabbat is called a remembrance of Creation; in the Deuteronomy version, it is called a remembrance of liberation from slavery.)

I became convinced that the reason the human race is in such danger of self-destruction is that for five hundred years—the modern era—the human race has not made Shabbat. Not rested from its work, technology, doing, inventing, in order to rest, reflect, rethink, reevaluate—in order to be. The playful message itself seemed to call for a playful medium: the language of myth and storytelling that adults would hear and kids could understand.

So in 1986, I wrote, and *Hadassah Magazine* published, "The Rest of Creation" (September 1986, p. 30). (By now, my kids had grown into their own interests. I was on my own.) The title is of course a pun that like most Jewish puns is serious. It addresses the most profound puzzle of Shabbat: Is it about resting from Creation or is it "the rest of"—the very last and necessary part of—Creation? The pun is also about the process of my writing on Creation, for this story is "the rest of" *Before There Was a Before*, in both senses.

For years now I have been telling "The Rest of Creation" as one in a group of "Tales of Tikkun" that Phyllis Berman and I wrote and tell—often at the beginning or end of Shabbat. Kids respond with joyful exuberance, shouting out new things for God to make and finally naming the new Day. Adults express a somewhat wry enjoyment as they "get" how the story speaks to them.

ime for a rest," declared God, as the sun sank low to end day six. And as the sunset purples turned to browns and oranges, God watched the quiet and began to hum a gentle song. First World joined in, and then all the other newly created beings: woman and man, cherry trees and turtles, ocean and night.

"What's next?" asked God. "All these six days, I have felt I was creating. Such joy! I want to do some more."

"Come," God invited the creatures. "Let's sit in a circle and help me work out the next things to create. What shall I make for day seven? And eight? And nine?"

The hippopotamus grunted, "Uh. Huh. Uh. Streams. Of water. For me. To soak in."

The bluebird gurgled, "A ribbon of blue in the sky, to match me."

The robin redbreast glared at her. "No, a ribbon of red in the sky, to match *me!*"

The Baltimore oriole sighed, "How about a ribbon of orange in the sky, for me—or yellow, for the canary? Or—here's the best idea—how about a ribbon in the sky of red *and* orange *and* yellow *and* green *and* blue: *all* the colors!"

The woman interrupted. "Wait," she said. "These all sound like nice ideas. The colors would be wonderful. But I want to tell you a story. It's about the colors, too. This afternoon in the Garden, I found some purple grapes and some red strawberries and some thick green leaves. When I squeezed them, juice came out with all the different colors. So I started to make a . . . a . . ." And she stopped.

"A picture," God said.

"Good word," she said, "a picture. It was beautiful. I put the juices on a flat, gray rock I found in the Garden, and I began to make a picture of the Garden. With the strawberry juice, I painted a red sun, and I mixed the green and the red together to make a brown tree trunk. It felt almost like making the Garden myself." And she smiled at God.

"So I put on more and more colors," she continued. "The picture got prettier and prettier. I got really excited, and I put on one more color—and poof, it wasn't pretty anymore! It was ruined.

"I sat and cried. I said to the picture, 'Be finished.' But the picture cried, too, and said, 'I'm just finished off.' I said to the picture, 'I'm done,' but the picture said 'I'm done in.'

"So I learned something: Before you do something more, ask yourself, is it already done? If it is, just stop. Right away. Catch your breath. Because if you don't stop when the picture is finished, you'll finish it off. If you stop when it's time to stop, you can start when it's time to start—again—to make something new.

"So now, God, I wonder: Maybe Your world is all finished up, for now. Maybe it's time to catch Your breath. Maybe You shouldn't do any more doing."

God looked all around the circle. "Then what will I make for the seventh day?" God asked.

"You could make *not making*," said the man.

"That's wonderful," said God and looked around the circle again. Then God's face began to look strange—the top like a frown, the bottom like a smile. "I see something new. *You* painted a picture. *You* told a story. *You* taught Me new wisdom. It really is time to rest.

"This day," God said, "will be called, 'Rest and catch your breath.' And what we'll do instead of working is—we'll sit in a circle, just as we are doing now. We'll talk, just talk, about what is work and what is rest."

"We'll sing to each other," said the World.

"We'll breathe with each other," said the oak tree.

"We'll dance with each other," said the walrus.

And the bat and the bumblebee began to fly in a circle dance around each other. They went up, up, up, in a spiral of delight, while God and the oak tree breathed in and out and in and out.

"Ahhh!" said the oak tree.

"Yhhhwwhh," said God.

BARKING DOGS

Peretz Wolf-Prusan

Peretz Wolf-Prusan, *a rabbi and educator, is the education director at Congregation Emanu-El in San Francisco. A native Californian, he received his rabbinic ordination from Hebrew Union College. In addition, he uses words when he applies his art of calligraphy of Hebrew letters and as a storyteller. He has published* A Guide to Hebrew Lettering *and* Art and Spirituality. *He lives in San Francisco with his wife, Rebecca, and their three children, Leora, Avital, and Noah.*

Glenn Triest Photographic

Presently, I am involved in small ways with the homeless. Many of these people lost their shelter for the lack of a few dollars, perhaps two missed rent payments following the loss of work. Many received help on the street from storefront social service agencies and emergency aid to families when their need cried out. But it would have been better if they could have been helped before they barked.

Storytelling, for me at least, is the creation of a teaching opportunity. Stories can cut like a knife through the fog of illusion, even denial. I tell this story in conjunction with my effort to bring people to a level of understanding regarding homelessness. San Francisco, like many other cities across the land, is full of barking.

This story takes a parabolic path; it loops back upon itself to reveal a contradiction. The earthly value of giving upon request is lower than the spiritual value of giving before asked. A tale of hasidic origins, it is a story I heard long ago and tell quite often.

I was recently standing before the entrance to the Western Wall with forty students and adults. I had in my pocket tzedakah money given to me by friends in the States to distribute. I approached several "solicitors" and gave them money from my tzedakah envelope. Later on, when a student expressed her discomfort with solicitors offering to make a blessing in exchange for a donation, I shared with her the story of the barking dogs. I revealed a bit of myself to her when I said that it took me years to understand that if I gave first, before being asked, then the need to descend into a "transaction" relationship was uncalled for. By having to ask for money, a product must be offered. By giving before asked, no product is requested. She and I agreed that the giving of tzedakah is a learned skill, to be practiced and improved.

---

n a shoddy street in a sad district of a great city, an old man closed his butcher shop. He was not known to many, and his shop had but a few customers. He latched the door, hitched his collar up against the cold, and went home, where he died in his sleep.

He died, as it would happen, at the same moment that a famous manufacturer, surrounded by family, friends, and servants, died in his sleep. Both souls appeared in heaven at the same time.

The famous man and the butcher stood side by side and watched in amazement as a multitude of cheering angels approached. They surrounded and sang to them. As one, the angels lifted the butcher on their shoulders and carried him away for his reward in this, the world to come.

"What," the manufacturer said aloud, "is this! I know who I am! I have given and given, whenever asked. Just call me, and I gave! My name is on plaques and proclamations all over the land! Who was this they carried away?"

An angel, sent to walk with the manufacturer to his reward, asked, "Do the dogs bark at night in your city?" "No, the manufacturer replied, "as a matter of fact, they do not." "It is because of that one," the angel replied. "He would feed the dogs scraps of meat each night. You gave when asked. That one gave dogs food before they barked."

THE SEER OF LUBLIN'S SHIRT

Diane Wolkstein

Diane Wolkstein *is an author, storyteller, and teacher for children and adults. Charles Kurault of "PBS Sunday Morning" recently did a special broadcast about her, honoring her twenty-five years of storytelling, writing, and teaching. She gives performances and workshops on storytelling at schools, festivals, and conferences. Her adult book,* The First Love Stories, *includes her own translation of "The Song of Songs." Exactly thirty years after Diane told the story of Esther in Paris, her version of Queen Esther's life will be published as a book*—Esther's Story. *It is her eighteenth. Diane lives in New York City.*

Rachel C. Zucker

Rabbi Shlomo Carlebach had the storyteller's most important gift: the ability to tell the story the listener's soul most needs to hear. My daughter Rachel grew up attending Shlomo's synagogue, but for the last several years she had refused to come for the holidays—partly because she had been away in college, but most recently, she was angry with God. Her best friend's boyfriend, Ben Eddins, a tall, strong boy, who was as gentle and kind as he was intelligent, had recently died at twenty years old of a heart attack. Last Yom Kippur, when Rachel came to synagogue, she looked through the prayer book, then she shut it and turned to me and said, "Mom, how can I pray to God after what happened?"

Just then Shlomo walked in. He hadn't seen Rachel in three years. He gave her a big greeting. He began to speak about the holiday. Then he said, "I have a story, a special one, for Rachel." We both blushed in surprise.

Shlomo spoke about the Radzymin rabbi, who lived in Poland in the eighteenth and nineteenth centuries. The Radzymin had recently learned from his kabbalistic studies how to bring people back from the dead, but he had sworn he would never use this knowledge. One evening the Radzymin passed the hut of a poor family and heard piteous weeping. He went inside. A woman was dying, surrounded by her eleven children, who were all crying— the youngest was only ten months old. Her poor husband was beside himself with grief, begging her to live.

At the sight of such grief, the Radzymin forgot his promise and brought the woman back to life. But then he fell to the ground, unconscious. He had been struck by the powers of heaven for disobeying his oath. When the Radzymin arrived in heaven, he was asked, "What right do you have to break your oath?" When he answered, "It is permissible to break an oath if it will save a life," he was told, "We will accept what you say if this is the only time you have ever broken a promise."

For two hours, the Radzymin lay on the ground as the holy court reviewed his whole life and every word he had spoken. After two hours, he was brought back to life, for they could not find one time he had ever broken a promise to anyone.

Rachel and I turned to each other in silent astonishment. Stories anoint the wounds, providing the first healing.

Shlomo Carlebach told "The Seer of Lublin's Shirt" on Yom Kippur many years ago in synagogue. When I first heard the story, my sympathy lay with the brazen character of the master thief. Recently, when Shlomo told the story again, my heart opened to the fool. The fool doesn't know. He's stymied—stuck. He zigzags here and there and only later does a path emerge, a meaning. A story.

Thirty years ago, in 1965, I went to Paris determined to become a pantomimist. My parents violently disapproved. They worried I would "get behind." I had no idea how I would support myself, but I was brazen. I took the first three jobs I found: dubbing foreign films, tutoring English, and teaching Sunday school to children at Temple Copernic. At the end of the year, to my surprise, I discovered that what I loved the most was telling Bible stories once a week, and especially the story of Esther, which we made into a wonderful Purim shpiel. I had traveled three thousand miles to discover I didn't want to be silent. I loved words. I wanted to speak. I wanted to tell sacred stories.

So often, Shlomo ended his stories with a sigh and said, "What do I know? What do we know?" Was the righteous Radzymin a fool to throw his promise to the winds to save the life of a peasant? Was Moishe a fool to want to bring joy to a drunkard? Was I a fool to go off to Paris instead of "getting on with it"? The detours throw us off the known path into chaos, but there we have an opportunity to discover the needs of our soul. It is these needs and our confusion that story often addresses. When Moishe, in "The Seer of Lublin's Shirt," no longer understands, a story arrives.

The joy of a good story is that it continues to speak to us over the years. As the years pass, I've begun to have greater and greater admiration for the fool.

"What do we know?" Shlomo asks.

If we are fortunate, a story answers. . . .

---

ne day as the other members of the congregation were leaving the synagogue, the Seer of Lublin noticed Moishe. Moishe was the last to leave, tripping over his feet, knocking over the chairs. He wore a shirt that had one yellow sleeve and one green sleeve. The back was black and the front was green and red. It was patched together from the last five shirts he had owned that had fallen into pieces. He looked so bedraggled that the Seer of Lublin could not bear it.

"Moishe," he called out. "Come here."

Shyly Moishe walked toward his rabbi. He had great respect for the Seer. It was believed that the Seer could see the soul of anyone who was standing before him. He could see their soul back to the moment it was created. He could see all the experiences it had had and everything it needed to be fixed.

"Wait here," the rabbi said, and he went into the back room where he slept and brought out one of his shirts. The sleeves, the cuff, the collar, the front and back were all one color, all blue, and he handed it to Moishe.

"For me?" Moishe said, overcome with delight and disbelief: a gift from his rabbi.

"For you," the Seer confirmed. "Wear it in good health. And try to be a *mensch*, Moishe."

Moishe put it on and was filled with joy. He walked down the road, turning his head as he walked so he could admire his shirt from all directions. What joy, a brand-new shirt and a gift from his beloved rabbi.

He whistled as he walked and was soon joined by Yoishe, the town drunkard. For a time, Yoishe watched Moishe stroke his new shirt and make circles with his neck so he could enjoy the sight of it. Then he commented, "Where'd you get the shirt?"

"My rabbi, the Seer of Lublin, gave it to me this morning after services."

"To you?"

"Yes, to me."

"Gee," Yoishe said, "I wish someone would give me a shirt. That's a beautiful shirt, Moishe. I love your shirt. I love it."

"You do?"

"I do. I love it. I really love it." And he reached out and stroked the sleeve of Moishe's shirt. "I wish I had a shirt like that."

"Well, do—do you want it?"

"Oh, I love it. I would be so happy."

"Well, then take it, it's for you."

"For me?"

"Sure," Moishe said, with great pleasure, thinking to himself that he had never before had the possibility to make someone else so happy.

Moishe took off his shirt and gave it to Yoishe.

Yoishe didn't even thank Moishe. He started down the road at breakneck speed. He ran until he came to the town tavern. He ran into the tavern and cried, "Do I have a bid for the Seer of Lublin's shirt?"

The bartender, who knew a good deal when he saw it, answered, "A year's supply of free drinks!"

"Sold!" Yoishele cried.

The next day the bartender took the shirt to the marketplace. He stood on the street and called out, "Do I have a bid for the shirt of the holy Seer of Lublin? Any woman who wears this shirt will surely get pregnant. Twins! Any man who wears this shirt will have his fortune double!"

At this moment the Seer of Lublin walked into the marketplace and heard the bartender cry: "Do I have a bid for the Seer of Lublin's shirt?" The rabbi walked closer and saw it was the blue shirt he had given to Moishe. It was sold for an outrageous amount. The rabbi shook his head in frustration, turned and saw Moishe, who was standing in his many-colored patched shirt and blushing under the gaze of his rabbi. The Seer gave him a thunderous look of disapproval and walked away.

"But Rabbi, Rabbi," Moishe ran after him, trying to explain.

The Seer waved Moishe away. "Not today, Moishe. It's enough. Not today."

Moishe was crushed. Crushed. He had disappointed his beloved rabbi.

What had he done? What was he to do with himself?

Oy. His feet took him without thinking to the town cemetery on top of the hill. Where else should he be?

He sat down on the earth and wept.

A stranger passing by stopped to comfort Moishe.

"I'm sorry to hear of the passing," he said. "Was it someone very close to you?"

"Myself."

The stranger looked at him.

"I'm no use—in fact, I'm bad use. Whenever I try to do good, it comes out badly."

"What has happened?" the stranger asked him.

And when the stranger heard Moishe's story, he said, "Now, let me tell you a story. . . . In our town, where I was born, there was a thief. But not just any thief—he was a master thief. He had only to look at you and your wallet would be gone. If he asked you the time, your watch would be gone. No one was exempt. He robbed from everyone in the town. He was a professional of the highest caliber. No one could catch him.

"He became wealthier and wealthier and was invited to join the synagogue. But soon after he joined the synagogue, he gave up his profession. It just didn't feel right anymore to him to continue to steal. But then he became poorer and poorer.

"Several months later, the richest man in the synagogue passed by the thief's house on the eve of the Sabbath. He saw the thief sitting on the steps of his house surrounded by his children and he saw they were nearly dying of hunger.

"The rich man sent the thief a good sum of money so he could buy food for the Sabbath. The next week he did the same, and the next week and the next. Every week he sent the thief money so he could celebrate the Sabbath with joy.

"Many years later it happened that both the rich man and the thief died at the same moment. Nearly everyone in the town attended the rich man's funeral. Only five people, if that many—all of them former apprentices—attended the thief's funeral.

"The rich man went to heaven. He stood outside the gates of paradise while his good and bad deeds were weighed. As he had so many sins, the scale dipped in the wrong direction. The rich man realized he had no chance.

"Just then, a breeze came up and he found himself inside the gates of paradise.

"'What happened?' he asked in astonishment. 'How did I get in?'

"He was told, 'Your friend, the thief, stole your sins.'"

APPENDIX 1

Other Works by the Contributors

BOOKS

Adelman, Penina V. *Miriam's Well: Rituals for Jewish Women Around the Year*. Fresh Meadows, NY: Biblio Press, 1986, revised ed., 1990.

———. *The Aleph Beit Bible: For Young Children and Grown-ups*. Los Angeles, CA: Aleph Design Group, 1994.

Bandes, Hanna. *Reb Aharon's Treasure*. Jerusalem: Targum Press/Feldheim New York, 1993.

———. *Sleepy River*. New York: Philomel Books, 1993.

Bresnick-Perry, Roslyn. *Leaving for America*. San Francisco, CA: Children's Book Press, 1992.

Buxbaum, Yitzhak. *Jewish Spiritual Practices*. Northvale, NJ: Jason Aronson, 1990.

———. *The Life and Teachings of Hillel*. Northvale, NJ: Jason Aronson, 1994.

———. *Storytelling and Spirituality in Judaism*. Northvale, NJ: Jason Aronson, 1994.

Carlebach, Rabbi Shlomo, and Susan Yael Mesinai. *Shlomo's Stories: Selected Tales*. Northvale, NJ: Jason Aronson, 1994.

Forest, Heather. *The Baker's Dozen: A Colonial American Tale*. New York: Harcourt Brace Jovanovich, 1989.

———. *The Woman Who Flummoxed the Fairies: An Old Tale from Scotland*. New York: Harcourt Brace Jovanovich, 1990.

Frankel, Ellen. *The Classic Tales: 4,000 Years of Jewish Lore*. Northvale, NJ: Jason Aronson, 1989.

Frankel, Ellen, and Betsy Platkin Teutsch. *The Encyclopedia of Jewish Symbols*. Northvale, NJ: Jason Aronson, 1992.

Gordon-Zaslow, Debra, and Maureen Cresci. *Creative Dramatics for Children*. New York: Scott, Foresman and Co., 1989.

Gottlieb, Lynn. *She Who Dwells Within: A New Vision of Women in Judaism*. New York: HarperCollins, 1994.

Grossman, Daniel. *Bible Play: Biblical Characters and Special Needs*. Los Angeles, CA: Torah Aura Productions, 1987.

Grossman, Daniel T., and Elayne Robinson Grossman. *Help Us Bake a Challah* (music for children). Cedarhurst, NY: Tara Publications, 1991.

Harrison, Annette. *Easy-To-Tell Stories for Young Children*. Jonesborough, TN: National Storytelling Press, 1992.

Harrison, Annette, and Jerilynn Changar. *Storytelling Activities Kit*. Englewood Cliffs, NJ: The Center for Applied Research in Education/Simon and Schuster, 1992.

Jaffe, Nina. *Canto Saquito! Sing, Little Sack: A Folktale from Puerto Rico*. New York: Bantam Books, 1993.

———. *In the Month of Kislev: A Story for Hanukkah*. New York: Viking Childrens' Books, 1992.

———. *The Univited Guest and Other Jewish Holiday Tales*. New York: Scholastic, Inc., 1993.

———. *Patakin: World Tales of Drums and Drummers*. New York: Henry Holt and Co., 1994.

———. *Older Brother, Younger Brother: A Korean Folktale*. New York: Viking Children's Books, 1995.

Jaffe, Nina, and Steven Zeitlin. *While Standing on One Foot: Puzzle Stories and Wisdom Tales from the Jewish Tradition*. New York: Henry Holt, 1993.

Lieberman, Syd. *The Wise Shoemaker of Studena*. Philadelphia, PA: Jewish Publication Society, 1994.

Mintz, Helen. *A Woman's Voice in Jewish Storytelling* [working title]. Vancouver, BC, Canada: Press Gang, 1996.

Rand, Baruch, and Barbara Rush. *Jews of Kurdistan*. Toledo, OH: Toledo Board of Jewish Education and AAJE, 1978.

Rosman, Steven M. *Sidrah Stories: A Torah Companion*. New York: UAHC, 1989.

———. *Deena the Damselfly*. New York: UAHC Press, 1992.

———. *The Bird of Paradise and Other Sabbath Tales*. New York: UAHC, 1994.

———. *Spiritual Parenting: A Guide for Parents and Teachers*. Wheaton, IL: Theosophical Publishing House, 1994.

———. *The Twenty-Two Gates to the Garden*. Northvale, NJ: Jason Aronson, 1994.

Rosman, Steven M., Kerry M. Olitzky, and David P. Kasakove. *When Your Jewish Child Asks Why: Answers for Tough Questions*. Hoboken, NJ: Ktav Publishing House, 1993.

———. Also see Schram, Peninnah, and Steven M. Rosman.

Rubinstein, Robert E. *Hints for Teaching Success in Middle School*. Englewood, CO: Teacher Ideas Press/Libraries Unlimited, 1994.

Rush, Barbara. *The Book of Jewish Women's Tales*. Northvale, NJ: Jason Aronson, 1994.

————. Also see Rand, Baruch, and Barbara Rush; Schwartz, Howard, and Barbara Rush.

Rush, Barbara, and Eliezer Marcus. *Seventy and One Tales for the Jewish Year: Folk Tales for the Festivals.* New York: AZYF, 1980.

Sanfield, Steve. *A Natural Man: The True Story of John Henry.* Boston: David R. Godine, 1986.

————. *The Adventures of High John the Conqueror.* New York: Orchard Books, 1989.

————. *The Feather Merchants and Other Tales of the Fools of Chelm.* New York: Orchard Books, 1991.

————. *Bit by Bit.* New York: Philomel, 1995.

————. *American Zen by a Guy Who Tried It.* Monterey, CA: Larkspur Press, 1994.

————. *Strudel, Strudel, Strudel.* New York: Orchard Books, 1995.

Schachter-Shalomi, Zalman M. (with Donald Gropman). *The First Step: A Guide for the New Jewish Spirit.* New York: Bantam Books, 1983.

————. *Fragments of Future Scroll: Hasidism for the Here and Now.* Philadelphia, PA: B'nai Or Press, 1983.

————, and Edward Hoffman. *Sparks of Light: Counseling in the Hasidic Tradition.* Boulder, CO: Shambhala, 1983.

————. *Spiritual Intimacy: A Study of Counseling in Hasidism.* Northvale, NJ: Jason Aronson, 1991.

————. *Paradigm Shift.* Northvale, NJ: Jason Aronson, 1993.

Schram, Peninnah. *The Big Sukkah.* Rockville, MD: Kar-Ben Copies, Inc., 1986.

————. *Jewish Stories One Generation Tells Another.* Northvale, NJ: Jason Aronson, 1987.

————. *Tales of Elijah the Prophet.* Northvale, NJ: Jason Aronson, 1991.

Schram, Peninnah, and Steven M. Rosman. *Eight Tales for Eight Nights: Stories for Chanukah.* Northvale, NJ: Jason Aronson Inc., 1990.

Schwartz, Cherie Karo. *My Lucky Dreidel: Hanukkah Stories, Songs, Poems, Crafts, Recipes, and Fun for Kids.* New York: Smithmark, 1994.

Schwartz, Howard, ed. *The Captive Soul of the Messiah.* New York: Schocken, 1983.

————. *Miriam's Tambourine: Jewish Folktales from Around the World.* New York: Oxford University Press, 1988.

————. *The Dream Assembly: Tales of Rabbi Zalman Schacter-Shalomi.* Nevada City, CA: Gateways, 1989.

———, ed. *Gates to the New City: A Treasury of Modern Jewish Tales*. Northvale, NJ: Jason Aronson, 1991.

———. *Lilith's Cave: Jewish Tales of the Supernatural*. New York: Oxford University Press, 1991.

———, ed. *Imperial Messages: One Hundred Modern Parables*. New York: Overlook Press, 1992.

———. *The Sabbath Lion*. New York: Harper and Row, 1992.

———. *Adam's Soul: The Collected Tales of Howard Schwartz*. Northvale, NJ: Jason Aronson, 1993.

———. *Gabriel's Palace: Jewish Mystical Tales*. New York: Oxford University Press, 1993.

———. *Elijah's Violin and Other Jewish Fairy Tales*. New York: Oxford University Press, 1994.

Schwartz, Howard, and Anthony Rudolf, eds. *Voices Within the Ark: The Modern Jewish Poets*. New York: Avon Books and Pushcart Press, 1980.

Schwartz, Howard, and Barbara Rush. *The Diamond Tree: Jewish Tales from Around the World*. New York: HarperCollins, 1991.

Shapiro, Rami M. *The One Minute Mentsch: Exercises for Spiritual Growth*. Miami, FL: New Paradigm Press, 1985.

———. *Tangents: Selected Poems 1978–1988*. Miami, FL: EnR Wordsmiths, 1988.

———. *Open Hands: A Guide to Dying, Death and Bereavement*. Miami, FL: Medic Publishing, 1990.

———. *Embracing Esau: A Jewish Look at Masculinity*. Miami, FL: Light House Press, 1991.

———. *Willow Baskets, Colored Glasses: Helping Friends through Mourning*. Miami, FL: Medic Publishing, 1991.

———. *The Assembler of Wisdom: Ecclesiastes*. Miami, FL: Light House Press, 1992.

———. *Last Breaths: A Guide for Aiding the Dying*. Miami, FL: Light House Press, 1993.

Shapiro, Rami M. *Teachings: Reflections on Pirke Avot*. Miami, FL: Light House Press, 1993.

Simms, Laura. *Moon and Otter and Frog*. New York: Hyperion Books, 1994.

———. *The Bone Man*. New York: Hyperion Books. Forthcoming.

———. *Rotten Teeth*. Boston: Little, Brown & Co. Forthcoming.

Simms, Laura, and Ruth Kozodoy. *Exploring Our Living Past Storybooks*. New York: Behrman House, 1979.

Teller, Hanoch. *Once Upon a Soul*. New York: NYC Publishing Co., 1984.

———. *Soul Survivors*. New York: NYC Publishing Co., 1985.

———. *"Souled!"* (Books 1 and 2). New York: NYC Publishing Co., 1986.

———. *Above the Bottom Line*. New York: NYC Publishing Co., 1988.

———. *Bridges of Steel, Ladders of Gold*. New York: NYC Publishing Co., 1990.

———. *Give Peace a Stance*. New York: NYC Publishing Co., 1992.

———. *A Matter of Principal*. New York: NYC Publishing Co., 1994.

Telushkin, Dvorah Menashe. *The Master of Dreams*. New York: William Morrow, 1995.

Waskow, Arthur. *Down-to-Earth Judaism: Food, Money, Sex and the Rest of Life*. New York: William Morrow, 1995.

Waskow, Arthur. *Seasons of Our Joy*. Boston: Beacon, 1982; rev. ed., 1991.

———. *These Holy Sparks: The Rebirth of the Jewish People*. New York: Harper and Row, 1983.

———. *Godwrestling*. Montpelier, VT: Jewish Lights, 1995.

Waskow, Arthur, and Phyllis Berman. *Tales of Tikkun*. Northvale, NJ: Jason Aronson. Forthcoming.

Waskow, Arthur, David Waskow, and Shoshana Waskow. *Before There Was a Before*. New York: Adama Books, 1984.

Waskow, Howard, and Arthur Waskow. *Becoming Brothers*. New York: Free Press, 1993.

Weiss, Avraham. *Women at Prayer: A Halakhic Analysis of Women's Prayer Groups*. Hoboken, NJ: Ktav Publishing House, 1990.

Wolf-Prusan, Peretz. *A Guide to Hebrew Lettering*. New York: UAHC, 1982.

Wolf-Prusan, Peretz, and Jan Rindfleisch, eds. *Art and Spirituality*. Cupertino, CA: Helen Euphrat Gallery, 1982.

Wolkstein, Diane. *The Red Lion*. New York: T. Y. Crowell, 1977.

———. *The Magic Orange Tree and Other Haitian Folktales*. New York: Alfred A. Knopf, 1978.

———. *The Banza*. New York: Dial Books, 1980.

———. *The Magic Wings*. New York: E. P. Dutton, 1983.

———. *The Legend of Sleepy Hollow*. New York: Morrow Junior Books, 1987.

———. *The First Love Stories: From Isis and Osiris to Tristan and Iseult*. New York: HarperCollins, 1991.

———. *Little Mouse's Painting*. New York: Morrow Junior Books, 1992.

———. *Step by Step*. New York: Morrow Junior Books, 1992.

———. *Esther's Story*. New York: Morrow Junior Books. Forthcoming.

———. *Oom Razoom, or, I Go I Know Not Where, Bring Back I Know Not What: A Russian Tale*. New York: Morrow Junior Books, 1991.

Wolkstein, Diane, and Samuel Noah Kramer. *Inanna: Queen of Heaven and Earth: Her Stories and Hymns from Sumer*. New York: Harper and Row, 1983.

STORY AND ESSAY COLLECTIONS

Homespun: Tales from America's Favorite Storytellers. Edited by Jimmy Neil Smith. New York: Crown Publishers, 1988. (See stories by Laura Simms and Diane Wolkstein.)

Joining In: An Anthology of Audience Participation Stories and How to Tell Them. Compiled by Teresa Miller with Anne Pellowski. Edited by Norma Livo. Cambridge, MA: Yellow Moon Press, 1988. (See stories by Heather Forest, Doug Lipman, Laura Simms, and Diane Wolkstein.)

The Invisible Thread. Edited by Diana Bletter and Lori Grinker. Philadelphia, PA: Jewish Publication Society, 1989. (See interview with Suzanne Benton and photos of her artworks.)

Best-Loved Stories Told at the National Storytelling Festival. (See stories by Syd Lieberman, Doug Lipman, Steve Sanfield, Peninnah Schram and Laura Simms.) *More Best-Loved Stories Told at the National Storytelling Festival*. (See stories by Heather Forest, Syd Lieberman, Doug Lipman, Steve Sanfield, Peninnah Schram, and Diane Wolkstein.) Jonesborough, TN: National Storytelling Press, 1991, 1992.

The Ghost and I: Scary Stories for Participatory Telling. Edited by Jennifer Justice. Cambridge, MA: Yellow Moon Press, 1992. (See stories by Heather Forest, Betty Lehrman, Doug Lipman, Robert E. Rubinstein, and Laura Simms.)

Spinning Tales, Weaving Hope: Stories of Peace, Justice and the Environment. Edited by Ed Brody et al. Philadelphia, PA: New Society Publisher, 1992. (See stories by Hanna Bandes, Heather Forest, Doug Lipman, and Peninnah Schram.)

The Storyteller's Companion to the Bible: Old Testament Women. Volume 4. Edited by Michael E. Williams. Nashville, TN: Abingdon Press, 1993. (See stories contributed by Betty Lehrman.)

Teacher's Read Aloud Anthology. 9 volumes. Margaret H. Lippert, Anthologist. New York: Macmillan/McGraw Hill School Publishing Co., 1993. (See stories by Doug Lipman, Peninnah Schram, Laura Simms, and Diane Wolkstein.)

Many Voices: True Tales from America's Past. Edited by Mary Weaver.

Jonesborough, TN: National Storytelling Press and School Book Fairs, 1994. (See stories by Hanna Bandes, Joel ben Izzy, Karen Golden, and Annette Harrison.)

The New Jewish Teachers Handbook. Edited by Audrey Friedman Marcus. Denver, CO: A.R.E., 1994. (See "Storytelling: Role and Technique," essay by Peninnah Schram.)

Reading Comprehension Workshop: Insights. Edited by Lynn W. Kloss. Paramus, NJ: Globe Fearson, 1994. (See story by Peninnah Schram.)

Ready-to-Tell Tales: Surefire Stories from America's Favorite Storytellers. Edited by David Holt and Bill Mooney. Little Rock, AK: August House, 1994. (See stories by Judith Black, Heather Forest, Doug Lipman, Steve Sanfield, Peninnah Schram, Laura Simms, and Diane Wolkstein.)

The Storyteller's Companion to the Bible: Old Testament Wisdom. Volume 5. Edited by Michael E. Williams. Nashville, TN: Abingdon Press, 1994. (See stories contributed by Peninnah Schram.)

Tales as Tools: Power of Story in the Classroom. Jonesborough, TN: National Storytelling Press, 1994. (See essays by Peninnah Schram.)

Across the Great Divide: From Orality to Print and Back Again. Edited by Carol Birch and Melissa Heckler. Little Rock, AK: August House, 1995. (See essays by Gerald Fierst, Peninnah Schram, and Laura Simms.)

The Complete Guide to Using Storytelling in the Library. Jonesborough, TN: National Storytelling Press, 1994. (See essay by Peninnah Schram.)

The Kids' Catalog of Jewish Holidays. Edited by David A. Adler. Philadelphia, PA: Jewish Publication Society, 1995. (See story by Peninnah Schram and Rachayl Eckstein Davis.)

Life Cycles: Jewish Women on Holidays and Communal Celebration. Volume 3. Edited by Rabbi Debra Orenstein. Woodstock, VT: Jewish Lights. Forthcoming. (See stories by Karen Golden.)

SPECIAL RESOURCES

Davis, Rachayl Eckstein. *See* Schram, Peninnah, and Rachayl Eckstein Davis.

Schram, Peninnah. *Elijah the Prophet Study Guide/Instant Lesson.* Los Angeles, CA: Torah Aura Productions, 1994; (800) BE-TORAH.

Schram, Peninnah, and Rachayl Eckstein Davis. "The Apple Tree's Discovery." Jewish New Year's card with story. Coalition for the

Advancement of Jewish Education (CAJE), 261 West 35 St., New York, NY 10001; (212) 268–4210.

Shore, Eliezer, ed. *Bas Ayin* (a journal that seeks to offer Torah articles of a personal and inspiring nature). *Bas Ayin*, 14 Hutchinson Ct., Great Neck, NY 11023; (516) 482-2989.

Torah Times: An Audio Magazine (Rabbi Shlomo Carlebach's teachings, songs, stories, and music). *Torah Times*, 63 West 38 St., Suite 1201, New York, NY 10018.

Waskow, Arthur, editor. *New Menorah* (a quarterly journal of the practice and theory of Jewish renewal). ALEPH: Alliance for Jewish Renewal, 7318 Germantown Ave., Philadelphia, PA 19119-1793; (215) 242–4074.

AUDIOTAPES

Adelman, Penina V. *This Is the Story: Original Songs and Midrashim about Jewish Women.*

A Song a Month (with Suri Levow-Krieger). Penina Adelman, 243 Upland Road, Newtonville, MA 02160, or Sounds Write Productions, Inc., 6685 Norman Lane, San Diego, CA 92120.

Ben Izzy, Joel. *Stories From Far Away.*

The Beggar King and other Tales from Around the World. SILO Music, P.O. Box 429, South Main St., Waterbury, VT 05676.

Benton, Suzanne. *Myths, Masks, Legends and Lifestory.* Suzanne Benton, 22 Donnelly Dr., Ridgefield, CT 06877.

Black, Judith. *Waiting for Elijah.*

Glad To Be Who I Am.

Hell for a Picnic.

Banned in the Western Suburbs.

The Home Front.

Adult Children of . . . Parents, Oops Ma! Judith Black, 33 Prospect St., Marblehead, MA 01945.

Bresnick-Perry, Roslyn. *Holiday Memories of a Shtetl Childhood: Gut Yom Tov, Gut Yor.*

A Real American Girl: Stories of Immigration and Assimilation. Roslyn Bresnick-Perry, 210 West 70 St., No. 307, New York, NY 10023.

Danoff, Susan. *Enchantments.*

The Invisible Way: Stories of Wisdom.

Women of Vision. Susan Danoff, P.O. Box 7311, Princeton, NJ 08543–7311.

Etshalom, Yitzchak. *Rest Area: Tales of the Road.*

    Burbank: Tales of the Road II. Yitzchak Etshalom, 1601 Beechwood Blvd., Pittsburgh, PA 15217.

    Family and Friends (original music by Y. Etshalom and performed by student and faculty of Los Angeles Hebrew High School). LAHHS, 5900 Sepulveda Blvd., Van Nuys, CA 91411.

Fierst, Gerald. *Jewish Tales of Magic and Mysticism.*

    Tikkun Olam: Stories to Heal the World (with Jonathan Feig on violin). Gerald Fierst, 222 Valley Road, Montclair, NJ 07042.

Forest, Heather. *Songspinner: Folktales and Fables Sung and Told.*

    Sing Me a Story.

    Tales of Womenfolk.

    Tales Around the Hearth.

    In the Eye of the Beholder.

    The Animals Could Talk: Aesop's Fables Musically Retold (tape and libretto, August House). Cartoon Opera, P.O. Box 354, Huntington, NY 11743.

Frankel, Ellen. *Classic Tales: Traditional Jewish Stories.* Ellen Frankel, 6678 Lincoln Dr., Philadelphia, PA 19119.

Golden, Karen. *Tales and Scales: Stories of Jewish Wisdom.* Golden Button Productions, 6152 W. Olympic Blvd., No. 9, Los Angeles, CA 90048.

Grayzel, Eva. *Proud to Be Jewish* (with Cantor Buzzy Walters). Eva Grayzel, 4245 Farmersville Ct., Easton, PA 18042–2346.

Grossman, Daniel, and Elayne Robinson Grossman. *Help Us Bake a Challah* (book and audiocassette). P.B.T. Creative Enterprises, 6 Lannigan Drive, Lawrenceville, NJ 08648.

Harrison, Annette. *Lilith's Cave: Jewish Tales of the Supernatural.*

    A Dash of Seasoning.

    Storytelling, American Style (with Perrin Stifel). Annette Harrison, 6370 Pershing Ave., St. Louis, MO 63130.

Ilsen, Eve Penner. *Tales of Mystery and Mussar.*

    Windows to Another World: Chassidic Story and Song. Eve Penner Ilsen, 3201 Wellington St., Philadelphia, PA 19149.

Jaffe, Nina. *The Three Riddles* (book and audiocassette). Nina Jaffe, 3901 Independence Ave, Bronx, NY 10463.

Lehrman, Betty. *Watermelon! and Other Stories.*

    Tales for the Telling.

    Jewish Tales from the Heart. Tales for the Telling, 99 Arlington St., Brighton, MA 02135.

Lieberman, Syd. *The Old Man and Other Stories.*
Joseph the Tailor and Other Jewish Tales.
A Winner and Other Stories.
Intrepid Birdmen.
The Johnstown Flood of 1889.
The Tell-Tale Heart. Syd Lieberman, 2522 Ashland, Evanston, IL 60201.
Lipman, Doug. *The Forgotten Story: Tales of Wise Jewish Men.*
Folktales of Strong Women.
Milk from the Bull's Horn.
One Little Candle: Participation Stories and Songs for Hanukkah.
Now We Are Free: Passover Participation Stories and Songs.
The Amazing Teddy Bear.
Keep on Shaking.
Tell It With Me.
Hopping Freights. Doug Lipman, P.O. Box 441195, W. Somerville, MA 02144.
Mara. *Seeing with My Ears.*
Storysong. MARA, P.O. Box 20181, San Jose, CA 95160–0181.
Rosman, Steven M. *Sidra Stories: A Torah Companion*, vol. 1. UAHC Press, 838 Fifth Ave, New York, NY 10021.
Rubinstein, Robert E. *The Rooster Who Would Be King and Other Healing Tales.*
The Day the Rabbi Stopped the Sun and Other Jewish Tales.
Tales of Mystery / Tales of Terror. Robert E. Rubinstein, 90 East 49 Ave., Eugene, OR 97405.
Rush, Barbara. *Barbara Rush Tells Stories from* The Diamond Tree. Barbara Rush, 24 Gaymor Lane, Commack, NY 11725.
Sanfield, Steve. *Could This Be Paradise?*
Steve Sanfield Live at the Sierra Storytelling Festival. Backlog Book Services, Box 694, North San Juan, CA 05960.
Schachter-Shalomi, Reb Zalman M. *Le Chayim—To Life!*
The Seven Beggars: A Tale of Rabbi Nahman of Bratslav.
Davenning with Reb Zalman: An Audio Siddur.
For Your Healing.
Your Glory Shines.
The Spiritual Elder.
The Tools of Spiritual Eldering. ALEPH, 7318 Germantown Ave., Philadelphia, PA 19119–1793.

Schwartz, Cherie Karo. *Worldwide Jewish Stories of Wishes and Wisdom.*

> *Miriam's Tambourine: Jewish Folktales from Around the World.* Cherie Karo Schwartz, 996 S. Florence St., Denver, CO 80231.

Simms, Laura. *Making Peace—Heart Uprising.*

> *Women and Wild Animals.*
> *Moon on Fire: Calling Forth the Power of the Feminine.*
> *Laura Simms Tells Stories Just Right for Kids.*
> *Stories: Old as the World, Fresh as the Rain.*
> *Incredible Journey.* Earwig Music Co., Inc., 1818 W. Pratt Blvd., Chicago, IL 60626.
> *Nightwalkers: Tales of the Visible and Invisible Worlds.*
> *Squeaky Door.*
> *Dance Without End.* Laura Simms Studio, 814 Broadway, New York, NY 10003.

Stone, Susan. *The Angel's Wings and Other Stories from* The Diamond Tree: Jewish Tales from Around the World. 1320 Wesley, Evanston, IL 60201.

Sutton, Joan. *The Jewish Holidays* (five audiocassettes for young children). Joan Sutton, 1451 15th Ave, San Francisco, CA 94118.

Teller, Hanoch. *The Sound of Soul I.*

> *The Sound of Soul II.* New York City Publishing Co., 37 West 37 St., New York, NY 10018.

Wolkstein, Diane. *The Story of Joseph.*

> *Romping.*
> *Hans Christian Andersen in Central Park.*
> *Eskimo Stories: Tales of Magic.*
> *The Epic of Inanna.*
> *Psyche and Eros.*
> *Fairy Tales from Estonia.*
> *Tales of the Hopi Indians.*
> *California Fairy Tales.*
> *The Banza.* Diane Wolkstein, 10 Patchin Place, New York, NY 10011.

AUDIOTAPE ANTHOLOGIES

Best-Loved Stories Told at the National Storytelling Festival. Volume 1: Steve Sanfield; Volume 2: Peninnah Schram. National Storytelling Association, P.O. Box 309, Jonesborough, TN 37659.

A Storytelling Treasury: Tales Told at the 10th-Anniversary National Storytelling Festival (set of five audiocassettes; selected and arranged by Carol Birch). (Hear recordings by Judith Black, Heather Forest, Syd Lieberman, Doug Lipman, Steve Sanfield, Peninnah Schram, Laura Simms, and Diane Wolkstein.) National Storytelling Association, P.O. Box 309, Jonesborough, TN 37659.

VIDEOTAPES

Suzanne Benton: Sculptor, Mask Performer, Printmaker. Suzanne Benton, 22 Donnelly Dr., Ridgefield, CT 06877.

Grayzel, Eva, and Suri Levow-Krieger. *The Secret in Bubbie's Attic.* Ergo Media Inc., P.O. Box 2037, Teaneck, NJ 07666.

Grossman, Daniel T. *Someone Is Listening: A Video Play.* United Synagogue, 155 Fifth Ave., New York, NY 10010.

Levow-Krieger, Suri. *See* Grayzel, Eva, and Suri Levow-Krieger.

Lipman, Doug. *Coaching Storytellers: A Demonstration Workshop.* Doug Lipman, P.O. Box 441195, West Somerville, MA 02144.

Price, Marilyn, and Jeffrey Schein. *Puppets and Paradigms.* Reconstructionist Press, P.O. Box 157, Rockaway Beach, NY 11693.

Schachter-Shalomi, Reb Zalman M. *Prayer from the Heart.*

Life Harvest: The Missing Piece to Wholeness. ALEPH: Alliance for Jewish Renewal, 7318 Germantown Ave., Philadelphia, PA 19119–1793.

Wolkstein, Diane. *Inanna.*

Stories in the Park. Cloudstone Productions, 10 Patchin Place, New York, NY 10011.

VIDEOTAPE ANTHOLOGY

The American Storytelling Series (eight videocassettes). H. W. Wilson Company, 950 University Ave., Bronx, NY 10452 (see performances of stories by Heather Forest and Diane Wolkstein).

APPENDIX 2
Storytelling Organizations

National Storytelling Association (NSA), P.O. Box 309, Jonesborough, TN 37659; (615) 753-2171 or (800) 525-4514. Also known as NAPPS. Publishes *The National Storytelling Magazine*.

The Jewish Storytelling Center, 92nd Street Y Library, 1395 Lexington Avenue, New York, NY 10128; (212) 415-5544. Peninnah Schram, founding director–Gerald Fierst, artistic director. Publishes *The Jewish Storytelling Newsletter*.

Jewish Storytelling Network of CAJE (Coalition for the Advancement of Jewish Education), coordinator Cherie Karo Schwartz, 996 S. Florence St., Denver, CO 80231; (303) 367–8099.

Jewish Storytelling Arts of Toronto, c/o Leslie Robbins, 96 Chudleigh Avenue, Toronto, Ontario, Canada M4R 1T3; (416) 483-3082.

Jewish Storytelling Coalition of Boston, c/o Bonnie Greenberg, 63 Gould Road, Newton, MA 02168; (617) 244-2884.

Minnesota Jewish Storytellers' Guild, c/o Lennie Major, 1432 Edmund Avenue, St. Paul, MN 55104; (612) 645-0825.

APPENDIX 3

Contributors' Addresses

Penina V. Adelman, 243 Upland Road, Newtonville, MA 02160

Hanna Bandes, P.O. Box 35416, Brighton, MA 02135 — 617 254-3846

Joel ben Izzy, 1715 La Loma St., Berkeley, CA 94709 — 510 883-0883

Suzanne Benton, 22 Donnelly Dr., Ridgefield, CT 06877 — 203 438-4650

Rabbi Saul J. Berman, 329 West 108 St., #1A, New York, NY 10025 — 212 663-3541

Judith Black, 33 Prospect St., Marblehead, MA 01945 — 617 631-4417

Rabbi Tsvi Blanchard, CLAL, 99 Park Ave., Suite C-300, New York, NY 10016–1599 — 212 867-8888

Renée Brachfeld, 4108 Military Rd. NW, Washington, DC 20015 — 202 362-3270

Jay Brand, P.O. Box 871, Reynoldsburg, OH 43068 — 614 868-8655

Roslyn Bresnick-Perry, 210 W. 70 St., 307, New York, NY 10023 — 212 724-2392

Yitzhak Buxbaum, 144-39 Sanford Ave, 6I, Flushing, NY 11355 — 718 539-5978

Susan Danoff, P.O. Box 7311, Princeton, NJ 08543–7311 — 609 921-0916

Rachayl Eckstein Davis, 3440 Fairway Rd., Oceanside, NY 11572 — 516 678-4681

Rabbi Yitzchak Etshalom, 1601 Beechwood Blvd., Pittsburg, PA 15217 — 412 422-4279

Gerald Fierst, 222 Valley Rd., Montclair, NJ 07042 — 201 746-4608

Heather Forest, P.O. Box 354, Huntington, NY 11743 — 516 271-2511

Ellen Frankel, 6670 Lincoln Dr., Philadelphia, PA 19119 — 215 843-0228

Cantor Nancy R. Ginsberg, Temple Beth-El, 70 Orchard Ave., Providence, RI 02906 — 401 331-6070

Karen Golden, 6152 West Olympic, No. 9, Los Angeles, CA 90048 — 213 933-4614

Rabbi James Stone Goodman, c/o Central Reform Congregation, 77 Maryland Plaza, St. Louis, MO 63108 — 314 361-3919

Debra Gordon-Zaslow, 692 Elkader St., Ashland, OR 97520 — 503 482-0088

Rabbi Lynn Gottlieb, 3309 Mountain Rd. NE,
    Albuquerque, NM 87106   505 268-9961
Eva Grayzel, 4245 Farmersville Court, Easton,
    PA 18042   215 258-3763
Rabbi Daniel T. Grossman, 6 Lannigan Dr.,
    Lawrenceville, NJ 08648   609 883-7416
Naftali Haleva, Eksercioglu Sok Yumurcak
    Apt. 30-11, Sisli, Istanbul, Turkey   90-212 2405610
Annette Harrison, 6370 Pershing Ave, St. Louis,
    MO 63130   314 725-7767
Lynn Hazan, 1401 W. Olive, No. 2, Chicago, IL 60660   312 728-1161
Merna Ann Hecht, 17904 Westside Highway, SW,
    Vashon, WA 98070   206 463-5653
Rabbi David Holtz, Temple Beth Abraham,
    25 LeRoy Ave., Tarrytown, NY 10591   914 631-1770
Eve Penner Ilsen, 3201 Wellington St., Philadelphia,
    PA 19149   215 332-3088
Nina Jaffe, c/o Bank Street College of Education,
    610 West 112 St., New York, NY 10025   212 875-4492
Betty Lehrman, 88 Flanagan Dr., Framingham,
    MA 01701   508 877-9738
Suri Levow-Krieger, 311 Hardenburgh Rd.,
    Demarest, NJ 07627   201 767-9480
Syd Lieberman, 2522 Ashland, Evanston, IL 60201   708 328-6281
Lisa Lipkin, 773 Blvd. E., Weehawken, NJ 07087   201 863-2812
Doug Lipman, P.O. Box 441195, West Somerville,
    MA 02144   617 391-3672
Lennie Major, 1432 Edmund Ave., St. Paul,
    MN 55104   612 645-0825
Mara, P.O. Box 20181, San Jose, CA 95160-0181   408 927-0964
Helen Mintz, 4007 Renton Ave., S., Seattle,
    WA 98108   206 723-1749
Marilyn Price, 2430 Prairie Ave., Evanston, IL 60201   708 869-6378
Leslie Robbins, 96 Chudleigh Ave., Toronto, Ontario
    M4R 1T3 Canada   416 483-3082
Rabbi Steven M. Rosman, 88 Starrs Plain Rd.,
    Danbury, CT 06810   203 792–6996
Rabbi Don Rosoff, 28 Blackwatch Trail, Morristown,
    NJ 07960   201 539-2558
                                                      or 201 539-4539
Charlie Roth, 57 East 11 St., New York,
    NY 10011-4605   212 420-0042

Robert E. Rubinstein, 90 E. 49 St., Eugene, OR 97405   503 344-8176
Barbara Rush, 28 Mitudela, Jerusalem, 96306 Israel   02 632-034
   or 24 Gaymor Lane, Commack, NY 11725   516 543-4535
Steve Sanfield, 22000 Lost River Rd., Nevada City,
   CA 95959   916 292-3353
Rabbi Zalman Schachter-Shalomi, ALEPH:
   Alliance for Jewish Renewal, 7318 Germantown
   Ave., Philadelphia, PA 19119   215 242-4074
Peninnah Schram, 1720 Morningview Drive,
   Yorktown Hts., NY 10598   914 962-9387
Rebecca Schram-Zafrany, 2/19 Shar Ha'arayot,
   Ashdod 77443 Israel *or* Peninnah Schram   08 556-410
Cherie Karo Schwartz, 996 S. Florence St., Denver,
   CO 80231   303 367-8099
Howard Schwartz, 13 Stacy Drive, St. Louis,
   MO 63132   314 997-4553
Shai Schwartz, Neve Shalom, DN Shimshon
   99761 Israel   02 917-502
Rabbi Rami M. Shapiro, P.O. Box 161238, Miami,
   FL 33116
Eliezer Shore, 14 Hutchinson Ct., Great Neck,
   NY 11023   516 482-2989
   or Rechov Yehoyariv 8, Shmuel HaNavi,
   Jerusalem 97354 Israel   02 813-549
Laura Simms, 814 Broadway, New York, NY 10003   212 674-3479
Devorah Spilman, 196 N. Carmelina Ave.,
   Los Angeles, CA 90049   310 472-5172
Susan Stone, 1320 Wesley Ave., Evanston, IL 60201   708 328-8159
Arthur Strimling, 504 8th St., Brooklyn, NY 11215   718 965-7187
Joan Sutton, 2349 Funston Ave., San Francisco,
   CA 94116   415 665–7628
Rabbi Susan Talve, Central Reform Congregation,
   77 Maryland Plaza, St. Louis, MO 63108   314 361-3919
Rabbi Hanoch Teller, Rechov Yehoyariv 4,
   Jerusalem, 97354 Israel   02 823-919
Dvorah Menashe Telushkin, 900 West End Ave.,
   New York, NY 10025   212 222-7136
Arthur Waskow, 6711 Lincoln Dr., Philadelphia,
   PA 19119   215 844-8494
Rabbi Avraham Weiss, Hebrew Institute
   of Riverdale, 3700 Henry Hudson Parkway,
   Bronx, NY 10463   718 796-4730

Rabbi Peretz Wolf-Prusan, Cong. Emanu-El,
    2 Lake St., San Francisco, CA 94118   415 751-2535
Diane Wolkstein, 10 Patchin Place, New York,
    NY 10011   212 929-6871

GLOSSARY

Unless otherwise noted, the following expressions are Hebrew. Nearly all of them are used in Yiddish as well. Ashkenazic pronunciation is indicated by (A), Sefardic pronunciation by (S), Yiddish by (Y), Hebrew by (H), Ladino (Judeo-Spanish) by (L). The vowel combination ei is pronounced a as in cake; ai is i as in kite. Kh and ch are as in the German, ich. Some of the spelling of Hebrew words within the stories may vary. For example, *chevra* may also be spelled *hevra*.

Abuelita   Dimutive form of "grandmother."
Agunah   A woman who cannot remarry under Jewish law because her husband has deserted her or because his death cannot be verified.
Ah sgula   Something that brings good fortune.
A lebn af dayn kop   Literally, "A life upon your head." It means, "Life should be filled with sunshine." Said affectionately.
Aleichem Shalom   Response to the greeting "Shalom Aleichem," Literally, Unto you be peace.
Aleph-beis (Y), Aleph-bet (H)   First two letters of Hebrew alphabet. Used to refer to entire alphabet.
Alter haim (Y)   The Old Country; literally, the old home.
Ayin   Nothing.
'Ayin   Eye.
Ayneni yodaya   Literally "I don't know."
Ba'alas chessed   A kind or charitable woman.
Ba'al midos   Someone who has good character or ethics.
Ba'al Shem Tov   The Master of the Good Name. Refers to Rabbi Israel, the founder of the chasidic movement in the eighteenth century. Also Balshem.
Balabusta   A housewife or head of a household; by extension, a super-homemaker.
Badchan, Badchanim (pl.)   A jester or merrymaker who entertained through song and rhyme; also at weddings in Eastern Europe.
Bakitzur   To make a long story short. In short.
Balshem   See Ba'al Shem Tov.
Bar Mitzvah   Son of the Commandment, occurs at thirteen years of age.
Baruch Hashem   Blessed is the Creator.

Beis (A)   Second Letter of the Hebrew alphabet.

Beit HaMedrash   House of Study; a part of every synagogue. In the talmudic age it was a school for higher rabbinic learning (study, discussion, and prayer). In posttalmudic times, most synagogues had a Beit HaMedrash, or else the synagogue itself would be referred to as the Beit HaMedrash, since they were places of study. Also called *Beit HaMidrash* or *Beit Midrash*.

Beit HaMikdash   The Holy Temple in Jerusalem.

Beit Midrash   House of Study; a part of every synagogue.

Ben Atar, Ibn Attar   Meaning "spice dealer." Name of an illustrious Moroccan family of rabbis and authors.

Ben Torah   Son of Torah, a Torah scholar.

Bereshis   "In the beginning." First word in Bible.

Beshert   Fate.

Besht   Acronym for Ba'al Shem Tov.

Bich'vodo u've'atzmo   The one and only, the honorable.

Bimah   An elevated place or platform in the synagogue where the rabbi and cantor stand and where the Torah is read.

Bobka   Russian coffee cake.

B'sha'a tova u'mutzlachas   In a good and successful timely hour.

B'tzelem Elohim   In the likeness of the Infinite One.

Bubbe (Y)   Grandmother.

Challah   A special white bread, usually braided, for Sabbath and holiday meals.

Chanukiah   See menorah.

Chanukiot   Plural for chanukiah or menorah.

Charoset   A mixture of chopped apples and nuts or of raisins and dates, seasoned with wine as a Passover Seder symbol for the clay bricks in Egypt.

Chassan   Bridegroom.

Chassanah   Wedding.

Chasidism   See Hasidism.

Cheder   "Room." The elementary school for Jewish boys in Eastern Europe.

Chelm   Imaginary town of fools in Jewish folklore (although there does exist a real town of Chelm in Poland).

Chevra   Friends.

Chumash   The first five books of the Torah.

Chuppa   Jewish wedding canopy. Can also refer to the entire wedding ceremony.

Chuzpadik   Brazen.

Cohen Gadol   The High Priest in the Temple.

Davven (Y)   To pray.

Dayenu   Enough.

Derash or drasha   A homily or teaching on the Torah.

Dieta   Ritual observance of the laws of family purity.

Dinar   A coin used in the Near East.

Eish Da'at   The fiery law; specifically refers to the letter of the Torah.

El atrian   Spices (Moroccan Arabic dialect).

Erev   The evening before the Shabbat or festival begins.

Eshet Chayil   "A Woman of valor." These are the first words of Proverbs 31:10–31 describing the virtuous wife. The verses are traditionally recited by a husband to his wife at the Shabbat table on Friday evening.

Etrog; etrogim (pl.) (s) or Esrog; esrogim (pl.) (A)   A citron used for holiday of Sukkot. If the pistil (*pittum* in Hebrew), the stem at one end of the esrog, is broken off, the esrog is unusable for ritual purposes.

Gabbai   The lay communal official of a synagogue who keeps order and hands out Torah honors; the word is part of the term *gabbai tzedakah* (charity warden).

Gadol   A great or righteous person.

Gehenna   Jewish version of Purgatory.

Gemara   Relevant discussion and elaboration on Mishna in the Talmud. The Mishna is the code of basic Jewish law redacted and arranged into six orders and subdivided into tractates by Rabbi Yehuda Hanasi c. 200 C.E. Contains the Oral Law transmitted for generations. The Talmud, the most sacred Jewish text after the Torah, is comprised of the Mishna and the Gemara.

Geulah   Redemption.

Geveret   Mrs. A form of address for women.

Gezunterheit (Y)   In good health.

Gimel   Third letter of the Hebrew alphabet.

Goldene medine (Y)   Literally, the golden land; America.

Gonif   Thief.

Guadaloupe   The name of Maria in New Mexico. She wears a blue dress covered with yellow stars and is usually encircled in flames.

Gut Yomtov (Y)   Good holiday.

Hadar   Glory.

Haftarah   A selection from the Prophets read following the Torah reading in the synagogue on Sabbath and holidays.

Hamantasch   Triangular pastry filled with poppy seed or fruit fillings and eaten at Purim. Named for the villain Haman. Literally means Haman's pocket.

Hashem God.

Hashgacha pratit God's guiding hand, in personal matters.

Hasid; Hasidim (pl.) A pious one. A member of a hasidic group.

Hasidishe Hasidic.

Hasidism The religious mystical movement founded by Rabbi Israel ben Eliezer, known as the Ba'al Shem Tov, in the eighteenth century in Poland.

Havdalah "Separation." The ceremony at the end of Sabbath and festivals to separate the holy day from the weekday. The ceremony includes blessings using a braided candle, a spice box, and wine.

Havurah; Havurot (pl.) Group of friends who meet for study and prayer.

Hevra Kadisha Aramaic for holy brotherhood. This communal organization performs the holy commandment of caring for and washing the dead person, accompanying the body to the grave, and burial. It is considered a great honor to become a member of this society.

Ilui A child prodigy.

Kabbala "That which is received." Jewish mystical tradition. Kabbala was most fully explored in the thirteenth-century book *Zohar* ("Book of Splendor") and in the writings of the fifteenth-century Jewish mystics of Safed.

Kallah Bride.

Kapporis Means "atonement." The custom on the eve of Yom Kippur (Day of Atonement) of swinging a fowl (rooster for a man, a hen for a woman) over the head several times while praying that the fowl, when slaughtered, will serve as a sacrificial substitute for the person.

Kashrut Pertaining to kosher preparation and foods.

Kavannah Insight; intent. The act of focusing one's thoughts and feelings during prayer or the performance of a commandment.

Kawmetz aleph-aw Rote teaching of Hebrew reading skills.

Kedusha Sanctification of God's name.

K'fitzat Haderekh The jumping of the way.

Khakhome (Y) Wise woman.

Kibbitz (Y) Banter.

Kiddush "Sanctification." The prayer recited over wine. Recited prior to Sabbath and holiday meals.

Kinderlakh (Y) Little children.

Kippa   Skull cap. Called a yarmulka in Yiddish.

Kita   Class.

Kita Bet   Second grade.

Klezmer (Y)   Street musicians.

Kol Nidre   Aramaic for "All Vows." This prayer for the annulment of vows made rashly to God by the worshiper is chanted by the cantor on the eve of Yom Kippur, the Day of Atonement. This prayer, chanted at the beginning of the service, is so important that the entire evening is referred to as *Kol Nidre*.

Kovod   Honor.

Krasavitza (Y) (Polish)   A beauty.

Kretchma (Russian)   Inn.

Kvel (Y)   To be delighted with pride and joy.

Kvetch   Complain.

Ladino   Judeo-Spanish language originally spoken by Jews in Spain. The Sephardim brought Ladino to the other countries where they settled after the expulsion from Spain in 1492.

Lamed-Vav Tzaddikim or Lamed Vavnikim   Thirty-six hidden saints by whose merit the world continues to exist.

Lantzmen (Y)   People who come from the same town or region.

Lebzar likhil   Black pepper in Moroccan Arabic dialect.

Lekach (Y)   Honey cake.

L'chaim   "To Life." A traditional Jewish toast at weddings and other joyous occasions.

Lizrok 'ayin   Literally "To throw an eye."

L'Shana Tova   "A good year." A greeting at Rosh Hashanah.

Lulav   A bundle of branches and leaves of three species: willow, myrtle, and palm. It is used along with the *etrog* during Sukkot to symbolize the fruit and trees and the natural beauty of Israel. Also see *etrog*.

Maariv   Evening prayer recited daily at sundown.

Ma'aseh   Story.

Maggid, Maggidim (pl.)   A traveling storytelling rabbi.

Mame (Y)   Mother.

Masoret   Tradition.

Matzoh   Unleavened bread eaten during the eight days of Passover to recall the haste with which the Jews left Egypt, since there was no time for the bread to rise. Matzoh meal is used to make matzoh balls, often added to soup.

Meidele (Y)   Little girl.

Mazel   Good luck.

M'chaya   Enjoyment. Literally means revives.

Mechutanim   In-laws. The parents of your child's spouse.

Melamed   Teacher.

Mellach   A walled community.

Menorah   The special candelabrum used specifically for Chanukah. It holds nine candles: one for each night of Chanukah and one for the *shamash* or servant candle used to light the others. Also called *chanukiah*.

Mensch (Y)   A holistic word that refers to the *human* in human being. A person who is compassionate and ethical and knows how to live in the right and good way.

Mezzuin   Person calling Moslems to prayer. Also refers to the prayer tower.

Mezzuzah   "Doorpost." A parchment scroll inscribed with two biblical passages and God's name and enclosed in a decorative case. It is attached to every doorpost in Jewish homes and serves to offer divine protection as well as to show loyalty to and identity with the Jewish tradition.

Midrash; midrashim (pl.)   A method of interpreting Scripture to bring out lessons through stories or homilies. A genre of rabbinic literature. The term refers both to the method of interpretation as well as to the literature itself. A midrash, sometimes in the form of a story or folktale, explains or "fills in the spaces between the words."

Mija (Spanish)   My daughter (used with affection).

Mi'Mitzrayim   From Egypt.

Mincha   Afternoon prayer recited daily between midday and before Maariv.

Minyan; Minyonim (pl.)   Quorum of ten adults necessary to recite certain prayers and perform certain ceremonies and services.

Mishna   The code of basic Jewish law (Halakhah) redacted and arranged into six orders and subdivided into tractates by Rabbi Yehuda Hanasi c. 200 c.e. Contains the Oral Law, which has been transmitted for generations.

Mishpukha   Family.

Misnagdim   The intellectual and moral movement rooted in the primacy of the study of Jewish Law, in opposition to the charismatic and emotional orientation of Chasidism.

Misstamme (Y)   Perhaps.

Mitzvah   A divine commandment. The term has also come to mean a good deed.

Mitzvot (S) or Mitzvos (A)   Plural of *mitzvah*. 613 *mitzvot* are the total number of biblical commandments.

Morah   Teacher.

Moshav   "Workers' settlement." A collective agricultural village where inhabitants have individual homes but cooperate in purchasing things and working the land.

Moshiach   Messiah.

Motzoi Shabbos   Saturday night after the Sabbath ends.

Musaf   The additional service on Sabbath and Festivals.

Nefesh   Animal nature of our being.

Neshamah; Neshamos (pl.)   Soul. Essential spiritual nature of our beings.

Nign; Nigunim (pl.)   A melody without words.

Nu   So.

Parasha   The weekly Torah reading for Sabbath services and on Mondays and Thursdays.

Pekl; pekele; peklekh (Y)   A bundle; a little bundle; bundles.

Peretz, Y. L. (1852–1915)   A founder of modern Yiddish literature and an important writer of Hebrew literature.

Peyos   Earlocks.

Pitom   Stem of the *etrog* (citron) used on Sukkot. Without the *pitom*, the *etrog* is not considered ritually usuable for the holiday. Also *pittum*. See **Etrog**.

Purim shpiel (Y)   Purim play based on the story of Esther.

Qvelling   Bursting with pride and joy. See *Kvel*.

Rabbonim   Rabbis.

Rael   Short for "Yisrael."

Reb   Rabbi, teacher, or learned man.

Rebbe (Y)   Rabbi. The leader of a chasidic community.

Rebbetzin (Y)   Rabbi's wife.

Rosh Chodesh   "Head of the month." The first day of each Hebrew month, which is celebrated as a minor holiday.

Ruggelach   Rolled pastry filled with cinnamon, raisins, and nuts.

Schmaltz   The renderings from an animal, such as goose fat.

Schmattes   Rags. Sometimes refers to old clothes.

Schnaps (Y)   Whiskey.

Schnorrer   Someone who begs or wheedles.

Seder   Literally, "order." It refers to the ceremony that follows an order of service (including the meal) that takes place in the home on the first two nights of Passover. (In Israel, only one seder is held.)

Seraphim   A certain group of angels.

Seuda Shelisheet   The third meal of the Sabbath preceding *Havdalah*, the concluding ceremony of the holy day.

Shabbat; Shabbatot (pl.); Shabbos (Y)   Sabbath.

Shadkhan   A matchmaker.

Shailos   Questions.

Shalom Aleichem   A greeting. Literally, "Peace be unto you." The response is "Aleichem Shalom."

Shamash   See menorah.

Shammas   The caretaker of the synagogue.

Shechina   The feminine aspect of God, characterized by compassion, watchfulness, and immanence. The Shechina is often described as having wings that shelter the people of Israel.

Shechting   Ritual slaughtering of animals for kosher food.

Shed; Shedim (masc. pl) and Shedot (fem. pl)   Demon

Sheitel   A wig.

Sheitel-macher   A wig maker.

Shidduch   A match for marriage.

Sh'tibles   See Shtiebl.

Shiva   The seven days of mourning following the burial.

Shleppers   Tagalongs.

Shma Yisrael   "Hear O Israel." The Jewish credo.

Shoah   Holocaust.

Shochet   A ritual slaughterer of animals for food. For food to be considered kosher, the animals must be slaughtered by a *shochet*.

Shofar   The ram's horn sounded on Rosh Hashanah and at the end of Yom Kippur to call people to repentance. According to tradition, the shofar will also be blown to announce the coming of the Messiah at the End of Days.

Shomer Shabbos   A Sabbath observer.

Shpiel   A skit or play.

Shtetl   A town.

Shtetle   A small town.

Shtiebl (Y)   A small synagogue.

Shuk   A marketplace.

Shul (Y)   A synagogue.

Simcha   A joyous occasion, especially a happy life-cycle event.

Sudario (L)   Order of the prayer service.

Sukkah   Booth used during the holiday of Sukkot.

Sukkos (Y)   Booths. Also refers to the harvest festival that begins on Tishri 15 and is known also as the Festival of Tabernacles.

Ta'am   Taste or flavor.

Ta'am Gan Eden   A taste of the Garden of Eden.

Tachles (Y)   Business.

Tallis (A)   A four-cornered prayer shawl with fringes (tzitzit), worn in the synagogue during morning services.

Talmida   A student.

Talmid chacham   Someone who is wise in the learning of Torah. A scholar of Torah.

Talmud   The commentaries on the Torah and the Oral Law that were transmitted through the generations and redacted in 500 c.e. There are two Talmuds: the Jerusalem Talmud and the Babylonian Talmud. The Babylonian Talmud has had the greatest influence on Jewish thought, study, and practice. It is a storehouse of Jewish history and customs containing both stories (*aggadah*) and the law (*halakhah*). The Talmud is the most sacred Jewish text after the Torah and is comprised of the Mishnah and the Gemara.

Tante (Y)   Aunt.

Tateh (Y)   Father.

Tehillim   Psalms.

Tefillin or T'filln   Phylacteries. They consist of two black leather boxes containing parchment inscribed with Bible verses and connected to leather straps. One is worn on the left arm and the other on the forehead during morning prayers, except on Shabbat and festivals.

Tefillot   Prayers. Tefilla (singular).

Teshuvah   Return. Also repentance.

Tia (Spanish)   Aunt.

Tikkun   Repair. Refers to spiritual repair or healing that helps make a person whole, not just in body but also in soul. When people discover that personal blessing, they become truly healed. Since each person is a microcosm of the universe, they then can "repair" the world, that is, fulfill the holy purpose of *tikkun olam* (repair of the world).

Tish   A table.

Torah   The first five books of the Bible and referred to as the Old Testament, the Pentateuch or *Chumash*. The Torah scroll is read aloud in the synagogue on Mondays, Thursdays, Sabbaths, and festivals as long as a *minyan*, a quorum of ten adults, is present. (In an Orthodox service the quorum must be ten men.) The Torah, the most sacred Jewish book, also can mean the entire body of Jewish teaching and literature.

Tselem Elokim   See B'tselem Elohim.

Tu B'Shvat   Jewish Arbor Day. The fifteenth of Hebrew month of Shvat.

Tzaddik   A righteous person. This title is given to a person known for deep faith and piety. The concept of the *tzaddik* became especially important in the chasidic movement of the eighteenth century, when the *tzaddik* was regarded as possessing extraordinary powers and could serve as an intermediary between God and man.

Tzedakah   Charity; Justice.

Tzimmes   A time-honored dish popular in Eastern Europe. It is usually a mixture of potatoes, prunes, and meat or made only of shredded carrots.

Tzitzit   The fringes attached to the four corners of the *tallis* as commanded in the Torah.

Yahrzeit   The anniversary of a person's death.

Yeshiva   Talmudic academy or school.

Yetzer ha-Ra   The evil spirit.

Yetzer ha-Tov   The good spirit.

Yid   Jew.

Yiddish   Jewish. The word also refers to the Yiddish (Judeo-Old German-Slavic-Hebrew) language spoken by Jews in Eastern Europe.

Yiddishkeit (Y)   Jewishness.

Yom Ha'atzmaut   Israel Independence Day celebrated on the fourth of the Hebrew month of Iyyar.

Yod   A pointer used for reading Torah.

Yom HaShoah   Day of Holocaust Remembrance.

Yoshev   A sitter.

z'l   *Zikhrono livrakhah*. "May his name be remembered"; said after mentioning the name of someone who has died.

CREDITS

435

About the Editor

Peninnah Schram, storyteller and author, is associate professor of speech and drama at Yeshiva University's Stern College and the founding director of the Jewish Storytelling Center. She travels, telling stories and conducting workshops on storytelling and the Jewish oral tradition. Peninnah's books include *Jewish Stories One Generation Tells Another*, *Tales of Elijah the Prophet*, and *Eight Tales for Eight Nights: Stories for Chanukah* (coauthored with Steven M. Rosman). A native of New London, Connecticut, she resides in the New York area.